TRADING

IN THE

GLOBAL
CURRENCY
MARKETS

SECOND EDITION

CORNELIUS LUCA

NEW YORK INSTITUTE OF FINANCE

NEW YORK • TORONTO • SYDNEY • TOKYO • SINGAPORE

NEW YORK INSTITUTE OF FINANCE
NYIF and New York Institute of Finance are trademarks of Executive Tax
Reports, Inc., used under license by Penguin Putnam Inc.

Library of Congress Cataloging-in-Publication Data

Luca, Cornelius.
    Trading in the global currency markets / Cornelius Luca.—2nd ed.
      p. cm.
    Includes bibliographical references and index.
    ISBN 0-7352-0146-3 (cloth)
    1. Foreign exchange market. 2. Investment analysis. I. Title.
  HG3851.L83   2000
  332.4'5—dc21   00-037244

To my wife, Sandra
and my daughter, Gwendolyn,
without whom this book would not be possible

Contents

13 Currency Crosses   208

14 Currency Futures   219

15 Currency Options   236

Preface

Foreign exchange trading took off in earnest as recently as 1973, when currencies were finally allowed to float freely. Apparently a new industry, its origins can actually be traced to ancient times, when foreign coins started to be exchanged. Since stocks and bonds took several more millennia to come into existence, foreign exchange is, in fact, the oldest financial market.

Few financial industries generate as much excitement and profit as currency exchange. Traders from around the world enter positions for weeks, days, hours, or only split seconds. The market can have explosive moves or steady flows. Money changes hands quickly, for a staggering daily average of 1 trillion U.S. dollars.

Foreign exchange profitability is legendary. George Soros' Quantum fund realized a profit in excess of 1 billion U.S. dollars for a couple of days' work in September 1992. And Hans U. Hufschmid of Salomon Brothers Inc. netted an income package of $28 million for 1993. Even by Wall Street standards, these numbers are heartstoppers.

It is impossible to envision a world without foreign exchange. Even the smallest transaction across borders triggers a currency exchange at one point or another. Whether importing or exporting raw materials, labor, manufactured goods, or services, foreign exchange is an integral part of the transaction.

In addition to the corporate demand, currency trading provides a leading source of income for most financial institutions. In terms of profitability, commercial banks have steadily switched their focus from lending to foreign exchange trading. Along with investment banks, they set up sophisticated individual trading rooms, somewhat resembling NASA mission control rooms.

The latest newcomer to the markets, the hedge fund, rose to prominence in the early 1990s. Extremely aggressive, hedge funds are able to concentrate billions of dollars into a single position, betting not only on a fund's capacity to "read" the market correctly, but also on its capability to "make" the market due to its sheer trade size. Because of the size of their positions, the leading hedge funds can also generate major market disruptions, such as the one in October 1998 that sent the dollar falling a mind-boggling 11.8 yen in a single day.

Despite its high trading volume and its fundamental role, the foreign exchange market is rarely in the limelight. Because only a tiny fraction of the transactions is conducted on regulated exchanges, the currency markets are generally less visible and receive less media coverage than stock or futures markets.

There are no geographic or temporal boundaries to foreign exchange. This is a vibrant, 24-hour market open to all eligible players. There are no official openings or closings, with the exception of the currency futures and the options on currency futures. If a trading session does not provide enough satisfaction, traders can deal after normal hours; and if there is a national holiday in one country, players are generally able to find other markets open.

This book will introduce you to all the significant aspects of foreign exchange in a practical manner, to best answer the typical questions:

Why do we trade currencies?

Who are the players?

What currencies do we trade?

What makes them move?

What instruments can we trade?

How can we use them?

How can we forecast currency behavior?

How do we access the pertinent information?

The book:

- presents the basis of foreign exchange and the factors that contributed to the growth of the industry, from market developments to technological breakthroughs.

- presents the historical developments in the market and how these elements have shaped the contemporary environment.

- focuses on the mechanics of the market, the major players and markets, the risks pertinent to foreign exchange, corporate trading, methods of trading execution, and dealing settlements.

- analyzes foreign exchange instruments and provides comprehensive coverage of the major option strategies.

- focuses on fundamental analysis, economic indicators vital to the financial markets that may be disregarded in the currency markets, and the mind of the trader, for a point of view different at times from the typical theoretical expectation.

- provides an exhaustive view of technical analysis, including an in-depth chart analysis comparing the major chart types, chart formations, and oscillators; and a comprehensive discussion of candlestick and point-and-figure charts as they apply to foreign currencies.

There are no miracle answers, of course—at least, not in this book. In fact, I generally shy away from rules of thumb. The only solid answer I favor is, "It depends." What you will learn is what makes the market move and traders tick.

You are presented here with a comprehensive set of trading tools, many of them on the cutting edge of technology. You will decide for yourself, "on what it all depends." With these tools, you will be able to make your own choices, test them, and ultimately use them for your own benefit.

Cornelius Luca

Acknowledgments

Many thanks to everyone at the New York Institute of Finance, especially to Robert Gulick, director of the Institute, and Dana Orenstein, seminar director, for all their gracious and professional cooperation over the years, along with past help from William Rini and Paul McQuarry. The help and support of Ellen Schneid Coleman and Sybil Grace from Prentice Hall and Fred Dahl, director of Inkwell Publishing Services, were vital for the successful completion of this book.

The revisions of several chapters and many of the illustrations have been made possible by the following:

Krishna Biltoo, Marketing Director, *Reuters International*

Suzanne Brown, Marketing Manager, *EBS*

Scott Cross, Account Executive, *FENICS® Software*

Michael Cuttone, Director, Enhanced Application Team, *Bridge Information Systems, Inc.*

Elizabeth DeMorse, Director of Marketing, *Bloomberg Financial*

Michael Duvally, Managing Editor, Financial Markets, *Bridge Information Systems, Inc.*

Robert Hafer, Publisher, Bridge CRB Futures Perspective, *Bridge Information Systems, Inc.*

Kurt Klein, Chief Editor, *FutureSource*

Oleg Litvak, Product Manager, *Bridge Information Systems, Inc.*

Janet Logan, Manager, *Reuters*

Paul Lowe, Executive Editor, *Bridge Information Systems, Inc.*

Darril Malloy, Manager, *Bloomberg Financial Markets*

Stephen Onstad, National Marketing Representative and New York
   Regional Manager, *CQG*

Kevin Pendley, Chicago Bureau Chief, *Bridge Information Systems, Inc.*

Robert Prechter, President, *Elliott Wave International*

Malcolm Rooney, Financial Engineer, *Spreadsheet Links Limited*

Melanie Stevens, Marketing and Advertising Assistant, *CQG*

Jonathan Stone, Financial Engineer, *Spreadsheet Links Limited*

1 What Is Foreign Exchange?

Foreign exchange is simultaneously a simple and a complex notion, depending on the end user. Despite the wide-ranging points of view, all foreign exchange has a common element. It is simply the mechanism that values foreign currencies in terms of another currency, providing a vital shock absorber for the international economic, financial, and political divergences. An exchange rate is therefore the price of one currency in terms of another.

WHY FOREIGN EXCHANGE OCCURS

At the most basic level, tourists around the world generate substantial foreign exchange flow. Whether the American tourists abroad taking advantage of the record high dollar in some years, or the foreign tourists in the United States benefiting from the record low dollar in other years, they all must convert their currencies to the local currencies to pay for traveling expenses. These small individual transactions generate important cash flow when compounded.

Investors around the world, large and small, are continuously hunting for investment opportunities. Whether in the securities markets, real estate, or bank deposits, any international investment must, at one point or another, go through foreign exchange.

An American shopper may buy an American-made silk tie in an American boutique. Chances are that the silk was produced abroad. Even if an American buys an American car from an American dealer, if the car was assembled in Canada or Mexico, foreign exchange was executed. The presence of foreign exchange in one or more stages of production is deeply ingrained, albeit not always obvious.

Global markets have become so competitive that corporations must continuously search the world for new markets and cheaper sources of raw materials and labor. The degree of international integration generates interest rate adjustments, which in turn affect foreign exchange rates.

Political changes are also major factors in foreign exchange. For instance, the fall of the Soviet Empire, despite its historic proportions, did not itself directly affect the foreign exchange market. However, a consequence of the fall, the unification of Germany, generated a long-term rally in the deutsche mark through 1995, based on expectations of future economic might and short-term high interest rates geared against inflation.

In terms of political or economic uncertainty, local currencies are quickly discarded in favor of safe-haven currencies, such as U.S. dollars or Swiss francs. For instance, in the war-torn former Yugoslavia, where inflation rampages at times at incredulous rates, the currencies of choice are U.S. dollars and, since 1999, euros.

In future chapters we will discuss in detail the major factors affecting the foreign exchange markets. For the time being, we must remember several of their general characteristics. The foreign exchange markets are:

- sensitive to a large and continuously changing number of factors,
- open to all players in the major currencies,
- large and liquid in the major currencies,
- concentrated on several currencies, and
- extremely efficient relative to other financial markets.

FACTORS THAT HAVE CONTRIBUTED TO FOREIGN EXCHANGE VOLUME GROWTH

Foreign exchange has experienced spectacular growth in volume ever since currencies were allowed to float freely against each other. While the daily turnover in 1977 was U.S. $5 billion, it increased to U.S. $600 billion in 1987, reached the U.S. $1 trillion mark in September 1992, and stabilized at around $1.5 trillion by the year 2000. (See Figure 1.1.)

Volume in foreign exchange cannot be measured directly the way it is in the stock market. Foreign exchange trading is generally conducted in a decentralized manner, with the notable exceptions of currency futures and options on currency futures. What is behind this spectacular growth in volume?

EXCHANGE RATE VOLATILITY

During the last days of the fixed exchange rates system, few envisioned the volatility potential of the currency markets. People generally assumed that economic forces needed only occasional self-adjustment in an otherwise quiet activity. Were they wrong! The unchecked increase of the U.S. dollar in the 1980s had a destructive effect on American exporters' international trade competitiveness. The U.S. dollar's record highs were capped in September 1985 and the currency was sent into a 10-year nosedive, which trimmed about 66 percent of its value against the Japanese yen. (See Figure 1.2.) The impact of the exchange rate activity on the international economy

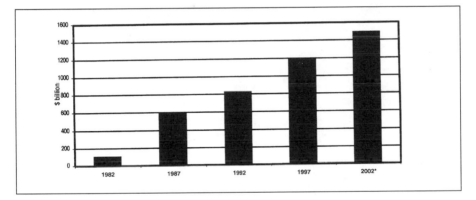

Figure 1.1. Daily turnover in FX between 1973 and 2000.

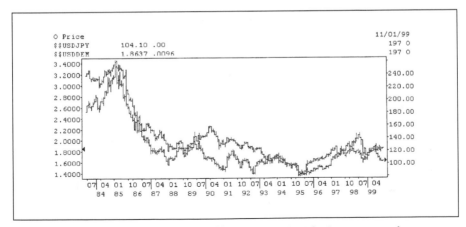

Figure 1.2. The U.S. dollar fell about 66 percent against the Japanese yen between 1985 and 1995. (*Source: Bridge Information Systems, Inc.*)

and trade is more difficult to gauge in the major economies. However, the Southeast Asian crisis of 1997–1998 that sharply devalued the regional currencies to unprecedented levels had a disastrous impact on their economies. (See Figures 1.3 and 1.4.)

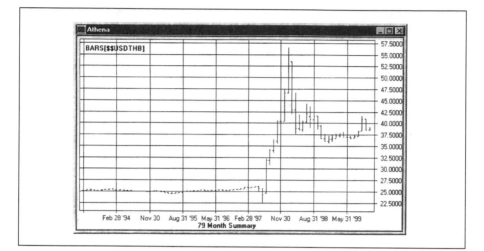

Figure 1.3. The Thai baht was the first to kick off the Southeast Asian crisis of 1997–1998. *(Source: Bridge Information Systems, Inc.)*

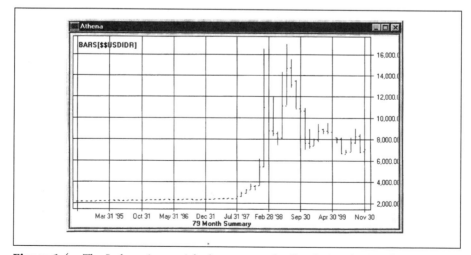

Figure 1.4. The Indonesian rupiah also came under fire during the Southeast Asian crisis of 1997–1998. *(Source: Bridge Information Systems, Inc.)*

For foreign exchange, currency volatility is a prime factor in the growth of volume. In fact, volatility is a sine qua non condition for trading. The only instruments that may be profitable under conditions of low volatility are currency options.

INTEREST RATE VOLATILITY

Economic internationalization generated a significant impact on interest rates as well. Willingly or not, economies became much more interrelated, a factor that exacerbated the need to change interest rates faster. Interest rates are generally changed in order to adjust the growth in the economy, and interest rate differentials have a substantial impact on exchange rates. (See Figure 1.5.) However, the correlation between the two is not mechanical. This is discussed in Chapter 17, which deals with fundamental analysis.

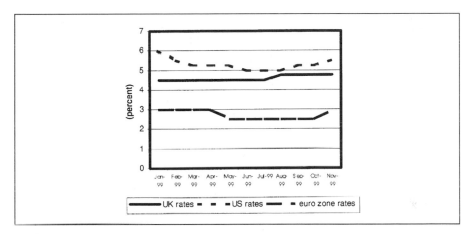

Figure 1.5.   The U.S., the U.K., and the euro-zone interest rates in 1999.

BUSINESS INTERNATIONALIZATION

In recent decades we have witnessed unprecedented internationalization in the business world. The competition has intensified, triggering a worldwide hunt for more markets and cheaper raw materials and labor. The pace of economic internationalization picked up even more in the 1990s, due to the fall of Communism in Europe and to up-and-down economic and financial development in both Southeast Asia and South America. These changes have been positive toward foreign exchange, since more transactional layers were added.

The New York or London or Tokyo markets' clear boundaries are being blurred by 24-hour trading and brokerage desks.

INCREASED CORPORATE INTEREST

Foreign exchange has been perceived by many corporations as a transaction cost, albeit a rather volatile one. This passive approach proved costly for many corporations, large and small. A successful performance of a product or service overseas may be pulled down from the profit point of view by adverse foreign exchange conditions. However, the opposite is true as well: An accurate handling of the foreign exchange may enhance the overall international performance of a product or service. Experience has proven over and over again that it is worth focusing not on what you pay for foreign exchange, but on what foreign exchange can pay to you. Proper handling of foreign exchange generally adds substantially to the rate of return. Therefore, interest in foreign exchange has increased dramatically in the past decade, although the full potential has not yet been reached. Many corporations are using currencies not only for hedging, but also for capitalizing on opportunities that exist solely in the currency markets.

INCREASED PLAYERS' SOPHISTICATION

Advances in technology, computer software, and telecommunications and increased experience have increased the level of players' sophistication. This enhanced traders' confidence in their ability to both generate profits and properly handle the exchange risks. Therefore, trading sophistication led toward volume increase.

DEVELOPMENTS IN TELECOMMUNICATIONS

In the 1970s and early 1980s, foreign exchange trading was mostly conducted via telephone, and to a much lesser extent on the telex machine. Both mediums are slow and error-prone. The introduction of automated dealing systems in the 1980s, of matching systems in the early 1990s, and of Internet trading in the late 1990s completely altered the way foreign exchange was conducted. The dealing systems are on-line computer systems that link banks on a one-to-one basis, while matching systems are electronic brokers. They are reliable and much faster, allowing traders to conduct four simultaneous trades, rather than one or a maximum of two on the phone. They are also safer, as players are able to see the deals that they execute. Finally, the dealing and matching systems have many other features that facilitate trading; they are presented in detail in Chapter 10. The dealing systems had a major role in expanding the foreign exchange business due to their reliability, speed, and safety. It may be difficult to recall the days before fax machines were introduced, but it is only fair to mention their share in helping foreign exchange to grow.

COMPUTER (HARDWARE AND SOFTWARE) DEVELOPMENT

Computers play a significant role at many stages of conducting foreign exchange. In addition to the dealing systems, matching systems simultaneously connect all players around the world, electronically duplicating the brokers' market.

The new front end–back office systems provide full accounting coverage, ticket writing, back office processing, and risk management implementation at a fraction of their previous cost.

Unlike the limited technical analysis of the early 1980s, advanced software now makes it possible to generate all types of charts, augment them with sophisticated technical studies, and put them at traders' fingertips on a continuous basis at a rather limited cost.

Also, currency options can hardly be traded professionally without the aid of computers, because complex strategies require the help of advanced software for pricing.

NEW FX INSTRUMENTS

Among the first new foreign exchange instruments were currency futures, which were developed on the Chicago International Monetary Market about two decades ago. New products in the currency options area continuously enrich foreign exchange. The gamut of options strategies has expanded significantly, as a result of the more sophisticated approach of corporations to foreign exchange trading. Options generally allow for customized strategies for both hedging and speculation.

PROFITABILITY

One of the biggest fears among equity players is the bear market. There is no such thing in the foreign exchange markets. Whether the U.S. dollar reaches record highs or record lows, the market is active and liquid. The foreign exchange market is concentrated in four major currencies—euro, Japanese yen, British pound, and Swiss franc—that are quoted against the U.S. dollar, ensuring a high degree of efficiency. Other financial markets tend to be fragmented among different issues and instruments, with much less liquidity available.

The major foreign exchange instrument is spot, which generally matures in two business days. The profit may be realized that quickly. Even the long-dated forward contracts mature a lot faster and more safely than most loans, the former bread-and-butter instrument for banks. That is why commercial banks have allocated significant resources to trade currencies. Even profits from the credit card business pale in comparison to the size of foreign exchange profits.

Historical
Development of
Foreign Exchange

F oreign exchange trading is a relatively new industry, having started only in 1973. However, it occurred in ancient times, as coins started to be exchanged among traders. This chapter deals with the more recent developments that shaped foreign exchange into the vibrant and complex market that exists today.

A HISTORICAL PERSPECTIVE

Foreign exchange trading as we know it began in earnest in 1973. Money, though, goes back a long time, more than 4500 years, to when the Egyptians coined the first metal money, and the Babylonians wrote the first bills and receipts. The incipient foreign exchange markets can be traced back to the ancient Middle East, where money changers initiated the exchange of coins. Later, during the Middle Ages, as the number of travelers increased, people realized that metal coins might be impractical. Because of highway robberies and the sheer weight of the coins, foreign exchange started to take shape. International merchant bankers devised bills of exchange, which were transferable third-party payments that allowed flexibility and growth in foreign exchange dealings.

Closer to the present, the twentieth century was comprised of periods of high volatility and of relative stability. Foreign exchange meant, mostly, commercial transactions. The idea of currency speculation has not always been regarded favorably. Money speculators were considered immoral and, at various times in history, they could even face imprisonment. In fact, as recently as the summer of 1993, following the Exchange Rate Mechanism's crisis, voices in Europe, especially France, only half-jokingly reminded us of the efficiency of the guillotine in combating currency speculators.

Extreme volatility and high speculation in foreign exchange immediately followed World War I; therefore, hedging with forward contracts became commonplace. The Great Depression, combined with the suspension of the gold standard in 1931, created a serious diminution in foreign exchange dealings. Nowadays, currencies around the world are generally quoted against the U.S. dollar. Things haven't always been this way. By the mid-1930s London had gained prominence as the leading center for foreign exchange. At the apex of the British empire, the pound was *the* currency to trade and to keep as a reserve currency. Beside quid, the pound has generally been known as cable, from the fact that in the old times foreign exchange was traded on the telex machines, or cable. In 1930, the Bank for International Settlements was established in Basel, Switzerland. Its goals were to oversee the financial efforts of the newly independent countries, along with providing monetary relief to countries experiencing temporary balance of payments difficulties. The implementation was not perfect. Governments were generally weak, yet reluctant to take advice. Financially, money was scarce, and the ghost of the Depression was everpresent. Germany was experiencing disastrous hyperinflation. It all seemed to create a perfect doomsday scenario. The political and economic disequilibria were overwhelming, and new geographic boundaries had to be drawn in the sand.

World War II had a crushing effect on the pound. The British economy was for all practical purposes destroyed; the empire was crumbling, and international confidence in the currency had sunk as a result of Germany's counterfeiting the pound in its all-out war effort against England.

In the period following the United States' entrance into the Second World War, the U.S. dollar became the prominent currency of the entire globe. Previously, the dollar had been perceived as a has-been, due to the Stock Market Crash of 1929 and the subsequent Great Depression. In fact, the United States had been reluctant to enter the war so soon after the painful rebalancing of the Depression-scarred economy. In the meantime, the ravages of war were turning Europe and Japan to ashes. The only country unscarred by war was the United States. It was only natural that the future had to be shaped by this country.

THE BRETTON WOODS ACCORD

Toward the end of the war, in July 1944, the Allies (the United States, Great Britain, and France) met at the United Nations Monetary and Financial Conference at Bretton Woods, New Hampshire to discuss and design the financial future of the new economic order. A North American location was selected because the United States was spearheading the Allies' war efforts and had the only major economy unscathed by the ravages of war.

In contrast to the volatility in foreign exchange markets that prevailed after World War I, the post–World War II period was designed to be stable, in part due to tight governmental controls on currency values. The objective was to bring about economic growth and prosperity internationally, through stable currencies. In order to implement it, the Bretton Woods Accord focused on two major building blocks: the pegging of currencies and the International Monetary Fund (IMF).

CURRENCY PEGGING

The major trading currencies were pegged to the U.S. dollar in the sense that they were allowed to fluctuate only one percent on either side of that rate. When a currency exceeded this range, marked by intervention points, the central bank in charge had to buy it or sell it, and thus bring it back into range. In turn, the U.S. dollar was pegged to gold at $35 per ounce. Thus, the U.S. dollar became the world's reserve currency.

The near-fixed monetary system served several purposes. First, it attempted to avoid the stop-and-go situation of the interwar era, when governments frequently tended to resort to floating exchange rates in the wake of economic pressures. Second, and at the time most important, the world needed a nurturing environment within which it could rebuild itself. With the majority of the world's industrial base gone up in smoke, major social disruptions, and the prewar political balance severely distorted, the last thing the world needed was currency speculation. Moreover, immediately after the war, there really weren't many currencies left, except the dollar. The world economy needed a warm and protective cocoon, and the Bretton Woods Accord provided that by keeping the currencies fixed against the U.S. dollar. The key requirement was the cooperation of the central banks to implement the intervention points. In addition to the technical aspect, this continuous and common effort was meant to assist in bringing together and eventually cementing long-lasting relationships among parties with divergent interests.

THE INTERNATIONAL MONETARY FUND (IMF)

The IMF is a cooperative institution that 182 countries have voluntarily joined. The purpose is to consult with one another to maintain a stable system of buying and selling their currencies, so that payments in foreign money can take place between countries smoothly and timely. Members of the IMF believe that open communication regarding policies that influence payments by the government and residents of one country to those of another is to everyone's advantage. They also believe that occasionally adjusting those policies, when fellow members agree that this is in the common interest, will help international trade to grow and will create more and higher-paying jobs in an expanding world economy.

The IMF lends money to members who have trouble meeting financial obligations to other members, on the condition that they undertake economic reforms to eliminate these difficulties for their own good and the good of the entire membership. However, the IMF has no effective authority over the domestic economic policies of its members. It cannot force a member government to spend more on schools and hospitals and less on military expenditures; but it can urge members to make the best use of scarce resources by refraining from financial excess. When members ignore this advice, the IMF can only try to persuade them of the domestic and international benefits of adopting policies favored by the membership as a whole.

The IMF has the authority only to require its members to disclose information on monetary and fiscal policies and to avoid, as far as possible, putting restrictions on the exchange of domestic for foreign currency and on making payments to other members.

Its members have given the IMF some authority over their payments policies, because these policies are of paramount importance to the flow of money between nations and because experience has confirmed that without a global monitoring agency, the modern system of payments in foreign currency simply does not work.

The International Monetary Fund (IMF), which has its headquarters in Washington, D.C., has the following general objectives, as presented in "The International Monetary Fund, Its Evolution, Organization and Activities—Pamphlet # 37—IMF":

- Promote international cooperation by providing the means for members to consult and collaborate on international monetary issues.
- Facilitate the growth of international trade and thus contribute to high levels of employment and real income among member nations.

- Promote stability of exchange rates and orderly exchange agreements, and [to] discourage competitive currency depreciation.

- Foster a multilateral system of international payments, and [to] seek the elimination of exchange restrictions that hinder the growth of world trade.

- Make financial resources available to members, on a temporary basis and with adequate safeguards, to permit them to correct payments imbalances without resorting to measures destructive to national and international prosperity.

Structure of the IMF

The Board of Governors and the Executive Board govern the Fund. The Board of Governors, which manages the Fund, consists of a governor and an alternate governor from each of the member countries. The Executive Board, which is in charge of implementing the daily activities, is comprised of 22 executive directors, representing one or more countries. A Managing Director leads the Executive Board.

Membership

The International Monetary Fund is open to all countries with a responsible foreign policy. Each of the 182 members is assigned a specific quota derived from the relative economic performance of each country. Members must pay 25 percent of this quota in standard reserve assets, such as U.S. dollars or SDRs, and the balance in their own currencies. The size of the quota limits both a member's voting rights and the amounts available to borrow. (See Figure 2.1.)

Borrowing Facilities

The funds thus raised are available to its members. These resources may be increased through borrowing. Members may borrow funds under the following five facilities:

1. *Reserve tranche* is the most common source of funds. This facility allows a member to draw on its own reserve asset quota at the time of payment. Although proof of need is required, the IMF may not challenge it.

2. *Credit tranche drawings* and *stand-by arrangements* are the standard form of IMF loans. Once approved by the Executive Board, the loans are available in four equal tranches of 25 percent of the individual quota. Each consecutive tranche is lent under increasingly stringent conditions linked to the implementation of sound

$$QUOTA = (0.02\ Y + 0.05R + 0.10M + 0.10V) * (1 + X/Y)$$

where

Y = national income as of 1940

R = gold and dollar balances

M = average imports during 1934–1938

V = maximum variation in exports during 1934–1938

X = average exports during 1934–1938

Figure 2.1. The formula used to determine the quota for the original members. *(Source: The International Letter, Federal Reserve of Chicago, October 5, 1984)*

economic policies. Loans are received either directly or over the period of the stand-by arrangement.

3. The *compensatory financing facility* extends financial help to countries with temporary problems generated by reductions in export revenues. The financial support consists of up to 83 percent of a specific quota.

4. The *buffer stock financing facility* is geared toward assisting the stocking up on primary commodities in order to ensure price stability in a specific commodity. To this end, up to 45 percent of the quota may be borrowed.

5. The *extended facility* is designed to assist members with financial problems in amounts or for periods exceeding the scope of the other facilities.

The Special Drawing Rights (SDRs)

The *special drawings rights* (SDRs) are international reserve assets created and allocated by the International Monetary Fund to supplement the existing reserve assets. The idea for the SDRs was born out of the necessity for a stable and consistent source of lending, independent of the traditional reserve assets, such as U.S. dollars. At the recommendation of the Group of Ten—the United States, Great Britain, West Germany, Belgium, the Netherlands, France, Italy, Japan, Canada, and Sweden—the SDRs were created at the IMF meeting in Rio de Janeiro in September 1967.

All the IMF members are eligible for allocations. The SDRs are used for payments and for obtaining currencies of other members.

The initial value of the SDR was calculated by the International Monetary Fund on a daily basis as the sum total of the weighted U.S. dollar values of the five currencies in the basket—the U.S. dollar, the deutsche mark, the British pound, the Japanese yen, and the French franc. (See Figure 2.2.) Effective January 1, 1999, the IMF replaced the currency amounts of deutsche mark and French franc in the Special Drawing Right (SDR) valuation basket with equivalent amounts of euro, based on the fixed conversion rates between the euro and the deutsche mark and French franc announced on December 31, 1998 by the European Council. (See Figure 2.3.)

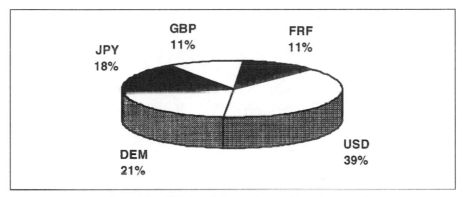

Figure 2.2. Valuation of the SDR (until December 1998). *(Source: The International Monetary Fund)*

Friday, August 13, 1999

Currency:	Currency amount under Rule 0-1	Exchange rate*	U.S. dollar equivalent	Percent change in exchange rate against U.S. dollar from previous calculation
Euro (Germany)	0.2280	1.06660	0.243185	0.310
Euro (France)	0.1239	1.06660	0.132152	0.310
Japanese yen	27.2000	114.90000	0.236728	0.940
Pounds sterling	0.1050	1.61230	0.169292	0.311
U. S. dollars	0.5821	1.00000	0.582100	
			1.363457	
		SDR1 = US$	1.36346	0.286**
		U.S.$1.00=SDR	0.733430	

* Exchange rates in terms of currency units per U.S. dollar except for the euro and the pound sterling which are expressed as U.S. dollars per currency unit.
** Percent change in value of SDR in terms of U.S. dollars from previous calculation.

                                                                    Prepared by Financial Relations Division

Figure 2.3. Valuation of the SDR (since January 1999). *(Source: The International Monetary Fund)*

The Test of the 1990s
The turbulent 1990s tested the IMF to the maximum with historical challenges. The IMF started the decade with a massive campaign to help the
countries of Central Europe, the Baltic countries, Russia, and the other
countries of the former Soviet Union in the difficult shift from centrally
planned to market economies. In mid-decade, a financial crisis erupted in
Mexico that showed the vulnerability of members to sudden shifts in market sentiment that lead to large and unpredictable capital outflows. Mexico
moved quickly to enact a strong program of policy adjustments and on
February 1, 1995, the IMF swiftly approved a record financing package for
a member country of $17.8 billion. This exceptional assistance was de-
signed to give confidence to the international financial community and to
stop contagion spreading from Mexico to other members.

The Asian financial crisis resulted in a record loan of $20.9 billion to
Korea in December 1997, as part of a major international support financial
package. Very large loans were also extended to Indonesia ($11.2 billion in
November 1997) and Thailand ($4.0 billion in August 1997). In July 1998,
serious economic and financial problems in Russia led to an $11.2 billion
IMF loan to Russia to enhance a previous $9.2 billion loan extended in
March 1996.

WHY THE BRETTON WOODS
ACCORD FAILED

Certainly, the Bretton Woods Accord was not a marriage made in heaven
for many of the participants. Some countries found the one-percent allowed
divergence from the value of the U.S. dollar to be constrictive. In addition,
under the gold standard, the price of gold was fixed by the United States at
U.S. $35 per ounce. This was dragging down on the American gold re-
serves and consequently on international confidence in the U.S. dollar.
Despite these problems, the Bretton Woods Accord lasted from 1944 to
1971, successful for most of its life. Under its auspices, a broken Europe
and Japan were able to reinvent themselves. From its inception, this system
had been mostly a one-nation show. Once recovered, though, both Europe
and Japan started to provide competition within the U.S. dollar block. The
expenses were rather high, and after 1965, the United States was perceived
as exporting inflation. By the late 1960s, the differences in the rates of
growth and the rates of inflation among the new major economies were
widening. To answer the international pressures, the intervention points
were underlined. But they could not provide the answer in 1971, when the

Bretton Woods system faltered, and they could not provide the answer 27 years later either, when the European Monetary System failed. The artificially designed ranges could not rein in the natural economic forces. In fact, they have just outlived their usefulness. Parallel to the demise of the Bretton Woods Accord, the United States abandoned pegging the price of gold, in effect annulling the gold standard.

AFTER BRETTON WOODS

Switching away from the fixed currency system after 27 years out of necessity, not by choice, was a difficult task. The Smithsonian Agreement, reached in Washington, D.C. in December 1971, had a transitional role in the free-floating markets. This agreement failed to address the real causes behind the international economic and financial pressures, focusing instead on increasing the ranges of currency fluctuations. From 1 percent, the fluctuation band for currencies relative to the U.S. dollar was expanded to 4.5 percent. Against each other, then, foreign currencies could fluctuate as much as 9 percent.

Parallel to the Washington efforts, the European Economic Community, established in 1957, tried to move away from the U.S. dollar block toward the deutsche mark block, by designing its own European monetary system. In April 1972, West Germany, France, Italy, the Netherlands, Belgium, and Luxembourg developed the European Joint Float. Under this system, the member currencies were allowed to fluctuate within a 2.25 percent band, known as *the snake*, against each other, and collectively within a 4.5 percent band, known as *the tunnel*, against the U.S. dollar.

Unfortunately, neither the Smithsonian Agreement nor the European Joint Float addressed the independent domestic problems of the member countries from the bottom up, attempting instead to focus solely on the large international picture and maintain it by artificially enforcing the intervention points. By 1973, both systems collapsed under heavy market pressures.

The idea of regional currency stability with the goal of financial independence from the U.S. dollar block persisted. By July 1978, the members of the European Community approved the plans for the European Monetary System—West Germany, France, Italy, the Netherlands, Belgium, Great Britain, Denmark, Ireland, and Luxembourg. The system was launched in March 1979, as a revamped European Joint Float or a mini Bretton Woods Accord. Additional features, such as the threshold of divergence, were designed to protect this monetary system from the fate of the previous ones. Judging from its expanded life span, until 1993 at least, the European

Monetary System was obviously better. However, the continued focus on the macroeconomic picture at the expense of the historically significant changes in Europe at country level, and the stubborn attempts to fix natural economic divergences by means of maintaining artificial intervention points, triggered the collapse of the EMS. The heralded but widely unexpected fall of the Communist system set off a series of economic imbalances difficult enough even to fully comprehend, let alone fix by means of intervention points. Seriously rocked by the British pound's exit under heavy foreign exchange selling in September 1992, the European Monetary System hit rock bottom at the end of July 1993. The traditional intervention bands were abandoned in favor of politically correct and insignificantly wide intervention bands. (For more details, refer to Chapter 3, the European Monetary Union.)

THE FREE-FLOATING FOREIGN EXCHANGE MARKETS

The 1973 double demise of the Smithsonian Agreement and the European Joint Float signified the official switch of the foreign exchange markets to free-floating. The switch occurred pretty much by default, since it was the only available option. However, it is important to keep in mind that currency free-floating was not, by any means, imposed. In other words, countries are free to peg, semipeg, or free-float their currencies. In fact, only in 1978 was free-floating officially mandated by the International Monetary Fund.

FREE-FLOATING

The major currencies, such as the U.S. dollar, move independently of other currencies. The currency may be traded by anybody so inclined. Its value is a function of the current supply and demand forces in the market, and there are no specific intervention points that have to be observed. Of course, the Federal Reserve Bank irregularly intervenes to change the value of the U.S. dollar, but no specific levels are ever imposed. (See Figure 2.4.) Naturally, free-floating currencies are in the heaviest trading demand. Free-floating is not the sine qua non condition for trading. Liquidity is also an indispensable condition.

CURRENCY BLOCKS

The major currencies tend to have a polarizing effect on currencies from smaller economies. Sometimes, this phenomenon occurs as a result of for-

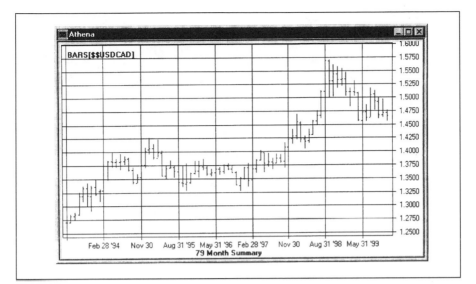

Figure 2.4. The value of the U.S. dollar against the Canadian dollar. *(Source: Bridge Information Systems, Inc.)*

mer colonial ties. For instance, the former British Empire was metamorphosed into the Commonwealth. Consequently, the currencies of the Commonwealth members, such as the Indian rupee, are closer to the British pound. At times, the polarizing effect is generated by the fact that the majority of a smaller economy's business is done with a single larger economy or with a group of economies. Therefore, currency blocks naturally occurred around the U.S. dollar, the British pound, the deutsche mark, and the French franc, at least before the last two merged into the euro.

SEMIPEGGED CURRENCIES

The semipegged currencies have gone the way of the dinosaurs. The standard example of semipegging used to be the member currencies of the European Monetary System. They were allowed to fluctuate within 2.25 percent or, exceptionally, within 6 percent intervention bands until July 31, 1993. Following the foreign exchange crisis of the summer of 1993, the new EMS intervention rates were expanded to a whopping 15 percent. Semipegging generally had a slowing-down effect on speculative currency trading. However, trading was enhanced when currencies reached the extreme values of the allowed range.

Since the beginning of 1999, the EMS' semipegging currencies morphed into the fully pegged values that form the euro.

PEGGED CURRENCIES

Moving away from the Bretton Woods Accord, some smaller economies naturally gyrated around larger economies with which they had the majority of their economic liaisons. For instance, many of the Caribbean nations, such as Jamaica, have pegged their currencies to the U.S. dollar. In addition, some countries have quasi-pegged their currencies to the U.S. dollar, by allowing minor divergences. For instance, the Saudi riyal spot exchange rate has been closely kept against the U.S. dollar at around 3.7500, although small divergences occurred. (See Figure 2.5.)

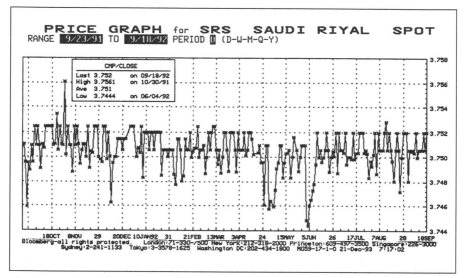

Figure 2.5. The U.S. dollar against the Saudi riyal is traded around 3.7500. *(Courtesy of Bloomberg)*

DIRTY FLOATING

Dirty floating, although not widespread, creates a phenomenon of inefficiency in an industry known to be very efficient. Although officially free-floating, some minor currencies are covertly and irregularly maneuvered by local governments and central banks to better suit domestic or even personal interests. For instance, one of the small countries that officially has a free-floating currency, regularly revalues its currency against the U.S. dollar prior to and during receiving oil shipments. The oil price is quoted in U.S. dollars, and the payment in this case is executed at the dock.

Therefore, the temporary revaluation of the domestic currency reduces the total oil bill. Although this type of inefficiency is potentially profitable in foreign exchange, the market size and the limited liquidity of small currencies greatly reduce the profit opportunities.

CURRENCY RESERVES

In times of economic or political uncertainty, people and corporations worldwide try to protect their investments and wealth by purchasing currencies or commodities perceived as safe haven instruments. In addition, certain international transactions are executed in currencies other than the domestic ones. These types of currencies are known as *currency reserves.* Prior to World War II, the reserve currency was the British pound. In the post–World War II era, the reserve currency around the world was the U.S. dollar. Currently, in addition to the U.S. dollar, other reserve currencies are the euro and, to a lesser extent, the Japanese yen. The portfolio of reserve currencies may change depending on specific international conditions, to include the Swiss franc.

AN OVERVIEW OF THE EMERGING MARKET CRISIS IN THE 1990S

Heavily interconnected Asian economies, such as Thailand, Indonesia, Malaysia, and South Korea, slowed down in the mid-1990s and became pressed to repay huge loans to struggling Japanese banks and other international investors. The situation was exacerbated by government corruption, poor banking practices, and lack of financial sophistication.

The crisis was initiated on July 2, 1997, when the Thai government devalued the baht, triggering a fund outflow from the whole region. Thailand became the first Asian country to turn to the International Monetary Fund for loans to keep its economy going. Soon after, South Korea and Indonesia found themselves in similar situations. The failing economies created social unrest and caused further damage to lenders and investors who were slow to pull their money.

In Japan, the government failed to agree on any kind of reform policy for the struggling banking system. In the United States, where effects of the "Asian flu" remained minimal, the Dow soared to above 9,000 points for the first time on April 6, 1998.

International investors turned bearish in other emerging markets like Brazil and Russia, fearing the problems in Asia could spread. Fears of international economic turmoil began to grow in the United States and Europe. In an effort to nip in the bud the potential impact of the crisis in the U.S., the U.S. Federal Reserve cut key interest rates.

By the end of the decade, Southeast Asia rebounded, but the region remained below the levels it had reached at its peak in the mid-1990s.

3 The European Monetary Union

The European Monetary Union (EMU) launched its much-planned euro on January 4, 1999, kicking off the most powerful union in times of peace. The introduction of the euro was made only in cyberspace, while the bills and coins were stored in safe boxes for release in 2002. This was just the first step in a long series of measures designed to fully integrate the richest economies of Western Europe in an all-out effort to compete head-to-head with the economic and financial might of the United States.

This chapter presents the historic path to the system, its characteristics, and its future in the international context of the twenty-first century.

HISTORICAL BACKGROUND

The creation of the European Monetary Union was the result of a long and continuous series of post–World War II efforts aimed at creating closer economic cooperation among the capitalist European countries. The European Community (EC) commission's officially stated goals were to improve the inter-European economic cooperation, create a regional area of monetary stability, and act as "a pole of stability in world currency markets."

Foreign exchange went through several ups and downs during the destabilized period between the World Wars but, by and large, foreign exchange speculation was not the name of the game, even when it was allowed. Such speculation still had a negative connotation, and it eventually became a punishable offense.

The end of World War II painted a ravaged picture of the former industrial and financial Europe. Foreign exchange was completely out of the picture, as currencies had lost their value. But even under better circumstances, trading would have been impossible, because currency fluctuations were tied in very narrow ranges against the U.S. dollar, under the Bretton Woods Accord of 1944. The accord had created a much-needed nurturing environment for the European economies. Currency stability was vital to the enormous task of rebuilding Europe.

The first steps in this rebuilding were taken in 1950, when the European Payment Union was instituted to facilitate the inter-European settlements of international trade transactions. In 1951, the Treaty of Paris established the European Coal and Steel Community, formed by West Germany, France, Italy, the Netherlands, Belgium, and Luxembourg. Great Britain declined to join. The purpose of the community was to promote inter-European trade in general, and to eliminate restrictions on the trade of coal and raw steel in particular.

The lesson one can draw from that early treaty is that the core lineup and the cultural gaps changed little over the past 50 years. From the very beginning, the de facto European leaders have been Germany (in its split version) and France, while the U.K. opted out. That was the case in 1951, and that remained the case on January 4, 1999.

The French National Assembly derailed plans for a joint European Defense Community in 1954. The lesson in this case is that French governments tend to have a more individualistic tone, which can spell trouble within unions in which members are supposed to strive for the good of the whole.

In 1957, the Treaty of Rome established the European Economic Community, with the same signatories as the European Coal and Steel Community. The stated goal of the European Economic Community was to eliminate customs duties and any barriers against the transit of capital, services, and people among the member nations. The EC also started to raise common tariff barriers against outsiders. To the young reader, these goals might sound tame. For the Europeans, however, the achievement of these goals represented enormous success in grinding down centuries-old rigidities, thus allowing the flexible flow of capital and labor, the basic requirements of a modern superpower.

The European Community consists of four executive and legislative bodies:

1. *The European Commission.* The executive body in charge of making and observing the enforcement of the policies. Since it lacks an enforcement arm, the commission must rely on individual governments to enforce the policies. There are 23 departments, such

as foreign affairs, competition policy, and agriculture. Each country selects its own representatives for four-year terms. The commission is based in Brussels and consists of 17 members.

2. *The Council of Ministers.* Makes the major policy decisions. It is composed of ministers from the 12 member nations. The presidency is held for six months by each of the members, in alphabetical order. The meetings take place in Brussels or in the capital of the nation holding the presidency.

3. *The European Parliament.* Reviews and amends legislative proposals and has the power to adopt or reject budget proposals. It consists of 518 elected members. It is based in Luxembourg, but the sessions take place in Strasbourg or Brussels.

4. *The European Court of Justice.* Settles disputes between the EC and the member nations. It consists of 13 members and is based in Luxembourg.

In 1963, the French–West German Treaty of Cooperation was signed. This pact was designed not only to end centuries of bellicose rivalry, but also to settle the postwar reconciliation between two major foes. The treaty, signed by President Charles de Gaulle and Chancellor Konrad Adenauer, stipulated that West Germany would lead economically through the cold war, and France, the former diplomatic powerhouse, would provide the political leadership. The premise of this treaty was obviously correct in an environment defined by a foreseeable long-term continuing cold war and a divided Germany. Later in this chapter, we discuss the implications for the modern era of this enormously expensive pact.

In 1964, a common agricultural market was instituted and uniform prices were introduced.

A conference of national leaders in 1969 set the objective of establishing a monetary union within the European Community. This goal was supposed to be implemented by 1980, when a common currency was planned to be used in Europe. The reasons for the proposed common currency unit were to stimulate inter-European trade and to weld together the individual member economies into an all-European superpower. Only this type of economy was perceived to be able to fully compete with the economies of the United States and Japan.

The monetary union strategy of semipegging the nation members' currencies allowed a 2 percent fluctuation against each other. Of course, by the end of 1971, the Bretton Woods Accord collapsed and was replaced for two years by a transitional system, the Smithsonian Agreement. This accord raised the stakes in the currency band of fluctuation, by allowing the currencies to move within 4.5 percent against the dollar or a hefty 9 percent against each other.

Faced with the prospect of a rapidly deteriorating international monetary system, the EC members established the European Joint Float Agreement in 1972. By 1973, Great Britain, Ireland, and Denmark were also members.

The agreement allowed the member currencies to move within a 2.25 percent fluctuation band. Due to its curvaceous movement, this band was nicknamed *the snake*. As a joint group, the agreement allowed these currencies to gyrate within a 4.5 percent band. This larger band was nicknamed *the tunnel*. All in all, the entire agreement became known as *the snake in the tunnel*.

The economic fundamentals did not provide much support to the monetary agreement. The members pursued independent economic policies. Consequently, one by one, the British pound, the Danish krone, and the Italian lira were forced out of the snake by early 1973. By and large, the Joint Agreement was gone, despite efforts to prolong its life. A little later in the same fateful year, the Smithsonian Agreement collapsed as well, due to immense pressure on the U.S. dollar.

However, the ideals of economic unification, planned to be achieved in large measure through foreign exchange stability, stayed all the contrarian forces and persevered through the engulfing tide of the free-floating markets.

THE EUROPEAN MONETARY SYSTEM

In 1978, the nine members of the European Community ratified a new plan for stability—the European Monetary System. After several inadvertent delays, the new system was established in 1979. Of the nine members, only seven were full members—West Germany, France, the Netherlands, Belgium, Luxembourg, Denmark, and Ireland. Great Britain did not participate in all of the arrangements and Italy joined under special conditions. Greece joined in 1981, Spain and Portugal in 1986. Great Britain joined the Exchange Rate Mechanism in 1990. Also in 1990, West Germany became Germany as a result of its political unification with East Germany.

FEATURES OF THE EMS

The European Currency Unit (ECU)
This currency was created by the European Monetary System with the eventual goal of replacing the individual European member currencies.

While insignificant in the currency trading community, the ECU's role was to pave the road for the high-powered euro and to create a light foundation for it. The European currency unit was a basket of the member currencies. As a composite unit, the ECU consisted of all the European Community currencies, which were individually weighted. The weights were a direct function of relative GDP and share of inter-EMS trading. These weights were examined every five years or upon request.

To obtain the individual currency in the ECU composition, the following calculations are made:

Composition =   ECU value × Weight × Currency exchange rate
                                                against the U.S. dollar

The ECU had two functions—monetary and accounting.

Under the *monetary function*, the ECU was considered to be a reserve currency. EMS central banks used it for loans and issued ECUs for debt settlement. The ECU was quoted in American terms, just like the British pound. Attempts to launch it on the Chicago Mercantile Exchange (CME) futures market in the mid-1980s failed.

Under the *accounting function*, the ECU price was used as a benchmark against which the member currencies were valued. The individual currency valuation was made at the fixing time in Europe and was based on the middle rate (the average between the bid and the offer).

The Bilateral Grid

The *bilateral grid* linked all of the central rates of the EMS currencies in terms of the ECU. A central rate is the average rate between the bid and the offer at fixing time. It was used on a daily basis to indicate whether the member currencies were observing the bands' fluctuation limits. These bands had been 2.25 percent for most of the members and 6 percent for Italy until 1990, and later for Spain until July 1993.

The extraordinary foreign exchange volatility of 1993 forced the EMS to expand the fluctuation band to 15 percent up or down against the central rate for all the members, and these enormously wide bands remained in place until the member currencies converged into the euro. Each central bank was responsible for shoring up its currency within the boundaries via FX intervention.

The Threshold of Divergence

The *threshold of divergence* was a very important safety feature of the EMS that was not transferred to the euro. This feature created an emergency exit for currencies that become the singular focus of various adverse forces. The threshold of divergence indicated when a specific country with pressured currency should take additional steps other than simple central bank intervention in the foreign exchange markets. These steps generally meant devaluation or revaluation of the currency and interest rate changes, rather than changes in economic policies.

This feature limited the responsibility of the rest of the EMS members toward the currency in trouble. Whereas the other countries provided support for the distressed currency in the short run, they stopped once the threshold of divergence was reached. Therefore, isolated problems became the sole responsibility of the specific country, and the financial and economic exposures of its peers were minimized. The threshold of divergence was set at 1.69 percent (with exceptions for countries in the wider 6 percent band, for which it was at 4.5 percent) from its ECU value.

It performed well in September 1992, when unusual selling pressure on the British pound set up all the defensive measures on the EMS. First, Bank of England attempted to support its battered currency by direct purchases in the interbank market. When this step failed, the other EMS members stepped in and also purchased the pound. This failed as well.

Due to the divergence of the British pound's price from the allowed percentage on the band, the threshold of divergence was activated. The other central banks halted their costly but unsuccessful support of the pound. Bank of England raised its base rate by a hefty 5 percent in the same day, trying to shore up the massive selling pressure. Yet the market was not impressed by the magnitude of the interest rate increase, as it understood that only the crisis, rather than economic policies, triggered the rate change. Therefore, the selling of the pound continued unabated.

With no alternative left, Bank of England was forced to pull its currency out of the Exchange Rate Mechanism (ERM) two years after joining it. Despite the high cost of trying to keep the pound within the permissible band (estimated to be anywhere between $6 and $20 billion), the threshold of divergence performed its emergency exit function, minimizing losses for the rest of the EMS members.

The European officials found no use for a safety exit within the euro, because there are no individual currencies to be targeted.

Supporting Credit Facilities
The supporting credit facilities offered the EMS' central banks an alternative to using their currency reserves for parity maintenance intervention. These facilities consisted of three different maturity loans:

    a. *short-term loans* (45 to 90 days) for virtually unlimited amounts;
    b. *medium-term loans* (90 to 270 days) from a limited ECU pool, based on each member's quota; and

c. *long-term loans* from a limited ECU pool, conditioned on the borrower's promise of following domestic economic policies to minimize the future need for this type of loan.

The European Monetary Cooperation Fund

The European Monetary Cooperation Fund was established to manage the EMS' credit arrangements. In order to increase the acceptance of the ECU, countries that hold more ECU deposits, or accept as loan repayment more than their share of ECU, receive interest on the excess ECU deposits, and vice versa. The interest rate is the weighted average of all the EMS members' discount rates.

PERFORMANCE OF THE EUROPEAN MONETARY SYSTEM

There was a short maiden voyage for the EMS before problems reminiscent of the time of the snake occurred. Divergences in the rate of growth and the rate of inflation among the members continued to generate unwanted changes in interest rates and economic policies. Yet despite many obstacles and several realignments, EMS had successfully sailed through the 1980s.

The 1990s were much stormier years for the European Monetary System. Despite long opposition to full economic union in Europe, starting in 1987, Great Britain successfully, if at a high domestic inflation cost, maneuvered the British pound to stay within the limits of the EMS. Great Britain had been a special member of the EMS since its inception, but not a member of the Exchange Rate Mechanism (ERM).

As one of the European powerhouses, Great Britain had to be close to the core of the discussions on the future of the European Monetary Union. Yet the British economy has been marked by high inflation and the British government opposed any type of economic or financial unification that would hinder national sovereignty, calculating that the perceived future political benefits of independence outweighed the short-term economic concerns. In September 1990, Great Britain joined the Exchange Rate Mechanism at the cross rate of sterling/deutsche mark 2.9500.

The move was widely perceived as beneficial for the British economy. Previously, the sterling/deutsche mark cross had become a sure bet to sell just under the 3.0000 level. Both the Bank of England and Bundesbank would intervene to protect that level. Upon the announcement, the foreign exchange market reacted aggressively by buying (or attempting to buy) large amounts of pounds, despite a simultaneous 1 percent cut in the base rate. The 3.0000 barrier was shattered in a matter of minutes.

The day was an embarrassing one for the cable traders, as it was virtually impossible to trade the currency. There aren't many instances in the careers of spot traders when they are totally unable to make a price.

From the very beginning, objections had been raised regarding the high cross rate of 2.9500 deutsche mark per pound at which Great Britain joined the ERM. The British position remained consistent, that the move was part of the long-term strategy of combating inflation.

Even after entering the ERM, the British government maintained its long-standing objections to advanced economic policy coordination and control, and to a single currency. Eventually, its position softened with regard to currency unification, but not toward European federalism.

By the end of 1991, with the shocks of the swift demise of the Communist block and the unexpected unification of Germany still in the process of psychological digestion, the skies over the EMS looked very calm and encouraging.

In February 1992, the 12 EMS members signed the European Union Treaty that created the European Union (EU), in the Dutch city of Maastricht. This was an ambitious agreement with the stated goal of forging a "closer union among the peoples of Europe." The 12 nations were Belgium, Denmark, France, Germany, Great Britain, Greece, Ireland, Italy, Luxembourg, the Netherlands, Portugal, and Spain. The Treaty consists of a series of amendments to the 1957 Treaty of Rome.

Some countries were reluctant to relinquish national control over their monetary policies, notably Denmark and Great Britain. On June 2, 1992, Danish voters narrowly rejected the Maastricht Treaty. However, the Danes voted their approval in May 1993. British voters ratified the treaty, but they did not generally support a common European currency. The European Union was established on November 1, 1993, after the treaty had been ratified by the 12 member states, which then became members of the EU. The EU retained the EC's Parliament, Council, Commission, and Court of Justice.

The Maastricht Treaty was to become law only upon ratification by all the EMS members, and was supposed to be implemented by January 1993, parallel to the establishing of the single European market. According to the Maastricht Treaty, the European Community leaders would have a central bank by 1994, a single currency by January of 1997 or January 1999, and a joint economic and foreign policy by 1999.

The convergence tests for the ERM members were based on inflation, interest rates, exchange rates, budget deficit, and debt stock. In terms of inflation, the individual country rate could not exceed the rate of 1.5 percent above the lowest three members in the previous year. Interest rates had to be kept within 2 percent above the lowest three members in the previous year. With regard to exchange rates, a country had to be an ERM bands member for two years, without realignment. The budget deficit could not exceed 3 percent of GDP. Finally, the outstanding stock of public sector debt could not be higher than 60 percent of GDP. One major economic indicator was not included in the criteria—unemployment. Result? Double-digit unemployment in the euro zone before and after the currency convergence of 1999.

Not all countries managed to clear the criteria; back-room politics were still in place. The German approach had been quite strict: Only those countries that cleared all criteria would enter the convergence in the first stage. The French attitude was that criteria meant a series of targets that all members would strive to achieve if they couldn't meet the deadline. The French version won. Therefore, two countries that failed to meet the targets—Italy and Belgium—still made the cut, while Greece did not.

THE EMS CRISES OF 1992–1993

As the costs of political change in Europe started to become apparent in the early 1990s, enthusiasm among the EMS members started to wear thin. In June 1992, as mentioned earlier, the Danish referendum had rejected the treaty. By September 1992, the British pound and the Italian lira had to be (temporarily, it was officially announced) withdrawn from the ERM. Red flags were raised. The foreign exchange shock of having the pound suspended from the ERM had a long-term impact. How could it happen?

A lot of fingers in the market pointed toward the Bundesbank's tight monetary policy. The traditional German distaste for inflation continued to be fueled by the specific inflationary characteristics of their nation's unification. With overheated consumer demand from the former East Germany, the Bundesbank had little choice but to pursue a high interest rate policy. The policy paid off domestically, but raised huge problems abroad. As the September 1992 events were unfolding, Germany produced only a .25 percent interest rate cut, far less than its neighbors' expectations.

Within a worldwide economic slowdown and East European political turmoil, each nation was looking to stay afloat economically. Faced with either the expensive choice of propping up their currencies to the agreed levels, or the economically suffocating choice of raising interest rates, most of the EMS members felt cornered. The monetary system, after all, was designed to reduce the currencies' gyrations, as the member economies converged. The feeling was that stronger currencies like the deutsche mark, the Dutch guilder, and the Belgian franc had to be revalued, while the other currencies had to be devalued.

Therefore, when the run on the EMS currencies finally occurred in September 1992, it looked more like a fait accomplit, rather than a totally unexpected surprise. What was surprising, though, was the velocity of the forces in play in the foreign exchange markets. It was no wonder that the average daily trading volume reached the U.S. $1 trillion level toward the end of 1992.

The pound sterling and the Italian lira were not, by any means, the only currencies affected negatively. The Spanish peseta, the Portuguese escudo, and the Irish punt were devalued; the Norwegian krone and the Finnish markka were allowed to fluctuate. The Swedish central bank raised a key interest rate by 500 percent (this is no typo!), before it gave up and let the Swedish krona fluctuate freely; and the Danish krone and the French franc came under increasing pressure. Allowing the currencies to gyrate according to the law of supply and demand is a de facto devaluation.

The Swedish krona and the Finnish markka are not, of course, members of the EMS. But because they had been planning to join the EMS, the Swedish and Finnish central banks maintained their respective currencies within the accepted bounds in order to show the necessary financial discipline and commitment.

What about the French franc? Relatively speaking, the French franc came under less pressure in the initial stages of the all-out sell-off of the EMS currencies. But sooner rather than later, the French franc became the selling target of traders around the world. The fundamentals had seemed to be supportive of the French franc. The French economy was in better shape than the economies of the other members. The increased independence of the Bank of France was perceived as a strong force behind the franc.

After targeting all of the weaker EMS currencies, triggering hefty devaluations across the board, the foreign exchange market finally focused on the core currency vis-à-vis the deutsche mark—the French franc. The French government policy of maintaining the franc in the ERM without devaluation, a policy known as the franc fort, was being tested.

As the French franc sell-off fury was unleashed, the French efforts had been matched by Germany's. To the chagrin of smaller members, the Bundesbank seemed much more inclined to help the French franc than their own currencies.

Was this a surprise? Not entirely. Behind it all was the French–West German Treaty of Cooperation. France and Germany had entered a deep-reaching pact covering their exact economic and political roles relative to each other. Thirty years later the pact was being put to the test on the foreign exchange markets.

The Bundesbank not only helped with vigorous foreign exchange market interventions; it also cut interest rates. Cutting the interest rates under pressure across the board, but specifically to support the French franc, was a first for the Bundesbank. Yet, despite the all-out joint efforts, the franc fort could not be saved.

The decision made by the ERM on the last weekend of July 1993 was to expand the previous fluctuation bands of 2.25 and 6 percent to 15 percent. Although it was stated to be a temporary decision, the future of the European Monetary System as envisioned at the Maastricht Treaty was, for a while, in jeopardy.

EMERGENCE OF THE EURO

Here are the official irrevocable locking rates of the 11 participating European currencies in the euro (EUR). The rates were proposed by the EU Commission and approved by EU finance ministers on December 31, 1998, ahead of the launch of the euro at midnight, January 1, 1999. The real starting date was Monday, January 4, 1999.

The conversion rates are:

1 EUR = 40.3399 BEF

1 EUR = 1.95583 DEM

1 EUR = 166.386 ESP

1 EUR = 6.55957 FRF

1 EUR = 0.787564 IEP

1 EUR = 1936.27 ITL

1 EUR = 40.3399 LUF

1 EUR = 2.20371 NLG

1 EUR = 13.7603 ATS

1 EUR = 200.482 PTE

1 EUR = 5.94573 FIM

On December 31, 1998, the Commission also set its final fixings of the ECU, which converted 1:1 with the euro at midnight, January 1, 1999. The Exchange Rate Mechanism (ERM-2) central rates for the Greek drachma and Danish krone were set on December 31, 1998, and are:

353.109 drachma per euro

7.46038 kroner per euro

Denmark will observe a narrow fluctuation margin of 2.25 percent around its central rate, while Greece's band is 15 percent. The other two EU countries outside the euro—the U.K. and Sweden—are also staying outside ERM-2, which is designed to link currencies outside the euro to the euro.

Europe's economic and political stability is a magnet for many European countries that have the right to apply to become members of the European Union. The countries that have applied are:

Malta: July 16, 1990

Switzerland: May 20, 1992 (shelved since the referendum on the European Economic Area of December 6, 1992)

Liechtenstein: September 28, 1992 (suspended because of the Swiss refusal to join the European Economic Area)

Hungary: March 31, 1994

Poland: April 5, 1994

Romania: June 22, 1995

Slovakia: June 27, 1995

Latvia: October 13, 1995

Estonia: November 24, 1995

Lithuania: December 8, 1995

Bulgaria: December 14, 1995

Czech Republic: January 17, 1996

Slovenia: June 10, 1996

In December 1997, the Luxembourg European Council decided to open negotiations in 1998 with six countries—Cyprus, the Czech Republic, Estonia, Hungary, Poland, and Slovenia. These six countries formed the "first wave" of applicant countries. A "second wave" would be made up of Bulgaria, Latvia, Lithuania, Romania, and Slovakia. Opening negotiations with these applicants would depend on their political and economic development.

As far as Turkey is concerned, the European Council concluded that the political and economic conditions allowing accession negotiations to be envisaged were not yet satisfied, and that the European strategy to prepare Turkey for accession should be continued.

DENOMINATIONS OF THE EURO

The euro bills are issued in denominations of 5, 10, 20, 50, 100, 200, and 500 euros. (See Figure 3.1.) Coins are issued in denominations of 1 and 2 euros, and 50, 20, 10, 5, 2, and 1 cent. (See Figure 3.2.)

THE AGENDA FOR TRANSITION TO THE EURO

1998

- May 2: Identification of the first wave of countries to adopt the single currency.
- July 1: Establishment of the European Central Bank (ECB).

1999

- January 1: Introduction of the euro; national currencies are treated as subdivisions of the euro.

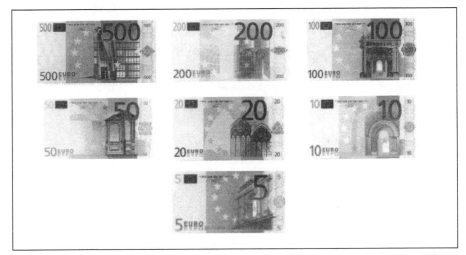

Figure 3.1. Euro bill denominations. *(Source: ECB)*

Figure 3.2. Euro coin denominations. *(Source: ECB)*

2000

- Foreign exchange transactions are in euros only.

2001

- The private sector is welcome, but not compelled, to use the euro.

2002

- January 1 (at the latest): Introduction of the euro coins and notes.
- July 1 (at the latest): Withdrawal of national coins and notes.
- The euro is the sole legal tender.
- All transactions are in euros.

WHAT IT ALL MEANS FOR THE EUROPEANS

As set out in the Maastricht Treaty, any national of a Member State is a citizen of the Union. The aim of European citizenship is to strengthen and consolidate European identity by greater involvement of the citizens in the Community integration process. Thanks to the single market, citizens enjoy a series of general rights in various areas such as the free movement of goods and services, consumer protection and public health, equal opportunities and treatment, access to jobs, and social protection.

There are four categories of specific provisions and rights attaching to citizenship in the European Union:

- freedom of movement and residence throughout the Union;
- the right to vote and stand as a candidate in municipal elections and in elections to the European Parliament in the state where the citizen resides;
- protection by the diplomatic and consular authorities of any Member State if the State of which the person is a national is a non-member country;
- the right to petition the European Parliament and apply to the Ombudsman.

The Amsterdam Treaty of 1997 completes the list of civic rights of Union citizens and clarifies the link between national citizenship and European citizenship.

The Treaty of Amsterdam

The Treaty of Amsterdam is the result of the Intergovernmental Conference launched at the Turin European Council on March 29, 1996. It was adopted at the Amsterdam European Council on June 16 and 17, 1997, then signed on October 2, 1997 by the Foreign Ministers of the 15 Member States. It is to be enforced after it has been ratified by all the Member States in accordance with their respective constitutional requirements.

From a legal angle, the purpose of the Treaty is to amend certain provisions of the Treaty on European Union, the Treaties establishing the European Communities, and certain related acts. It does not substitute for the other Treaties but adds to them.

The Troïka

The Troïka consists of the Member State that currently holds the Presidency of the Council, the Member State that held it for the preceding six months, and the Member State that will hold it for the next six months. The Troïka is assisted by the Commission and represents the Union in external relations coming under the common foreign and security policy.

When the Treaty of Amsterdam is fully enforced, the Troïka will cease to exist in its present form. It will be replaced by a system whereby the Presidency is assisted by the Secretary-General of the Council, in the capacity as High Representative for the common foreign and security policy, and by the Member State that is next in line for the Presidency.

Architecture of Europe

This refers to the various organizations, institutions, treaties, and traditional relations making up the European area within which members work together on problems of shared interest.

The Treaty on European Union formed three pillars, which established an essential part of this architecture:

1. the European Community,
2. the common foreign and security policy, and
3. cooperation in the fields of justice and home affairs.

Matters falling within the second and third pillars are handled by the Community institutions (the European Council, the Council, the Commission, the European Parliament, etc.), but intergovernmental procedures apply.

THE EUROPEAN CENTRAL BANK (ECB)

The European Central Bank was set up on June 1, 1998. Since the introduction of the single currency on January 1, 1999, the ECB has been responsible for carrying out the Community's monetary policy. As to practicalities, the ECB's decision-making bodies (the Governing Council and the Executive Board) will run a European System of Central Banks (ESCB) whose tasks will be to manage the money in circulation, conduct foreign exchange operations, hold and manage the Member States' official foreign reserves, and promote the smooth operation of payment systems. The ECB is the successor to the European Monetary Institute (EMI).

OBJECTIVES AND TASKS OF THE ESCB

The primary objective of the European System of Central Banks, as defined in Article 2 of the Statute of the European System of Central Banks and of the European Central Bank, is to maintain price stability. Without prejudice to the primary objective of price stability, the ESCB shall support the general economic policies in the Community with a view to contributing to the achievement of the objectives of the Community. In pursuing its objectives, the ESCB shall act in accordance with the principle of an open market economy with free competition, favoring an efficient allocation of resources.

The basic tasks to be carried out by the ESCB are:

- defining and implementing the monetary policy of the Community;
- conducting foreign exchange operations;
- holding and managing the official foreign reserves of the participating Member States;
- promoting the smooth operation of payment systems; and
- contributing to the smooth conduct of policies pursued by the competent authorities relating to the prudential supervision of credit institutions and the stability of the financial system.

In addition, the ESCB has an advisory role vis-à-vis the Community and national authorities on matters that fall within its field of competence, particularly where Community or national legislation is concerned. Finally, in order to undertake the tasks of the ESCB, the ECB, assisted by the NCBs, shall collect the necessary statistical information either from competent national authorities or directly from economic agents.

MONETARY FUNCTIONS AND OPERATIONS OF THE ESCB

The ESCB Statute specifies the monetary functions and operations of the ESCB. On the basis of these provisions, the European Monetary Institute (EMI) prepared an operational framework for the ESCB's monetary policy. The Governing Council of the ECB will make the final decision on the operational framework. The Governing Council of the ECB may decide not to use all the available options or may change certain features of the instruments and procedures presented here.

MONETARY POLICY INSTRUMENTS

The operational framework consists of a set of instruments; the ESCB will conduct open market operations, offer standing facilities, and may require credit institutions to hold minimum reserves on accounts with the ESCB.

Open Market Operations

Open market operations play an important role in steering interest rates, managing the liquidity situation in the market, and signaling the stance of monetary policy. Five types of instruments are available to the ESCB for conducting open market operations. The most important instruments are reverse transactions (applicable on the basis of repurchase agreements or collateralized loans). The ESCB may also use outright transactions, issue debt certificates, initiate foreign exchange swaps, and collect fixed-term deposits. Open market operations are initiated by the ECB, which also decides on the instrument to be used and the terms and conditions for the execution of such operations. With regard to their aim, regularity, and procedures, the ESCB open market operations can be divided into four categories—main refinancing operations, longer-term refinancing operations, fine-tuning operations, and structural operations.

- The *main refinancing operations* are regular liquidity-providing reverse transactions with a weekly frequency and a maturity of two weeks. They will be executed by the national central banks on the basis of standard tenders and according to a prespecified calendar. The main refinancing operations will play a pivotal role in pursuing the purposes of ESCB open market operations and will provide the bulk of refinancing to the financial sector.
- The *longer-term refinancing operations* are liquidity-providing reverse transactions with a monthly frequency and a maturity of three months. They will be executed by the national central banks

on the basis of standard tenders and according to a prespecified calendar. These operations aim to provide counterparties with additional longer-term refinancing. As a rule, the ESCB will not intend to send signals to the market by means of these operations and will therefore normally act as a rate taker.

- *Fine-tuning operations* can be executed on an ad hoc basis with the aim of both managing the liquidity situation in the market and steering interest rates, in particular, in order to smooth the effects on interest rates caused by unexpected liquidity fluctuations. Fine-tuning operations will primarily be executed as reverse transactions, but may also take the form of outright transactions, foreign exchange swaps, and the collection of fixed-term deposits. The instruments and procedures applied in the conduct of fine-tuning operations will be adapted to the types of transactions and the specific objectives pursued in performing the operations. Fine-tuning operations will normally be executed by the national central banks through quick tenders or bilateral procedures. The Governing Council of the ECB will decide whether, under exceptional circumstances, fine-tuning bilateral operations may be executed by the ECB itself.

- In addition, the ESCB may carry out *structural operations* through the issuance of debt certificates, reverse transactions, and outright transactions. These operations will be executed whenever the ECB wishes to adjust the structural position of the ESCB vis-à-vis the financial sector (on a regular or non-regular basis). Structural operations in the form of reverse transactions and the issuance of debt instruments will be carried out by the national central banks through standard tenders. Structural operations in the form of outright transactions will be executed through bilateral procedures.

Standing Facilities
Standing facilities aim to provide and absorb overnight liquidity, signal the general stance of monetary policy, and regulate overnight market interest rates. Two standing facilities, which will be administered in a decentralized manner by the national central banks, will be available to eligible counterparties on their own initiative:

- Counterparties will be able to use the *marginal lending facility* to obtain overnight liquidity from the national central banks against eligible assets. The interest rate on the marginal lending facility will normally provide a ceiling for the overnight market interest rate.

- Counterparties will be able to use the *deposit facility* to make overnight deposits with the national central banks. The interest rate on the deposit facility will normally provide a floor for the overnight market interest rate.

Minimum Reserves

Preparatory work has been carried out with a view to enabling the ESCB to impose minimum reserves as from the start of Stage Three. It will be up to the Governing Council of the ECB to decide whether minimum reserves will actually be applied. Any minimum reserves system would be intended to pursue the aims of stabilizing money market interest rates, creating (or enlarging) a structural liquidity shortage, and possibly contributing to the control of monetary expansion. The reserve requirement of each institution would be determined in relation to elements of its balance sheet. In order to pursue the aim of stabilizing interest rates, the ESCB's minimum reserves system would enable institutions to make use of averaging provisions. This implies that compliance with the reserve requirement would be determined on the basis of the institutions' average daily reserve holdings over a one-month maintenance period.

COUNTERPARTIES

The ESCB monetary policy framework is formulated with a view to ensuring the participation of a broad range of counterparties. If minimum reserves are applied, only institutions subject to minimum reserves may access the standing facilities and participate in open market operations based on standard tenders. If no minimum reserves are applied, the range of counterparties will broadly correspond to credit institutions in the euro area. The ESCB may select a limited number of counterparties to participate in fine-tuning operations. For outright transactions, no restrictions will be placed a priori on the range of counterparties. Active players in the foreign exchange market will be used for foreign exchange swaps conducted for monetary policy purposes.

UNDERLYING ASSETS

Pursuant to Article 18.1 of the ESCB Statute, all ESCB credit operations have to be based on adequate collateral. The ESCB will allow a wide range of assets to underlie its operations. A distinction is made, essentially for purposes internal to the ESCB, between two categories of eligible assets:

tier one and tier two respectively. Tier one consists of marketable debt instruments that meet uniform Monetary Union-wide eligibility criteria specified by the ECB. Tier two consists of additional assets, marketable and non-marketable, that are of particular importance for national financial markets and banking systems and for which eligibility criteria are established by the national central banks, subject to ECB approval. No distinction will be made between the two tiers with regard to the quality of the assets and their eligibility for the various types of ESCB monetary policy operations (except for the fact that tier two assets are normally not used in outright transactions). The eligibility criteria for underlying assets to ESCB monetary policy operations are the same as those applied by the ESCB for underlying assets to intraday credit. Furthermore, ESCB counterparties may use eligible assets on a cross-border basis; they may borrow from the central bank of the Member State in which they are established by making use of assets located in another Member State.

ORGANIZATION OF THE EUROPEAN SYSTEM OF CENTRAL BANKS

The ESCB is composed of the European Central Bank and the EU national central banks (NCBs). The NCBs of the Member States that do not participate in the euro area, however, are members of the ESCB with a special status. While they are allowed to conduct their respective national monetary policies, they do not take part in the decision making regarding the single monetary policy for the euro area and the implementation of such decisions.

The ESCB is governed by the decision-making bodies of the ECB—the Governing Council, the Executive Board, and the General Council.

The *Governing Council* comprises all the members of the Executive Board and the governors of the NCBs of the Member States without a derogation, those NCBs that participate fully in the Monetary Union. The main responsibilities of the Governing Council are:

- to adopt the guidelines and make the decisions necessary to ensure the performance of the tasks entrusted to the ESCB; and
- to formulate the monetary policy of the Community, including, as appropriate, decisions relating to intermediate monetary objectives, key interest rates, and the supply of reserves in the ESCB, and to establish the necessary guidelines for their implementation.

The *Executive Board* comprises the President, the Vice President, and four other members, all chosen from among persons of recognized standing and professional experience in monetary or banking matters. They are appointed by common accord of the governments of the Member States at the level of the Heads of State or Government, on a recommendation from the European Council after it has consulted the European Parliament and the Governing Council of the ECB (the Council of the European Monetary Institute for the first appointments). The main responsibilities of the Executive Board are:

- to implement monetary policy in accordance with the guidelines and decisions laid down by the Governing Council of the ECB and, in doing so, to give the necessary instructions to the NCBs; and

- to execute those powers that have been delegated to it by the Governing Council of the ECB.

The *General Council* comprises the President, the Vice President, and the governors of all the NCBs—of Member States both with and without a derogation. The General Council performs the tasks that the ECB took over from the European Monetary Institute (EMI) and that, owing to the derogation of one or more Member States, still have to be performed in the third stage. The General Council also contributes to:

- the ESCB's advisory functions;

- the collection of statistical information;

- the preparation of the ECB's quarterly and annual reports and weekly consolidated financial statements;

- the establishment of the necessary rules for standardizing the accounting and reporting of operations undertaken by the NCBs;

- the taking of measures relating to the establishment of the key for the ECB's capital subscription other than those already laid down in the Treaty;

- the laying down of the conditions of employment of the ECB's staff; and

- the necessary preparations for irrevocably fixing the exchange rates of the currencies of the Member States with a derogation against the euro.

THE ESCB IS AN INDEPENDENT SYSTEM

When performing ESCB-related tasks, neither the ECB, nor an NCB, nor any member of their decision-making bodies may seek or take instructions from any external body. The Community institutions and bodies and the governments of the Member States may not seek to influence the members of the decision-making bodies of the ECB or of the NCBs in the performance of their tasks. The ESCB Statute provides several measures to ensure security of tenure for NCB governors and members of the Executive Board:

- a minimum renewable term of office for governors of five years;
- a minimum non-renewable term of office for members of the Executive Board of eight years (it should be noted that a system of staggered appointments is foreseen for the first Executive Board for members other than the President in order to ensure continuity);
- removal from office is only possible in the event of incapacity or serious misconduct; and
- the European Court of Justice is competent to settle any disputes.

CONCLUSION

There is no doubt in anybody's mind that the unification of 354 million people, along with a joint GDP that is 20 percent more than the United States' and 50 percent more than Japan's, present the European Monetary Union with a very attractive goal. The European block is not only better suited to compete with the United States and Japan; it's also situated to become the world economic leader.

Achieving such a mighty goal cannot, in the long run, avoid economic and political realities. Despite the efforts toward economic convergence, the facts show that old-fashioned divergences, in terms of economic growth and inflation, labor immobility, high unemployment, and cultural differences, are recurring problems.

ECONOMIC DIVERGENCE

The divergent economic trends and the consequent need for divergent policies cannot help but emphasize the social differences, generally disregarded by most studies. The political unification of Germany, which capitalized on the opportunity presented by the weakening of the Communist grip in Europe, acted as a litmus test. Despite a common language, culture, and heritage, the unification proved to be an economically burdensome undertaking.

When a similar experiment is envisioned on an 11-nation scale (with all those nations being very different), the logistics appear in a very special perspective. Of course, these barriers are slowly melting away, but are they disappearing fast enough for this generation?

Labor rigidities present another issue of substance, as typically only the youngest employees are able and willing to relocate and work in a foreign land. Even with the well-known linguistic skills many Europeans enjoy, not all are willing to adapt to slower or faster working schedules than their domestic ones. With social systems providing comfortable benefits that are incomprehensible by U.S. standards, employees are understandably reluctant to take a leap into a different trading environment.

Unemployment rates remain at ridiculously high levels at the start of the twenty-first century. This is a challenge for an aspiring world economic leader. The European governments are hard-pressed to find means of creating jobs, while reducing social benefits and encouraging labor mobility.

Convergence has been the buzzword for decades, but it was natural convergence that was meant. When the reality of the economic fundamentals is denied, it is only a matter of time before the forces of the free markets make the necessary adjustments. Simply, artificial mechanisms have a limited life.

IMPACT ON THE FOREIGN EXCHANGE MARKET

The preparations for the euro included drastic trimming of jobs in the foreign exchange dealing rooms, as the EMS currency traders were no longer needed. Moreover, many money-center banks closed their branches in continental Europe and consolidated in London. After these drastic adjustments were made, the pruned FX community rebounded. Since the spring of 1999, after a short period of accommodation with trading the euro, volume has picked up considerably, albeit more focused on a handful of currencies than in the early 1990s. Along with electronic trading, the introduction of the euro has generated more efficiency in the currency markets. The FX markets started to roll with a vengeance in the new trading environment.

4 Currency Characteristics

This chapter describes the most-traded currencies and the ISO codes used to refer to them.

THE ISO CODES

The foreign exchange operations and most financial information services do not refer to currencies by their full name. Rather, they use standardized codes, developed by the International Organization for Standardization (ISO) and known as the ISO codes. For example, the U.S. dollar is coded USD and the euro is coded EUR. (See Figure 4.1.) Codification is a practical necessity in the complex global environment of the foreign exchange markets. Throughout this book, we refer to currencies alternatively by their full names and their codes. Figure 4.2 shows the ISO codes for the most traded foreign currencies.

Traders, customer traders, and back-office clerks use the ISO codes extensively for inputting and processing data. The codes are used on an individual basis or, more commonly, in currency pairs. For instance, U.S. dollar/Swiss franc is entered as USD/CHF.

The ISO abbreviations are not used, however, in normal conversations. Traders use nicknames for the currencies. The U.S. dollar is known as the *buck* or *greenback*. The British pound sterling is generally called *cable* or, less commonly, *quid*. The Swiss franc is commonly referred to as *swissy*; the Australian dollar is called *aussie*, and the New Zealand dollar, *kiwi*.

MarketWatch					
Symbol	Last	Chg	Low	High	Time
$$EURUSD	1.0657	−.0050	1.0640	1.0730	15:05
$$USDJPY	115.20	.42	114.47	115.43	15:02
$$GBPUSD	1.6101	−.0037	1.6074	1.6184	15:05
$$USDCHF	1.5031	.0071	1.4938	1.5058	14:56
$$USDCAD	1.4873	−.0103	1.4863	1.4983	15:02
$$AUDUSD	.6487	−.0020	.6461	.6537	15:04

Figure 4.1. The MarketWatch in Bridge displays ISO currency codes. *(Source: Bridge Information Systems, Inc.)*

ISO CODES	
US dollar	USD
Euro	EUR
Japanese yen	JPY
Swiss franc	CHF
Sterling	GBP
Canadian dollar	CAD
Australian dollar	AUD
New Zealand dollar	NZD

Figure 4.2. Examples of ISO codes.

THE U.S. DOLLAR

The United States dollar is the world's main currency. All currencies are generally quoted in U.S. dollar terms. In current dollar terms, the role of the U.S. dollar rose to 87 percent on one side of the transactions in 1998 from over 83 percent in 1995. That doesn't come as a surprise, since commodities and international debt are quoted in terms of the dollar.

In terms of international economic and political unrest, the U.S. dollar is the main safe-haven currency. This feature was proven particularly well during the Southeast Asian crisis of 1997–1998, when panicked investors in the beleaguered region dumped the crisis-stricken currencies in favor of dollars.

The U.S. dollar is no longer backed by gold, but by the sheer size of the United States' economy and its leading financial markets. Although challenged by the euro zone and Japanese competition, the United States remains the preeminent economy in the world, and the dollar is the world's financial standard. In the long run, the dollar is also underpinned by the predominant U.S. military force, which has been vital in putting out numerous regional political fires, thus encouraging a pro-market perspective. It doesn't hurt that the U.S. has the upper hand in the microchip and software industries, while our ample available land provides an advantage that cannot be matched by either Europe or Japan.

The U.S. dollar became the leading currency toward the end of the Second World War and was at the center of the Bretton Woods Accord, as the other currencies were virtually pegged against it. (Room for fluctuation against the dollar was a symbolic 1 percent.) The breakdown of the Bretton Woods system in 1971 and the introduction of the euro in 1999 reduced the dollar's importance only marginally.

The currency was devalued by approximately 60 percent between September 1985 and March-April 1995 in a relief effort for American exporters and in an attempt to rebalance the trade deficit. In 1995, the U.S. dollar reached record lows against the Swiss franc, deutsche mark, and Japanese yen (see Figures 4.3, 4.4, and 4.5) but not against the pound (see Figure 4.6). There are no restrictions on foreign exchange in the United States, and the Federal Reserve employs a minimum of interference, although it intervenes under special circumstances.

The major currencies traded against the U.S. dollar are the euro, Japanese yen, British pound, and Swiss franc.

THE EURO

The euro has replaced the deutsche mark as the second currency of resort since January 4, 1999. The currency, which was expected to perform better than the sum of its components, is steadily gaining acceptance as a major currency. The euro failed to live up to the heavy propaganda that preceded its introduction, and plunged consistently in 1999, falling below parity with the dollar for the first time. (See Figure 4.7.) European officials went to great lengths to emphasize the great euro potential, but the long-term outlook carried little weight for spot traders, who rightfully focused on the euro zone economic malaise at the time.

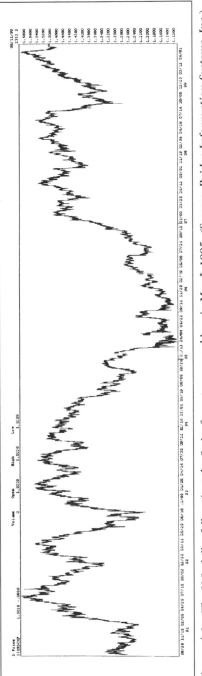

Figure 4.3. The U.S. dollar fell against the Swiss franc to a record low in March 1995. (*Source: Bridge Information Systems, Inc.*)

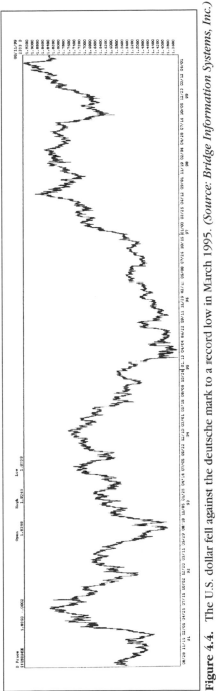

Figure 4.4. The U.S. dollar fell against the deutsche mark to a record low in March 1995. (*Source: Bridge Information Systems, Inc.*)

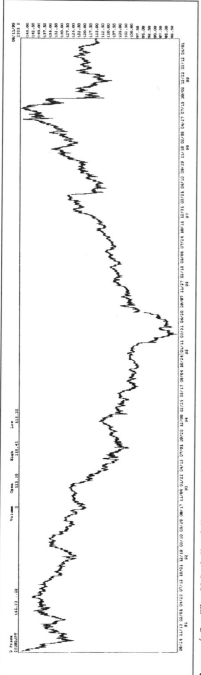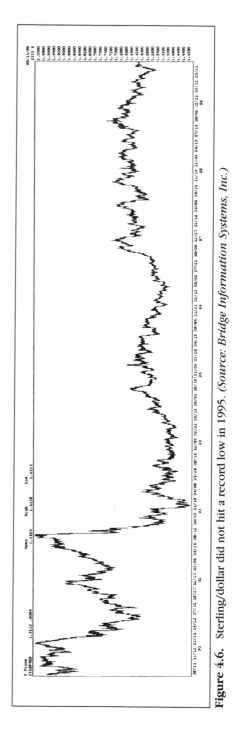

Figure 4.5. The U.S. dollar fell against the Japanese yen to a record low in April 1995. (*Source: Bridge Information Systems, Inc.*)

Figure 4.6. Sterling/dollar did not hit a record low in 1995. (*Source: Bridge Information Systems, Inc.*)

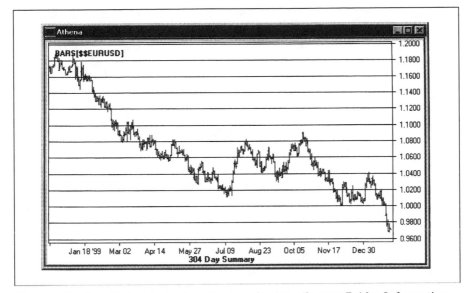

Figure 4.7. Euro/dollar's behavior after introduction. *(Source: Bridge Information Systems, Inc.)*

The euro was designed to become the premier currency in trading by simply being quoted in American terms. The type of quote means that you will see the euro as the first, or base, currency in an exchange rate, such as euro/dollar, euro/yen, and euro/Canadian dollar. The currency is exposed now to a wide variety of economic and political factors stemming from the 11 diverse members of the EMU, a drastic change from the responsibilities a currency generally encounters from a single economy. This approach changes the rules of the game, despite repeated assurances from European officials that the euro zone concept is similar to that of the United States. Their stated position disregards the bloody European history and the diversity of languages, culture, and work habits.

Like the U.S. dollar, the euro has a strong international presence stemming from members of the European Monetary Union. The currency remains plagued by unequal growth, high unemployment, and government resistance to structural changes. The pair was also weighed in 1999 and 2000 by outflows from foreign investors, particularly Japanese, who were forced to liquidate their losing investments in euro-denominated assets.

Moreover, European money managers rebalanced their portfolios and reduced their euro exposure as their needs for hedging currency risk in Europe declined.

THE JAPANESE YEN

The Japanese yen is the third most traded currency in the world; it has a much smaller international presence than the U.S. dollar or the euro. The yen is very liquid around the world, practically around the clock.

As some foreign companies found the Japanese market tough to crack, the natural demand to trade the yen concentrated mostly among the Japanese *keiretsu*, the economic and financial conglomerates. The yen is theoretically sensitive to changes in the price or structure of the raw material markets. However, after absorbing the oil *shoku* of 1973, the Japanese economy learned how to weather this type of crisis successfully. Therefore, the Kuwait takeover in 1990 failed to affect the oil price, the Japanese economy, and consequently, the Japanese yen. Let's not forget that the commodity-producing countries are more dependent on Japan than the other way around.

The yen is much more sensitive to the fortunes of the Nikkei index, the Japanese stock market, and the real estate market. The 1989 attempt of the Bank of Japan to deflate the double bubble in these two markets had a negative effect on the Japanese yen, although the impact was short-lived. Between 1989 and 1995, Japan had had more than its share of political scandals, from old-fashioned geisha affairs to bribery at the highest government levels. The political scandals had a much smaller impact on the currency, as traders became confused about the significance of those events vis-à-vis the traditional Japanese political arena. The lack of significant resolve generated a lack of interest in the foreign exchange market.

The Dollar/Japanese yen reached record lows in April 1995, after comments by newly elected President Bill Clinton and his Secretary of the Treasury Lloyd Bentsen emphasized that the yen should reflect the might of the Japanese economy. (See Figure 4.5.) The motivation of those statements was the worsening U.S. trade deficit with Japan. The yen had previously been revalued following the G-5's Plaza Accord of September 1985, precisely for the same purpose. However, the yen high of around 80, reached in April 1995, failed to stick or make a serious dent in the Japanese trade surplus with the United States. (See Figure 4.8.)

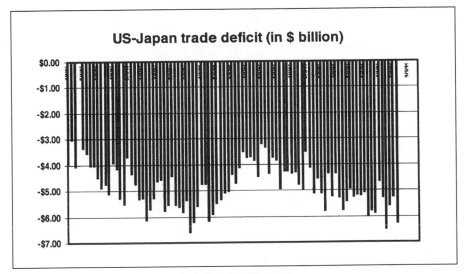

Figure 4.8. The U.S.–Japan trade deficit (1992–1999).

Why is the yen quoted at a rate different in format from the other major currencies? In post–World War II Japan, American occupation forces had to decide on a new exchange rate for the yen. Because the day starts in Asia and the Japanese flag displays the sun, this idea was extrapolated to foreign exchange. The sun is represented as a circle, circles have 360 degrees, so the dollar-yen spot exchange rate became 360. Et voila!

THE BRITISH POUND

At the start of the new millennium, the pound sterling commands 6 percent of the world market, which places it in a distant third against the dollar, behind the euro and the yen. The majority of the pound transactions take placet in the largest foreign exchange market—London—with volume decreasing significantly in the U.S. market, and slowing down to a trickle in Asia. Therefore, in the New York market, many banks have to stop quoting the pound (*cable*) at noon.

Until the end of World War II, the pound was the currency of reference. Its nickname, *cable*, is derived from the telex machine, which was used to trade it in its heyday. The currency is heavily traded against the euro and the U.S. dollar, but has a spotty presence against other currencies.

The pound's behavior resembles a roller coaster, due to its domestic problems and to its love-hate relationship with the European Monetary Union.

The two-year bout with the Exchange Rate Mechanism, between 1990 and 1992, had a soothing effect on the British pound, as it generally had to follow the deutsche mark's fluctuations, but the crisis conditions that precipitated the pound's withdrawal from the ERM had a psychological effect on the currency.

Prior to the introduction of the euro, both the pound and the Swiss franc benefited from any doubts about the currency convergence, just to be dumped when these question mark problems dissipated. After the introduction of the euro, Bank of England played a game of catch, slashing interest rates in rapid succession, not only to revive its moribund economy, but also to bring the high U.K. rates closer to the lower rates in the euro zone. But the central bank had to reverse policy and tighten rates. The pound could join the euro in the early 2000s, provided that the U.K. referendum is positive.

Although it isn't obvious, the pound is a petrocurrency. Therefore, cable can be sensitive to oil price gyrations.

THE SWISS FRANC

The Swiss franc is the only currency of a major European country that belongs neither to the European Monetary Union nor to the G-7 countries. This position is, however, typical of Switzerland, a country known for its neutrality.

Although the Swiss economy is relatively small, the Swiss franc is one of the four major currencies, despite its tiny 2 percent market share. Why? The Swiss franc closely resembles the strength and quality of the Swiss economy and finance. Switzerland has no political exposure to the former Soviet Union, and its financial exposure to the Eastern European region in general was reduced. However, it has a very close economic relationship with Germany, and thus to the euro zone. Therefore, in terms of political uncertainty in the East, the Swiss franc is favored generally over the euro. (See Figure 4.9.)

Moreover, a Swiss referendum rejected the possibility of joining the EMU, to the chagrin of Switzerland's neighbors. When the EMS came un-

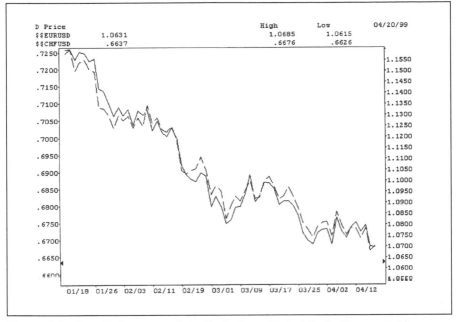

Figure 4.9. Euro/dollar versus dollar/Swiss franc (dotted line). *(Source: Bridge Information Systems, Inc.)*

der unprecedented pressure in 1993, swissy was one of the precious few European currencies that did not come under pressure.

The Swiss banking system has had an unusually high reputation for service. Although its infamous secrecy laws have been very helpful, the banking service goes well beyond that, maintaining a widespread network of customers around the world. The issue of reimbursing Jewish survivors and heirs for accounts lost during the Second World War dulled the shine of the Swiss banks in the late 1990s, but their eventual cooperation produced the desired settlement.

Typically, it is believed that the Swiss franc is a stable currency. From a foreign exchange point of view, this is simply not true. The Swiss franc closely resembles the patterns of the euro, but lacks its liquidity. As the demand for it exceeds supply, swissy can be more volatile than the euro.

The outlook for both the pound and the Swiss franc is cloudy at the beginning of the millennium. Economists are at loggerheads about whether these two major currencies can survive independently in a Europe dominated by the euro.

THE MAJOR FOREIGN EXCHANGE MARKETS

The foreign exchange markets function nonstop, 24 hours a day. The cash markets are fully decentralized, unlike the markets for currency futures and options on currency futures, which trade on special exchanges. There are no official opening and closing hours for foreign exchange trading. However, in the New York market, for instance, the unofficial standard trading hours are 8:30 AM to 3 PM EDT. Outside these hours, banks are not obliged to make prices, although most of them will quote, particularly in the electronic systems.

Although the market never closes except on weekends and holidays, traders find it rather hard to get a currency quote in the New York market after 4:30 PM EDT, because Auckland starts trading between 3 and 4 PM EDT. California attempted to fill this time niche in the late 1980s, but was unable to do so because of the limited number of banks in the region.

The advance in telecommunications greatly blurred the differences among the foreign exchange markets. From the trader's point of view, the main significance of the market relates to the presence of liquidity, since more players generate more trades. Otherwise, there is little practical difference, as traders only have to use a different code when calling out directly.

However, the presence of local customers and money markets still keeps the regional foreign exchange markets separated.

The London market had the most significant growth in foreign exchange from 1995 to 1998, as a result of the FX consolidation away from continental Europe prior to the euro launch. More dollars and euros are traded in London than in either New York or Frankfurt.

The major markets are London, with 32 percent of the market; New York, with 18 percent; and Tokyo, with 8 percent. Singapore follows with 7 percent; Germany has 5 percent; and Switzerland, France, and Hong Kong have 4 percent each. (See Figure 4.10.)

THE MAJOR PLAYERS

The major players in the foreign exchange arena are commercial banks, investment banks, central banks, trading institutions, hedge funds, corporations, high net-worth individuals, and individual investors. (See Figure 4.11.)

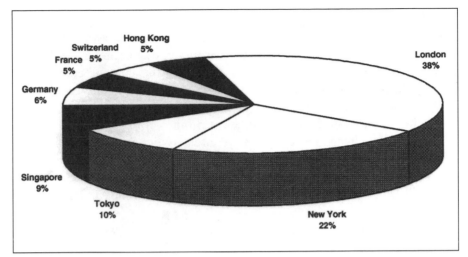

Figure 4.10. The major foreign exchange markets as of 2000.

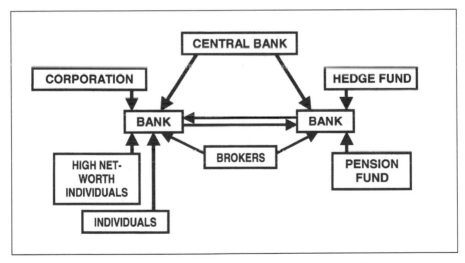

Figure 4.11. Diagram of the major players in foreign exchange trading.

COMMERCIAL AND INVESTMENT BANKS

Commercial and investment banks are the natural players, as all other participants must deal with banks if they want to trade foreign exchange. Currency trading started as a service added to the core of commercial banking business—deposits and loans. As currencies were allowed to float freely and as the writing of loans became more of a practice than an exception, banks had to look for other sources of profit.

Foreign exchange has the perfect characteristics for banks. It is profitable; the spot market provides limited credit exposure; the forward market provides significantly less credit exposure than loans; and, because worldwide interest is concentrated on a handful of currencies, the liquidity is excellent.

Commercial and investment banks are in the FX market on behalf of both their customers and themselves.

CENTRAL BANKS

Central banks represent a different type of player. Although they are the largest banks on an individual basis in most instances, central banks are not in the market for the money. They are actually nonprofit organizations. The major central banks do not speculate. Their main purpose regarding foreign exchange is to provide adequate trading conditions. They may also intervene in the market in an attempt to adjust economic or financial imbalances, and also for commercial reasons.

Although profit is not their aim, central banks tend to be profitable, because they generally trade on a long-term basis. For instance, all major central banks sold U.S. dollars against the yen in the aftermath of the Plaza Accord in September 1985, when the exchange rates were around 245 yen per dollar, and they bought back from around 121 yen per dollar in January 1988 to 80 yen per dollar in April 1995.

The currency crises of September 1992 and July 1993 had an exceptionally negative impact on the profitability of the European central banks.

HEDGE FUNDS

Hedge funds are relative newcomers to foreign exchange trading. They consist of partnerships of high net-worth investors that invest at least $1 million. Using this money as collateral, the funds borrow a multiple of the seed money. The funds research potential investments in markets worldwide and focus their capital on one or a few instruments. They bring to the market significant amounts of currency and flexibility. More funds are entering the currency markets as international investment opportunities increase.

The impact on the markets of the large funds, such as George Soros's Quantum group of funds, is a matter of study for the regulatory bodies. Soros's fund grossed over $1 billion in profits in September 1992 against the British pound, and lost $600 million on a long dollar/yen position in February 1994. History books will describe the havoc created in October 1998, when a leading hedge fund was forced out of its positions, sending dollar/yen into an 11.8-yen vortex.

CORPORATIONS

Corporations used to have a love–hate relationship with foreign exchange that was difficult to manage and looked chaotic. The internationalization of business and increased competitiveness forced them to take a closer look at foreign exchange. Corporations are becoming increasingly sophisticated at risk management. The days when hedging decisions were made on an all-or-nothing basis seem to be gone. Some corporations go beyond their commercial needs and take speculative positions, as opportunities occur.

HIGH NET-WORTH INDIVIDUALS

High net-worth individuals access foreign exchange markets through either investment banks or private banking departments. Private banking is generally geared toward European, Asian, and South American investors. The North American individual interest in foreign exchange is still under par.

INDIVIDUALS

Individuals have a limited impact on a one-on-one basis. Most of their transactions are not speculative and are generally related to travel expenses or purchasing foreign-made products. However, when compounded, the individual trading interest may be substantial. For instance, until 1985, summer vacations triggered sell-offs of U.S. dollars against the European currencies by American tourists. The strong dollar encouraged traveling abroad and, consequently, purchases of foreign currencies. The opposite has been true in the 1990s. The weak dollar encouraged foreign tourists to visit America and, therefore, enhanced dollar purchases. Figure 4.12 estimates the market share of the major currency markets in 2000.

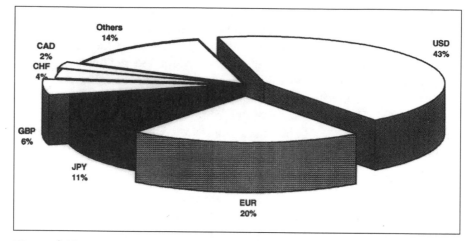

Figure 4.12. Estimated market share of the major currency markets in 2000.

CONCLUSION

Foreign exchange trading can be a profitable game. The larger the amounts in play, the greater the opportunity to be profitable. But it can also be an expensive game. In addition to the capital requirement, trading implementation is generally expensive. The support systems come with high price tags, from the phone turrets resembling hotel phone switching stations to computers and software; and the list can continue. Commercial and investment banks have deep pockets, so they can withstand temporary unrealized losses and even real setbacks.

Generally, the currency markets do not yet easily attract individuals. Foreign exchange trading is still misunderstood at the personal investment level, and is more often than not dismissed superficially as "really nuts" or as gambling. Forays in the right direction have already been made, as investment and commercial banks, along with some trading companies, offer individual investors and speculators the opportunity to participate in currency trading.

The potential for this market segment has not yet been reached. As foreign exchange financial information becomes more available at mass levels via personal computers, individual investors are likely to be attracted, given the opportunities for quick profits.

The futures exchanges provide the best setup for individual traders, or locals, as they are known. Locals buy or lease a seat on the organized exchange of the Chicago Mercantile Exchange and trade currency futures contracts directly.

5 Foreign Exchange Risks

Foreign exchange is not only a very profitable industry, it is also a risky business. The multitude of players, trading increasingly sophisticated instruments in staggering amounts, naturally exacerbates the trading risks. It is therefore vital to understand where the risks lie in order to develop the correct policies to manage these risks.

The main categories of foreign exchange risk are:

1. exchange rate risk,
2. interest rate risk,
3. credit risk, and
4. country (sovereign) risk.

Although these risks apply to the foreign exchange market as a whole, they apply selectively to the different instruments.

EXCHANGE RATE RISK

Exchange rate risk is the effect of the continuous shift in the worldwide market supply and demand balance on an outstanding foreign exchange position. This risk is pertinent to spot, forward outrights, futures, and options. These instruments have one element in common—the spot price. Forward outrights, futures, and options are all derivative instruments. Spot deals mature in two business days. Forward outrights and futures

mature past two business days. Options are drawn on both forward outrights and futures.

A trader opens a position by either buying or selling a foreign currency. For the period it is outstanding, the position will be subject to all the
price changes. The position will be *closed* or *covered* when the trader executes the opposite deal (sell, if first bought, and vice versa) for the same
amount of currency.

Exchange risk does not apply to swaps directly. In a swap deal, a
party buys and sells the same amount of the same currency with the same
counterparty, at different exchange rates and different value dates. Since
the same amount of foreign currency is simultaneously bought and sold,
there is no exchange risk per se. However, the exchange risk will find its
way to the swaps as well, via large spot price fluctuations.

The formula (discussed in Chapter 12) for calculating the forward
points, which are applied to the spot rates in order to determine the forward
rates, also includes the spot price. Should the spot rate change dramatically,
the forward points will also be affected. Volatility is by no means the en-
emy of the trader; it is in fact the vital element that creates the market.
Without continuous price fluctuations, trading would not be possible.
However, price volatility is good only when it is used properly.

COMPOUNDING THE RISK

From the managerial point of view, the *gross dealing exposure* should be
measured by adding together the absolute values of all the outstanding exposures. At any given time, a dealing room may be short in some currencies and long in others (or even in the same ones). Since the positions are
kept in the same currency, say U.S. dollars, the positions will partly or
completely offset each other.

However, from the point of view of volatility, this offsetting process
is not sound. Currencies move in different degrees of correlation relative to
each other. Incidental tendencies for moving in tandem do not reduce the
overall exchange risk. Therefore, the gross dealing exposure must always
be kept in absolute values, and its total size must be carefully managed.

EXCHANGE RISK MANAGEMENT AT MICRO LEVEL

Exchange risks start with the traders. A good trader knows to cut losses
short and ride profitable positions. In order to ensure that losses are kept
within manageable limits, certain systems are in place. The most popular
measures are the *position limit* and the *loss limit*.

There are two types of position limits: daylight and overnight.

1. The *daylight position limit* refers to the maximum amount of a certain currency a trader is allowed to carry at any single time during the regular trading hours. There is no rule or average regarding the magnitude of the position; each bank and each treasurer may have a different policy. Each trader should have a trading limit, regardless of his or her level of profitability or seniority. The limit should reflect both the trader's level of trading skills and the amount at which a trader peaks. It is less important whether the daylight limit is $5 million or $50 million than whether the trader can provide a peak performance with the respective position.

2. The *overnight position limit* refers to any outstanding position kept overnight by traders. As a rule of thumb, overnight limits should be smaller than daylight limits. Again, the limits are a function of the policy of the banks and their treasurers, along with the skills of the traders and their specific areas of expertise. The majority of foreign exchange traders do not hold overnight positions.

Most of the trading occurs in the spot market, in terms of both total volume and number of deals, and the spot positions generally have a life span of seconds to hours.

The limits, daylight or overnight, may be increased (or decreased) temporarily by a senior officer from the treasury to better encompass special market conditions. For instance, the "kidnapping" of Mikhail Gorbachev, then Soviet president, triggered a sharp rally in the dollar against the deutsche mark. (See Figure 5.1.) The political crisis was difficult to gauge because of the lack of precedent. Despite the magnitude of the rally, many players curtailed foreign exchange trading because they feared the lack of liquidity. Normal position limits were temporarily reduced in order to avoid unacceptable levels of exchange risks. Of course, this action further reduced the liquidity. The point is that this type of market behavior is a reality and, therefore, it must be addressed properly.

The *loss limit* is a measure designed to avoid unsustainable losses made by traders; it is enforced by the senior officers in the dealing room. The loss limits are selected on a daily and monthly basis by top management. Psychologically, this measure is of great help, as it removes the added pressure on the trader of deciding on the size of the loss to take in an already hectic environment.

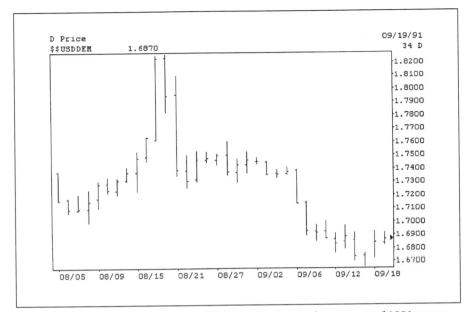

Figure 5.1. The "kidnapping" of Mikhail Gorbachev in the summer of 1991 generated a significant rally in the U.S. dollar/deutsche mark. *(Source: Bridge Information Systems, Inc.)*

Exchange Risk Management at the Macro Level

Management is responsible for designing a clear set of rules encompassing the policies of risk management in a trading entity. These rules refer to the dealing room's objectives, the methods of implementation, and the general approaches to extraordinary trading circumstances. The risk management policies must be revised regularly, or in reaction to unusual market developments. Flexibility and speed of adjustment are vital requirements in the fast-changing financial markets.

In the case of derivatives, and especially in the case of options, market participants should enter master agreements with each other. These agreements document all the outstanding and future transactions and provide for closeout and settlement netting.

The International Foreign Exchange Master Agreement reprinted here (as of November 1993) was designed by the Foreign Exchange Committee and the British Bankers' Association.

INTERNATIONAL FOREIGN EXCHANGE
MASTER AGREEMENT

MASTER AGREEMENT dated as of _____, 19___ , by
and between _____, a _____,
and _____, a _____.

Section 1. Definitions

Unless otherwise required by the context, the following terms shall have the following meanings in the Agreement:

"*Agreement*" has the meaning given to it in Section 2.2.

"*Base Currency*" means as to a Party the Currency agreed as such in relation to it in Part VIII of the Schedule hereto.

"*Base Currency Rate*" means as to a Party and any amount the cost (expressed as a percentage rate per annum) at which that Party would be able to fund that amount from such sources and for such periods as it may in its reasonable discretion from time to time decide, as determined in good faith by it.

"*Business Day*" means (i) a day which is a Local Banking Day for the applicable Designated Office of both Parties, or (ii) solely in relation to delivery of a Currency, a day which is a Local Banking Day in relation to that Currency.

"*Close-Out Amount*" has the meaning given to it in Section 5.1.

"*Close-Out Date*" means a day on which, pursuant to the provisions of Section 5.1, the Non-Defaulting Party closes out and liquidates Currency Obligations or such a close-out and liquidation occurs automatically.

"*Closing Gain*" means, as to the Non-Defaulting Party, the difference described as such in relation to a particular Value Date under the provisions of Section 5.1.

"*Closing Loss*" means, as to the Non-Defaulting Party, the difference described as such in relation to a particular Value Date under the provisions of Section 5.1.

"*Confirmation*" means a writing (including telex, facsimile or other electronic means from which it is possible to produce a hard copy) evidencing an FX Transaction governed by the Agreement which shall specify (i) the Parties thereto and their Designated Offices through which they are respectively acting, (ii) the amounts of the Currencies being bought or sold and by which Party, (iii) the Value Date, and (iv) any other term generally included in such a writing in accordance with the practice of the relevant foreign exchange market.

"*Credit Support Document*" means, as to a Party (the "first Party"), a guaranty, hypothecation agreement, margin or security agreement or document, or any other document containing an obligation of a third party ("Credit Support Provider") or of the first Party in favor of the other Party supporting any obligations of the first Party hereunder.

"*Credit Support Provider*" has the meaning given to it in the definition of Credit Support Document.

"*Currency*" means money denominated in the lawful currency of any country or the euro.

"*Currency Obligation*" means any obligation of a Party to deliver a Currency pursuant to an FX Transaction governed by the Agreement, or pursuant to the application of Sections 3.3 (a) or 3.3 (b).

"*Custodian*" has the meaning given to it in the definition of Event of Default.

"*Defaulting Party*" has the meaning given to it in the definition of Event of Default.

"*Designated Office(s)*" means, as to a Party, the office(s) specified in Part II of the Schedule hereto, as such Schedule may be modified from time to time by agreement of the Parties.

"*Effective Date*" means the date of this Master Agreement.

"*Event of Default*" means the occurrence of any of the following with respect to a Party (the "Defaulting Party", the other Party being the "Non-Defaulting Party"):

(i) the Defaulting Party shall default in any payment under the Agreement to the Non-Defaulting Party with respect to any sum when due under any Currency Obligation or pursuant to the Agreement and such failure shall continue for two (2) Business Days after written notice of non-payment given by the Non-Defaulting Party to the Defaulting Party;

(ii) the Defaulting Party shall commence a voluntary case or other proceeding seeking liquidation, reorganization or other similar relief with respect to itself or to its debts under any bankruptcy, insolvency or similar law, or seeking the appointment of a trustee, receiver, liquidator, conservator, administrator, custodian or other similar official (each, a "Custodian") of it or any substantial part of its assets; or shall take any corporate action to authorize any of the foregoing;

(iii) an involuntary case or other proceeding shall be commenced against the Defaulting Party seeking liquidation, reorganization or other similar relief with respect to it or its debts under any bankruptcy, insolvency or similar law or seeking the appointment of a Custodian of it or any substantial part of its assets, and such involuntary case or other proceeding is not dismissed within five (5) days of its institution or presentation;

(iv) the Defaulting Party is bankrupt or insolvent, as defined under any bankruptcy or insolvency law applicable to such Party;

(v) the Defaulting Party shall otherwise be unable to pay its debts as they become due;

(vi) the Defaulting Party or any Custodian acting on behalf of the Defaulting Party shall disaffirm, disclaim or repudiate any Currency Obligation;

(vii) (a) any representation or warranty made or deemed made by the Defaulting Party pursuant to the Agreement or pursuant to any Credit Support Document shall prove to have been false or misleading in any material respect as at the time it was made or given and one (1) Business Day has elapsed after the Non-Defaulting Party has given the Defaulting Party written notice thereof, or (b) the Defaulting Party fails to perform or comply with any obligation assumed by it under the Agreement (other than an obligation to make payment of the kind referred to in Clause (i) of this definition of Event of Default), and such failure is continuing thirty (30) days after the Non-Defaulting Party has given the Defaulting Party written notice thereof;

(viii) the Defaulting Party consolidates or amalgamates with or merges into or transfers all or substantially all its assets to another entity and (a) the creditworthiness of the resulting, surviving or transferee entity is materially weaker than that of the Defaulting Party prior to such action, or (b) at the time of such consolidation, amalgamation, merger or transfer the resulting, surviving or transferee entity fails to assume all the obligations of the Defaulting Party under the Agreement by operation of law or pursuant to an agreement satisfactory to the Non-Defaulting Party;

(ix) by reason of any default, or event of default or other similar condition or event, any Specified Indebtedness (being Specified Indebtedness of an amount which, when expressed in the Currency of the Threshold Amount, is in aggregate equal to or in excess of the Threshold Amount) of the Defaulting Party or any Credit Support Provider in relation to it: (a) is not paid on the due date therefor and remains unpaid after any applicable grace period has elapsed, or (b) becomes, or becomes capable at any time of being declared, due and payable under agreements or instruments evidencing such Specified Indebtedness before it would otherwise have been due and payable.

(x) the Defaulting Party is in breach of or default under any Specified Transaction and any applicable grace period has elapsed, and there occurs any liquidation or early termination of, or acceleration of obligations under that Specified Transaction or the Defaulting Party (or any Custodian on its behalf) disaffirms, disclaims or repudiates the whole or any part of a Specified Transaction; or

(xi) (a) any Credit Support Provider in relation to the Defaulting Party or the Defaulting Party itself fails to comply with or perform any agreement or obligation to be complied with or performed by it in accordance with the applicable Credit Support Document and such failure is continuing after any applicable grace period has elapsed; (b) any Credit Support Document relating to the Defaulting Party expires or ceases to be in full force and effect prior to the satisfaction of all obligations of the Defaulting Party under the Agreement, unless otherwise agreed in writing by the Non-Defaulting Party; (c) the Defaulting Party or its Credit Support Provider (or, in either case, any Custodian acting on its behalf) disaffirms, disclaims or repudiates, in whole or in part, or challenges the validity of, the Credit Support Document; (d) any representation or warranty made or deemed made by any Credit Support Provider pursuant to any Credit Support Document shall prove to have been false or misleading in any material respect as at the time it was made or given or deemed made or given and one (1) Business Day has elapsed after the Non-Defaulting Party has given the Defaulting Party written notice thereof; or (e) any event set out in (ii) to (vi) or (viii) to (x) above occurs in respect of the Credit Support Provider.

"*FX Transaction*" means any transaction between the Parties for the purchase by one Party of an agreed amount in one Currency against the sale by it to the other of an agreed amount in another Currency both such amounts being deliverable on the same Value Date, and in respect of which transaction the Parties have agreed (whether orally, electronically or in writing): the Currencies involved, the amounts of such Currencies to be purchased and sold, which Party will purchase which Currency and the Value Date.

"*Local Banking Day*" means (i) for any Currency, a day on which commercial banks effect deliveries of that Currency in accordance with the market practice of the relevant foreign exchange market, and (ii) for any Party, a day in the location of the applicable Designated Office of such Party on which commercial banks in that location are not authorized or required by law to close.

"*Master Agreement*" means the terms and conditions set forth in this master agreement.

"*Matched Pair Novation Netting Office(s)*" means in respect of a Party the Designated Office(s) specified in Part V of the Schedule, as such Schedule may be modified from time to time by agreement of the Parties.

"*Non-Defaulting Party*" has the meaning given to it in the definition of Event of Default.

"*Novation Netting Office(s)*" means in respect of a Party the Designated Office(s) specified in Part IV of the Schedule, as such Schedule may be modified from time to time by agreement of the Parties.

"*Parties*" means the parties to the Agreement and shall include their successors and permitted assigns (but without prejudice to the application of Clause (viii) of the definition of Event of Default); and the term "Party" shall mean whichever of the Parties is appropriate in the context in which such expression may be used.

"*Proceedings*" means any suit, action or other proceedings relating to the Agreement.

"*Settlement Netting Office(s)*" means, in respect of a Party, the Designated Office(s) specified in Part III of the Schedule, as such Schedule may be modified from time to time by agreement of the Parties.

"*Specified Indebtedness*" means any obligation (whether present or future, contingent or otherwise, as principal or surety or otherwise) in respect of borrowed money, other than in respect of deposits received.

"*Specified Transaction*" means any transaction (including an agreement with respect thereto) between one Party to the Agreement (or any Credit Support Provider of such Party) and the other Party to the Agreement (or any Credit Support Provider of such Party) which is a rate swap transaction, basis swap, forward rate transaction, commodity swap, commodity option, equity or equity linked swap, equity or equity index option, bond option, interest rate option, foreign exchange transaction, cap transaction, floor transaction, collar transaction, currency swap transaction, cross-currency rate swap transaction, currency option or any other similar transaction (including any option with respect to any of these transactions) or any combination of any of the foregoing transactions.

"*Split Settlement*" has the meaning given to it in the definition of Value Date.

"*Threshold Amount*" means the amount specified as such for each Party in Part IX of the Schedule.

"*Value Date*" means, with respect to any FX Transaction, the Business Day (or where market practice in the relevant foreign exchange market in relation to the two Currencies involved provides for delivery of one Currency on one date which is a Local Banking Day in relation to that Currency but not to the other Currency and for delivery of the other Currency on the next Local Banking Day in relation to that other Currency ("Split Settlement") the two Local Banking Days in accordance with that market practice) agreed by the Parties for delivery of the Currencies to be purchased and sold pursuant to such FX Transaction, and, with respect to any Currency Obligation, the Business Day (or, in the case of Split Settlement, Local Banking Day) upon which the obligation to deliver Currency pursuant to such Currency Obligation is to be performed.

Section 2. FX Transactions

2.1. *Scope of the Agreement.* a) Unless otherwise agreed in writing by the Parties, each FX Transaction entered into between two Designated Offices of the Parties on or after the Effective Date shall be governed by the Agreement. (b) All FX Transactions between any two Designated Offices of the Parties outstanding on the Effective Date which are identified in Part I of the Schedule shall be FX Transactions governed by the Agreement and every obligation of the Parties thereunder to deliver a Currency shall be a Currency Obligation under the Agreement.

2.2. *Single Agreement.* This Master Agreement, the particular terms agreed between the Parties in relation to each and every FX Transaction governed by this Master Agreement (and, insofar as such terms are recorded in a Confirmation, each such Confirmation), the Schedule to this Master Agreement and all amendments to any of such items shall together form the agreement between the Parties (the "Agreement") and shall together constitute a single agreement between the Parties. The Parties acknowledge that all FX Transactions governed by the Agreement are entered into in reliance upon the fact that all items constitute a single agreement between the Parties.

2.3. *Confirmations.* FX Transactions governed by the Agreement shall be promptly confirmed by the Parties by Confirmations exchanged by mail, telex, facsimile or other electronic means. The failure by a Party to issue a Confirmation shall not prejudice or invalidate the terms of any FX Transaction governed by the Agreement.

Section 3. Settlement and Netting

3.1 *Settlement.* Subject to Section 3.2, each Party shall deliver to the other Party the amount of the Currency to be delivered by it under each Currency Obligation on the Value Date for such Currency Obligation.

3.2 *Net Settlement/Payment Netting.* If on any Value Date more than one delivery of a particular Currency is to be made between a pair of Settlement Netting Offices, then each Party shall aggregate the amounts of such Currency deliverable by it and only the difference between these aggregate amounts shall be delivered by the Party owing the larger aggregate amount to the other Party, and, if the aggregate amounts are equal, no delivery of the Currency shall be made.

3.3. *Novation Netting.*

(a) *By Currency.* If the Parties enter into an FX Transaction governed by the Agreement through a pair of Novation Netting Offices giving rise to a Currency Obligation for the same Value Date and in the same Currency as a then existing Currency Obligation between the same pair of Novation Netting Offices, then immediately upon entering into such FX Transaction, each such Currency Obligation shall automatically and without further action be individually cancelled and simultaneously replaced by a new Currency Obligation for such Value Date determined as follows: the amounts of such Currency that would otherwise have been deliverable by each Party on such Value Date shall be aggregated and the Party with the larger aggregate amount shall have a new Currency Obligation to deliver to the other Party the amount of such Currency by which its aggregate amount exceeds the other Party's aggregate amount, provided that if the aggregate amounts are equal, no new Currency Obligation shall arise. This Clause (a) shall not affect any other Currency Obligation of a Party to deliver any different Currency on the same Value Date.

(b) *By Matched Pair.* If the Parties enter into an FX Transaction governed by the Agreement between a pair of Matched Pair Novation Netting Offices then the provisions of Section 3.3 (a) shall apply only in respect of Currency Obligations arising by virtue of FX Transactions governed by the Agreement entered into between such pair of Matched Pair Novation Netting Offices and involving the same pair of Currencies and the same Value Date.

3.4 *General*

(a) *Inapplicability of Sections 3.2 and 3.3.* The provisions of Sections 3.2 and 3.3 shall not apply if a Close-Out Date has occurred or an involuntary case or other proceeding of the kind described in Clause (iii) of the definition of Event of Default has occurred without being dismissed in relation to either Party.

(b) *Failure to Record.* The provisions of Section 3.3 shall apply notwithstanding that either Party may fail to record the new Currency Obligations in its books.

(c) *Cutoff Date and Time.* The provisions of Section 3.3 are subject to any cut-off date and cut-off time agreed between the applicable Novation Netting Offices and Matched Pair Novation Netting Offices of the Parties.

Section 4. Representations, Warranties and Covenants

4.1 *Representations and Warranties.* Each Party represents and warrants to the other Party as of the date of the Agreement and as of the date of each FX Transaction governed by the Agreement that: (i) it has authority to enter into the Agreement and such FX Transaction; (ii) the persons executing the Agreement and entering into such FX Transaction have been duly authorized to do so; (iii) the Agreement and the Currency Obligations created under the Agreement are binding upon it and enforceable against it in accordance with their terms (subject to applicable principles of equity) and do not and will not violate the terms of any agreements to which such Party is bound; (iv) no Event of Default has occurred and is continuing with respect to it; and (v) it acts as principal in entering into each and every FX Transaction governed by the Agreement.

4.2 *Covenants.* Each Party covenants to the other Party that: (i) it will at all times obtain and comply with the terms of and do all that is necessary to maintain in full force and effect all authorizations, approvals, licenses and consents required to enable it to lawfully perform its obligations under the Agreement; and (ii) it will promptly notify the other Party of the occurrence of any Event of Default with respect to itself or any Credit Support Provider in relation to it.

Section 5. Close-Out and Liquidation

5.1. *Circumstances of Close-Out and Liquidation.* If an Event of Default has occurred and is continuing, then the Non-Defaulting Party shall have the right to close-out and liquidate in the manner described below all, but not less than all, outstanding Currency Obligations (except to the extent that in the good faith opinion of the Non-Defaulting Party certain of such Currency Obligations may not be closed-out and liquidated under applicable law), by notice to the Defaulting Party. If "Automatic Termination" is specified as applying to a Party in Part VI of the Schedule, then, in the case of an Event of Default specified in Clauses (ii) or (iii) of the definition thereof with respect to such Party, such close-out and liquidation shall be automatic as to all outstanding Currency

Obligations. Where such close-out and liquidation is to be effected, it shall be effected by:

(i) closing out each outstanding Currency Obligation (including any Currency Obligation which has not been performed and in respect of which the Value Date is on or precedes the Close-Out Date) so that each such Currency Obligation is cancelled and the Non-Defaulting Party shall calculate in good faith with respect to each such cancelled Currency Obligation, the Closing Gain or, as appropriate, the Closing Loss, as follows:

(x) for each Currency Obligation in a Currency other than the Non-Defaulting Party's Base Currency calculate a "Close-Out Amount" by converting:

(A) in the case of a Currency Obligation whose Value Date is the same as or is later than the Close-Out Date, the amount of such Currency Obligation; or

(B) in the case of a Currency Obligation whose Value Date precedes the Close-Out Date, the amount of such Currency Obligation increased, to the extent permitted by applicable law, by adding interest thereto from the Value Date to the Close-Out Date at the rate representing the cost (expressed as a percentage rate per annum) at which the Non-Defaulting Party would have been able, on such Value Date, to fund the amount of such Currency Obligation for the period from the Value Date to the Close-Out Date.

(y) determine in relation to each Value Date: (A) the sum of all Close-Out Amounts relating to Currency Obligations under which, and of all Currency Obligations in the Non-Defaulting Party's Base Currency under which, the Non-Defaulting Party would otherwise have been obliged to deliver the relevant amount to the Defaulting Party on that Value Date, adding (to the extent permitted by applicable law), in the case of a Currency Obligation in the Non-Defaulting Party's Base Currency whose Value Date precedes the Close-Out Date, interest for the period from the Value Date to the Close-Out Date at the Non-Defaulting Party's Base Currency Rate as at such Value Date for such period; and (B) the sum of all Close-Out Amounts relating to Currency Obligations under which, and of all Currency Obligations in the Non-Defaulting Party's Base Currency under which, the Non-Defaulting Party would otherwise have been entitled to receive the relevant amount on that Value Date, adding (to the extent permitted by applicable law), in the case of a Currency Obligation in the Non-Defaulting Party's Base Currency whose Value Date precedes the Close-Out Date, interest for the period from the Value Date to the Close-Out Date at the Non-Defaulting Party's Base Currency Rate as at such Value Date for such period;

(z) if the sum determined under (y) (A) is greater than the sum determined under (y) (B), the difference shall be the Closing Loss for such Value Date; if the sum determined under (y) (A) is less than the sum determined under (y) (B), the difference shall be the Closing Gain for such Value Date;

(ii) to the extent permitted by applicable law, adjusting the Closing Gain or Closing Loss for each Value Date falling after the Close-Out Date to present value by discounting the Closing Gain or Closing Loss from the Value Date to the Close-Out Date, at the Non-Defaulting Party's Base Currency Rate, or at such other rate as may be prescribed by applicable law;

(iii) aggregating the following amounts so that all such amounts are netted into a single liquidated amount payable by or to the Non-Defaulting Party:(x) the sum of the Closing Gains for all Value Dates (discounted to present value, where appropriate, in accordance with the provisions of Clause (ii) of this Section 5.1) (which for the purposes of this aggregation shall be a positive figure) and (y) the sum of the Closing Losses for all Value Dates (discounted to present value, where appropriate, in accordance with the provisions of Clause (ii) of this Section 5.1) (which for the purposes of the aggregation shall be a negative figure); and

(iv) if the resulting net amount is positive, it shall be payable by the Defaulting Party to the Non-Defaulting Party, and if it is negative, then the absolute value of such amount shall be payable by the Non-Defaulting Party to the Defaulting Party.

5.2 *Calculation of Interest.* Any addition of interest or discounting required under Clause (i) or (ii) of Section 5.1 shall be calculated on the basis of the actual number of days elapsed and of a year of such number of days as is customary for transactions involving the relevant Currency in the relevant foreign exchange market.

5.3 *Other FX Transactions.* Where close-out and liquidation occurs in accordance with Section 5.1, the Non-Defaulting Party shall also be entitled to close-out and liquidate, to the extent permitted by applicable law, any other FX Transactions entered into between the Parties which are then outstanding in accordance with the provisions of Section 5.1, as if each obligation of a Party to deliver a Currency thereunder were a Currency Obligation.

5.4. *Payment and Late Interest.* The amount payable by one Party to the other Party pursuant to the provisions of Sections 5.1 and 5.3 shall be paid by the close of business on the Business Day following such close-out and liquidation (converted as required by applicable law into any other Currency, any costs of such conversion to be borne by, and deducted from any payment to, the Defaulting Party). To the extent permitted by applicable law, any amounts required to be paid under Sections 5.1 or 5.3 and not paid on the due date therefor, shall bear interest at the Non-Defaulting Party's Base Currency Rate plus 1% per annum (or, if conversion is required by applicable law into some other Currency, either (x) the average rate at which overnight deposits in such other Currency are offered by major banks in the London interbank market as of 11:00 a.m. (London time) plus 1% per annum or (y) such other rate as may be prescribed by such applicable law) for each day for which such amount remains unpaid.

5.5. *Suspension of Obligations.* Without prejudice to the foregoing, so long as a Party shall be in default in payment or performance to the Non-Defaulting Party under the Agreement and so long as the Non-Defaulting Party has not exercised its rights under Section 5.1, the Non-Defaulting Party may, at its election and without penalty, suspend its obligation to perform under the Agreement.

5.6. *Expenses.* The Defaulting Party shall reimburse the Non-Defaulting Party in respect of all out-of-pocket expenses incurred by the Non-Defaulting Party (including fees and disbursements of counsel, including attorneys who may be employees of the Non-Defaulting Party) in connection with any reasonable collection or other enforcement proceedings related to the payments required under this Section 5.

5.7. *Reasonable Pre-Estimate.* The Parties agree that the amounts recoverable under this Section 5 are a reasonable pre-estimate of loss and not a penalty. Such amounts are payable for the loss of bargain and the loss of protection against future risks and, except as otherwise provided in the Agreement, neither Party will be entitled to recover any additional damages as a consequence of such losses.

5.8. *No Limitation of Other Rights; Set-Off.* The Non-Defaulting party's rights under this Section 5 shall be in addition to, and not in limitation or exclusion of, any other rights which the Non-Defaulting Party may have (whether by agreement, operation of law or otherwise). To the extent not prohibited by applicable law, the Non-Defaulting Party shall have a general right of set-off with respect to all amounts owed by each Party to the other Party, whether due and payable or not due and payable (provided that any amount not due and payable at the time of such set-off shall, if appropriate, be discounted to present value in a commercially reasonable manner by the Non-Defaulting Party). The Non-Defaulting Party's rights under this Section 5.8 are subject to Section 5.7.

Section 6. Illegality, Impossibility and Force Majeure

If either Party is prevented from or hindered or delayed by reason of force majeure or act of State in the delivery or receipt of any Currency in respect of a Currency Obligation or if it becomes or, in the good faith judgment of one of the Parties, may become unlawful or impossible for either Party to deliver or receive any Currency which is the subject of a Currency Obligation, then either Party may, by notice to the other Party, require the close-out and liquidation of each affected Currency Obligation in accordance with the provisions of Sections 5.1, 5.2 and 5.4 and, for the purposes of enabling the calculations prescribed by Sections 5.1, 5.2 and 5.4 to be effected, the Party unaffected by such force majeure, act of State, illegality or impossibility (or if both Parties are so affected, whichever Party gave the relevant notice) shall effect the relevant calculations as if it were the Non-Defaulting Party. Nothing in this Section 6 shall be taken as indicating that the Party treated as the Defaulting Party for the purposes of calculations required hereby has committed any breach or default.

Section 7. Parties to Rely on Their Own Expertise

Each Party shall enter into each FX Transaction governed by the Agreement in reliance only upon its own judgment. Neither Party holds itself out as advising, or any of its employees or agents as having the authority to advise, the other Party as to whether or not it should enter into any such FX Transaction or as to any subsequent actions relating thereto or on any other commercial matters concerned with any FX Transaction governed by the Agreement, and neither Party shall have any responsibility or liability whatsoever in respect of any advise of this nature given, or views expressed, by it or any of such persons to the other Party, whether or not such advise is given or such views are expressed at the request of the other Party.

Section 8. Miscellaneous

8.1 *Currency Indemnity*. The receipt or recovery by either Party (the "first Party") of any amount in respect of an obligation of the other Party (the "second Party") in a Currency other than that in which such amount was due, whether pursuant to a judgment of any court or pursuant to Section 5 or 6, shall discharge such obligation only to the extent that on the first day on which the first Party is open for business immediately following such receipt, the first Party shall be able, in accordance with normal banking practice, to purchase the Currency in which such amount was due with the Currency received. If the amount so purchasable shall be less than the original amount of the Currency in which such amount was due, the second Party shall, as a separate obligation and notwithstanding any judgment of any court, indemnify the first Party against any loss sustained by it. The second Party shall in any event indemnify the first Party against any costs incurred by it in making any such purchase of Currency.

8.2 *Assignments*. Neither Party may assign, transfer or charge, or purport to assign, transfer or charge, its rights or its obligations under the Agreement or any interest therein without the prior written consent of the other Party, and any purported assignment, transfer or charge in violation of this Section 8.2 shall be void.

8.3. *Telephonic Recording*. The Parties agree that each may electronically record all telephonic conversations between them and that any such tape recordings may be submitted in evidence in any Proceedings relating to the Agreement. In the event of any dispute between the Parties as to the terms of an FX Transaction governed by the Agreement or the Currency Obligations thereby created, the Parties may use electronic recordings between the persons who entered into such FX Transaction as the preferred evidence of the terms of such FX Transaction, notwithstanding the existence of any writing to the contrary.

8.4. *No Obligation.* Neither Party to this Agreement shall be required to enter into any FX Transaction with the other.

8.5. *Notices.* Unless otherwise agreed, all notices, instructions and other communications to be given to a Party under the Agreement shall be given to the address, telex (if confirmed by the appropriate answerback), facsimile (confirmed if requested) or telephone number and to the individual or department specified by such Party in Part VII of the Schedule attached hereto. Unless otherwise specified, any notice, instruction or other communication given in accordance with this Section 8.5 shall be effective upon receipt.

8.6. *Termination.* Each of the Parties hereto may terminate this Agreement at any time by seven days' prior written notice to the other Party delivered as prescribed above, and termination shall be effective at the end of such seventh day; provided, however, that any such termination shall not affect any outstanding Currency Obligations, and the provisions of the Agreement shall continue to apply until all the obligations of each Party to the other under the Agreement have been fully performed.

8.7. *Severability.* In the event any one or more of the provisions contained in the Agreement should be held invalid, illegal or unenforceable in any respect under the law of any jurisdiction, the validity, legality and enforceability of the remaining provisions under the law of such jurisdiction, and the validity, legality and enforceability of such and any other provisions under the law of any other jurisdiction, shall not in any way be affected or impaired thereby.

8.8. *Waiver.* No indulgence or concession granted by a Party and no omission or delay on the part of a Party in exercising any right, power or privilege under the Agreement shall operate as a waiver thereof, nor shall any single or partial exercise of any such right, power or privilege preclude any other or further exercise thereof or the exercise of any other right, power or privilege.

8.9. *Master Agreement.* Where one of the Parties to the Agreement is domiciled in the United States, the Parties intend that the Agreement shall be a master agreement, as defined in 11 U.S.C. Section 101(55)(C) and 12 U.S.C. Section 1832(e)(8)(D)(vii).

8.10. *Time of Essence.* Time shall be of the essence in the Agreement.

8.11. *Headings.* Headings in the Agreement are for ease of reference only.

8.12 *Wire Transfers.* Every payment or delivery of Currency to be made by a Party under the Agreement shall be made by wire transfer, or its equivalent, of same day (or immediately available) and freely transferable funds to the bank account designated by the other Party for such purpose.

8.13. *Adequate Assurances.* If the Parties have so agreed in Part X of the Schedule, the failure by a Party ("first Party") to give adequate assurances of its ability to perform any of its obligations under the Agreement within two (2) Business Days of a written request to do so when the other Party ("second Party") has reasonable grounds for insecurity shall be an Event of Default under the Agreement, in which case during the pendency of a reasonable request by the second Party to the first Party for adequate assurances of the first Party's ability to perform its obligations under the Agreement, the second Party may, at its election and without penalty, suspend its obligations under the Agreement.

8.14. *FDICIA Representation.* If the Parties have so agreed in Part XI of the Schedule, each Party represents and warrants to the other Party that it is a financial institution under the provisions of Title IV of the Federal Deposit Insurance Corporation Improvement Act of 1991 ("FDICIA"), and the Parties agree that this Agreement shall be a netting contract, as defined in FDICIA, and each receipt or payment or delivery obligation under the Agreement shall be a covered contractual payment entitlement or covered contractual payment obligation, respectively, as defined in and subject to FDICIA.

8.15. *Confirmation Procedures.* In relation to Confirmations, unless either Party objects to the terms contained in any Confirmation within three (3) Business Days of receipt thereof, or such shorter time as may be appropriate given the Value Date of the FX Transaction, the terms of such Confirmation shall be deemed correct and accepted absent manifest error, unless a corrected Confirmation is sent by a Party within such three Business Days, or shorter period, as appropriate, in which case the Party receiving such corrected Confirmation shall have three (3) Business Days, or shorter period, as appropriate, after receipt thereof to object to the terms contained in such corrected Confirmation. In the event of any conflict between the terms of a Confirmation and this Master Agreement, the terms of this Master Agreement shall prevail, and the Confirmation shall not modify the terms of this Master Agreement.

8.16 *Amendments.* No amendment, modification or waiver of the Agreement will be effective unless in writing executed by each of the Parties.

Section 9. Law and Jurisdiction

9.1 *Governing Law.* The Agreement shall be governed by, and construed in accordance with the laws of [the State of New York] [England and Wales] without giving effect to conflict of laws provisions.

9.2 *Consent to Jurisdiction.* With respect to any Proceedings, each Party irrevocably (i) [submits to the non-exclusive jurisdiction of the courts of the State of New York and the United States District Court located in the Borough of Manhattan in New York City,] [agrees for the benefit of the other Party that the courts of England shall have jurisdiction to determine any Proceedings and irrevocably submits to the jurisdiction of the English courts], and (ii) waives any objection which it may have at any time to the laying of venue of any

Proceedings brought in any such court, waives any claim that such Proceedings have been brought in an inconvenient forum and further waives the right to object, with respect to such Proceedings, that such court does not have jurisdiction over such Party. Nothing in the Agreement precludes either Party from bringing Proceedings in any other jurisdiction nor will the bringing of Proceedings in any one or more jurisdictions preclude the bringing of Proceedings in any other jurisdiction.

9.3. *Waiver of Immunities*. Each Party irrevocably waives to the fullest extent permitted by applicable law, with respect to itself and its revenues and assets (irrespective of their use or intended use) all immunity on the grounds of sovereignty or other similar grounds from (i) suite, (ii) jurisdiction of any courts, (iii) relief by way of injunction, order for specific performance or for recovery of property, (iv) attachment of its assets (whether before or after judgment) and (v) execution or enforcement of any judgment to which it or its revenues or assets might otherwise be entitled in any Proceedings in the courts of any jurisdiction, and irrevocably agrees to the extent permitted by applicable law that it will not claim any such immunity in any Proceedings. Each Party consents generally in respect of any Proceedings to the giving of any relief or the issue of any process in connection with such Proceedings, including, without limitation, the making, enforcement or execution against any property whatsoever of any order or judgment which may be made or given in such Proceedings.

9.4. *Waiver of Jury Trial*. Each Party hereby irrevocably waives any and all right to trial by jury in any Proceedings.

IN WITNESS WHEREOF, the Parties have caused the Agreement to be duly executed by their respective authorized officers as of the date first written above.

By _____

Name:

Title:

By_____

Name:

Title:

Schedule

Part I: *Scope of Agreement.* The Agreement shall apply to [all] [the following] FX Transactions outstanding between any two Designated Offices of the Parties on the Effective Date.

Part II: *Designated Offices.* Each of the following shall be a Designated Office:

Part III: *Settlement Netting Offices.* Net settlement provisions of Section 3.2 shall apply to the following Settlement Netting Offices:

Part IV: *Novation Netting Offices.* Netting by novation provisions of Section 3.3 (a) shall apply to the following Novation Netting Offices and shall apply to [all FX Transactions] [FX Transactions with a Value Date more than two Business Days after the day on which the Parties enter into an FX Transaction]:

Part V: *Matched Pair Novation Netting Offices.* Matched pair netting by novation provisions of Section 3.3(b) shall apply to the following Matched Pair Novation Netting Offices and shall apply to [all FX Transactions] [FX Transactions with a Value Date more than two Business Days after the day on which the Parties enter into an FX Transaction]:

Part VI: *Automatic Termination.* The "Automatic Termination" provision in Section 5.1 [shall] [shall not] apply to _____ and [shall] [shall not] apply to _____

Part VII: *Notices*

Address:

Telephone Numbers:

Telex Number:

Facsimile Numbers:

Name of Individual or Department to Whom Notices are to be sent:

Part VIII: *Base Currency*

Part IX: *Threshold Amount*

The Threshold Amount applicable to _____ shall be:

The Threshold Amount applicable to _____ shall be:

Part X: *Adequate Assurances.* The provisions of Section 8.13 [shall] [shall not] apply to the Agreement.

Part XI: *FDICIA Representations.* The provisions of Section 8.14 [shall] [shall not] apply to the Agreement.

TOTAL CURRENCY EXPOSURE VERSUS FOREIGN EXCHANGE TRADING

Banks and institutions involved in foreign exchange generally have two main sources of transactions—the total currency exposure and the actual foreign exchange trading. The total currency exposure, consisting of all the foreign denominated assets and liabilities, is generally separated from the daily trading activity for management purposes. The total currency exposure may be subject to position limits as well.

SOURCES OF RISK AND REVENUES

Foreign exchange instruments have different rates of profitability and different degrees of risk. It is management's responsibility to select the most profitable instruments, relative to the present or projected trading capability of the desk, and identify the specific risks associated with each instrument. Only a clear understanding of business conditions enables management to design the proper risk management policies.

MARKING-TO-MARKET

Marking-to-market is the common valuation procedure used to calculate the foreign exchange exposure at current market prices.

In the past, positions and profit and loss were calculated only on an end-of-day basis. Currently, nearly all trading desks use front end–back office computerized systems that are plugged into the on-line financial services and provide a continuous marking-to-market. The failure to execute a marking-to-market on at least a daily basis may have disastrous consequences. Unchecked high volatility in the foreign exchange markets is highly likely to generate insurmountably adverse trading conditions.

In the United States foreign exchange markets, the most common time for selecting the *end-of-day revaluation* rates is 3 PM EDT, which coincides with the end of the trading day on the currency futures exchanges. The common practice is to use the middle rate of a specific spot rate or forward spread, which is the arithmetic average of the bid and offer. If and when administrative costs are necessary, adjustments to these revaluations must be allowed. Using the 3 PM rates does not mean that trading is halted at that time.

The exchange rates used for revaluations should be obtained in an objective manner. Generally, the rates should be printed and updated in the computerized systems by an independent source, such as the back office. In the larger dealing rooms, the front end–back office systems linked to the on-line financial services execute this function, as already described. Common sources of information on exchange rates in the spot market are pages

263–266 of Telerate (Figure 5.2) and EFX= on Reuters (Figure 5.3). This approach is important in order to avoid unrealistically favorable rates input by a trader, who may want to improve an unrealized P&L, for instance. Certainly, any unrealized P&L figures have only a limited significance, but they may provide substantial warning signals. The lack of "raised red flags" may trigger serious surprises when the P&L is finally realized.

VALUE AT RISK

According to *Derivatives: Practices and Principles*, *value at risk* refers to "the expected loss from an adverse market movement with a specified probability over a particular period of time." Commonly, the potential adverse change in the value of a portfolio on a daily basis may be calculated with a probability of 97.5 percent, when using two standard deviations.

The determination of the value at risk is significant, especially for more complex foreign currency portfolios, because the results may be compared to the current financial and human resources, thus allowing for decisions on the most adequate set of risk management rules.

STRESS TESTS

Although players generally understand the unexpected rises in foreign exchange volatility, few could have forecasted the dollar/yen collapse in October 1998. (See Figure 5.4.) That development generated some big winners, but also big losers. To better respond to this type of situation, it is imperative that management request periodic stress tests, designed to check and prepare the traders' handling of their positions vis-à-vis periods of unusually high or low currency volatility. The historical volatility specific for each instrument is readily available from the financial services. (See Figure 5.5.)

```
Telerate                                                    Mon Aug 09 15:06:43 1999
                              Analytics/Pages

· 08/09     15:00 NYC     [TELERATE GLOBAL CURRENCY COMPOSITE]          PAGE 263

                     TELERATE GARBAN DATA - PAGES 4645-4699
 PAGE  BANK          GBP          GMT   PAGE  BANK          JPY          GMT
 2460 B N Z      WEL 1.6055 -65  18:56  3150 R B C      TOR 115.15 -25  18:05
 7601 BARCLAYS   LDN 1.6042 -52  16:28   820 CITIBANK   N Y 115.17 -27  18:58
  820 CITIBANK   N Y 1.6058 -68  18:57   855 UBS WDR    C T 115.35 -45  17:40
 3551 D G BANK   FFT 1.6040 -50  16:29  2460 B N Z      WEL 115.18 -25  18:56
 3150 R B C      TOR 1.6055 -65  18:45  3217 SOC GEN    PAR 115.39 -44  16:59
 HI 23:18    1.6130- 1.6015  13:12 LO   HI 13:39    115.49- 115.02   8:33 LO
 PAGE  BANK          EUR          GMT   PAGE  BANK          CHF          GMT
  820 CITIBANK   N Y 1.0704 -11  19:00  3150 R B C      TOR 1.4955 -65  18:53
  855 UBS WDR    C T 1.0706 -08  17:48   820 CITIBANK   N Y 1.4953 -63  19:00
  718 RADA FX    N Y 1.0707 -11  17:48  3551 D G BANK   FFT 1.4948 -58  16:28
 3150 R B C      TOR 1.0705 -10  18:33  3505 UBS WDR    ZUR 1.4949 -59  16:00
 3668 C ITALIAN  MIL 1.0706 -11  17:00  7601 BARCLAYS   LDN 1.4948 -58  16:27
 HI 23:24    1.0755- 1.0684  13:08 LO   HI 13:38    1.4985- 1.4918   2:51 LO
```

Figure 5.2. Pages 263–266 of Telerate are a major source of FX information. *(Source: Telerate, Inc.)*

```
Telerate                                              Mon Aug 09 15:06:50 1999
                                Analytics/Pages

08/09    15:00 NYC    [ADDITIONAL EUROPEAN CURRENCIES]              PAGE 264
                        [SEE ALSO 265 266]
     BANK                          GMT       BANK                       GMT
CZK  CITIBANK   PRG 33.992 -35    14:33  DKK CITIBANK   N Y 6.9490 -40  18:32
     C S O B    PRG 33.883 -01    18:35      RADA FX    N Y 6.9520 -50  17:46
     RADA FX    N Y 33.956 -06    17:45      SE BANKEN  STK 6.9473 -513 16:59
     BANK                          GMT       BANK                       GMT
PLN  RABOBANK   WAW 3.9640 -660   09:06  NOK RADA FX    N Y 7.7275 -25  16:38
     P M Y      GBL 3.9550 -600   15:06      U B N      OSL 7.7340 -00  15:02
     CHRSTIANA  OSL 3.9529 -89    11:42      CITIBANK   N Y 7.7185 -80  18:32
     BANK                          GMT       BANK                       GMT
SKK  SLOV SPO   BRA 41.805 -905   15:07  SEK CITIBANK   N Y 8.2245 -40  18:32
     C S O B    BRA 41.779 -900   19:00      UBS WDR    C T 8.2950 -50  14:43
     CITIBANK   BRA 41.739-833    19:00      RADA FX    N Y 8.2170 -20  16:39
     BANK                          GMT       BANK                       GMT
HUF  HYPO BK    BUD 236.30   40   06:33  RUB I M B      MOS 25.35/25.55 08:55
     DRESDNER   BUD 540.31 -5225  11:48      OKOBANK    HEL 25.08 - 25.09 13:50
```

```
Telerate                                              Mon Aug 09 15:06:57 1999
                                Analytics/Pages

08/09    16:00 NYC    [TELERATE CURRENCY MARKET PRICES]             PAGE 266
[ ]  BANK       CTR   BID - ASK   GMT      BANK       CTR  BID - ASK   GMT
ARS  TELERATE   GBL 0.9990-1.0000 12:12 INR RADA FX   N Y 43.39-49     17:37

BHD  RADA FX    N Y 0.37695-05    17:36 ILS 1ST INTL  TLV 4.1694 -764  19:00

BRL  TELERATE   GBL 1.84   -1.85  17:46 KES BARCLAYS  LDN 73.70/50     06:44

GRD  PIRAEUS    ATH 303.45 -75    18:59 KRW RADA FX   N Y 1198-1203    17:37

HKD  RADA FX    N Y 7.7626-30     17:37 KWD RADA FX   N Y 0.30455-75   17:37

TRL  T E B      IST 432860/33310  14:26 MYR RADA FX   N Y 3.7886-06    17:37

IDR  RADA FX    N Y 7040-7090     17:39 THB RADA FX   N Y 37.800 860   17:39
     [DIRECTORY OF SWIFT CODES  P 24480]
```

```
Telerate                                              Mon Aug 09 15:07:06 1999
                                Analytics/Pages

08/09    15:01 NYC    [TELERATE  CURRENCY MARKET PRICES]            P  266
[ ]  BANK       CTR   BID - ASK   GMT      BANK       CTR  BID - ASK   GMT
MXN  BANAMEX    MEX 9.4750/4850  18:44 PGK A N Z      MEL 0.3870 -70   20:30

NZD  NAT BK NZ  WEL 0.5288 -95   19:00 QAR RADA FX    N Y 3.6395 -425  17:45

PHP  RADA FX    N Y 39.08 -28    17:38 SEK CITIBANK   N Y 8.2245 -40   18:32

TWD  INDOSUEZ   TPE 32.135 -146  06:38 AED RADA FX    N Y 3.6726 -31   17:36

SAR  A B C      BAH 3.7503 -06   07:12 VEB RADA FX    N Y 613.25-25    17:40

SGD  RADA FX    N Y 1.6675 -85   17:39 CNY BROKER     GBL 8.2765 -2775 02:56

ZAR  CITIBANK   N Y 6.1640 -90   18:59 OMR CITIBANK   BAH 0.38490-10   08:20
        [DIRECTORY OF SWIFT CODES, P 24480]
```

Figure 5.2. *(Continued)*

```
EFX=                  Latest  Spots
RIC                 BIDSASK  CONTRIB      LOC SRCE DEAL    TIME  HIGH      LOW
EUR=      ↑    1.0711S18   CITIBANK      NYC CINX CITN    14:06 1.0735    1.0684
JPY=      ↓  115.15S5.25   ROYAL BK CAN  TOR RBCT RBCT*J  14:05 115.50    114.99
GBP=      ↑    1.6040S50   CITIBANK      NYC CINX CITN*G  13:59 1.6100    1.6010
CHF=      ↓    1.4945S55   ROYAL BK CAN  TOR RBCT RBCT*C  14:08 1.4986    1.4910
DEM=      ↓    1.8248S60   REUTERS       RTR RTRS         14:10 1.8306    1.8219
FRF=      ↓    6.1201S41   REUTERS       RTR RTRS         14:10 6.1396    6.1105
NLG=      ↓    2.0561S74   REUTERS       RTR RTRS         14:10 2.0626    2.0528
ITL=      ↓ 1806.56S7.74   REUTERS       RTR RTRS         14:10 1812.31   1803.70
BEF=      ↓   37.638S662   REUTERS       RTR RTRS         14:10 37.757    37.578
XAU=      ↓  257.10S7.60   REPUBLIC NAT  NYC RNBG RNBA    14:10 257.50    255.95
XAG=      ↑    5.31S5.34   REPUBLIC NAT  NYC RNBG RNBA    14:09 5.39      5.30
IEP=      ↑    1.3600S09   REUTERS       RTR RTRS         14:10 1.3631    1.3566
AUD=      ↑    0.6536S41   CITIBANK      NYC CINX CICM*T  13:59 0.6540    0.6497
CAD=      ↓    1.5021S31   BK OF NS      TOR BNST BNST*R  14:04 1.5045    1.4976
ATS=      ↓   12.8385S69   REUTERS       RTR RTRS         14:10 12.8794   12.8182
ESP=      ↓  155.24S5.34   REUTERS       RTR RTRS         14:10 155.73    154.99
SEK=      ↑    8.2210S10   SE BANKEN     NYC SEBN SEBN*S  13:54 8.2365    8.1811
NOK=      ↑    7.7172S92   SE BANKEN     NYC SEBN SEBN*L  13:54 7.7668    7.7020
DKK=      ↓    6.9463S83   SE BANKEN     NYC SEBN SEBN*H  13:54 6.9655    6.9328
FIM=      ↓    5.5474S11   REUTERS       RTR RTRS         14:10 5.5651    5.5386
PTE=      ↓  187.05S7.17   REUTERS       RTR RTRS         14:10 187.65    186.76
GRD=      ↓  303.23S3.52   PIRAEUS       ATH BPGR PIRE    14:09 306.48    302.93
RUB=      ↑   25.100S300   OGRES KOM BK  RIX OGRE OKBR    13:07 25.6000   24.8100
TRL=      ↓ 432460S3010   KOCBANK       IST KOCT KOCT    14:08 433050    431870
ISK=      ↓   72.70S2.80   BUNADARBANKI  RVK BUNA         14:08 72.90     72.77
```

Figure 5.3. EFX= is a common source of spot exchange rates used for revaluation purposes. *(Source: Reuters)*

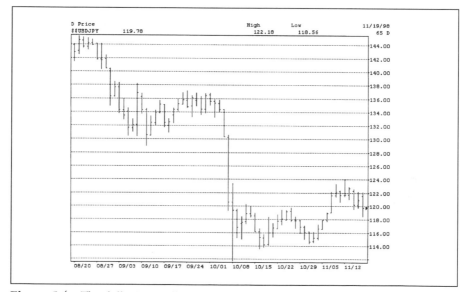

Figure 5.4. The dollar/yen collapse in October 1998 exemplifies the unexpectedly high volatility in foreign exchange. *(Source: Bridge Information Systems, Inc.)*

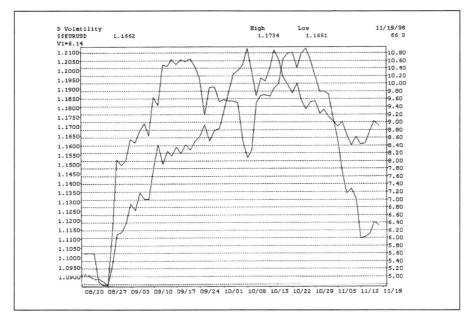

D Volatility		High	Low	11/19/98
$$EURUSD	1.1662	1.1734	1.1661	66 D
V1=6.14				

Figure 5.5. The historical volatility of the euro/dollar rate. *(Source: Bridge Information Systems, Inc.)*

EXCHANGE RISK MANAGEMENT IMPLEMENTATION

The position and loss limits are very basic management and control tools that can now be implemented better and more conveniently with the help of computerized systems. After all transactions are entered in the system, the treasurer and the chief trader have continuous, instantaneous, and comprehensive access to accurate figures for all the positions and the profit and loss. In addition, this information may be relayed from all the international branches into the headquarters terminals.

INTEREST RATE RISK

Interest rate risk refers to the profit and loss generated by fluctuations in the forward spreads, along with forward amount mismatches and maturity gaps among transactions in the foreign exchange book. This risk is pertinent to currency swaps, forward outrights, futures, and options.

An *amount mismatch* between a spot deal and a forward outright deal may occur during a deal between the spot trader and a customer. If the customer asks for an odd amount dated forward, the spot trader will most likely cover in the spot market in the closest standard amount possible. The difference between the spot and the forward amounts is a mismatch.

For instance, if a customer buys USD/CAD 910,000 in forward outright, a trader will most likely cover USD/CAD 1,000,000 in the spot market, because it is easier to trade an even amount, and will adjust the forward pips later. However, there is an amount mismatched of USD/CAD 90,000.

A typical *maturity gap* occurs when a customer deals in an odd maturity (say 32 days) and the trader covers in one month (assume 31 days). Another typical example occurs when a forward outright deal is covered with a spot deal. This is done frequently to avoid the exchange risk. Although the exchange risk is annulled, as the same amount of foreign currency was bought and sold, for the duration of time the maturity dates are different, the party that covered only the spot side of the deal is exposed to any changes in either of the applicable interest rates (the interest rate differential).

For small exchange books, maturity mismatches may easily be avoided. For an active forward desk, despite increasingly sophisticated computer systems, the complete elimination of maturity gaps is virtually impossible. However, this may not be a serious problem if the amounts involved in these mismatches are small.

On a daily basis, traders balance the net payments and receipts for each currency through a special type of swap, called *tomorrow/next* or *rollover*. This type of swap, discussed in detail in Chapter 12, is geared toward the changing, or rolling over, of the old spot date to the new spot date. It is a powerful and convenient tool for handling the flow of maturing trades.

RISK MANAGEMENT IMPLEMENTATION

To minimize interest rate risk, management sets limits on the total size of mismatches. The policies differ among banks, but a common approach is to separate the mismatches, based on their maturity dates, into up to six months and past six months. All the transactions are entered in computerized systems in order to calculate the positions for all the delivery dates and the P&L. Continuous analysis of the interest rate environment is necessary to forecast any changes that may impact on the outstanding gaps. The results of this approach are good, but not perfect.

CREDIT RISK

Credit risk refers to the possibility that an outstanding currency position may not be repaid as agreed, due to a voluntary or involuntary action by a counterparty. Insolvency or prohibition of foreign exchange transactions may trigger the failure. An example is the sudden insolvency of Drexel Burnham of New York, the high-riding junk bond leader of the 1980s. Although more commonly associated with loan departments, credit or settlement risk also pertains to the foreign exchange markets.

The maturity dates may be closer than for loans, but the same characteristics apply. Credit problems occur not only in the long-dated forward contracts, but also in spot contracts, for which payments are due in only two business days. Both the credit and the trading departments are responsible for managing credit risk, which is present in all foreign exchange instruments except currency futures and options on currency futures.

In these cases, trading occurs on regulated exchanges, such as the Chicago IMM, where all trades are settled by the clearinghouse. On such exchanges, traders of all sizes can deal without any credit concern.

In order to minimize the credit risk for instruments traded off regulated exchanges, the potential and active customers' creditworthiness is essential because commercial and investment banks, trading companies, and banks' customers must have credit lines with each other to be able to trade. Even after the credit lines are extended, the counterparties' financial soundness should be continuously monitored.

Traders should use Foreign Exchange Master Agreements to document FX transactions in derivative products. A sample of an International FX Master Agreement as drafted by the British Bankers' Association and the Foreign Exchange Committee is provided in the Exchange Rate Risk section of this chapter.

Two forms of credit risk are replacement risk and settlement risk.

1. *Replacement risk* occurs when counterparties of the failed bank find their books unbalanced to the extent of their exposure to the insolvent party. In order to rebalance their books, these banks must enter new transactions.

2. *Settlement risk* occurs because of the time zones separating nations. Consequently, currencies may be credited at different times during the day. Australian and New Zealand dollars are credited first, then Japanese yen, followed by the European currencies and ending with the U.S. dollar. Therefore, payment may be made to a party that will declare insolvency (or be declared insolvent) immediately after, but prior to executing its own payments.

In this case, we are no longer facing exchange risk; we are facing a sudden disappearance of capital. Foreign exchange traders usually deal in multiples of $1 million, but these amounts mean little more than tokens. Money is neither seen nor touched. It only exists as an electronic surrealism.

The counterparty's payment failure, however, zooms the concept of money back into reality at a chilling speed. Although rare and therefore easy to forget, the two major cases, Bankhaus I. D. Herstatt, a small private German bank, and BCCI, sent out clear signals about the seriousness of the situation. After closing down BCCI, Bank of England telexed the news to all the major commercial banks and wished them good luck in recouping their losses through litigation. Some of the losses may be recovered eventually, but the magnitude of the losses incurred by a large, select group of major banks emphasizes the need for better credit risk control.

In addition to opening lines of credit selectively and constantly monitoring the creditworthiness of the counterparties, another measure is available. In assessing the credit risk, end users must consider not only the market value of their currency portfolios, but also the potential exposure of these portfolios. The potential exposure may be determined through probability analysis over the time to maturity of the outstanding position.

NETTING

Netting is a process that enables institutions to settle only their net positions with one another at the end of the day, in a single transaction, not trade by trade. It is a safer procedure, as the cash flow at maturity is clearly reduced. If a bank shows signs of payment difficulty, a group of large banks will provide short-term backing from a common reserve pool. In addition, the forward credit lines are not filled, providing room for more business.

Finally, netting is distinctly cheaper. Settlement netting should fall under a single comprehensive master agreement with each counterparty, in order to provide the maximum legal coverage for credit exposure.

IMPLEMENTATION

The computerized systems currently available are very useful in implementing credit risk policies. Credit lines are easily monitored. In addition, the matching systems introduced in foreign exchange since April 1993 are used by traders for credit policy implementation as well. Traders input the total line of credit for a specific counterparty. During the trading session, the line of credit is automatically adjusted. If the line is fully used, the system will prevent the trader from further dealing with that counterparty. After maturity, the credit line reverts to its original level.

COUNTRY RISK

Country (sovereign) risk refers to the government's interference in the foreign exchange markets. Although theoretically present in all foreign exchange instruments, currency futures are, for all practical purposes, excepted from country risk, because the major currency futures markets are located in the United States.

This type of risk should not be confused with the risk of intervention of the central banks in the foreign exchange markets, which pertains to exchange risk. Country risk occurs when governments interfere for such reasons as currency shortage, tightening control over the banking system, freezing foreign funds on deposit, or war.

The example of Kuwait's takeover by Iraq, when foreign exchange transactions (along with all other transactions) were abruptly severed, signifies the difficulty of separating credit from country risk. Of course, this example had a happy ending—at least in the financial markets. The National Bank of Kuwait, which also had a set of books in London, made all the outstanding payments. Another example is the U.S. freezing of Iranian deposits in U.S. banks following the Iranian government's overthrow and the taking of American hostages.

The impact of restrictions on foreign exchange is generally high if they interfere with the normal payments setup. The failure to receive an expected payment due to government interference amounts to the insolvency of an individual bank or institution, a situation described under credit risk. However, the scale is magnified with country risk, as more banks or institutions are affected.

Since the 1980s, the trend among the major countries has been one of liberalization. Switzerland and Japan are among the countries that relaxed monetary controls. Sweden also relaxed its controls over the krona forward market. But outside the major economies, controls on foreign exchange activities are still present and actively implemented.

From the trader's point of view, it is very important to know or be able to anticipate any restrictive changes concerning the free flow of currencies. If this is possible, though trading in the affected currency will dry up considerably, it is still a manageable situation. The problem occurs at its fullest if there is an element of surprise, because the recovery of funds through litigation is a lengthy and frustrating undertaking.

Country risk falls under the joint responsibility of the treasurer and the credit department.

CONCLUSION

Foreign exchange has skyrocketed in daily turnover from a mere $5 billion in 1977 to a staggering U.S.$1.5 trillion in 1998. The industry is thus far subject to limited regulation, save for currency futures. In addition to these factors, the spot market moves at breakneck speed. For instance, a major exchange rate may change in value 18,000 times daily. In this huge and rapidly moving trading environment, risks may be substantial, so it is imperative to have sophisticated and experienced management able to impose sound policies that are best suited for the capacity of each particular trading entity.

The introduction of front end–back office systems has greatly facilitated the implementation of risk management. Instantaneous, accurate, and comprehensive information on positions, P&L, and credit lines is available to aid in this management task.

6 Central Banks

Generally speaking, a central bank's role is to direct the domestic monetary policy of its country. Under the monetary policy, the central bank manages the flow of money and credit that is provided to the economy. Therefore, the role of the central bank vis-à-vis the economy is paramount.

When discussing the subject of the central bank in the context of foreign exchange, there is a tendency to focus on market interventions. While interventions are very important, they represent only a fraction of the total role the central banks exercise in affecting the foreign exchange market.

Before we go any further, though, let's take a look at the United States' Federal Reserve.

THE FEDERAL RESERVE

HISTORICAL BACKGROUND

The Federal Reserve (the Fed) was established in 1913, when Congress passed the Federal Reserve Act. The act held that the role of the Federal Reserve was "to furnish an elastic currency, to afford the means of rediscounting commercial paper, to establish a more effective supervision of banking in the United States, and for other purposes."

The act instituted a decentralized system, consisting of the Federal Reserve Board in Washington and 12 regional Federal Reserve banks around the country. These banks around the country had sufficient autonomy to manage financial conditions in their districts. They were also managed by governors.

In 1923, the Open Market Investment Committee (OMIC) was established to coordinate the Reserve Bank operations. It was composed of the governors of the Federal Reserve Banks in New York, Boston, Philadelphia, Chicago and Cleveland. In 1930, the OMIC was replaced by the Open Market Policy Conference (OMPC). It consisted of the governors and members of the Board of the 12 Federal Reserve banks.

The strains of World War I, the stock market crash of 1929, and the subsequent Depression of the 1930s, along with a better understanding of the effects of monetary tools, were all important factors behind changes established by the Roosevelt Administration in 1933. Among those changes were the creation of the Federal Deposit Insurance Corporation (FDIC), the formal recognition of the Open Market Policy Conference (OMPC) already established in 1930, and empowering the Board to change the member bank reserve requirements.

The Banking Act of 1935 reshaped the structure of the Federal Reserve System into its current form. The Board was renamed the Board of Governors of the Federal Reserve System. The Board of Governors now consisted of seven Governors, one of whom was Chairman of the Board. Also, the Treasury Secretary and the Comptroller of the Currency were disassociated from the Board meetings. The titles of the regional Reserve Bank governors were changed to presidents, and the OPMC's name was switched to its current name, the Federal Open Market Committee (FOMC).

The autonomy of the regional Reserve Banks was curtailed with regard to government debt transaction without FOMC permission. The act also held that the Board must use its powers to generate an appropriate environment for business stability.

The Federal Reserve Bank is independent of Congress and the President. However, all Federal Reserve Governors are selected by the President and must be ratified by Congress.

In contemporary times, Paul Volcker, the Fed Chairman in 1979, linked economic performance to the growth rates of the *money supply (M1)*. M1 is composed of currency in circulation (outside the Treasury, the Fed, and depositary institutions), travelers checks, demand deposits, and other checkable deposits [negotiable order of withdrawal (NOW) accounts, automatic transfer service (ATS) accounts, etc.]. In 1980, the Depositary Institutions Deregulation and Money Control Act (MCA) simplified the structure of the reserve requirements and allowed the elimination of interest rate ceilings on most of the deposits (the exception was demand deposits). By 1982, however, M1 as an economic indicator was dropped in favor of *M2*. M2 consists of M1 plus repurchase agreements, overnight eurodollars, money market deposit accounts, savings and time deposits (in amounts under $100,000), and balances in general purposes. Since then, the FOMC has had a love–hate relationship with M2's ability to be a reliable economic indicator.

M3 is composed of M2 plus time deposits over $100,000, term eurodollar deposits, and all balances in institutional money market mutual funds.

THE FEDERAL RESERVE'S ROLE IN FOREIGN EXCHANGE

Like the other central banks, the Federal Reserve affects the foreign exchange markets in three general areas:

1. the discount rate,
2. the money market instruments, and
3. foreign exchange operations.

DISCOUNT RATE

The *discount rate* is the interest rate at which eligible depositary institutions may borrow funds directly from the Federal Reserve Banks. This rate is controlled by the Federal Reserve and is not subject to trading. It is a benchmark interest rate. (See Figure 6.1.)

Prime Rate

The *prime rate* is the rate used by commercial banks as a base for retail loan rates. (See Figure 6.2.) The prime rate is based on the discount rate; it is always higher than the discount rate. The correlation between the two is not constant. For instance, if the discount rate is increased, it is sure that the prime rate will increase as well. If the discount rate is cut, the prime rate may not follow, giving the banks an extra spread for profit.

THE MONEY MARKET INSTRUMENTS

The money market instruments tend to have a generally marginal impact on foreign exchange. Among these instruments, the most significant are federal funds, repurchase agreements, and eurodollars.

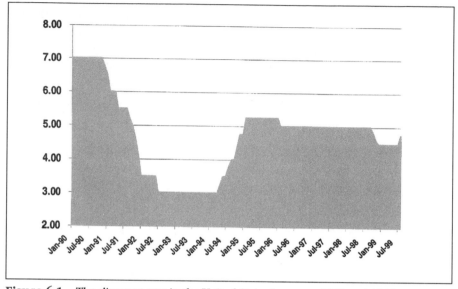

Figure 6.1. The discount rate in the United States between 1979 and 1999.

Federal Funds

Federal funds, largely known as Fed funds, are the immediately available reserve balances at the federal reserves. The Fed funds are widely used by commercial banks or large corporations to lend to each other, mostly on an overnight basis. (See Figure 6.3.) Although the Fed establishes their level, the prices fluctuate because they are being traded in the market. The Fed funds levels are available from the on-line financial services. Typically, traders find them on Reuters or Telerate, page 5.

Foreign exchange traders generally are not concerned on a daily basis with the Fed funds prices. However, changes in their levels are considered warnings of potential changes in the discount rate. Therefore, at times, the Fed funds prices may be a trading signal for the foreign exchange markets.

This scenario came to life in February 1994. The pressure on the Federal Reserve in the United States with regard to openness on activity in Fed funds, led Alan Greenspan, the Fed's Chairman, to announce an increase in the Fed funds. This direct approach was unprecedented and generated unusually volatile market conditions in foreign exchange.

Repurchase Agreements

Repurchase agreements (repos) are almost daily operations executed by the Federal Reserve. A repurchase agreement between the Federal Reserve and a government securities dealer consists of the Fed's purchasing a security for immediate delivery, with an agreement to sell the same security back at the same price at a predetermined date in the future (usually within 15 days), and at a specific rate of interest. This arrangement amounts to a temporary injection of reserves into the banking system. The impact on the foreign exchange market is that the dollar *should* weaken. The repurchase agreements may be either customer repos or system repos.

Telerate   Analytics/Pages   Mon Aug 09 17:51:56 1999

[TELERATE DATA SERVICE]   PAGE 125
[PRIME RATE HISTORY--MAY 20, 1985 TO PRESENT] SOURCE: FRB H.15

DATE	RATE	DATE	RATE	DATE	RATE
07/01/99-PRESENT	8.00	12/23/91-07/01/92	6.50	02/02/88-05/10/88	8.50
11/18/98-06/30/99	7.75	11/06/91-12/20/91	7.50	11/05/87-02/01/88	8.75
10/16/98-11/17/98	8.00	09/13/91-11/05/91	8.00	10/22/87-11/04/87	9.00
09/30/98-10/15/98	8.25	05/01/91-09/12/91	8.50	10/07/87-10/21/87	9.25
03/26/97-09/29/98	8.50	02/04/91-04/30/91	9.00	09/04/87-10/06/87	8.75
02/01/96-03/25/97	8.25	01/02/91-02/01/91	9.50	05/15/87-09/03/87	8.25
12/20/95-01/31/96	8.50	01/08/90-12/31/90	10.00	05/01/87-05/14/87	8.00
07/07/95-12/19/95	8.75	07/31/89-01/07/90	10.50	04/01/87-04/30/87	7.75
02/01/95-07/06/95	9.00	06/05/89-07/28/89	11.00	08/26/86-03/31/87	7.50
11/15/94-01/31/95	8.50	02/24/89-06/02/89	11.50	07/11/86-08/25/86	8.00
08/16/94-11/14/94	7.75	02/10/89-02/23/89	11.00	04/21/86-07/10/86	8.50
05/17/94-08/15/94	7.25	11/28/88-02/09/89	10.50	03/07/86-04/20/86	9.00
04/19/94-05/16/94	6.75	08/11/88-11/27/88	10.00	06/18/85-03/06/86	9.50
03/24/94-04/18/94	6.25	07/14/88-08/10/88	9.50	05/20/85-06/17/85	10.00
07/02/92-03/23/94	6.00	05/11/88-07/14/88	9.00	[CONTINUED NEXT PAGE]	

Telerate   Analytics/Pages   Mon Aug 09 17:52:05 1999

[TELERATE DATA SERVICE]   PAGE 126
[PRIME RATE HISTORY--APR 30, 1981 TO MAY 17, 1985] SOURCE: FRB NY

DATE	RATE	DATE	RATE	DATE	RATE
01/15/85-05/17/85	10.50	10/14/82-11/21/82	12.00	11/17/81-11/17/81	16.50
12/20/84-01/16/85	10.75	10/07/82-11/13/82	13.00	11/09/81-11/16/81	17.00
11/28/84-12/19/84	11.25	08/23/82-10/06/82	13.50	11/03/81-11/08/81	17.50
11/09/84-11/27/84	11.75	08/18/82-08/22/82	14.00	10/13/81-11/02/81	18.00
10/29/84-11/08/84	12.00	08/16/82-08/17/82	14.50	10/05/81-10/12/81	19.00
10/17/84-10/28/84	12.50	08/02/82-08/15/82	15.00	09/22/81-10/04/81	19.50
09/27/84-10/16/84	12.75	07/29/82-08/01/82	15.50	09/15/81-09/21/81	20.00
06/25/84-09/26/84	13.00	07/20/82-08/28/82	16.00	07/08/81-09/14/81	20.50
05/08/84-06/24/84	12.50	02/23/82-07/19/82	16.50	06/03/81-07/07/81	20.00
04/05/84-05/07/84	12.00	02/18/82-02/22/82	17.00	05/22/81-06/02/81	20.50
03/19/84-04/04/84	11.50	02/02/82-02/17/82	16.50	05/19/81-05/21/81	20.00
08/08/83-03/18/84	11.00	12/01/81-02/01/82	15.75	05/11/81-05/18/81	19.50
02/28/83-08/05/83	10.50	11/24/81-11/30/81	16.00	05/04/81-05/10/81	19.00
01/11/83-02/25/83	11.00	11/20/81-11/23/81	16.50	04/30/81-05/03/81	18.00
11/22/82-01/10/83	11.50	11/17/81-11/19/81	17.00	[CONTINUED NEXT PAGE]	

Figure 6.2. The prime rate in the United States between 1982 and 1999. *(Source: Telerate, Inc.)*

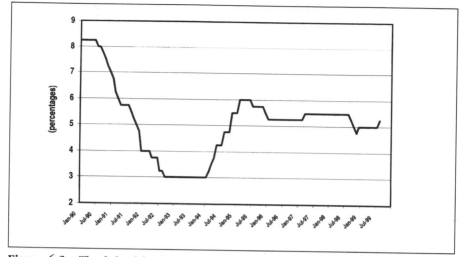

Figure 6.3. The federal funds rates in the United States between 1990 and 1999.

Matched Sale-Purchase Agreements

Matched sale-purchase agreements are just the opposite of repurchase agreements. When executing a matched sale-purchase agreement, the Fed sells a security for immediate delivery to a dealer or a foreign central bank, with the agreement to buy back the same security at the same price at a predetermined time in the future (generally within 7 days). This arrangement amounts to a temporary drain of reserves. The impact on the foreign exchange market is that the dollar *should* strengthen. These types of operations usually occur in mid-morning

The repo activities generally have only a limited impact on foreign exchange trading. The Fed watchers have become quite adroit and their forecasts are very accurate. Foreign exchange traders generally discount these daily operations; but when the Fed refrains from its expected operation or executes the opposite type of repos, they see this as a trading signal.

The New York Federal Reserve Bank as directed by the FOMC executes these open market operations.

Eurodollars

Eurodollars are dollar-denominated deposits at commercial banks outside the United States. All currency deposits outside the country of origin are called *eurocurrencies*. These deposits do not have to be placed in Europe. Therefore, yen deposits outside Japan are euroyen, British pounds outside

England are known as eurosterling, etc. Eurodollars have the largest share of the eurocurrency market.

The name eurodollar seems to have been coined inadvertently by a French branch of a Soviet bank, La Banque Commerciale pour l'Europe du Nord, S.A., which had as its international cable code "Eurobank." Somehow, the name stuck with traders and has been used ever since.

Currency deposits outside the issuing country are not a novelty. At all times throughout history, some foreign currencies had more panache for their holders. In the beginning of the twentieth century, the most popular eurocurrency was the eurosterling, because the British pound was the currency of reference around the world. The end of World War II brought the end of the supremacy of the pound and indirectly helped the rise of the eurodollar market.

In the postwar period, money was scarce. The U.S. dollar was the major currency, and demand for it was widespread. The Communist countries, especially the former Soviet Union, kept dollar deposits in London. Events in 1957—debilitating British inflation and the Suez crisis—triggered capital controls in the United Kingdom. But the Soviet Union was in no rush to move its dollar deposits from London to New York, because it feared that the United States would to freeze these deposits in retaliation for the expropriation of American property in the Soviet Union.

United States legislation was also instrumental in the growth of this market. The Federal Reserve had passed Regulation Q, which prohibited payment of interest on demand deposits and prescribed maximum rates that banks can pay on time deposits. These ceilings had been imposed since 1933 by the United States government. According to *A Guide to Federal Reserve Regulations*, published by the Board of Governors of the Federal Reserve System, "federal law prohibits the payment of interest on demand deposits by member banks." Regulation Q defined "interest" and restated the prohibitions. In addition, Regulation Q included rules governing the advertising of deposits by member banks. Regulation Q is no longer applicable.

When the European countries returned to free convertibility in 1958, U.S. dollars were still kept in deposits in Europe, to avoid the capped interest rates in the United States. In addition, the investment opportunities were better in Europe, where the economies had been rebuilt. Finally, the eurodollar deposits filled the niche for short-term money market instruments in Europe.

Eurodollar deposits can be created by any depositors of U.S. dollars outside the United States, regardless of whether they are American or not. For instance, they could be foreign holders of U.S. dollar deposits at American banks transferring these deposits to foreign banks, or American citizens receiving checks drawn on accounts in U.S. banks and depositing them in foreign banks.

Eurocurrencies' rates are used by forward traders to calculate the forward spread. The formula for the forward spread is:

$$\frac{\text{Forward}}{\text{spread}} = [\text{Spot rate} \times (\text{Eurocurrency} - \text{Eurodollar})] \times \frac{\text{No. of days}}{360}$$

If the result is a positive number, then the forward spread is at a premium, and it is added to the spot price. Conversely, if the result is negative, then the spread is at discount, and it is subtracted from the spot rate. Forward spreads are covered in detail in Chapter 12.

FOREIGN EXCHANGE OPERATIONS

The major central banks are involved in foreign exchange operations in more ways than intervening in the open market. Their operations include payments among central banks or to international agencies. In addition, the Federal Reserve has entered a series of currency swap arrangements with other central banks since 1962. For instance, to help the allied war effort against Iraq's invasion of Kuwait in 1990–1991, payments were executed by the Bundesbank and Bank of Japan to the Federal Reserve. Also, payments to the Worldbank or the United Nations are executed through central banks.

When learning of large currency fluctuations in which the central banks are involved, one cannot help but wonder whether these banks have been motivated by profit. After all, central banks have access to arguably the largest trading capital around. It is very important to dispel this myth. *The major central banks do not engage in speculative trading.* Intervention in the United States foreign exchange markets by the U.S. Treasury and the Federal Reserve is geared toward restoring orderly conditions in the market or influencing the exchange rates. It is not geared toward affecting the reserves.

If, for intervention purposes, the Federal Reserve buys dollars, then it drains reserves. If it sells, then it adds reserves. The intervention is split between the Federal Reserve and the Treasury. If the Treasury pays for its portion in currencies from the Exchange Stabilization Fund, the intervention will not have any impact on the reserves. If the intervention is financed through a sale of special drawing rights (SDRs) from the International Monetary Fund (IMF), then it adds reserves. The change in reserves occurs because the sale of the SDRs, which are financial assets, creates money. Reserves are also increased if the Treasury exchanges foreign currencies for U.S. dollars with the Federal Reserve with the agreement to repurchase them at the same rate. This technique, called warehousing, adds reserves because the Treasury invests the funds.

The Foreign Exchange Desk at the Federal Reserve Bank of New York executes the actual intervention. There are two types of foreign exchange interventions: naked intervention and sterilized intervention.

Naked intervention, or *unsterilized intervention*, refers to the sole foreign exchange activity. All that takes place is the intervention itself, in which the Federal Reserve either buys or sells U.S. dollars against a foreign currency. In addition to the impact on the foreign exchange market, there is also a monetary effect on the money supply. If the money supply is impacted, then consequent adjustments must be made in interest rates, in prices, and at all levels of the economy. Therefore, a naked foreign exchange intervention has a long-term effect.

Sterilized intervention neutralizes its impact on the money supply. As there are rather few central banks that want the impact of their intervention in the foreign exchange markets to affect all corners of their economy, sterilized interventions have been the tool of choice. This holds true for the Federal Reserve as well.

The sterilized intervention involves an additional step to the original currency transaction. This step consists of a sale of government securities that offsets the reserve addition that occurs due to the intervention. It may be easier to visualize it if you think that the central bank will finance the sale of a currency through the sale of a number of government securities.

In addition to selling government instruments to balance the reserve injection, a central bank has two other alternatives—printing money and writing a check to itself. Although central banks are entitled to do so, these are not actual alternatives to be considered, because of the grave consequences on inflation.

Because a sterilized intervention only generates an impact on the supply and demand of a certain currency, its impact will tend to have a short- to medium-term effect.

REASONS FOR FOREIGN EXCHANGE INTERVENTIONS

It is vital for traders to understand the reason behind central banks' interventions so they can protect their outstanding positions and capitalize on the opportunity. Some assume that central banks typically intervene to protect their currencies. This is not always a valid assumption. Central banks intervene for the following reasons:

- to provide market liquidity,
- to protect a certain level,
- to slow down movements, or
- to reverse a trend.

Providing Market Liquidity

When a crisis hits a currency pair, the FX market might become disorderly, with one of the price sides, bid or offer, disappearing. A central bank might intervene to provide the missing side of the price. There is no guarantee the bank will operate this way, but it is an operation it might undertake on special occasions. Therefore, the impact is likely to be short-lived, as the central bank's goal would be to provide a safety exit for traders who got caught the wrong way, not to change the direction of the market.

Protecting a Certain Level

Central banks have long since lost their 1980s ability to tell the market what range it can trade in. Range or level protection took a further step back after the ranges of the EMS currencies against the deutsche mark merged into the euro at the end of 1998. Nevertheless, central banks still attempt to support certain levels, although on a spotty basis. The Bank of Japan is a typical example, as its major exporters can be sufficiently influential in convincing the bank to act to protect their interest.

Slowing Down Operations

Central banks will execute slow-down operations when they don't mind either the direction or the exchange level, but rather the speed of movement. When a currency falls too fast, for instance, the bank might buy small amounts to slow down the descent. Traders can use the opportunity to load up on cheap currency and then sell it back after the intervention.

Reversing a Trend

Few central banks are ready and willing to intervene with this lofty goal in mind. FX markets are too big and sophisticated to give up the fight hands down. The best example of when central banks were successful was the complex, joint, and long-term intervention that followed the Plaza Accord that reversed the dollar uptrend. Traders can benefit from such an operation by joining the side of the central banks.

AN OVERVIEW OF THE CENTRAL BANKS OF THE OTHER G-7 COUNTRIES

In the wake of World War II, both Germany and Japan were helped to develop new financial systems. Both countries created central banks that were fundamentally similar to the Federal Reserve. Along the line, their scope was customized to their domestic needs and they diverged from their model.

THE EUROPEAN CENTRAL BANK (ECB)

The European Central Bank was set up on June 1, 1998 to oversee the ascent of the euro. During the transition to the third stage of economic and monetary union (introduction of the single currency on January 1, 1999), it was responsible for carrying out the Community's monetary policy. The ECB, which is an independent entity, supervises the activity of individual member European central banks, such as Deutsche Bundesbank, Banque de France, and Ufficio Italiano dei Cambi. The ECB's decision-making bodies run a European System of Central Banks whose task is to manage the money in circulation, conduct foreign exchange operations, hold and manage the Member States' official foreign reserves, and promote the smooth operation of payment systems. The ECB is the successor to the European Monetary Institute (EMI).

THE DEUTSCHE BUNDESBANK (BUBA)

The German central bank, widely known as the Bundesbank, was the model for the ECB. The Bundesbank was a very independent entity, dedicated to a stable currency, low inflation, and a controlled money supply. The hyperinflation that developed in Germany after World War I created a fertile economic and political scenario for the rise of an extremist political party and for the start of World War II. The Bundesbank's charter obligated it to avoid any such economic chaos.

THE BANK OF JAPAN (BOJ)

The Bank of Japan has deviated from the Federal Reserve model in terms of independence. Although its Policy Board is still fully in charge of monetary policy, changes are still subject to the approval of the Ministry of Finance (MOF). The BOJ targets the M2 aggregate. On a quarterly basis, the BOJ releases its Tankan economic survey. Tankan is the Japanese equivalent of the American tan book, which presents the state of the economy. The Tankan's findings are not automatic triggers of monetary policy changes. Generally, the lack of independence of a central bank signals inflation. This is not the case in Japan, and it is yet another example of how different fiscal or economic policies can have opposite effects in separate environments.

BANK OF ENGLAND (BOE)

The Bank of England may be characterized as a less independent central bank, because the government may overrule its decision.

The BOE has not had an easy tenure. Despite the fact that British inflation was high through 1991, reaching double-digit rates in the late 1980s,
the Bank of England did a marvelous job of proving to the world that it was
able to maneuver the pound into mirroring the Exchange Rate Mechanism.

After joining the ERM late in 1990, the BOE was instrumental in
keeping the pound within its 6 percent allowed range against the deutsche
mark, but the pound had a short stay in the Exchange Rate Mechanism.
The divergence between the artificially high interest rates linked to ERM
commitments and Britain's weak domestic economy triggered a massive
sell-off of the pound in September 1992. (See Figure 6.4.)

Despite significant losses in foreign exchange, rumored to exceed
$100 billion, the BOE was able to support the battered British economy by
drastically lowering the interest rates.

After the euro came into being, the BOE steadily trimmed the base
rates in a double-pronged effort to stimulate the waning U.K. economy and
bring its rates closer to the lower euro-zone rates. The latter goal would enable the U.K. to join the euro zone, provided a domestic referendum produced a positive vote.

BANQUE DE FRANCE/BANK OF FRANCE (BOF)

The Bank of France has joint responsibility, with the Ministry of Finance,
to conduct domestic monetary policy. Their main goals are noninflationary

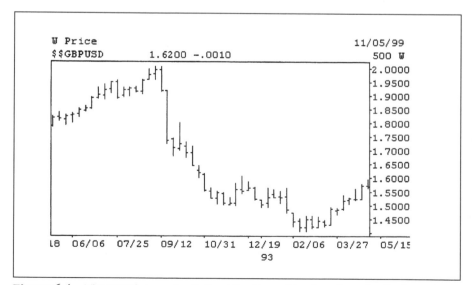

Figure 6.4.   The British pound activity at the time of its drop from the Exchange Rate
Mechanism. *(Source: Bridge Information Systems, Inc.)*

growth and external account equilibrium. France has become a major player in the foreign exchange markets since the ravages of the ERM crisis of July 1993, when the French franc fell victim to the foreign exchange markets.

Ufficio Italiano dei Cambi/Bank of Italy (BOI)

The Bank of Italy is in charge of the monetary policy, financial intermediaries, and foreign exchange. Like the other former European Monetary System central banks, BOI's responsibilities shifted domestically following the ERM crisis. Along with the Bundesbank and Bank of France, the Bank of Italy is now part of the European System of Central Banks (ESCB).

Bank of Canada (BOC)

The Bank of Canada is an independent central bank that has a tight rein on its currency. Due to its complex economic relations with the United States, the Canadian dollar has a strong connection to the U.S. dollar. The BOC intervenes more frequently than the other G7 central banks to shore up the fluctuations of its Canadian dollar. The central bank changed its intervention policy in 1999 after admitting that its previous mechanical policy, of intervening in increments of only $50 million at a set price based on the previous closing, was not working. (See Figure 6.5.)

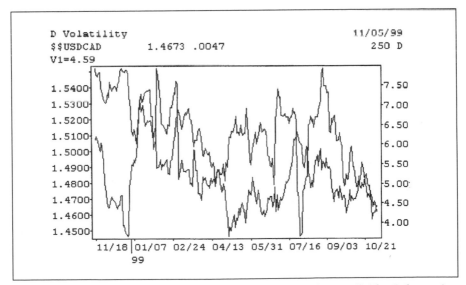

Figure 6.5. The volatility of U.S. dollar/Canadian dollar. *(Source: Bridge Information Systems, Inc.)*

Price Structure and Foreign Exchange Terminology

7

This chapter presents the typical terminology in foreign exchange, from bids and offers in different instruments to the leave orders left by corporations and in the interbank market. Whereas the definitions of bids and offers are very basic and generally known in the spot market, the definitions can change in the case of other instruments. The differences are explained in this chapter.

SPOT MARKET

A *spot deal* takes place between two parties who deliver a certain amount of different currencies to each other, based on an agreed exchange rate, within two business days of the deal date. The exception is the Canadian dollar, in which the spot delivery is executed within one business day.

Let's take an example in the spot market. A bank quotes the USD/CHF at 1.4955/60 on a monitor. In this case, the bank's *bid* is 1.4955 (left side), which means that the bank is interested in buying USD/CHF at this price. The bank's *offer* is 1.4960 (right side), which means that the bank is interested in selling USD/CHF at this price. The difference between the bid and the offer is called the *spread*. In our example, the spread between 1.4955 and 1.4960 is five pips. A *pip* is the last decimal of the exchange rate. It is the fourth decimal of the exchange rate in the case of currencies such as the euro, and the second in the case of the Japanese yen.

Keep in mind that the prices on the monitors are not binding. Although accurate, they are displayed as suggested prices only. If a bank posts the prices during a slow market, it is possible that it will also quote those rates in interbank dealing. Naturally, banks are generally unable to update prices in a fast market, allowing for gaps between the monitor rates and the quoted prices.

A customer calls this bank for a price in USD/CHF and is quoted 1.4955/60. If the customer wants to buy, he or she will take the offer at 1.4960. If selling, the customer will sell at 1.4955. Conversely, if you set the price of 1.4955/60, then your bid is 1.4955, and your offer is 1.4960.

FORWARD MARKET

A *forward transaction* takes place between two parties who deliver a certain amount of different currencies to each other, based on an agreed exchange rate, past two business days of the deal date. In the forward market, a trader must be a little more careful about the meaning of bids and offers. If you quote a forward price in foreign currency, your bid is on the left side and the offer on the right side, provided that the amount traded is quoted in foreign currency. If the amount is quoted in U.S. dollars, then the right side is your bid and the left side is your offer. In order to cope with this sometimes confusing reversal, just remember that buying U.S. dollars is equivalent to selling foreign currency, and vice versa.

> *Example:*
> USD/JPY
>
> Spot price   150.00–150.05
>
> Forward price   20–25
>
> If you quote 20–25, a counterparty can sell you Japanese yen 250,000,000 at 20 (your bid for foreign currency), or buy Japanese yen 250,000,000 at 25 (your offer for foreign currency), just as in the spot market. However, the counterparty can also sell you $2,000,000 at 25 (your bid for U.S. dollars), or buy $2,000,000 at 20 (your offer for U.S. dollars).

We discuss forward pricing in appropriate detail in Chapter 12.

FUTURES MARKET

Currency futures are a special case of forward outright transactions, or exchange deals that mature past the spot value date. In the spot and forward markets, currencies are quoted either in European terms (i.e., Japanese yen), or in American terms (i.e., British pound), depending on the generally accepted norm.

In the futures market, prices are quoted only in American terms. The bids and offers are quoted similarly to spot prices—the bid is on the left side, and the offer is on the right side. For example, if you quote Japanese futures at .8000–.8010, it means that you want to buy at .8000 and sell at .8010. If you want to trade, and this price is quoted to you by another party, you can sell at .8000 and buy at .8010.

FOREIGN EXCHANGE TERMS

Communicating in the foreign exchange markets is an exact and minimalist matter. It could not have been any other way, given the high volatility and the high number of daily transactions.

SELLING

To sell, the following terms are used:

- If you hit a bid, you say:
  "Yours."
  "I give you."
  "I sell."

- If you want to sell in the brokers' market without hitting the bid, then you say:
  "Offer join for X amount of currency."
  "I sell X amount of currency at (a lower offer than the current one)."

Joining or improving the offer does not guarantee the execution.

BUYING

To buy, the following terms are used:

- If you take an offer, you say:
  "Mine."
  "I take."
  "I buy."

- If you want to buy in the brokers' market without taking the offer, you say:

"Join the bid for *X* amount of currency."

"I buy *X* amount of currency at (a higher bid than the current one)."

Of course, joining the bid or improving the bid in the brokers' market does not guarantee execution.

PRICE CHANGING

If you want to change the price, several options are available to you.

1. On the dealing machine, you hit the "Interrupt" key. Once this appears on the screen, the price is no longer valid.
2. On the dealing machine or on the phone, you can say "Change" or "Off" to withdraw your price.

If the counterparty still wants a quote, he or she will ask you either "How now?" or "How are you left?" or "Where are you now?" Of course, you cannot answer, "I'm left heartbroken" or, "Downtown," to some traders' chagrin.

LEAVE ORDERS

Corporations, high net-worth individuals, and banks leave currency trading orders with other banks, trading companies, and brokers because they cannot trade directly in the interbank market. Of course, they also have the option to request a two-way price and trade on that quote.

Even banks leave orders with other banks, either because it is not efficient for them to trade certain currencies or because they want to maximize the chance of execution by working their orders 24 hours a day. For instance, a bank specializing in the Scandinavian currencies that receives an unusual request for a Japanese yen item might be better off leaving the order with another bank that has an active Japanese yen desk, rather than allocating untrained personnel to follow that yen item.

Working currency orders around the clock is a common practice among large banks. If the orders are not executed in a certain market, the orders are transferred to a branch, a subsidiary, or another bank in the next time zone. Provided that those orders are still not executed, then the transfer will continue to the next time zone, until the time circle is complete—New York, then Sydney or Tokyo or Singapore or Hong Kong, then London or Frankfurt or Zurich.

Order execution is obviously very important. To be properly done, it is important for the parties involved to agree on the assignment of risk before the order transfer. Both parties must be clear on what they want and what they can expect from each other.

There are two types of leave orders—profit-taking and stop-loss.

Profit-Taking Orders

Profit-taking orders may mean two different things. First, as the name states, a trader who is long (had bought) USD/JPY 5 million at 104.00, leaves an order to sell USD/JPY 5 million at 105.00, as the trader wants to sell at a price currently unavailable to realize a profit. In this case, the trader had a position prior to leaving this order. This is an exit or position closing order.

Second, a trader may leave an order to buy or sell a currency at a price currently unavailable, without having a prior position. For instance, a trader may believe that if the GBP/USD reaches 2.0000, it is a good selling opportunity, and so leaves a selling order overnight to sell GBP/USD 3 million at that level. This is an entry order.

How does one check on the execution of the leave orders? For a bank, the best approach is to ask several brokers what the overnight trading ranges were and check the low on the matching systems. For a corporation, the best approach is to ask several banks what the overnight trading ranges were. If the order is well within the trading range, there is no problem.

Potential problems occur when the leave order falls on the extremes of the overnight ranges. For instance, a bank's leave order is to buy euro/dollar 5 million at 1.0500, and the overnight range in one broker is 1.0500–1.0650, and 1.0501–1.0647 in another. The bank with which the order was left says that at 1.0500 only EUR/USD 2 million were bought for someone else. The leave order was, regrettably, not executed.

Was your order executed or not?

The bank with which the order was left must have access to at least one of the brokers for whom the low was 1.0500. Also, the two banks should have agreed on the execution rules in advance. If the agreed-upon format gives the counterparty execution latitude, then the bank leaving the order has most of the risk.

Some banks prefer to consider the order executed, based solely on price range, not on liquidity. Therefore, if 1.0500 was given in the brokers' market, then the order was filled, despite the fact that only one broker reported that level as the low. In this case, the bank executing the order takes the full risk.

Why would a bank take this approach? Perhaps the bank would like to improve the trading relationship with the counterparty; or it might have a large book of customers, which enables it to protect itself. If there are several orders to buy around 1.0500, EUR/USD 90 million at 1.0520, EUR/USD 200 million at 1.0510, and EUR/USD 120 million at 1.0505, for instance, the chances that 1.5000 will be given are rather small.

Both approaches are valid, as long as the parties agree beforehand on the assignment of risk.

Stop-Loss Orders

Stop-loss orders generally are position exiting orders under adverse market conditions. Following up on the previous example, assume you bought EUR/USD 5 million at 1.0500. The EUR/USD was very steady throughout the day. You left two overnight orders: a profit-taking order to sell EUR/USD 5 million at 1.0600, and a stop-loss order to sell EUR/USD at 1.0400. If your forecast that the EUR/USD will rally to 1.0600 is wrong, then you will limit your loss on the downside by closing your position at or below 1.0400.

Stop-loss orders can also be used as position entry orders. If you don't have a current outstanding position, and if you expect the market to make a significant move once a certain level breaks, you can leave a so-called stop-loss order close to that specific level to enter a position.

For instance, let's assume that your previous order to buy EUR/USD 5 million at 1.0500 was not executed overnight. During your trading day, however, the EUR/USD fell to 1.0440 and remained there for the balance of your trading day. You still expect the EUR/USD to rally, but you are afraid that the 1.0500 level turned from a support level into a resistance level once it was broken. Therefore, you may leave an overnight stop-loss order to buy EUR/USD 5 million at 1.0515.

Please notice that the order is placed at a higher level than the initial 1.0500. This is done to avoid potential resistance at 1.0500.

It is more difficult to execute stop-loss orders than profit-taking orders. Chances are that stops are placed at significant levels that are used by many other traders. Once those levels are reached, large stop-loss orders are going to be triggered, making it close to impossible to execute your order precisely at the requested level. Therefore, it is extremely important to have clear agreements on the type of execution.

There are four types of stop-loss order execution: next best price, at the price, discretion for range to trader, and at best.

- *Next Best Price*. The stop-loss order kicks in *after* the requested level was reached. The trader executing the order must trade on the next available price. Under this format, the risk is borne fully by the customer, who has no guarantee as to whether the order will be filled 3 or 30 pips away from the targeted price. This approach may leave room for argument, as the trader may return the customer a worse execution than the actual market deal.

For example, if the stop-loss order is to sell GBP/USD 3 million at 1.5000, a fill will have to be acceptable at 1.4990, but not at 1.5000. The customer wants to be sure that the 1.5000 support level was really broken before exiting the position.

This type of stop-loss order is most common.

- *At the Price.* The stop-loss order must be executed at the precise requested level, regardless of market conditions. The full risk is in the executor's court. This type of stop-loss order can only be executed by banks or trading firms. For example, if the stop-loss order is to sell GBP/USD 3 million at 1.5000, even if the market dropped to 1.4900 under very hectic conditions and 1.5000 bid was never posted, the order is considered to be filled.

Traders may take a position to try to execute the order even if the specific price is not available in the market, but brokers cannot. If the price is not available, a broker simply cannot execute the order. The price is said to have gapped out. This approach is rarely implemented.

- *Discretion for Range to Trader.* This approach is an imperfect hybrid of the first two types of stop-loss orders. The trader—either a bank or a trading firm, but not a broker—has a number of discretionary pips within which the order has to be filled. The customer usually decides the number of discretionary pips, and whether the currency price must be traded before execution.

For example, if the stop-loss order is to sell GBP/USD 3 million at 1.5000, the customer may do one of two things:

1. Instruct the trader to wait until 1.5000 is given, wait until 1.5000 is offered, and then fill the order within 5 pips from the level. In other words, the stop-loss order is shifted from 1.5000 to 1.4995.

2. Instruct the trader to fill the order at any price between 1.5000 and 1.4995.

The downside is that, realistically, it is close to impossible to fill a stop-loss order only a handful of pips away from a significant price level, especially if that level must first be traded and then offered, as in our example. Therefore, the trader's discretionary buffer pips are canceled, and most of the risk is borne by the trader.

- *At Best.* Both profit taking and stop-loss orders can be executed *at best.* This means that the trader wants to trade regardless of the price. This type of order is placed in a fast market, where specific price levels cannot be traded and the need for exiting or entering a market takes precedence over the choice of price.

CURRENCY FIXINGS

Currency fixings are a solely European currency market phenomenon. (See Figure 7.1.) They are executed on a daily basis via an open auction in which all players, regardless of size, are welcome to participate with any amount. Unlike regular trading, there is no anonymity, as all bids and offers are openly displayed. The highest bid and lowest offer are averaged to calculate the daily currency fixings.

ECB		ECB		ECB		BANK OF PORTUGAL	
AUD	1.5570	EEK	15.6466	NZD	1.9988	BRL	1.7496
CAD	1.4182	GBP	0.61950	PLN	4.1038	CVE	110.264
CHF	1.6083	GRD	332.30	SEK	8.4845	MOP	7.8123
CYP	0.57554	HUF	255.59	SIT	200.7612	ZAR	6.1098
CZK	35.778	JPY	105.78	USD	0.9748		
DKK	7.4428	NOK	8.0175				

Figure 7.1. Example of a daily currency fixing by Bank of Portugal in euros. *(Source: Bridge Information Systems, Inc.)*

The fixings are used by a variety of players. Companies that have a limited foreign exchange exposure and want to avoid either going through a bank or setting up their own desk find the daily operations to be convenient. Large banks may use the fixings to square off either small exposures incurred during the day from customer business, or small positions resulting from netting.

The fixings provide reference levels that are important in Europe. The foreign exchange fixings executed in Frankfurt are used as reference points for the daily end-of-day revaluations. In addition, they are used as legal agreements and as a basis for foreign exchange agreements between banks and customers.

These agreements are executed by the banks at three different levels:

- *At the fixing* is the best price and is used in the interbank trades.
- *At 20 pips spread* is the improved corporate spread for the most important customers.
- *At 40 pips spread* is reserved for smaller customers.

Customers generally try to negotiate better spreads with their banks.

Currency fixings are not executed in England or the United States. Japan canceled currency fixings in the late 1980s.

8 Corporate Trading

Willingly or not, corporations have become significant players in foreign exchange. While currency hedging still constitutes the majority of their interest, market speculation is becoming an increasingly attractive activity among corporations of different sizes. Foreign exchange is slowly evolving from its old status as a cost of business to a legitimate source of profit.

THE ROLE OF FOREIGN EXCHANGE FOR CORPORATIONS

Professional traders start from no position and virtually buy the risk; but corporations start from a given position and try to minimize the risk. Corporate customers do not trade among themselves the way banks do. They reach the market via commercial or investment banks.

Corporate interest in foreign exchange derives from several sources. First, companies may need to make payments for raw materials, labor, advertising, distribution, or profit repatriation, to name a few of the typical natural needs to exchange currencies. Second, future expected payments might be hedged in order to eliminate or minimize the risk of adverse currency movement. Finally, corporations may want to enhance their performance by entering foreign exchange markets purely to take advantage of expected currency fluctuations—in other words, to speculate. As speculation in foreign currency is quickly losing its shady connotation, corporations are increasingly joining the ranks of commercial and investment banks, the major foreign exchange players.

Unlike banks, corporations do not trade in-and-out all day long. Their outlook tends to be longer-term, not spot-oriented. The longer-term approach is valid for hedging, covering their commercial needs, and speculation.

TYPES OF CORPORATIONS

There are many types of companies involved in foreign exchange: small and large, single foreign currency oriented and multicurrency oriented, national and multinational. There are product makers, such as electronic services and software; consumer service firms, such as travel agencies; and investment companies, such as equity funds. Corporations may have a temporary or long-term interest in international business.

Due to the complexity and speed that characterize the contemporary economy, these factors may overlap or quickly change. For instance, many equity and fixed income funds used to have a predominant focus on local markets. Some of the more internationally oriented funds had diversified primarily in the G-7 countries—the United States, Germany, Japan, the United Kingdom, France, Italy, and Canada. Economic and political developments since 1989, notably the fall of Communism in Eastern Europe and the economic rebirth in South America and Southeast Asia, created new high-growth stock markets and, consequently, new investment opportunities for equity and fixed income funds.

TYPES OF EXPOSURE

Exposure reflects the potential effect of currency fluctuations on shareholders' equity.

There are three types of exposure: transaction or exchange exposure, economic exposure, and translation exposure.

TRANSACTION EXPOSURE

Transaction or *exchange exposure*, which is equivalent to exchange risk in the interbank market, reflects the potential profit and loss generated by current foreign exchange transactions of both national and international corporations. For instance, let's consider the situation of an American travel agency, catering to British travelers, that sold trips to the United States in August 1992. The travel payments were received by the agency at a time when the British pound fetched about 2 U.S. dollars. Only days later, in early September 1992, the GBP/USD rate was 1.70, and by December 1992, only 1.50. (See Figure 8.1.) The repatriation of the receipts from British pounds to U.S. dollars registered a loss of approximately 15 percent within days.

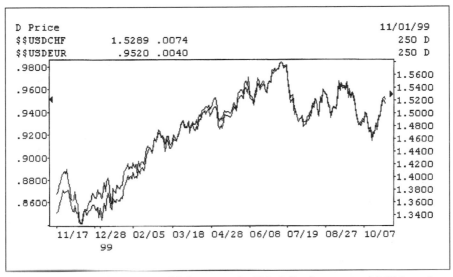

Figure 8.1. The sterling pound fell against the U.S. dollar from around 2.00 in early September 1992 to 1.50 by December 1992, as a result of the crisis in the European Monetary System. *(Source: Bridge Information Systems, Inc.)*

MANAGING TRANSACTION EXPOSURE

To manage the exposure generated by currency transaction, management must have a clear set of rules in place. Several questions must be answered thoroughly.

- Do we want the risk?
- Can we shift the risk?
- If we can't shift the risk, how much risk do we want to accept?
- What is our expectation for each of the currencies to which we have an exposure?
- What is the best strategy for handling the currency exposure?
- How can we implement this strategy?

In the case of the travel agency, it seems that the exposure risk was acceptable, probably for economic reasons such as competitive prices for the trip. The risk could have been shifted if the prices had been charged in U.S. dollars rather than British pounds. But speaking realistically, it is not feasible to charge a vacation fee in a foreign currency. Another approach could have been to enter a partnership with a British travel agency and convince that agency to take the currency risk. Provided that neither of these approaches had been taken, the agency would have to decide whether it wanted to keep the British pounds in a British bank at a higher rate than in the United States, with full, partial, or no hedging, or exchange the money into U.S. dollars at once.

In order to make this decision, management would have to form a view on the behavior of the British pound vis-à-vis the U.S. dollar. A historical chart of the past decade would have indicated that the British pound had been overvalued against the U.S. dollar above the rate of 2.0. Additional fundamental information regarding the state of the British economy vis-à-vis the American and European economies would have shown weak results. A fair conclusion would have been that the British pound was headed down. Therefore, management could have sold the cable in the spot market for U.S. dollars at the earliest possible time, or could have entered a forward outright deal based on a GBP/USD spot exchange rate of about 2.00.

In addition to the security of hedging, the forward outright transaction would have been advantageous from two points of view. First, the agency would have had more time to collect the British pounds. Second, the cable could have been deposited in a British bank, provided that the cash was not needed for payments. Certainly, management could customize these approaches by executing both spot and forward outright transactions for fractions of the total receipts.

The abrupt fall of cable against both the U.S. dollar and the European currencies was generated by the unexpected EMS crisis. However, the crisis itself was triggered by the same imbalance of the fundamentals, which could have been noticed by the management of the travel agency.

Therefore, if management expects the foreign currency to devalue versus the base currency, then the position in the foreign currency must be exchanged quickly at the current rates. Conversely, should the management expect the base currency to ease vis-à-vis the foreign currency, then the position should be translated to the base currency at a later date.

These approaches assume that the receipts in foreign currency, in our example British pounds, have to be repatriated into the base currency, U.S. dollars. However, if the foreign currency receipts can be invested in the foreign currency, the transaction exposure is eliminated, reduced, or postponed, depending on the situation.

ECONOMIC EXPOSURE

Economic exposure reflects the impact of foreign exchange fluctuations on the future competitive position of national and international companies.

For instance, let's take the example of IBM personal computers. Developed in the United States, they had the largest segment of the world market in the early 1980s. The high and increasing value of the U.S. dollar in this period had a strong negative effect on IBM's capacity to export PCs abroad. This was a window of opportunity for the competition, which managed to assemble surprisingly accurate clones at much lower prices. IBM not only reacted slowly to what seemed to be meek competition in the international markets, but ended up seeing its share of the domestic market reduced as well.

By the time the G-5 countries capped the U.S. dollar's rise in September 1985 and eventually devalued it by 50 percent in December 1987, IBM had already lost its competitive edge in personal computers. It is certainly unfair to blame all of IBM's problems in the personal computer market solely on unfavorable exchange rates. Even later, when the dollar reached record lows against the yen, providing American exporters with the opportunity to return the favor, it was precisely the American personal computer makers—including IBM—who were slow to take advantage of the currency edge in the Japanese consumer market.

MANAGING ECONOMIC EXPOSURE

Managing economic exposure is a complex and long-term task. The decision depends on the degree of elasticity of demand for specific goods, the time available for adjustment, and the direction of the base currency relative to the operational foreign currency. The base currency is the currency against which other currencies are quoted. The rule of thumb is, the more inelastic the demand, the longer the time needed for adjustment.

If demand for a product is strong in a particular market, a price increase will have a limited negative impact on demand. An example may be the demand for American-made airplanes. Despite the strength of the U.S. dollar in the mid-1980s, the demand for American commercial airplanes was not really affected. Of course, the industry's nearly monopolistic position in the world helped as well.

At the other end of the spectrum, an elastic demand, such as American consumers' demand for cars, had a significantly negative impact on the domestic market share of American car makers faced with Japanese competition. Naturally, the shoddy quality of American cars in the 1970s and early 1980s, along with the oil crisis, were also significant factors.

Time for adjustment is crucial. Management may consider importing parts or even building assembly plants abroad in order to take advantage of the lower prices generated by the exchange rates. For instance, when faced with steeply declining profits due to the revaluation of the yen against the U.S. dollar, Japanese producers built assembly plants for consumer electronic products in Southeast Asia, where currencies were pegged or semi-pegged to U.S. dollars, and even directly in the United States, in the case of some auto assembly plants.

Where does foreign exchange fit in this puzzle? Consumers tend to care less about the exchange rate of their domestic currency than they do about their domestic prices, even though this rate is a significant determinant of the total price of the product. When faced with the choice between a domestic product and an import, consumers generally focus on which product has better features and a better price.

Management must have a good sense of the direction of the base currency relative to the operating currency. Based on an accurate analysis of the price elasticity of demand, expected exchange rate direction, and time to adjust, management should be able to set a sound long-term strategy. Current economic, financial, and political events must be continually monitored in order to better adjust this strategy.

A flexible approach to minimizing economic exposure is paramount, given the potentially severe swings in the currency markets.

TRANSLATION EXPOSURE

Multinational companies naturally have a variety of multiple currency exposures generated by their international subsidiaries and branches. For consolidation purposes, all these exposures are translated into a single currency—the base currency. *Translation exposure* reflects the risk of change in the consolidated corporate earnings as a result of past volatility in the base currency. Currency fluctuations may be sizable enough to generate challenging problems for corporate management. Several accounting rules attempted to solve this thorny issue.

FASB 8

Originally, the accounting rules regarding foreign exchange were standardized in 1975 under the Financial Accounting Standards Board's Statement Number 8 (FASB 8). FASB 8 set the procedures for foreign currency translations into U.S. dollars in the consolidated balance sheets of U.S. multinational corporations.

The immediate effect of this rule was to increase the volatility of the P&L and of the balance sheet statements as a direct result of the exchange rates' volatility. FASB 8 came under heavy criticism because the foreign exchange P&L was directly reported into income, generating volatility in corporate earnings.

FASB 52

In order to answer these concerns, a new, complex set of rules was designed in 1981, under the Financial Accounting Standards Board's Statement Number 52 (FASB 52), and it is currently in use. The FASB's main objective is to move the foreign exchange P&L from current income into shareholders' equity.

The P&L resulting from foreign exchange translations is generally contained in an equity account until the investment is liquidated. However, the translation of the foreign exchange P&L may be deferred if the affiliate is a separate entity. This approach is taken for corporations that operate in currencies other than the U.S. dollar. The operating currency, usually the local currency, is called the functional currency. When a corporation has several units, it may use different functional currencies.

However, if one of the functional currencies happens to be a highly inflationary one, management should remeasure the results in the reporting currency. In addition, if the functional currency is actually U.S. dollars, then the foreign exchange fluctuations are reflected in current income, in effect using FASB 8.

HEDGING

To hedge or not to hedge, that is the question. The answer depends on a variety of factors, because some corporate investors are comfortable with a full currency hedge while others disregard hedging as useless and costly. Hedging decisions vary, depending on the time frame, the volatility of currency, the market view on the specific currency, management's level of sophistication, and the level of risk each company is willing to take.

The expected time frame of the position to maturity is an important factor in deciding whether to hedge. Certain equity fund managers are reluctant to hedge the currency side of investments held for three or more years—the general consensus of long term—but are eager to hedge short-term investments.

What is best? It depends. In the short term, the British pound lost 15 percent of its value within days in September 1992, and 25 percent in about two months. (See Figure 8.1.) One and a half years later, the currency was quoted at the same levels. In September 1985, the U.S. dollar was exchanged for 3 deutsche marks. In the long term, about 10 years later, the

U.S. dollar could fetch only 1.34 deutsche marks, or less than 50 percent of its old value.

It should be stressed that time, as a hedging factor, should only be considered along with the type of currency and the view of the specific currency. Used alone, the time factor may be unreliable.

Some currencies are more volatile than others. The management of a German company operating in both Switzerland and Japan may not feel hard-pressed enough to hedge the Swiss franc (CHF) against the euro, but it would surely consider it against the yen (JPY). While the Swiss franc tends to have a high correlation with the euro (see Figure 8.2) due to their economic links, generating more subdued fluctuations on the EUR/CHF cross (see Figure 8.3), the correlation between euro and yen is much lower (see Figure 8.4), which allows for much more fluctuation on the EUR/JPY cross (see Figure 8.5).

If management perceives that the operating currency is expected to perform adversely, and therefore that the outstanding position is at risk, then it must decide on a hedging strategy. To achieve an accurate view of the market, management should use the forecasting techniques explained in Chapters 17 to 28.

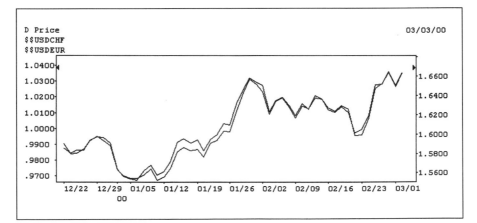

Figure 8.2. Euro/dollar and dollar/Swiss franc tend to trade in a similar fashion. *(Source: Bridge Information Systems, Inc.)*

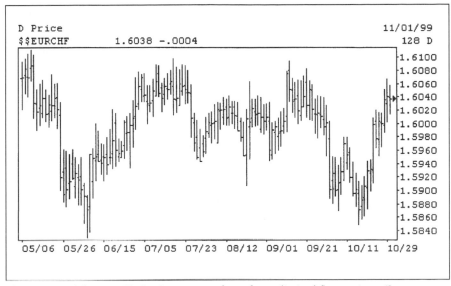

Figure 8.3. The euro/Swiss franc cross-chart shows limited fluctuation. *(Source: Bridge Information Systems, Inc.)*

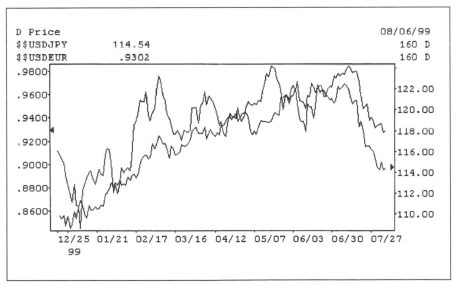

Figure 8.4. Euro/dollar and dollar/yen tend to trade in a dissimilar fashion. *(Source: Bridge Information Systems, Inc.)*

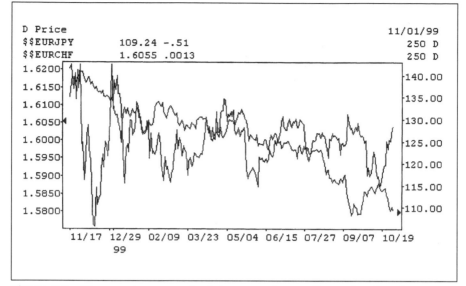

```
D Price                                               11/01/99
$$EURJPY         109.24 -.51                            250 D
$$EURCHF         1.6055  .0013                          250 D
```

Figure 8.5. The euro /yen cross-chart shows much more fluctuation than the euro/Swiss franc cross-chart. *(Source: Bridge Information Systems, Inc.)*

Management's level of sophistication, both in personnel and equipment, is crucial in making hedging decisions. The implementation of a hedging strategy, or the performance of the unhedged outstanding positions, must be closely monitored. At the simplest level, the position must be marked to the market at least on a daily basis. The individuals in charge must have the necessary skills, along with full access to the decision support systems, such as on-line monitors displaying the running rates and information and adequate software for management and control. Contingency plans for unexpected developments must be in place.

If the outstanding position is not fully or entirely hedged, stop-loss orders must be established and enforced. Conversely, the hedge may be raised if it prevents the outstanding position from generating a profit, and if the elimination of the hedge itself does not neutralize the expected profit.

The level of risk that management is willing to accept differs considerably among companies. It depends on the corporate objective regarding a specific position, the degree of diversification within the compound position, and the financial capacity to withstand adverse market behavior.

In terms of corporate objective, management must determine whether the hedge is passive—that is, purely designed to insulate the outstanding position from the foreign exchange fluctuation—or active, meaning that it is designed to enhance the profit of the original position. The objective of a passive hedge is to realize a profit and loss as close to zero as possible. This type of hedge may be achieved through forward outright, futures, swaps, or options contracts. An active hedge may come into existence only under adverse currency conditions. This type of hedge may be implemented through stop-loss orders in both the spot and forward markets, along with currency options.

HOW FOREIGN EXCHANGE IS EXECUTED

Corporations do not generally trade among themselves. Although exceptions occur, intercorporate foreign exchange is very limited. Corporations reach the currency markets through commercial and investment banks. (See Figure 8.6.) Corporate customers trade in two ways: ask for a price and trade directly, or leave an order with the bank.

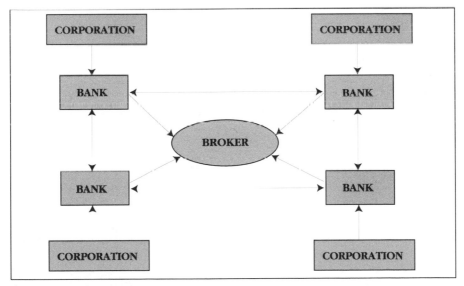

Figure 8.6. Corporate customers do not trade among themselves. They reach the foreign exchange markets through commercial and investment banks. In turn, banks trade with each other directly and through brokers.

Corporations do not usually contact the traders directly. The two parties are generally linked by the banks' sales force. The sales force, or the corporate traders, have a multitude of tasks. They make cold calls to prospective customers, advise, take orders from customers and pass them to traders, and confirm the orders' execution with the customers. (See Figure 8.7.)

Corporate customers are very important to banks. Foreign exchange traders welcome the orders as a means of gauging cash flow and for enhancing their own profits. When the size of the orders is large, a trader gets a good "feeling" about the cash flow.

Patterns of profit repatriation, for instance, are often quite important, at least in the short term. An example is the profit repatriation by Japanese companies, a commercial need. The Japanese fiscal semesters end in March and September. In order to repatriate their profits, Japanese companies must purchase yen, generally against U.S. dollars, prior to these dates. Once the new fiscal semesters start in April and October, the Japanese yen is sold again for hedging purposes.

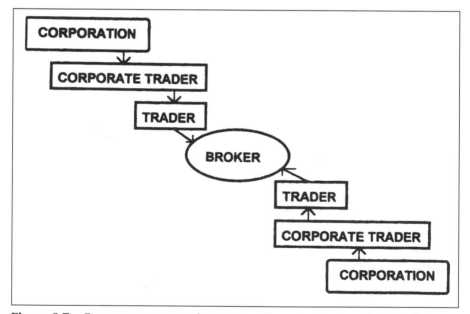

Figure 8.7. Corporate customers do not generally contact traders directly. The two parties are linked by the banks' corporate traders. Corporate traders make cold calls for prospective customers; take orders from customers and pass them to the trading desk; confirm the orders that were executed; and advise their corporate customers.

This type of pattern is generally important to foreign exchange traders not only in terms of temporal repetition, but also in terms of transaction size. Because the total of Japanese exports to the United States is so large, it follows that the amounts of U.S. dollars that must be sold for Japanese yen are quite significant.

As part of their daily strategy, traders also use corporate orders. If the orders are placed at crucial support or resistance levels, traders may also trade at these levels after customer orders are filled. Therefore, both players—the corporation and the trader—will benefit from the execution of the customer's orders.

The quality of the price that banks quote their customers is a function of several factors. First, it depends on the importance the bank's management attaches to specific customers. Customers gain in stature when they trade regularly, avoiding calls only to pick the tops and bottoms, and share significant information. The sales force generally reciprocates not only by getting better prices from traders ("Special price for this customer, mate!"), but also by quickly informing the customer of unusual market changes before the rest of the market is informed. The opposite is true when corporations have a habit of pulling orders off just before execution or throwing their weight around with the sales force.

Second, the quote for the customer reflects the position of the bank, along with the individual position. Therefore, the quote may reflect marginal (about 1 to 5 pips) skews from the running market prices. Finally, the quote to the corporate customer must reflect the long-term importance of the business relationship.

Some banks quote their customers the market running prices, similar to quoting in the interbank. The spread between the bid and offer is tight, around 5 pips. This approach generally occurs in the case of larger orders. In this case, there is no commission for the bank. If the orders are large, for instance over $50 million, then the trader may not gain 1 or 2 pips, but will benefit from the flow information instead.

Other banks have an understanding with their customers to quote the running market prices. Once the deals are executed, the banks charge a fixed commission of 1 or 2 pips. This approach, which ensures some income for the bank, encourages the trader to quote the price without any personal distortion. This approach seems to be the fairest to all parties involved. The company receives the "real" price, the trader does not have to disrupt his or her trading trying to "read" the customer, and the corporate salesperson does not have to skew the price, because the commission is built in.

Yet another quoting approach is to widen the spread between the bid and the offer. This approach limits the risk of the trader, since it offers the buffer of several pips against any adverse currency fluctuations.

The general consensus regarding the prices quoted by banks to corporate customers is that the larger the amounts, the tighter the spread of the quotes. In the interbank market, it is more difficult to trade $500,000 than $10 million. To partly compensate for small size, some traders quote spreads of 10 pips or more for small amounts.

In the past, corporations would call the banks and tell them not only the currency and amount they wanted to trade, but also whether they wanted to buy or sell. Currently, few large companies will mention which side they need, if they want to trade directly, and some of them behave similarly to the large banks. They call several banks at the same time and pick the most advantageous price. This approach is not warmly received by traders because they have no margin of profit if the deal is executed, and no information if the deal goes to a different bank.

When a customer has a relatively small order to execute, perhaps less than $1 million, it is more advantageous to mention the side of interest. When this is done, traders tend to quote a better price than the customary ones reserved for small amounts.

A professional, courteous, and quick response by the sales force usually goes a long way in cementing long-term, stable business relationships.

DIFFERENT POINTS OF VIEW

In the regular foreign exchange market, the major market participants are traders, corporate traders, corporations, and brokers. Let's see how their points of view differ.

Traders
Traders attempt to translate the impact of different fundamental and technical factors on the currencies and to seize the opportunities in these markets. They need volatility. The direction of the market and the price levels are very important to traders.

Corporate Traders
The economic and technical data and market behavior are important to corporate traders only for advisory purposes. They need some volatility to generate more corporate sales, but they prefer moderate volatility in a two-way market, which attracts more customer orders.

Corporations
Generally, corporations do not like volatility. They already have a natural trading demand stemming from their business. Since currencies fluctuate nevertheless, corporations must be actively involved in foreign exchange to hedge their positions. Therefore, direction and price levels are important to them.

Brokers
Brokers need market volatility. Volatility gets the market busy, and busy traders execute more deals through brokers. However, excessive volatility has a negative impact on the business. Few trades go through when the market is trading under extreme conditions. The direction of the market and the price levels are irrelevant to brokers. The best daily market is one with moderately volatile two-way activity.

9 Foreign Exchange Settlement

An average $1.4 trillion changes hands every day in the foreign exchange markets, often under volatile conditions. The execution of these payments among hundreds of banks around the world is a staggering task. Conversely, the failure to generate timely and accurate payments is sanctioned by steep fines. This chapter focuses on the operational aspect of foreign exchange, a vital part of the trading process.

THE ROLE OF THE BACK OFFICE

Foreign exchange transactions do not end when the trader agrees with another party to buy or sell a certain currency. The details of the trade have to be processed, and the amounts agreed to be exchanged must be debited and credited. The responsibility for all these activities is in the hands of the Foreign Exchange Trading Operations Department, or the back office.

The department is physically separated from the dealing room for internal control. In fact, as communications developments have made it possible, some back offices have been moved to different locations altogether in an effort to save on real estate costs.

Let's take a look at the document that initiates the responsibilities of the operations department: the *trade ticket*. Every single foreign exchange trade is entered on a ticket. The ticket has a printed serial number if the deal is executed in a commercial bank. There is no sequential number on tickets in investment banks.

The information entered on the ticket can be separated into two categories: information for the trader and information for foreign exchange accounting and operations.

The most significant information to the trader is the name and amount of the base currency, the exchange rate, and the side of the deal (buying or selling).

Note: Assume that the trader knows both what currency was quoted against the fixed currency (for instance JPY against the USD) and the maturity date (spot, one month, etc.).

Base, or fixed, currency is the primary currency, which is traded against another. Generally, the fixed currency is the USD, but it may also be one of the Commonwealth currencies, such as the British pound or the Canadian dollar (CAD) on a cross-deal. If you trade USD/JPY 1,000,000, then the fixed currency is the USD. If the trade is done in GBP/USD 5,000,000, then the base currency is GBP. If you trade CAD/JPY, then the base currency is CAD.

The information necessary for foreign exchange accounting and operations is:

1. The name and the location (city) of the counterparty.

2. The transaction (deal) date.

3. The maturity date (or dates in the case of swaps).

4. The name and amount of the base currency.

5. All relevant exchange rates. (There are several exchange rates in the case of cross, forward outright, and swap transactions.)

6. Buying or selling the fixed (base) currency.

7. The other foreign currency name and amount.

8. The name of the trader.

9. The method of execution: brokers' market or direct dealing. (If the deal was executed in the brokers' market, the trader must enter the name of the brokerage house or matching system. This information allows the back office to make the correct commission payments. In the case of a direct deal, the form of telecommunication must be specified—dealing system, phone, or telex. If the deal is transacted on the dealing system, the name of the dealing system must be entered.)

10. Payment and receiving instructions (P&R) must be entered for overseas counterparties only. The details of FX transactions with parties on the same continent are confirmed by phone.

Until the mid-1980s, tickets used to be written by hand. (See Figure 9.1.) Needless to say, the process was error-prone and it slowed down the trading operation considerably. Starting in the late 1980s, dealing rooms began to turn "paperless," as tickets were electronically produced and kept in the computer's memory. (See Figure 9.2.) The workload of the back office has been greatly reduced, as most of the relevant information is input in the front office and sent electronically to the operations department. Processing is executed quickly and accurately by the computerized system.

Let's move to the operations department to see how it processes this information.

After the time of the trade but the same day, the department staff goes through several steps. They check all the details of the tickets generated by traders, and they calculate any missing amounts and exchange rates (if applicable). After the tickets are filled and checked, the back office confirms every deal by phone with the counterparties located on the same continent. If the deals are executed over the dealing or matching systems, the trading tickets are checked against the printed confirmations generated by these systems, regardless of the location of the counterparty. An increasing number of banks have the electronic trades automatically downloaded into their systems. If the deals are executed through brokers, traders bear the responsibility of getting the telex confirmations for all deals with overseas counterparties.

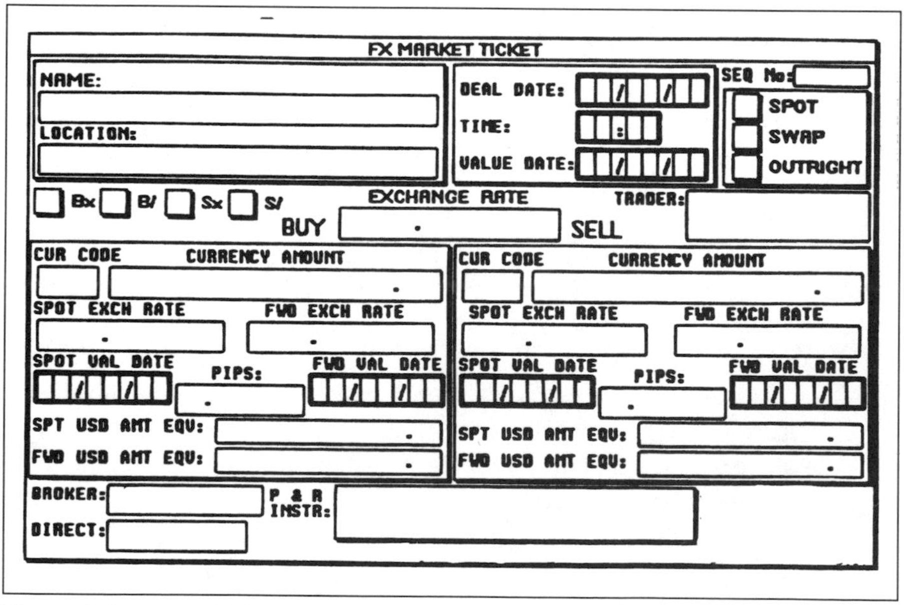
FX MARKET TICKET

NAME:

LOCATION:

DEAL DATE: / /

TIME: :

VALUE DATE: / /

SEQ No:

SPOT

SWAP

OUTRIGHT

Bx B/ Sx S/

EXCHANGE RATE

BUY .

SELL

TRADER:

CUR CODE CURRENCY AMOUNT .

SPOT EXCH RATE .

FWD EXCH RATE .

SPOT VAL DATE / /

PIPS: .

FWD VAL DATE / /

SPT USD AMT EQU: .

FWD USD AMT EQU: .

CUR CODE CURRENCY AMOUNT .

SPOT EXCH RATE .

FWD EXCH RATE .

SPOT VAL DATE / /

PIPS: .

FWD VAL DATE / /

SPT USD AMT EQU: .

FWD USD AMT EQU: .

BROKER:

DIRECT:

P & R INSTR:

Figure 9.1. A typical foreign exchange trade ticket.

Electronically produced Foreign Exchange Screen/Ticket

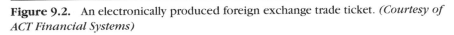

```
                        OMARK L&D/FX/FXA    MODULE
10:50 AM                                                        10/08/93
                        FX LEVEL-2 INPUT / MAINTENANCE
   Branch: PARIS            Trade:      886          Type: F     □ Action:


   Trade: 10/08/93                  Value: 11/11/93
     Sell: USD            88,833.12    Spot: 5.0            M
     Buy : FRF           444,165.60   Dealt: 5.0
                                     Status: Input 2 Instr B


     PC:           Salesperson:             Trader: TEST        Deal Method: P
     Port:             Brok:                A/C Type:           Conf Rcv Method:
     DID:              Ref.:                Fees:
     Cust: BANK IRL                         Brkrg:
     Pay:
     Narr:

F10 Xmit       PF2 Help       PF3 Print      PF4 Quit      F17 Explode    F18 Query
```

Figure 9.2. An electronically produced foreign exchange trade ticket. *(Courtesy of ACT Financial Systems)*

After the time of the trade but before maturity, the department sends the payment instructions via automated systems. The system used for foreign currencies is named the Society of Worldwide Interbank Financial Telecommunications (SWIFT). The system used for U.S. dollars is called the Clearing House Interbank Payments System (CHIPS). The dollar payment instructions may also be sent by another system called Fedwire, which links Fed banks to depositary institutions.

In addition, the back office checks to make sure that all the outstanding contracts have been matched and reports any discrepancies. A separate unit specializes in investigating the discrepancies.

After the time of the trade but on the maturity day, the department checks to see if the money credited to its own bank is in the *nostro* or *clearing account* as instructed, and reports if it is not credited.

NOSTRO ACCOUNT

A *nostro account,* or *clearing account,* is the account for each foreign currency in the country of origin maintained by the financial institutions for purchase and receiving (P&R) purposes. For instance, all banks have nostro accounts for yen in Japan, either with a Japanese bank or with a Japanese branch of a foreign bank. As an example, let's say that the First Bank of IOU/New York has its CAD nostro account either in its Canadian branch or in a Canadian bank.

SWIFT

Until 1977, all foreign exchange transactions were settled by following instructions from banks sent via cable messages, known as *cable transfers*. This method was extremely labor-intensive and consequently error-prone. The steep increase in foreign exchange trading volume has generated extreme pressure on operations departments that are forced to use cable transfers, which were developed in the 1920s. In September 1977, the SWIFT (Society of Worldwide Interbank Financial Telecommunications) automated system was set up in order to send standardized payment instructions for foreign currencies among European and North American banks. The system proved to be an instant success.

Since the late 1980s, SWIFT has been expanding outside these geographical boundaries, and some 3000 institutions around the world are currently connected to the system.

SWIFT IMPLEMENTATION

There are two types of messages—*financial messages* between SWIFT users and *system messages* between users and the SWIFT system. SWIFT messages have a common structure:

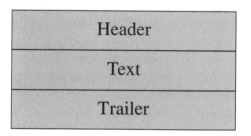

Functions required in the *computer-based terminal* (CBT) for message exchange are:

- connection with mainframe computer;
- message transmission;
- message reception; and
- application management.

In the *regional processor* (RGP), messages from a number of users are concentrated, encrypted, and sent to the applicable Operating Center for processing. In the Operating Center, the SWIFT system executes four processes on the messages. They are:

- Check the syntax of the messages.
- Construct a new header to convert the message to the output form.
- Add trailers to the messages.
- Copy and encrypt for storage.

Validation of the message to the sender is expressed as:

- ACK = positive acknowledgment, or
- NAK = negative acknowledgment.

Trailers are added to an output message if additional information is necessary. For instance, if the sender is uncertain that the original SWIFT message was received, a new message will be generated, bearing the trailer PDM (possible duplication message). *Message numbering* is done automatically via an Input Sequence Number (ISN) added to every message sent. Therefore, safety, accuracy, and ease of processing are insured. *Encryption* ensures privacy for all the messages sent through SWIFT, and these messages remain private even to SWIFT.

TYPES OF SWIFT FX MESSAGES

Foreign Exchange:

- MT300 FX confirmation (see Figure 9.3)
- MT305 Foreign currency option (see Figure 9.4)

General

- MT 390   Advice of Charges, Interest, and Other Adjustment
- MT 391   Request for Payment of Charges, Interest Rate, and Other Expenses
- MT 392   Request for Cancellation
- MT 395   Queries
- MT 396   Answers
- MT 398   Proprietary Message
- MT 399   Free Format Message
- MT 935   Rate Change Advice

In MT 300 FX confirmations:

- For actual transfers of funds, use MT 202/203/205.
- For confirmation of credits and debits, use MT 900/910/950.

ADVISORY BILATERAL FOREIGN EXCHANGE NETTING SERVICE

Netting is a service that enables institutions to settle their net positions with one another at the end of the day in a single transaction instead of at the time each trade is executed.

This process has definite advantages. It is cheaper, as there is only one deal to process versus tens of deals on a daily basis. In addition, it is a valuable safety feature, as banks must make only one payment on the net balance with another bank. If this bank shows any sign of payment difficulty, a group of large banks, known as a *banking cooperative*, will provide short-term backing from a common reserve pool.

M/O	TAG	FIELD NAME
Sequence A—Conditions of the Contract		
M	20	Transaction Reference Number
M	21	Related Reference
M	22	Code/Common Reference
M	30	Date Contract Agreed/Amended
M	36	Exchange Rate
O	72	Sender to Receiver Information
Sequence B—Amount Bought		
M	32R	Value Date, Currency Code, Amount Bought
O	56a	Intermediary
M	57a	Account with Institution
Sequence C—Amount Sold		
M	33P	Value Date, Currency Code, Amount Sold
O	53a	Sender's Correspondent
O	56a	Intermediary
M	57a	Account with Institution
M= Mandatory	O = Optional	

Figure 9.3. MT 300 FX Confirmation Format Specifications

M/O	TAG	FIELD NAME
M	20	Transaction Reference Number
M	21	Related Reference
M	22	Code/Common Reference
M	23	Further Identification
M	30	Date Contract Agreed/Amended
O	31C	Earliest Exercise Date
M	31G	Expiry Date
O	31E	Final Settlement Date
M	26F	Settlement Type
M	32B	Underlying Currency and Amount
M	36	Strike Price
M	33B	Counter Currency and Amount
O	37K	Premium Price
M	34a	Premium Payment
O	53a	Sender's Correspondent
O	56a	Intermediary
M	57a	Account with Institution
O	77 D	Terms and Conditions
O	72	Sender to Receiver Information
M= Mandatory		O = Optional

Figure 9.4. MT 305 FX Option Confirmation Format Specifications

Foreign exchange netting is implemented through ACCORD (discussed next) from SWIFT.

ACCORD

ACCORD is a central, computerized system used by banks and brokers to confirm and match foreign exchange and money market trades.

These operations used to be executed primarily by phone and telex. Currently, the majority of foreign exchange trades are confirmed through SWIFT's ACCORD service because of the system's advantages. It improves efficiency, gives a rapid and accurate picture of settlement positions, spots errors quickly, and greatly reduces operational costs (fines and labor costs). Figures 9.5, 9.6, and 9.7 show ACCORD services.

NUMBER	NAME	PRODUCTION
SMT 371	Report of Matched Confirmations	Daily/intermittently/on request
SMT 372	Detailed Report of Confirmations	On request
SMT 373	Report of Unmatched Confirmations	Daily/intermittently/on request
SMT 374	Report of Mismatched Confirmations	Immediately/intermittently/on request

Figure 9.5. Submessage and Message Types

AccordWorkstation—Work Queue (Accord) Confirmation List

Deal	Account Status	Counterparty	Subscriber	Our TFN	Attention	Filed
MT300	Matched	BARCAU2SXXX	Y	FS00830893035		✓
MT300	Matched	BARCAU2SXXX	Y	FS13969211135		✓
MT300	Matched	BBRU.S.GSGXXX	N	FS13969011135	✓	
MT300	Matched	BBRU.S.GSGXXX	N	FF13942411135	✓	
MT300	Matched	BKNZNZ22XXX	Y	FFS00836273035		✓
MT300	Matched	BKNZNZ22XXX	Y	FS13968421135		✓
MT300	Matched	BKTRAU2SXXX	Y	FS13967681135		✓

Figure 9.6. Work Queue (ACCORD) Confirmation List

Number	Name	Production
MT 970	Netting Statement	Daily/regularly/on request
MT 971	Netting Balance Report	Daily/on request
MT 972	Netting Interim Statement	Daily/regularly/on request

Figure 9.7. ACCORD Netting Service—Reports

CHIPS

Foreign exchange dollar settlements are executed through a computerized system called CHIPS (Clearing House Interbank Payments System). CHIPS is owned by 11 large New York City banks, and links 122 New York City depository institutions that pay and receive dollar funds from their correspondent banks around the world.

To get a sense of the magnitude of U.S. dollar transactions volume and of the importance of the system, let's compare the total number of transactions versus the total volume of these transactions in the United States.

Number of Payments (in U.S. dollars):

85% cash

13% checks

2% electronic transfers

Volume of Payments (in U.S. dollars):

99% electronic transfers

1% cash and checks

CHIPS and the Federal Reserve's network have 80 percent of the total worldwide dollar transfers business. There are several reasons for the growth in CHIPS' volume:

1. The expansion of government securities, a market that was automated in 1980 to finance the federal deficit.
2. The growth of the world economy and the increased number of countries participating.
3. The low price of execution makes the payment method feasible in a high-volume environment.
4. The high speed of execution is vital to heavy-volume markets.
5. Safety is a sine qua non condition for the execution. In order to ensure the safety of the extraordinarily large amounts of money being transferred, the system is protected by sophisticated (and generally undisclosed) methods.
6. Accuracy is yet another sine qua non condition for execution. Without it, speed and price are inconsequential features.
7. Reliability of the system has been proven over and over again. The foreign exchange market is continuously subjected to large moves and waves of heavy trading. CHIPS is fully able to process the trades.

CHIPS helps execute some 100,000 to 300,000 transactions a day. To minimize the number of transactions on a bank-to-bank basis, the settlements are netted.

Multilateral clearing of accounts through CHIPS depends on each bank's ability to meet its obligations.

Since 1990, the banks have been required by the Federal Reserve to put up securities as collateral against risk of failure of any participant bank. The members' failure would thus be absorbed as a group at settlement time and the losses would be settled later through negotiation or litigation.

CHIPS operates between 7 AM and 4:30 PM (EDT). After all the payments and receipts have been executed through CHIPS, the transfers are final when the CHIPS settle at the Federal Reserves, generally by 6 PM (EDT).

FEDWIRE

Settlement in U.S. dollars may also be made via *Fedwire*, a settlement system and communication network that links the Fed banks to all the depository institutions that want to link up to the Fed.

The main Fedwire features are:

- Securities are transferred free or DVP (delivery versus payment).
- Balances due are paid transaction by transaction, not by netting.
- Fedwire money transfers are final, unlike CHIPS transfers, which are not final until CHIPS settles.

Fedwire is used for five types of trades:

- large payments and receipts of Fed funds from CHIPS settlement;
- Fed funds;
- eurodollar transactions;
- securities delivery; and
- funds transfer.

INTERBANK COMPENSATION

Although there is no standard method per se currently enforced around the world, the majority of the international banks apply the same set of compensation rules. The U.S. Council on International Banking, Inc. provides Interbank Compensation Rules to its 360 members around the world. Their rules are also followed by numerous other banks. The importance of standard (or close to standard, in this case) procedures goes beyond the financial costs; the clarity and fairness of the rules is paramount for maintaining good business relationships in a volatile financial environment. (The compensation rules, courtesy of the U.S. Council on International Banking, Inc., are reprinted at the end of this chapter.)

CONCLUSION

The operations, or back office, department has a vital role in the continuously moving and changing world of foreign exchange. Simply, the trading activity cannot survive in its absence. Traders focus, fairly enough, on dealing. The foreign exchange transaction is not over until payment and receipt of foreign currencies around the world are accurately executed. Traders deal millions and billions day in and day out, but the real value of these enormous amounts is not always fully perceived. Nevertheless, it is the back office's responsibility to make sure that all these amounts are properly debited and credited. Only then is trading activity complete.

The introduction of computerized front end–back office systems in the late 1980s lightened the work schedule of the back office. However, increases in volume and instrument sophistication will keep back offices around the world quite busy for the foreseeable future.

Appendix: U.S. Council on International Banking Compensation and Indemnity and Compensation Rules (Effective: 1/2/90)*

Part I. General

Rule I.1. Scope. The U.S. Council on International Banking's Interbank Compensation Rules, (the "Rules") govern the settlement of claims for compensation between U.S. Council on International Banking member banks ("banks"), including their head offices and overseas branches, but excluding their subsidiaries, arising from interbank funds payments (other than ACH payments) in United States dollars regardless of:

i.. the original source or ultimate beneficiary of any payment, whether foreign or domestic;

ii. the manner of payment (e.g., Fedwire, CHIPS, check, telex);

iii. the type of funds involved (e.g., same day funds, next day funds);

iv. the nature of the underlying transaction (e.g., securities transaction, foreign exchange); or

v. the departments of the banks involved in initiating, processing or receiving the transaction.

---

*Courtesy of U.S. Council on International Banking, Inc. One World Trade Center, Suite 1963, New York, NY 10048, (212) 466-3352.

Rule I.2. Nature of the Rules. a. Not every possible situation involving a claim for compensation is explicitly addressed. Notwithstanding any provision of these Rules, when a claim for compensation meriting special attention is identified, it is expected that the banks involved will settle such claim so that no bank shall be unjustly enriched or injured by the actions of another member bank.

b. Unless otherwise specified, compensation in connection with a claim meriting special attention shall not exceed the benefit derived by the bank obligated to pay compensation. This limitation may be invoked, for example, in the case of Rule 3, 4 or 5 of Part II, if a beneficiary withdraws the funds from its account so that its bank does not have use of funds.

c. Payment or attempted payment of compensation pursuant to these Rules does not constitute and should not be construed as an admission of negligence or fault on the part of any of the banks involved.

Rule I.3. Manner of Payment. Compensation under the Rules shall be paid in United States dollars. A compensation payment may be made by CHIPS, Fedwire or check. Banks may alter the manner of payment of compensation by prior mutual agreement.

Rule I.4. Ordering Parties/Beneficiaries. The Rules do not confer any right or responsibility on any person, entity or organization not a member of the U.S. Council on International Banking.

Rule I.5. Third Parties. The Rules do not apply to claims for compensation arising from actions of third parties who are non-members of the U.S. Council on International Banking.

Rule I.6. Disputes. Disagreements which arise between member banks, over the application of the rules, may be submitted in writing to the U.S. Council on International Banking Rules Committee for arbitration.

Part II: Interbank Funds Payments
Rule II.1. Definitions.

a. "Business day" means a Monday, Tuesday, Wednesday, Thursday or Friday which is not a day on which banking institutions in the United States are authorized or obligated by law or executive order to close.

b. "Fed. Funds Rate" means the average of each day's Federal Funds rate, as published on a daily basis by the Federal Reserve Bank of New York, for the days that a bank must include in the applicable formula(s) in calculating compensation. The daily Fed. Funds Rate for any day on which a published rate is not available shall be deemed to be the same as the immediately preceding published rate.

Rule II.2. Back Valuation. a. A bank which sent a payment may request the bank which received the payment to back value such payment. Generally, such request is accompanied by a payment for the amount of compensation owed pursuant to the formula below. If compensation is paid, the receiving bank is obligated to back value the payment to the date requested, unless i) its customer instructs it not to back value such payment; ii) the account has been closed; iii) the sending bank requests a back valuation to a date more than one year prior to the payment date; or iv) the compensation payment is received more than one year after the payment date.

b. The rules do not require the sending bank to obtain back value. The rules only stipulate the amount required when back valuation is requested by the sending bank.

c. If the receiving bank back values the payment pursuant to the request of the sending bank, the sending bank must pay the receiving bank compensation according to the following formula (without regard to whether or not the beneficiary's account was actually in an overdraft position):

$$\text{Compensation} = \frac{\substack{\text{(Dollar Amount of Payment)} \times \text{(Fed. Funds Rate)} \times \\ \text{(No. of Days Back Valued)} + \$200^*}}{360}$$

Rule II.3. Forward Valuation. a. A bank which sent a payment may request the bank which received the payment to adjust the payment to a future value date. The receiving bank is not obligated to make such an adjustment.

b. If a receiving bank adjusts the payment to a future value date pursuant to the request of the sending bank, the receiving bank must, upon receiving a claim for compensation within 60 days from the date on which the requested adjustment was made, pay the sending bank compensation according to the following formula:

$$\text{Compensation} = \frac{\substack{\text{(Dollar Amount of Payment)} \times \text{(100\%-Reserve} \\ \text{Requirement)} \times \text{(Fed. Funds Rate)} \times \\ \text{(No. of days Forward Value)} - \$200^{**}}}{360}$$

---

*$200 fee is paid to the bank which was requested to make the adjustment to compensate it for its administrative costs in back valuing a payment.

**The $200 deduction is allowed to compensate the receiving bank for its administrative costs in adjusting a payment to a future date. The receiving bank is not entitled to the $200 deduction for forward valuation if a request for a change of beneficiary (Rule 5) also accompanies a request for forward valuation. However, the receiving bank is entitled to the $200 fee for amending the beneficiary.

Rule II.4. Return of Payment "Missent Payment." a. There may be circumstances in which a bank that has sent a payment may request the bank that received such payment to return the funds. For example, a bank that has i) sent a payment that should not have been sent; ii) sent a payment to the wrong bank; or iii) sent a duplicated payment or has made an over-payment (each such payment or part thereof constituting an overpayment is hereafter referred to as a "missent payment"), may request the bank which received the payment to return it. To induce the receiving bank to return a missent payment the sending bank may issue an Indemnity conforming to the format of the U.S. Council on International Banking's Compensation Indemnity and Responses (the Indemnity) (Appendix A). The receiving bank is not obligated to return the payment in reliance on the Indemnity.

b. Except as provided under Rule 7 of this Part II (Netting of Compensation), if a receiving bank returns a missent payment, it shall, upon receiving a claim for compensation within 60 days from the date on which it returned the missent payment, pay the sending bank compensation according to the following formula:

$$\text{Compensation} = \frac{\begin{array}{c}\text{(Dollar Amount of Payment)} \times \text{(100\%-Reserve} \\ \text{Requirement)} \times \text{(Fed. Funds Rate)} \times \text{(No. of} \\ \text{days not to exceed 180)} - \text{Applicable Deduction}\end{array}}{360}$$

c. A request for compensation received beyond 60 days from the date the missent payment was returned, need not be honored by the receiving bank.

d. A request for compensation included in the body of the Indemnity is a legitimate claim under the new Rules and fulfills the 60 day requirement.

e. If a missent payment is retained by the receiving bank for more than 180 days, the Fed. Funds Rate means the Fed. Funds Rate in effect during the most recent 180 day time period.

Appendix: U.S. Council on International Banking Compensation and Indemnity and Responses (the "Indemnity")

   1. Purpose. In order to induce a bank receiving a payment (the "Receiving Bank") to return in an expeditious manner, a payment sent to the wrong bank, an overpayment, a duplicated payment or to adjust a credit to the correct account on a payment made to the correct Receiving Bank but for credit to an incorrect or no account, the bank sending such a payment (the "Paying Bank") may issue the Indemnity which appears below to the Receiving Bank. The Receiving Bank may, but is not obligated to act as a result of the Indemnity. The Indemnity may be issued only in connection with payments made in United States dollars.

   2. Method of Transmission. A Paying Bank should transmit the Indemnity and a Receiving Bank should transmit any response or release thereof, by telex, S.W.I.F.T., any other mutually agreed upon means of electronic transmission, or by letter. It is recommended that the Indemnity be sent by means of electronic transmission. If transmitted by telex, the telex must be tested. If transmitted by S.W.I.F.T. or any other means of electronic transmission, the transmission must be authenticated. If transmitted by letter, the letter must be executed by an authorized signatory of the sender and must be hand delivered to the receiver by an authorized messenger from the sender. The receiver shall acknowledge in writing receipt of such a letter. Such acknowledgement shall be considered proof that such letter was properly delivered by the sender to the receiver. If transmitted by letter, each Indemnity must be enclosed in a readily identifiable envelope addressed to the Receiving Bank clearly marked with the notation "Indemnity."

   3. "Format." a. The Indemnity must be in the following format:

REF.NO. _____

INDEMNITY

   With reference to our payment date _____ by means of (Fedwire # _____, (CHIPS#_____), (S.W.I.F.T._____), or (check # _____), for U.S. $_____ in your favor for the account of _____, by order of _____, we request that you:

[   ] Adjust the credit from the acount of _____ to the account of _____;

[   ] Refund the amount of U.S. $_____, which was intended for you;

[   ] Refund the amount of U.S. $_____, because the afore-mentioned payment was a duplication of (Fedwire #_____), (CHIPS #_____), (S.W.I.F.T. #_____), or (check #_____);

[   ] Refund the amount of U.S. $_____, which was an over-payment. The correct amount should be U.S. $_____;

[   ] Pay us compensation calculated pursuant to the U.S. Council on International Banking's Interbank Compensation Rules from (payment date) to the date on which you fulfill this request.

In consideration of your complying with the terms of this Indemnity we agree to indemnify you, your officers and employees against any and all claims, liabilities, losses, expenses, (including the reasonable fees and disbursements of your counsel) suits or damages resulting therefrom (each of the foregoing is hereinafter referred to as "loss").

You agree to notify us of any such loss within ten (10) business days of your receipt of notification of any such loss.

We represent and warrant that we are duly authorized by all necessary and appropriate corporate action to execute this Indemnity and that this Indemnity is a valid and legally binding obligation of our bank.

Pursuant to a Recall of Funds notification as provided under the U.S. Council on International Banking's Compensation Indemnity and Responses we will return on demand the amount refunded by you or reimburse you on demand for the amount of the adjustment.

You agree to contact your customer immediately to obtain its debit authorization. Upon receiving such debit authorization, our obligations under this Indemnity will cease and you will notify us of your release hereunder. Please make the appropriate response to this Indemnity.

b. The Indemnity may be sent in an abbreviated format when it bears the statement: "We agree to indemnify you according to the Compensation Indemnity and Responses contained in the U.S. Council on International Banking's Guideline for Issuing and Responding to an Indemnity." Such statement will be deemed to incorporate the entire text of the Indemnity set forth above. The following information must also be provided in the abbreviated format:

1. Date of transfer
2. Amount of transfer
3. Method of transfer

4. Payment system identification

    a) Fedwire number

    b) CHIPS number

    c) S.W.I.F.T. number

    d) Check number

    e) Account number or name of party to whom payment was originally sent

    f) Account number or name of party to be credited

5. By order party

6. Description of action requested (including claim for compensation).

c. The Indemnity may be sent by using structured format transaction codes established by procedures in the CHIPS Systems and Operations Manual for CHIPS participants to send and receive such indemnities. Such procedures permit the Paying Bank to cause CHIPS to transmit to the receiving bank a CHIPS Service Message that contains either the statement: "We indemnify you under NYCHA or USCIB Compensation Rules as applicable (Ref. No. _____)" or a structured format transaction code established by such Manual for such indemnities. Such CHIPS Service Message will be deemed to incorporate the entire text of the U.S. Council on International Banking Indemnity set forth in its Compensation Rules between a New York Clearing House Association member bank and a USCIB member bank or between two USCIB member banks. The following information must also be provided in the CHIPS Service Message:

1. Identification of the CHIPS payment message by which the transfer was made as follows:

    a. Paying Bank's payment sequence number ("PSN")

    b. Amount of transfer

    c. Date of transfer

2. Identification of the parties (by name or account number or both where available) as follows:

    a. Party to whom payment was originally sent

    b. By order party

    c. Party to whom corrected payment shall be made (if applicable).

4. Responses. a. When a Receiving Bank determines it will return principal pursuant to an Indemnity, principal should be returned by CHIPS or Fedwire; and the Receiving Bank should notify the Paying Bank as follows: "Returning your (Fedwire #_____), (CHIPS #_____), (S.W.I.F.T. # _____), or (check #_____) dated for $_____ pursuant to your Indemnity Ref. No. _____ dated _____. (We are forwarding the appropriate compensation.)"

  b. When in reliance on an Indemnity a Receiving Bank determines to adjust the beneficiary's account and account number, the Receiving Bank should notify the Paying Bank as follows: "On (date), we adjusted your (Fedwire #_____), (CHIPS #_____), (S.W.I.F.T. # _____),or (check # _____) to read (beneficiary and amount) pursuant to your Indemnity Ref. No. _____ dated _____. Please forward compensation of $ _____."

  c. When a Receiving Bank determines to take no action on an Indemnity because it contains insufficient information or is not in the standard format, the Receiving Bank should notify the Paying Bank as follows: "Your Indemnity delivered by (S.W.I.F.T., telex, letter) Ref. No. _____ dated _____ for $ _____ covering instructions via (Fedwire # _____). (CHIPS # _____), (S.W.I.F.T. # _____), or (check # _____) dated _____ by order of _____ cannot be acted upon because it contains (Incorrect Format, Incomplete Information, or Inappropriate Transmittal)."

  d. When Receiving Bank in its sole discretion determines not to take action requested by XXX Indemnity, the Receiving Bank shall notify the Paying Bank as follows: "We have determined to take no action pursuant to your Indemnity delivered by (S.W.I.F.T., telex, letter) Ref. No. _____ dated _____ for $ _____ covering instructions via (Fedwire #_____), (CHIPS #_____), (S.W.I.F.T. # _____), or (check # _____) dated _____ by order of _____. (We are treating the matter as an inquiry and are to-day, (date), seeking debit authorization from our customer. We shall advise you of its response)."

5. Confirmation. If the Receiving Bank determines to take the action requested by the Indemnity, it shall attempt to procure confirmation of its action from the party whose account was debited. The Receiving Bank shall notify such party as follows: "On (date), we debited your account #_____ for $_____ in reversal of a credit entry dated _____, our Ref. No._____, cutomer Ref. No.

_____ by the order of _____ for the order of _____. The paying bank notified us that it had incorrectly instructed us to credit your account. Please confirm to us that you have no objection to our debiting your account to correct said error."

6. Release. After the Receiving Bank has obtained debit authorization from its customer, the Paying Bank is released from its liabilities and obligations under the Indemnity. The Receiving Bank must notify the Paying Bank as follows promptly upon obtaining said debit authorization: "We hereby notify you that you have been released from all obligations and liabilities arising from and in connection with your Indemnity delivered by (S.W.I.F.T., telex letter) Ref. No._____ dated for $_____ covering instructions via (Fedwire # _____), (CHIPS #_____), (S.W.I.F.T. #_____), or (check #_____) dated _____ by order of _____."

Once the Receiving Bank has received debit authorization from its customer or notifies the Paying Bank that it releases the Paying Bank of its obligations and liabilities arising from and in connection with such Indemnity, the Paying Bank, shall no longer be liable to the Receiving Bank on the Indemnity in connection with any matter related to, or arising from such Indemnity.

7. Recall of Funds. If the beneficiary whose account has been debited by the Receiving Bank pursuant to a request in the Indemnity from a Paying Bank, requests the return of the amount so debited, the Paying Bank must, as the case may be, return, or reimburse the Receiving Bank for such amount upon receipt of the following notice from the Receiving Bank: "Please (return to us or reimburse us) in the amount of $ which we refunded to you via (Fedwire #_____), (CHIPS #_____), or (check #_____) (or credited to the account of _____) pursuant to the Indemnity delivered by (S.W.I.F.T., telex, letter) Ref. No._____, dated _____ covering instructions via (Fedwire #_____), (CHIPS _____), (S.W.I.F.T. #_____), or (check #_____) dated _____ by order of _____because our customer has demanded a return of funds."

10 Conducting Foreign Exchange Trading

Foreign exchange trading is conducted directly, bank-to-bank, or with the help of an intermediary. Until April 1992, the interbank intermediary had always been the foreign exchange broker. Since then, matching systems, or electronic brokers, have replaced most of the traditional brokers' business.

Technological breakthroughs have changed the manner of trading foreign exchange directly as well. The telephone, the communication tool of choice after the breakup of the Bretton Woods Accord and the consequent shift from fixed rates to free-floating rates, has been replaced by dealing and matching systems, which are computer terminals that link the world of finance. These systems have almost entirely replaced phone trading in the larger dealing rooms. Currently, direct dealing is a complementary method.

THE BROKERS' MARKET

THE ROLE OF CURRENCY BROKERS

First, I would like to emphasize the difference between an equity brokerage house and a foreign exchange brokerage house. Equity brokerage houses trade for both customers and themselves. They service both individuals and institutions. The institutions may be mutual funds, other investment banks, manufacturing companies, and so on.

Foreign exchange brokers do not take positions for themselves; they only service banks. Their roles are:

1. bringing together buyers and sellers in the market,
2. optimizing the price they show to their customers, and
3. quickly, accurately, and faithfully executing the traders' orders.

Because they neither assume financial responsibility nor trade for themselves, foreign exchange brokers are not subject to any regulatory requirements per se. Their primary customers are commercial and investment banks.

The majority of their business is executed via phone. The phone lines between brokers and banks are dedicated, or direct, and are usually installed free of charge by the broker. This is a direct result of the competition from both matching and dealing systems. Having a direct phone line means that neither the bank nor the broker has to dial a phone number; they simply pick up the phone and trade. These dedicated phone lines can be used only by the broker and the individual bank where they were installed.

Although brokers charge commissions, traders are highly unlikely to miss a deal because of fee considerations. It is much more important to enter a profitable deal or to timely cut a losing position than to miss the opportunity in order to avoid a broker's commission.

Brokers charge a commission that is paid equally by the buyer and the seller. This helps to ensure the impartiality of the broker. Brokerage is paid per million of U.S. dollars, or British pounds, Australian dollars, etc. The fees are negotiated on an individual basis by the bank and the brokerage firm. They start at $8 per million of foreign currency.

SETUP

A foreign exchange brokerage firm has direct lines to banks around the world. Most foreign exchange is executed through an *open box system*—a microphone in front of the broker that continuously transmits everything he or she says on the direct phone lines to the speaker boxes in the banks. This way, all banks can hear all the deals being executed. Because of the open box system used by brokers, a trader is able to hear all prices quoted; whether the bid was hit or the offer taken; and the following price. What the trader will not be able to hear is the amounts of particular bids and offers and the names of the banks showing the prices. Prices are anonymous The anonymity of the banks that are trading in the market ensures the market's efficiency, as all banks have a fair chance to trade.

CHARACTERISTICS OF THE CURRENCY BROKERS' PRICE

Let's see how brokers show their customers the prices made by other customers. The broker requests either two-way (bid and offer) prices or one-way (bid or offer) prices from his or her customers. Traders show different prices because they "read" the market differently; they have different expectations and different interests. A broker who has more than one price on one or both sides will automatically optimize the price. In other words, the broker will always show the highest bid and the lowest offer. Therefore, the market has access to the narrowest spread possible.

For example, a broker on the spot USD/JPY desk receives the following prices from different banks:

Bank	Bid	Offer
Nonaggresiva	117.10	117.20
Bidda	117.12	117.22
Offerta	117.11	117.17
Taurus	117.12	117.19
Notinterestida	117.10	—
Southoriented	117.07	117.17
Uponthefence	—	117.20

The highest bid is 117.12, shown by banks Bidda and Taurus, and the lowest offer is 117.17, shown by banks Offerta and Southoriented. Consequently, the optimized price is 117.12–117.17.

Once the broker announces the price, all the other prices, the runners-up, are automatically off, and the broker will not use them regardless of the direction of the market, unless the original trader or traders renew their prices.

Note that, as in the example, traders may show only one side of the price. This is characteristic only of the brokers' market, as one-sided prices are not generally quoted in the direct market. This dealing approach is less aggressive, and from the trader's point of view, this option is attractive because it involves less risk.

One of the advantages of trading in the brokers' market is that traders have more trading options than in the direct market. Let's take a closer look at these options, using the same broker's spot price: USD/JPY 117.12–117.17.

When attempting to buy USD/JPY before it rallies, a trader has three alternatives:

1. Take the offer at 117.17.

This is identical to the alternative in the direct market. This option provides the highest degree of certainty for executing the deal. Brokers' prices are in competition with the interbank's prices if they both show an identical price. The broker's advantage is ready availability, which is vital in a fast market. The downside is that there is no guarantee that the full amount asked by the trader will be executed.

For instance, a trader trying to buy USD/JPY 10,000,000 from the broker may only be able to buy USD/JPY 6,000,000, the only amount that the broker had in the offer at that moment.

Taking the offer is an aggressive approach, and the trader will have to deal on the price shown to him or her. The cost consists of the spread between the bid and the offer, but there is no commission to pay when dealing direct.

2. Join the bid at 117.12.

This alternative provides the least certainty of having the deal executed. If you join a bid, you will have to have your deal executed behind previous bids. Brokers use the prices on a first come, first served basis. In other words, joining the bid is equivalent to joining an invisible queue in the attempt to buy U.S. dollars against yen. The trader does not know who is at the front of the queue or how many millions of dollars are posted in the particular bid. Brokers quote only the running price, not the amount. Therefore, it is impossible for a trader to know the size of the bid (or offer, for that matter). It may be an uncertain undertaking to wait for someone to hit your bid for the exact number of dollars you want to buy.

Joining the bid is the most defensive approach, but provides a price cost advantage. If your bid is hit and the USD/JPY does indeed go up as you expected, the profit will be higher by the spread between the bid and the offer, i.e., 5 pips.

3. Improve the bid, anywhere between 117.13 and 117.16.

This middle-of-the-road alternative has several advantages. By marginally improving (raising) the bid, the trader can be sure of having the best bid. Anyone joining the bid will not know the size of the bid, and will just have to wait to have an order executed in turn.

Although it's a defensive tool, improving the bid provides more certainty than joining the bid. Generally speaking, the more a trader improves the bid, the better the chances of having it dealt on.

The opposite options are available if the trader were to sell USD/JPY, on expectations of poor economic data:

1. Hit the bid at 117.12.
2. Join the offer at 117.17.
3. Improve the offer by lowering the offer to between 117.16 and 117.13.

We've said that price anonymity is an important characteristic of the brokers' market. Let's assume, for example, that the market is passing through a stagnant period that is not rich in fundamental or technical signals. Fundamental and technical analyses are used for forecasting the future direction of the currency. A trader might test the market by hitting a bid for a small amount to see if there is any reaction. If you knew there was a large amount in the bid, the trader would have done just the opposite, choosing the path of least resistance.

Sticking with the spot USD/JPY example, let's add some U.S. dollar amounts to the previous bids and offers.

Bank	Bid Price	Bid Amount	Offer Price	Offer Amount
Nonaggresiva	117.10	$5,000,000	117.20	$20,000,000
Bidda	117.12	$40,000,000	117.22	$5,000,000
Offerta	117.11	$5,000,000	117.17	$3,000,000
Taurus	117.12	$150,000,000	117.19	$3,500,000
Noninterestida	117.10	$15,000,000		
Southoriented	117.07	$20,000,000	117.17	$2,000,000
Uponthefence	117.20	$5,000,000		
Bid	**117.12**	**$190,000,000**	**117.17**	**$5,000,000**

Although prices are almost always anonymous, brokers will state the amounts on a price in two specific instances:

1. When the size of the bid or offer is less than the usual marketable amount of $5,000,000; in this case, the broker will say "On small" or "On tiny" or specify the amount, especially if it is an odd amount.
2. When a customer expressly asks the broker to look around for a specific amount, most likely late in the afternoon (after 3 PM in the New York market).

Among traders, a bank name may have special significance. When the name of the party showing a price belongs to one of the aggressive market makers, this bit of information may be construed as a signal to take their side.

Although there are some exceptions, anonymity provides market efficiency by providing each player a fair trading opportunity.

BROKERS' SWITCHES

Because prices are anonymous, traders cannot know who the counterparty is. Although a deal is transacted, names will not be accepted if the banks do not have sufficient credit lines with each other or if there is any kind of dispute between the banks. In this situation, it is the responsibility of the broker to switch, or wash, that name. The broker will look for a third party that can deal with both organizations and is willing to execute two artificial trades by buying from one and selling to the other at the same price.

Brokers cannot be forced into taking a principal's role if the name switch takes longer than anticipated.

Example:

In the brokers' market, Bank Ichisan buys USD/JPY 10,000,000 at 150.00 from Bank Niisan. The two banks cannot accept each other's names. The broker calls on Bank Sansan, which has lines of credit with both Bank Ichisan and Bank Niisan. Bank Sansan will sell USD/JPY 10,000,000 to Bank Ichisan at 150.00 and it will also buy USD/JPY 10,000,000 from Bank Niisan at 150.00. Bank Sansan, in effect, bought and sold the same amount of USD/JPY at the same rate, with no bearing on its P&L. The original deal was a good deal; the only thing that changed was the name of the counterparty.

SWITCHING PIPS

Switching pips is a peculiar situation that may, theoretically, lead brokers to take minor positions. At times, due to turbulence in the market, price liquidity decreases while demand increases. This imbalance creates additional trading tension.

Brokers scramble to bring fresh prices to the market in these circumstances. Due to the rapid trading activity, a trader who wanted to buy, for instance, EUR/USD at 1.1017, may end up buying at 1.1019, because of the difference between supply and demand. Backtracking to our example of the brokers' price structure, you can see that the amount of EUR/USD in the 1.1017 offer side is minuscule. Once that happens, it is likely that the selling trader will quickly demand that the 1.1019 offer be shown. But if the offer is not properly shown by the broker, or not properly understood by the buying trader, the buyer may ask for compensation—from the broker—for the 2 pips on each of the millions of euro traded.

The broker cannot have a position, but has to maintain the business relationship with the specific bank. So the broker must either look for a similar mistake on the opposite side or, more realistically, ask a friendly trader for a "pips" loan until that error occurs again. The logic in this case is flawed and unbalanced on the trader's side, because it is common knowledge that brokers cannot enter trading positions. It is rather difficult to be sure whether the broker is just trying to accommodate a difficult trader or is creating a financial position for personal gain.

The Federal Reserve attempted to resolve this Catch-22 situation for brokers. On August 1, 1990, the Fed advised both brokers and traders to cease all "pips" borrowing activity. This should have been an example of fences making good neighbors, an attempt to clarify brokers' professional boundaries and, therefore, to protect them against undue pressure from traders.

In reality, exceptions may occur.

LIQUIDITY

Another advantage of the brokers' market is that brokers might provide a broader selection of banks to their customers. This adds to price liquidity. For example, the dealing room of an American bank wants to trade in the afternoon, but because of the time differences, European and Asian banks are not trading at the same time as the American banks. However, some European and Asian banks have overnight desks that operate at limited capacity. Their primary function, however, is to execute orders and not to make markets. So their orders are usually placed with brokers who can deal with the American banks, adding to the liquidity of the market.

LACK OF TRADING RECIPROCITY

Dealing with brokers has other advantages, especially for smaller banks. One of these is the fact that direct trading is based on the idea of reciprocity. If Banque Deuxieme calls Banque Premiere, then Banque Premiere will call back Banque Deuxieme. But Banque Deuxieme may not like to be called back, especially if Banque Deuxieme is a smaller bank with a limited exposure to foreign exchange and Banque Premiere is a major market maker. A bank will be able to trade with fewer dealers if it trades primarily through the brokers' market.

For smaller banks, using the brokers' market may also translate to savings on personnel costs; the cost of training and maintaining an in-house staff qualified to handle a constant flow of calls to and from other banks can be quite high.

ETHICS

The structure of the price—the amounts of currency on either side of the price—is very important information. However, the only party with access to this information is the broker. Theoretically, a broker could be the best trader, knowing the short-term supply and demand on each of the major currencies. One must remember, however, that foreign exchange brokers always act as impartial intermediaries and never take positions for themselves.

A brokerage firm enforces this rule carefully in order to maintain its reputation with its clients. A broker engaging in any type of unethical activity runs the risk that traders will simply stop trading with him or her. Brokers, like other foreign exchange participants, observe high standards of professionalism and ethics.

OTHER SERVICES

In order to provide better service under the pressure of increasing competition, brokers offer additional services, such as posting their rates for the major currencies on different monitors, quoting outside the unofficially "official" trading hours of 8:30 AM EDT to 3PM EDT, quoting exotic currencies, and even providing elements of technical analysis.

POTENTIAL DISADVANTAGES

Despite all their ordinary and extraordinary efforts, brokers are not always able to provide either a two-way or a one-sided price. Not only do they have a small market share, but in periods of high price volatility, banks may not wish to take on extra risk by showing a full or even a partial price in the brokers' market. Therefore, there are times when brokers are not able to provide prices.

DIRECT DEALING

TRADING RECIPROCITY

Direct dealing is an aggressive approach to trading. It is based on trading reciprocity. A market maker—the bank making or quoting a price—expects the bank that is calling to reciprocate with respect to making a price when called upon.

Making a price doesn't mean making just any price. What a trader expects and is expected to provide in turn is a fast quote with a tight spread between the bid and the offer. Reciprocity requires that banks develop market relationships. These relationships are very important when the caller needs extra service, such as a quote outside the regular trading time, a faster quote in an illiquid market, or a price on an odd amount.

There are some exceptions to full reciprocity, such as situations in which banks reach an understanding to quote each other a handful of different currencies. This occurs when smaller banks specialize in one or two currencies, but may call larger banks on an irregular basis for prices in other currencies.

CHARACTERISTICS OF THE INTERBANK CURRENCY PRICE

Unlike the brokers' market, quotes in the interbank market are always two-way prices.

When making a market, a bank will quote, or show, only a bid and an offer, known as a spread, to the other bank. Just like the broker, the market maker will not quote the big figure of the exchange rate, which is assumed to be known by all the players. For example, the rate of 116.10–15 will be quoted as 10–15.

The similarity stops here. The calling bank will only have the option of hitting the bid or taking the offer of the price being quoted. The alternatives available in the brokers' market of joining or improving one of the price's sides are no longer available. The price cannot be negotiated. The calling party must decide quickly whether to trade on the price or not. Postponing the answer beyond 20 seconds or so usually triggers the price annulment.

Because the price quoted by a single bank may not be negotiated, a trader looking to improve the price only has the option of increasing the pool of prices by calling several banks simultaneously or in close sequence and selecting the best price.

For instance, if a trader from Bank Aggresiva is looking to buy EUR/USD in the direct market, then the trader will call out, mentioning the currency and the amount needed, and get the following prices:

Bank	Bid	Offer
Nonaggresiva	1.1010	1.1020
Bidda	1.1012	1.1022
Offerta	1.1011	1.1017
Taurus	1.1012	1.1019
Supersouth	1.1010	1.1015

The cheapest, or lowest, offer is quoted by Bank Supersouth at 1.1015, and the trader from Bank Aggresiva will buy EUR/USD at this price.

In a fast market, direct trading may be the only option for getting a price, as the brokers may be bypassed by risk-averse traders. The quoting banks, under these conditions, may be slower than their customary zapping speed, and may also show wider spreads than usual. Yet availability may replace price quality as the traders' top priority.

DISCRETION

Direct dealing provides more trading discretion, as compared to dealing in the brokers' market. Sometimes traders take advantage of this characteristic. When a bank needs to trade a large amount of currency quickly, it may simultaneously call a number of banks and hit all or the majority of their prices in rapid succession. Although not endorsed by all participants, this strategy of lining up banks is an accepted reality of the market.

The downside of direct trading is that it may interfere with individual trading flows. Let's say that a trader expects the USD/JPY to go up and, consequently, the trader buys USD/JPY 10,000,000. Soon, another trader calls directly, asks for a price in USD/JPY, and buys USD/JPY 10,000,000 from the first trader. Immediately after, the USD/JPY suddenly rallies, but the first trader is not long USD/JPY anymore. Therefore, the trader must develop defensive trading skills.

In order to be able to pick up all the direct calls accurately and call out to trade, a trading desk needs experienced and reliable trading support.

HOW THE BUSINESS IS EXECUTED

Direct dealing used to be conducted mostly on the phone. The balance was executed by telex. Phone dealing was error-prone and slow. Most traders or their assistants could make only one phone deal at a time, or rarely, two. When the phone rang, the identity of the caller and the reason for calling were not known. Moreover, despite the rather limited vocabulary used by traders, communication errors occurred often, due to the noisy and tense trading environment. Dealing errors were difficult to prove and even more difficult to settle. The unofficial working policy was to share the resulting cost of the error equally.

In order to increase dealing safety, most banks tapped the phone lines on which trading was conducted. This measure was helpful in recording all the transaction details and enabling the dealers to allocate the responsibility for errors fairly. But tape recorders were unable to prevent trading errors. Direct dealing was forever changed in the mid-1980s, by the introduction of dealing systems.

DEALING SYSTEMS

Dealing systems are on-line computers that link the contributing banks around the world on a one-on-one basis. This type of service is provided by Reuters. (See Figures 10.1 and 10.2.) The performance of dealing systems is characterized by speed, reliability, and safety.

SPEED

The receiving bank is able to see on its monitor what bank is calling and for what amount. This feature is not only convenient; it also enhances speed, as the call will be picked up by the specific currency trader, rather than randomly.

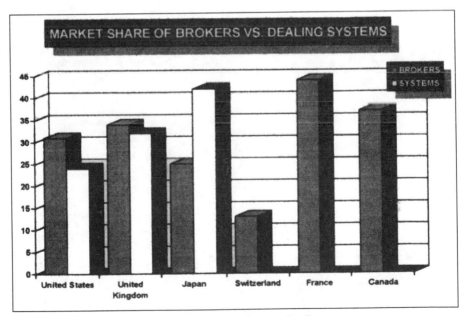

Figure 10.1. Market share of brokers versus Reuters Dealing system.

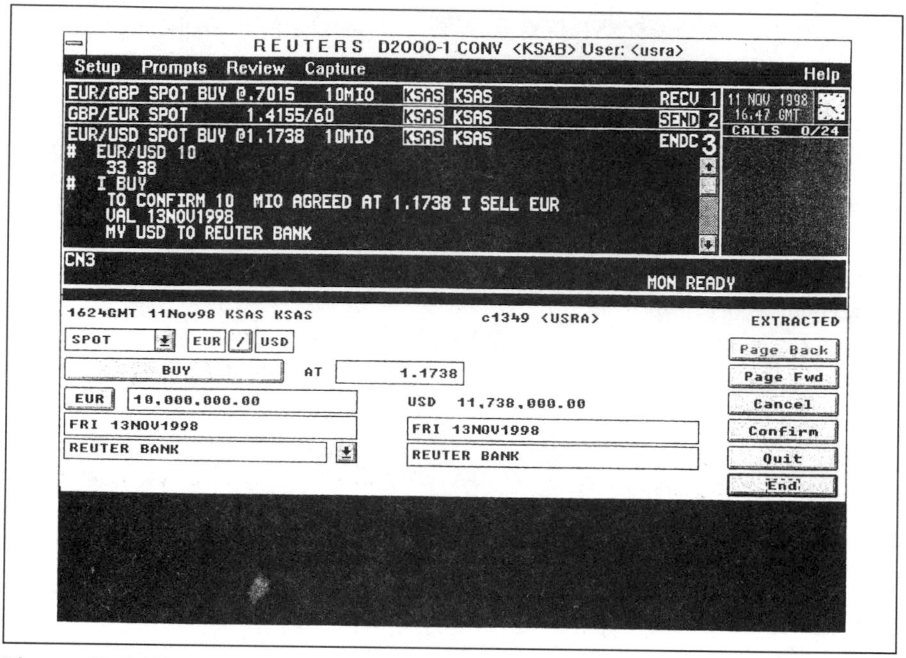

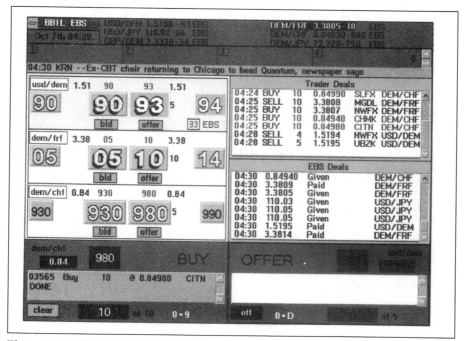

Figure 10.2. The Reuters Dealing 3000 system. *(Source: Reuters)*

Figure 10.3. The EBS system. *(Source: EBS)*

A trader is able to hold up to 24 simultaneous conversations on the Reuters dealing system. That's quite a departure from struggling to handle two phone dealings in the best case. The deals are clearly posted on the screen. Switching among the calls is accomplished by a single stroke of a key on the keyboard.

Accessing a bank through a dealing system is much faster than making a phone call, even using a speed dialer. Even simultaneously accessing four banks may require only a single keystroke. Immediately following the trade execution, further information regarding value dates, payment and receiving, and even greetings may be exchanged.

Instead of typing all this information, useful time is saved by using preset keys. Executing four trades totaling $40 million or more in about 30 seconds is common among foreign exchange traders. That's fast!

RELIABILITY

Dealing systems are indispensable trading tools, and they are continuously being improved in order to offer maximum support to the dealer's main function: trading. The software is very reliable in picking up the big figure of the exchange rates and the standard value dates. In addition, it is extremely precise and fast in contacting other parties, switching among conversations, and accessing the database.

SAFETY

The trader is in continuous visual contact with the information exchanged on the monitor. It is easier to see than hear this information, especially when switching among conversations.

Traders use only the last two digits of the bid and offer. When confirming, however, all the information must be fully expressed. The software picks up the big figure, not only saving time but also ensuring that typing errors do not occur. Because all the payment and receiving information is stored in memory, the trader or assistant is prevented from inadvertently sending the wrong instructions.

At the end of the conversation, all the details are saved and stored in the database, ready to be conveniently retrieved at any time. If an error still occurs, it is significantly faster and easier to retrieve the details from a dealing system than from a tape recorder. Immediately following the end of communication, the entire trade or conversation is printed on at least one printer. Dealing tickets may be printed or, as is increasingly the case, electronically generated in paperless systems.

Most banks use a combination of brokers and direct dealing systems. Both approaches reach the same banks, but not the same parties, because corporations, for instance, cannot deal in the brokers' market. Traders develop personal relationships with both brokers and traders in the markets, but select their trading medium based on price quality, not on personal feelings. The market share between dealing systems and brokers fluctuates based on market conditions. Fast market conditions are beneficial to dealing systems, whereas regular market conditions are more beneficial to brokers.

MATCHING SYSTEMS

The biggest competition to voice brokers has come from the introduction of electronic matching systems, which are, in effect, electronic brokers. They are EBS and Reuters. Unlike dealing systems, on which trading is not anonymous and is conducted on a one-on-one basis, matching systems are anonymous and individual traders deal against the rest of the market, similar to dealing in the brokers' market.

Unlike the brokers' market, there are no individuals to bring the prices to the market, and liquidity may be limited at times. Several incentive programs that lower the commissions are geared to increasing liquidity levels nearer to those on dealing systems. Matching systems are well-suited for trading smaller amounts as well, because brokers generally shy away from trading amounts under $3 million.

The dealing systems' characteristics of speed, reliability, and safety are replicated in the matching systems. In addition, credit lines are automatically managed by the systems. Traders input the total credit line for each counterparty. When the credit line has been reached, the system automatically disallows dealing with the particular party by displaying credit restrictions, or shows the trader only the price made by banks that have open lines of credit. As soon as the credit line is restored, the system allows the bank to deal again. Figure 10.3 shows EBS, and Figure 10.4 displays the Reuters matching system.

In the interbank market, traders deal directly with dealing systems, matching systems, and brokers in a complementary fashion. Traders take advantage of the large and sophisticated brokers' market, the level of certainty in direct dealing, and the electronic sophistication of matching systems. Corporations do not use matching systems.

Few players use only one trading venue. Increased competition among these venues brings further efficiency to the foreign exchange markets. Although they are important, the differences in commissions between brokers and dealing systems are secondary, because traders focus on the best or fastest price available.

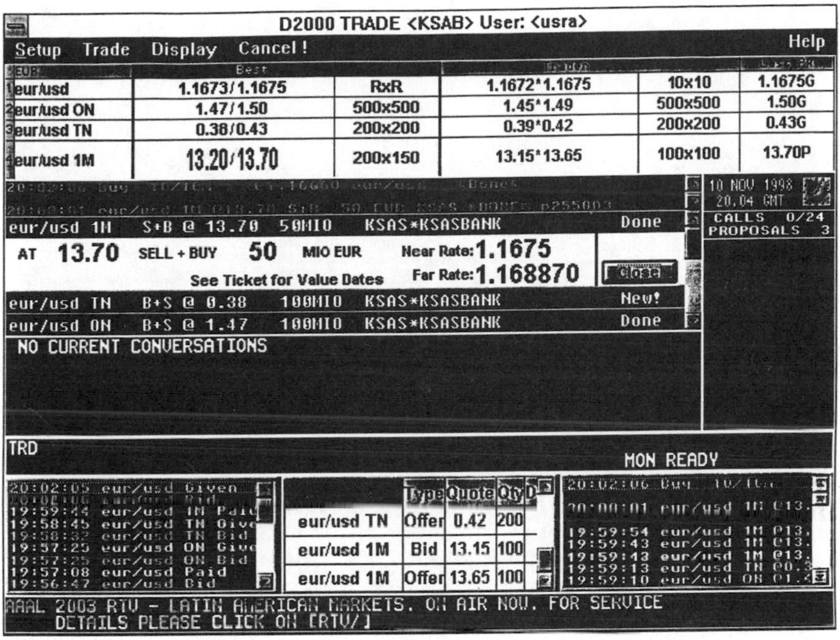

D2000 TRADE <KSAB> User: <usra>

Setup   Trade   Display   Cancel !   Help

	Best		Best		
1 eur/usd	1.1673/1.1675	RxR	1.1672*1.1675	10x10	1.1675G
2 eur/usd ON	1.47/1.50	500x500	1.45*1.49	500x500	1.50G
3 eur/usd TN	0.38/0.43	200x200	0.39*0.42	200x200	0.43G
4 eur/usd 1M	13.20/13.70	200x150	13.15*13.65	100x100	13.70P

20:02:06 Buy 10/10.   1.16660   Donex
20:00:01 eur/usd 1M 013.70 S+B 50 EUR KSAS +DONEx p255003

10 NOV 1998
20.04 GMT

eur/usd 1M   S+B @ 13.70   50MIO   KSAS*KSASBANK   Done   CALLS   0/24
                                                                    PROPOSALS   3
AT 13.70 SELL + BUY   50   MIO EUR   Near Rate: 1.1675
            See Ticket for Value Dates   Far Rate: 1.168870   Close

eur/usd TN   B+S @ 0.38   100MIO   KSAS*KSASBANK   New!
eur/usd ON   B+S @ 1.47   100MIO   KSAS*KSASBANK   Done
NO CURRENT CONVERSATIONS

TRD
                                                          MON READY

20:02:05 eur/usd Given | Type | Quote | Qty | 20:02:06 Buy 10/10.
20:02:06 eur/usd Bid | eur/usd TN | Offer | 0.42 | 200 | 20:00:01 eur/usd 1M 013.
19:59:44 eur/usd 1M Paid | | | | 19:59:54 eur/usd 1M 013.
19:58:45 eur/usd TN Give | eur/usd 1M | Bid | 13.15 | 100 | 19:59:43 eur/usd 1M 013.
19:58:32 eur/usd TN Bid | | | | 19:59:43 eur/usd 1M 013.
19:57:25 eur/usd ON Give | eur/usd 1M | Offer | 13.65 | 100 | 19:59:13 eur/usd 1M 013.
19:57:25 eur/usd ON Bid | | | | 19:59:13 eur/usd TN 00.3
19:57:08 eur/usd Paid | | | | 19:59:10 eur/usd ON 01.4
19:56:47 eur/usd Bid

AAAL 2003 RTV - LATIN AMERICAN MARKETS. ON AIR NOW. FOR SERVICE
       DETAILS PLEASE CLICK ON [RTV/]

Figure 10.4. The Reuters Matching System. *(Source: Reuters)*

11 The Spot Market

C urrency spot trading is the most popular foreign currency instrument around the world, making up 37 percent of the total activity.
(See Figure 11.1.) The fast-paced spot market is not for the faint-
hearted, as it features high volatility and quick profits (and losses). This
chapter examines how spot trading works and explains how savvy traders
stay on top of this exciting market.

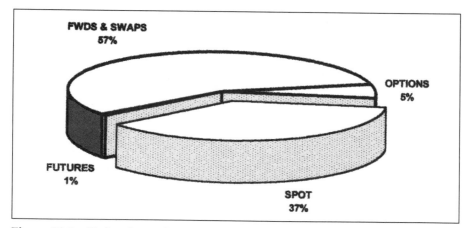

Figure 11.1. Market share of spot trading. *(Source: Bridge Information Systems, Inc.)*

THE FOREIGN CURRENCY SPOT MARKETPLACE

A spot deal consists of a bilateral contract whereby a party delivers a specified amount of a given currency against receipt of a specified amount of another currency from a counterparty, based on an agreed exchange rate, within two business days of the deal date. The exception is the Canadian dollar, in which the spot delivery is executed next business day.

Note that the name "spot" does not mean that the currency exchange occurs the same business day the deal is executed. Currency transactions that require same-day delivery are called *cash transactions*. The two-day spot delivery for currencies was developed long before technological breakthroughs in information processing. This time period was necessary to check out all transactions' details among counterparties. Although technologically feasible, the contemporary markets did not find it necessary to reduce the time to make payments. Human errors still occur and they need to be fixed before delivery. When currency deliveries are made to the wrong party, fines are imposed.

Traders check out all daily transactions executed through brokers at the end of each day, and the back office compares all trading details against printed records when possible. Moreover, the netting agreements developed in the major trading centers such as New York eliminate the need for executing payments for each individual trade. A single net payment is made at the end of the day to another counterparty. (Netting agreements are discussed in detail in Chapter 9.) These processes eliminate the possibility of making payments before the end of the day. Occasionally, brokers submit incorrect names. The majority of name errors are generally fixed by the end of the day. However, some counterparty names won't be changed until the next business day. Consequently, for all practical purposes, payments could not be executed the same day.

In terms of volume, currencies around the world are traded mostly against the U.S. dollar, because the U.S. dollar is the currency of reference. The U.S. dollar's role as currency of reference reflects the United States' economic and political position in the international arena. The other major currencies are the euro, followed by the Japanese yen, the British pound, and the Swiss franc. Other currencies with significant spot market shares are the Canadian dollar and the Australian dollar.

In addition, a significant share of trading takes place in the currencies crosses, a non-dollar instrument whereby foreign currencies are quoted against other foreign currencies, such as euro against Japanese yen.

There are good reasons for the popularity of currency spot trading. Profits (or losses) are realized quickly in the spot market, due to market volatility. In addition, since spot deals mature in only two business days, the time exposure to credit risk is limited. Turnover in the spot market has been increasing dramatically, thanks to the combination of inherent profitability and reduced credit risk.

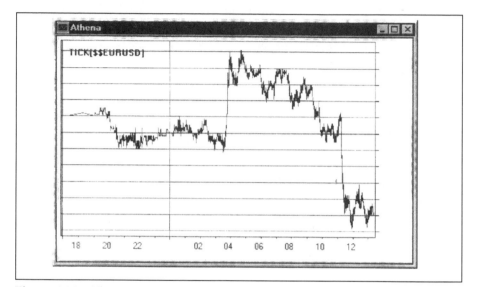

Figure 11.2. The exchange rate in a major currency, such as the euro, may change up to 18,000 times in an active trading day. *(Source: Bridge Information Systems, Inc.)*

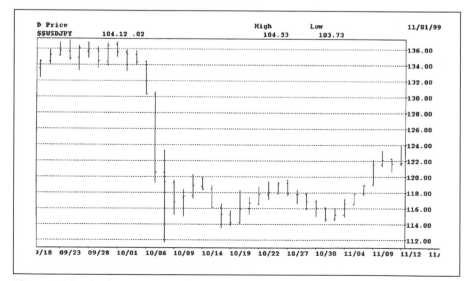

Figure 11.3. Dollar/yen in October 1998. *(Source: Bridge Information Systems, Inc.)*

The spot market is characterized by high liquidity and high volatility. In an active global trading day (24 hours), the euro/dollar exchange rate may change its value 18,000 times. (See Figure 11.2.) How quickly does the exchange rate move? There is no easy answer, and trying to determine an average time is not useful. An exchange rate may "fly" 200 pips in a matter of seconds if the market gets wind of a significant event. For example, when dollar/yen collapsed under the pressure of long liquidation by hedge funds in October 1998, the dollar shed nearly 12 yen on the day. (See Figure 11.3.)

On the other hand, the exchange rate may remain quite static for extended periods of time, even in excess of an hour, when one market is almost finished trading and waiting for the next market to take over. This is a common occurrence toward the end of the New York trading day. Since California failed in the late 1980s to provide the link between the New York and Tokyo markets, there is a technical trading gap between around 4:30 PM and 6 PM EDT. In the New York market, the majority of transactions occur between 8 AM and 12 PM, when the New York and European markets overlap. The activity drops sharply in the afternoon, over 50 percent in fact, when New York loses the international trading support. (See Figure 11.4.) Overnight trading is limited, as very few banks have overnight desks. Most of the banks send their overnight orders to branches or other banks that operate in the active time zones.

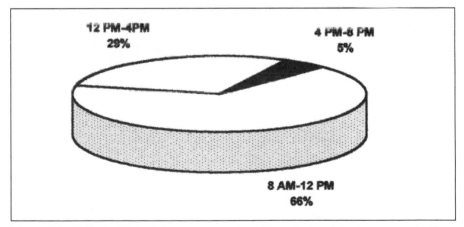

Figure 11.4. In the United States spot market, the majority of deals are executed between 8 AM and noon, when European traders are still active. The turnover drops in the afternoon as liquidity dries up. Overnight activity is limited. *(Source: Bridge Information Systems, Inc.)*

TYPICAL SPOT TRADES

In the spot market, any amount may be traded, odd or even, denominated in U.S. dollars or in foreign currency. However, the standard tends to be USD 10,000,000. Unless otherwise specified, a call for spot USD/JPY will be interpreted as for USD/JPY 10,000,000. If the caller tries to execute a different amount, even if it is smaller, the deal may be fully canceled by the market maker. Therefore, the caller must make sure to mention beforehand the amount he or she wants to trade if it differs from the standard.

Not all players trade USD 10,000,000. Other typical amounts traded are US$5 million and US$3 million lots.

THE MAJOR PLAYERS

The major players in the spot market are naturally the commercial banks and the investment banks, followed by hedge funds and corporate customers. In the interbank market, the majority of the deals are international, reflecting worldwide exchange rate competition and advanced telecommunication systems. However, corporate customers tend to focus their foreign exchange activity domestically, or to trade through foreign banks operating in the same time zone. Although the hedge funds' and corporate customers' business in foreign exchange has been growing, banks remain the predominant trading force.

EXECUTING THE TRADE

In executing their deals, spot traders have a language of their own. They use a concise code to get their point across quickly and accurately, leaving no room for interpretation.

Let's take a look at a typical spot trade:

Example:
A trader from Banca Prima, who just heard from one of her market contacts that a large investment bank is buying EUR/USD, calls AllesBanken on Monday, August 1.

Banca Prima: "EUR 10 PLS." In direct (and polite) translation, this means: "May I have a spot price in EUR/USD 10 million, please?"

AllesBanken's trader replies: "35–40. " In a more complete translation, this may stand for "My price for the above amount is 1.1035–40." The big figure (in our case 1.10) is rarely stated, as traders are presumed to know where the market is.

If Banca Prima's trader likes the price and wants to buy EUR/USD at 40, she will press a preset key (B, for instance) and the software will

automatically display on the screen in capital letters: "I BUY
EUR/USD 10,000,000 AT 1.1040 VALUE AUGUST 3. MY USD TO
Banca Prima/NEW YORK. THANKS VERY MUCH FOR YOUR
NICE PRICE."

Finally, AllesBanken confirms the deal by pressing a preset key for
confirmation. The software will display the following: "TO CON-
FIRM I SELL USD 10,000,000 AT 1.1040 VALUE AUGUST 3. MY
EUR TO AllesBanken/FFT. THKS FOR CALLING. BIFN." BIFN
stands for "Bye for now." The deal is done.

If the spot trade is done via a dedicated phone line, an increasingly
disappearing act, the same information is exchanged, although the format
may be slightly different.

Example:

Banca Prima calls AllesBanken: "Spot euro in 10, please."

AllesBanken replies: "35–40."

Banca Prima: "Mine" (or "I buy" or "I take").

AllesBanken: "All right, I sell you 10 at 40. Big figure is 1.10. All
agreed, please?"

Banca Prima: "Yep, all agreed. Thanks, friend. Ciao."

AllesBanken: "Aufwiedersehen."

PROFIT AND LOSS

What spot currency trader doesn't dream of being "turbocharged" from an
abysmal loss to a stellar profit by the "divine" intervention of a central bank?
The scenario involves three players. In order of their stage entry, they are:

1. A rather aggressive customer, who is looking to sell a large
   amount of USD/JPY to a bank, on expectation of worsening trade
   relationships between the United States and Japan and a consequent appreciation of the Japanese yen.
2. A weathered currency trader, who is aware of the U.S.–Japan
   trade frictions but believes that the Japanese yen is too strong, and
   expects the U.S. dollar to strengthen against the yen.
3. A "divine" central bank, who fears that the foreign exchange market is getting out of hand in its buying of the Japanese yen.

The customer, Ichiban, calls First International for a price in
USD/JPY 100 million. The trader, Don Joe, quotes 121.40–50. Ichiban

sells USD 100 million against JPY at 121.40. As Don scrambles for cover, being able to sell only USD 20 million at 121.40, the USD/JPY suddenly drops to 120.60. Understandably tense, Don is just preparing to cut his loss when the Bank of Japan intervenes, lifting the USD/JPY to 122.40, 100 pips higher than where he bought. Don Joe sells the balance of the US$80 million, realizing a profit of about $781,250, and he instantly becomes a folk hero in the wild world of foreign exchange. Despite its dreamlike quality, this scenario accurately described the market behavior of the USD/JPY in April 1994.

The bottom line is important in all financial markets, but in currency spot trading the antes always seem to be higher as a result of the demand from all around the world.

The profit and loss can be either *realized* or *unrealized*. The realized P&L is a certain amount of money netted when a position is closed. The unrealized P&L consists of an uncertain amount of money that an outstanding position would roughly generate if it were closed at the current rate. The unrealized P&L changes continuously in tandem with the exchange rate.

Let's take a look at the calculations. For the currencies quoted in European terms, the spot profit and loss (P&L) is calculated as follows:

$$P\&L = \frac{(\text{Selling average rate} - \text{Buying average rate}) * \text{US dollar amount}}{\text{Closing/revaluation rate}}$$

Example:
Banca Due, which had no previous position in USD/JPY, executed six deals today. The trader first sold USD/JPY 10,000,000 at 117.25 before the release of economic data, expecting the figure to be worse than expected. The trader was correct, but the dollar fell only 25 pips. The trader took the profit by buying USD/JPY 10,000,000 at 117.00. As the USD started to rebound, two different banks called directly on the dealing system and sold to Banca Due USD/JPY 10,000,000 each at 117.10 and 117.05, respectively. However, the USD/JPY rebounded, and the trader at Banca Due took profit by selling USD/JPY 10,000,000 at 117.30 and USD/JPY 10,000,000 at 117.35.

Buy	Sell
USD/JPY 10,000,000 at 117.00	USD/ JPY 10,000,000 at 117.25
USD/JPY 10,000,000 at 117.10	USD/ JPY 10,000,000 at 117.30
USD/JPY 10,000,000 at 117.05	USD/ JPY 10,000,000 at 117.35

The end-of-day revaluation rate, or closing rate, is 117.20. This rate is necessary for the P&L calculation for the currencies quoted in European terms.

The average buying rate is 117.05 for USD/ JPY 30,000,000. The calculation of the average is made as follows:

$$\frac{(10,000,000*117.00 + 10,000,000*117.10 + 10,000,000*117.05)}{30,000,000} = 117.05$$

The average selling rate is 117.30 for USD/ JPY 30,000,000. The calculation of the average is made as follows:

$$\frac{(10,000,000*117.25 + 10,000,000*117.30 + 10,000,000*117.35)}{30,000,000} = 117.30$$

$$P\&L = \frac{[(117.30 - 117.05)*30,000,000]}{117.20} = USD\ 63,993.17$$

For the currencies quoted in American terms, such as the British pound, the spot profit and loss (P&L) is calculated as follows:

P&L = (Selling average rate − Buying average rate)*Foreign currency amount

Example:
Banco Tres, which had no previous position in GBP/USD, executed six transactions today. First it bought GBP/USD 10,000,000 at 1.5000 as the currency broke a significant resistance line. Rumors that Bank of England is buying GBP prompted Banco Tres to buy another GBP/USD 10,000,000 at 1.5005 and GBP/USD 10,000,000 at 1.5010. The profit was taken at 1.5025, 1.5030 and 1.5035 for GBP/USD 10,000,000 each, when the rumors were denied.

Buy	*Sell*
GBP/USD 10,000,000 at 1.5000	GBP/USD 10,000,000 at 1.5025
GBP/USD 10,000,000 at 1.5010	GBP/USD 10,000,000 at 1.5030
GBP/USD 10,000,000 at 1.5005	GBP/USD 10,000,000 at 1.5035

The end-of-day revaluation rate is irrelevant for the realized profit and loss in the case of currencies quoted in American terms.

The average buying rate is 1.5005 for GBP/USD 30,000,000. The calculation of the average is made as follows:

$$\frac{(10,000,000 * 1.5000 + 10,000,000 * 1.5010 + 10,000,000 * 1.5005)}{30,000,000} = 1.5005$$

The average selling rate is 1.5030 for GBP/USD 30,000,000. The calculation of the average is made as follows:

$$\frac{(10,000,000 * 1.5025 + 10,000,000 * 1.5030 + 10,000,000 * 1.5035)}{30,000,000} = 1.5030$$

$$P\&L = (1.5030 - 1.5005) * 30,000,000 = USD\ 75,000.00$$

The unrealized P&L is calculated by using the same formulas. The missing rate is replaced by the revaluation rate, and the missing amount will equal the outstanding position.

Example:

La Premiere Banque has a previous long position of USD/CHF 10,000,000 at 1.4510. The position was correct, and the USD/CHF is higher today. Today, it executes six additional trades in USD/CHF. The market moves in a tight range, but the trader is able to buy USD/CHF 10,000,000 at 1.4600 and sell it back at 1.4625; sell USD/CHF 10,000,000 at 1.4630 and buy back at 1.4610; buy again USD/CHF 10,000,000 at 1.4605 and sell this amount at 1.4635. Expecting the USD/CHF to continue to appreciate, the trader continues to hold a long USD/CHF 10,000,000 position.

Previous position: + USD/CHF 10,000,000 at 1.4510

Buy	*Sell*
USD/CHF 10,000,000 at 1.4600	USD/CHF 10,000,000 at 1.4625
USD/CHF 10,000,000 at 1.4610	USD/CHF 10,000,000 at 1.4630
USD/CHF 10,000,000 at 1.4605	USD/CHF 10,000,000 at 1.4635

The end-of-day revaluation rate is 1.4620. For the unrealized P&L, the end-of-day or closing rate is important for supplementing the missing exchange rate for currencies quoted in both European and American terms.

The average buying rate is 1.458125 for USD/CHF 40,000,000. The calculation of the average is made as follows:

$$\frac{(10,000,000 * 1.4510 + 10,000,000 * 1.4600 + 10,000,000 * 1.4610 + 10,000,000 * 1.4605)}{40,000,000} = 1.458125$$

The average selling rate is 1.4630 for USD/CHF 30,000,000. The calculation of the average is made as follows:

$$\frac{(10,000,000*1.4625 + 10,000,000*1.4630 + 10,000,000*1.4635)}{30,000,000} = 1.4630$$

$$\text{P\&L realized} = \frac{[(1.4630 - 1.458125)*30,000,000]}{1.4620} = \text{USD } 100,034.20$$

$$\text{P\&L unrealized} = \frac{[(1.4620 - 1.458125)*10,000,000]}{1.4620} = \text{USD } 26,504.79$$

SOURCES OF INFORMATION

Foreign exchange traders are information traders. Consequently, traders generally have multiple monitors displaying the most recent rates and events from around the world. The major sources of information are Bridge Information Systems, Telerate, Reuters, and Bloomberg. Generally, spot currency traders watch pages EFX= on Reuters (see Figure 11.5) and 263 (see Figure 11.6) and 262 (see Figure 11.7) on Telerate and MarketWatch on Bridge (see Figure 11.8).

	Latest Spots							
	BIDSASK	CONTRIB	LOC	SRCE	DEAL	TIME	HIGH	LOW
↑	1.0711S18	CITIBANK	NYC	CINX	CITN	14:06	1.0735	1.0684
↓	115.15S5.25	ROYAL BK CAN	TOR	RBCT	RBCT*J	14:05	115.50	114.98
↑	1.6040S50	CITIBANK	NYC	CINX	CITN*G	13:59	1.6100	1.6010
↓	1.4945S55	ROYAL BK CAN	TOR	RBCT	RBCT*C	14:08	1.4986	1.4910
↓	1.8248S60	REUTERS	RTR	RTRS		14:10	1.8308	1.8219
↓	6.1201S41	REUTERS	RTR	RTRS		14:10	6.1396	6.1105
↓	2.0561S74	REUTERS	RTR	RTRS		14:10	2.0626	2.0528
↓	1806.56S7.74	REUTERS	RTR	RTRS		14:10	1812.31	1803.70
↓	37.630S662	REUTERS	RTR	RTRS		14:10	37.757	37.578
↓	257.10S7.60	REPUBLIC NAT	NYC	RNBG	RNBA	14:10	257.50	255.95
↑	5.31S5.34	REPUBLIC NAT	NYC	RNBG	RNBA	14:09	5.39	5.30
↑	1.3600S09	REUTERS	RTR	RTRS		14:10	1.3631	1.3566
↑	0.6536S41	CITIBANK	NYC	CINX	CICM*T	13:59	0.6540	0.6497
↓	1.5021S31	BK OF NS	TOR	BNST	BNST*R	14:04	1.5045	1.4976
↓	12.8385S69	REUTERS	RTR	RTRS		14:10	12.8794	12.8182
↓	155.24S5.34	REUTERS	RTR	RTRS		14:10	155.73	154.99
↑	8.2210S10	SE BANKEN	NYC	SEBN	SEBN*S	13:54	8.2365	8.1811
↑	7.7172S92	SE BANKEN	NYC	SEBN	SEBN*L	13:54	7.7668	7.7020
↓	6.9463S83	SE BANKEN	NYC	SEBN	SEBN*H	13:54	6.9655	6.9328
↓	5.5474S11	REUTERS	RTR	RTRS		14:10	5.5651	5.5386
↓	187.05S7.17	REUTERS	RTR	RTRS		14:10	187.65	186.76
↓	303.23S3.52	PIRAEUS	ATH	BPGR	PIRE	14:09	306.48	302.93
↑	25.100S300	OGRES KOM BK	RIX	OGRE	OKBR	13:07	25.6000	24.8100
↓	432460S3010	KOCBANK	IST	KOCT	KOCT	14:08	433050	431870
↓	72.70S2.80	BUNADARBANKI	RVK	BUNA		14:08	72.90	72.77

Figure 11.5. Page EFX=. *(Source: Reuters)*

These pages display the most recent spot rates in the major currencies. Page 263 on Telerate posts the most recent five quotes in each of the four major currencies: euro, Japanese yen, Swiss franc, and British pound; while page 262 posts the most recent quotes in seven major currencies: euro, Japanese yen, Swiss franc, British pound, Australian dollar, New Zealand dollar, Canadian dollar, and the major currency crosses—

```
11/11    10:49 NYC      [TELERATE GLOBAL CURRENCY COMPOSITE]                263

                    TELERATE GARBAN DATA - PAGES 4645-4699
PAGE  BANK            GBP        GMT    PAGE  BANK             JPY         GMT
 7601 BARCLAYS    LDN 1.6218 -28 15:49   3670 B C I        MIL 104.84 -89 15:49
 3414 ZUERCHER    ZUR 1.6218 -23 15:49   3551 D G BANK     FFT 104.84 -89 15:49
 3551 D G BANK    FFT 1.6220 -30 15:49   3505 UBS WDR      ZUR 104.85 -89 15:48
 3150 R B C       TOR 1.6220 -30 15:43   3414 ZUERCHER     ZUR 104.82 -87 15:49
 3505 UBS WDR     ZUR 1.6219 -29 15:48   7601 BARCLAYS     LDN 104.82 -92 15:48
 HI 23:38    1.6285- 1.6216  15:07 LO    HI  8:20   105.31- 104.50  23:20 LO
PAGE  BANK            EUR        GMT    PAGE  BANK             CHF         GMT
 3986 CHASE       LDN 1.0405 -10 15:48   3670 B C I        MIL 1.5445 -50 15:49
 3668 C ITALIAN   MIL 1.0411 -13 15:49   3551 D G BANK     FFT 1.5445 -50 15:49
 3620 BHF BANK    FFT 1.0410 -15 15:49   3986 CHASE        LDN 1.5445 -50 15:48
47389 ING BANK    AMS 1.0410 -14 15:49   3505 UBS WDR      ZUR 1.5444 -54 15:49
 3414 ZUERCHER    ZUR 1.0410 -15 15:49   7601 BARCLAYS     LDN 1.5442 -52 15:48
 HI 07:54    1.0448- 1.0400  12:21 LO    HI 12:20    1.5465- 1.5382   9:00 LO
```

Figure 11.6.   Page 263. *(Source: Bridge Information Systems, Inc.)*

```
11/11    10:57 NYC    [ TELERATE GLOBAL CURRENCY COMPOSITE]           PAGE 262
        BANK        CTR    SPOT     GMT  PREV1 PREV2   GMT   HIGH - LOW      GMT
EUR  ING BANK   AMS 1.0403 -07  15:56 03-07 01-11 22:03  1.0449-1.0401  12:19
JPY  CITIBANK   N Y 104.85 -95  15:56 85-99 86-96 08:20  105.31-104.50  23:20
GBP  CITIBANK   N Y 1.6218 -28  14:56 21-24 18-28 22:00  1.6286-1.6219  12:00
CHF  CITIBANK   N Y 1.5452 -62  15:56 50-64 58-68 12:20  1.5465-1.5382  09:00
AUD  UBS WDR    ZUR 0.6428 -33  15:56 27-32 29-34 09:19  0.6436-0.6416  06:47
NZD  BARCLAYS   LDN 0.5134 -44  15:53 34-39 34-41 09:24  0.5140-0.5123  01:03
CAD  BARCLAYS   LDN 1.4650 -60  15:56 48-58 50-60 22:39  1.4683-1.4655  15:51
HKD  DAO HENG   H K 7.7615 -22  14:43 15-25 17-22 09:21  7.7717-7.7690  00:02
       CROSS RATES           HIGH-LOW        3 MONTH DEPOSITS   6 MONTH DEPOSITS
EUR/JPY  109.13 -17    109.92-109.00    USD     5.88- 5.98        5.72- 5.84
EUR/CHF  1.6081 -85    1.6109-1.6043    EUR     3.40- 3.46        3.38- 3.48
EUR/GBP  0.6409 -19    0.6420-0.6408    JPY     0.05- 0.15        0.05- 0.15
GBP/JPY  170.13 -23    171.27-170.03    GBP     5.65- 5.75        5.85- 5.95
CHF/JPY   67.85 -89     68.39- 67.80    TBOND 100.12-16 6.088  GLD 296.10-296.85
AUD/NZD  1.2506 -20    1.2541-1.2490    BRENT   DEC    2375-80  SILV  5.13- 5.16
AUD/JPY   67.43 -49     67.72- 67.09    SIMEX  MAR00 EURO$ 94.1200 EUROJPYS99.850
```

Figure 11.7.   Page 262. *(Source: Bridge Information Systems, Inc.)*

Telerate		MarketWatch		
Symbol	Last	Chg	Low	High
$$USDJPY	114.71	– .99	114.60	115.93
$$EURUSD	1.0569	.0001	1.0545	1.0604
$$GBPUSD	1.5982	–.0058	1.5965	1.6113
$$AUDUSD	.6502	–.0020	.5489	.6543
$$USDCHF	1.5150	–.0011	1.5105	1.5194
$$EURJPY	121.27	– 1.03	121.06	122.58
$$USDCAD	1.5150	–.0011	1.5105	1.5194

Figure 11.8. MarketWatch. *(Source: Bridge Information Systems, Inc.)*

euro/Japanese yen, euro/Swiss franc, euro/sterling, British pound/Japanese yen, Swiss franc/Japanese yen, Australian dollar/New Zealand dollar, and Australian dollar/Japanese yen—along with other financial information.

The information available on the monitors is supplemented by traders' personal networking. The objective of networking is twofold: Find out whether any large customer orders went through, and try to "feel" the mood of the market. This type of information is not available on the regular monitor pages. By the time rumors about large transactions reach the monitors, the market effect is generally diminished. Sometimes, large transactions in some currencies may have an impact on another currency. For instance, a large buying order of Swiss franc against Japanese yen may slow down an otherwise bullish U.S. dollar against euro. Swiss franc and euro are highly correlated. Therefore, the strength of the Swiss franc extrapolates to the euro as well.

STOP-LOSS

Cutting losses is painful for every trader. The ability to cut one's losses in time is the sign of a seasoned trader. Good traders are too busy trying to "read" the market to waste time on blind hope. Lesser traders become trapped, hoping for the daily miracle. They dismiss a profitable trading pattern as lucky. Even good traders may lose on numerous individual transactions. However, the losing trades are cut quickly, while the profitable trades are allowed to "run."

CHARACTERISTICS OF A
SPOT TRADER

To be successful, spot traders must embody seemingly opposite traits. They must be simultaneously flexible and firm, patient and quick to react.

Why are such contradictory qualities necessary in the current spot market?

Traders have, or at least should have, a view on the market, a scenario, a plan. This view must be backed by some reasons: fundamental factors, such as the state of the domestic economy relative to other significant economies; chart signals; or a combination of the two. Having a set plan gives the trader mental toughness and a psychological basis that will provide direction in an otherwise chaotic environment.

With the scenario in place, the trader starts trading, and the market behavior seems to coincide with the plan. But all of a sudden, the exchange rate starts moving abruptly in the "wrong" direction. There is a rumor in the market that a central bank is intervening. The trader feels that his or her view is still fundamentally correct, that in time the market will indeed trade the "right" way. In the short term, however, what is the trader to do?

Imagine yourself hearing on the radio that a train is out of control, quickly running to the railroad tracks, and you are waiting right in the middle, believing that the train will still be able to stop. If you are correct, that's nice; but if you are wrong, you have a problem. A good spot trader soon learns that staying alive is essential to being profitable. A single encounter with the runaway train of the exchange market may prove dangerous to the trader's health. Therefore, while it is important that a trader have a specific market view and go about implementing it, it is equally important to be fast and flexible enough to adjust to changing market conditions.

The spot trader must be able to quickly distinguish between a major adverse change and a temporary move. If the trader is long (bought) $5 million against yen at 120.00 and the exchange rate moves a little lower, to 119.50, the trader may want to buy $5 million more at the lower price while supporting the bids, or simply wait it out if the move seems to be minor. If buying more, the new average price will be 119.75, so the rate must move up by only 25 pips for the trader to break even. Of course, if the trader is wrong, then the long position will be twice as large as the original one in a falling market.

The reverse is true for a perceived significant adverse exchange rate move. The trader must be able to quickly cut the loss and wait, or reverse the position. If the same long $5 million against yen at 120.00 position is in place, and the trader decides that 120.00 was toppish, he or she may decide at 119.70 to either cut the position by selling $5 million against yen, or fully reverse the position by selling $10 million against yen. The new position is short by $5 million against yen.

Spot traders must be able to readily cut through the abundance of information, and quickly value only the significant factors. This ability is mostly an acquired trait, an art rather than a science. There is only so much quantification to be done. Beyond that, it is up to the trader to mentally process the information and implement the results.

TYPES OF TRADERS

Some traders have a strategic approach, and others trade "in-and-out" all day long. Both types of traders play a significant role in the market. The strategic players, or proprietary traders, focus more on the "big picture." They tend to trade larger positions and keep them for much longer periods of time. The "in-and-out" traders, who constitute the largest group, provide daily liquidity in the market. They rarely have a strong view on the market, focusing instead on the daily market flow. Their profit margin per deal is generally lower than that of the strategic traders, but they make more deals.

Traders may also be categorized by the level of risk they are able to manage. There is no magic formula for determining the optimum level of risk for each trader. This level can be determined only through trial and error. It is less important to know how much risk a trader is willing to take; it is vital to know at what level the trader's performance peaks. The size of the individual position should therefore reflect not the size of the trader's ego, but his or her capacity to maximize trading performance. This decision is made by the chief trader.

The more risk-averse traders take positions after the release of economic data, for instance, rather than going with a position into the number. Most traders do the former, because they need reinforcement from the market behavior. Fewer traders will take positions before the release of economic data. Ultimately, it is the trader's performance that counts—the return on investment—not his or her thirst for risk taking.

CONCLUSION

Once spot traders decide on a plan, they must stick to their guns, oblivious to any extraneous distractions. Sometimes, a trader would like to go long in a specific currency. Before that happens, however, another counterparty calls and buys from our original trader, who is now short, contrary to the plan. If squaring off now, the trader may incur a small loss, so he or she decides to wait a little longer in order to break even. Once that happens, our trader will go back to the main plan of going long on that currency. But the currency is moving higher, the loss is getting bigger, and the trader remains stuck further with a losing position. No matter how much our trader complains about the unfairness of the market, about the frustration of having the right idea but being pushed in the wrong position, nothing will change. Therefore, a trader must remember to follow his or her own judgment. Even if small losses result, successful traders exit positions that do not fit their trading view. If the situation is not clear, it is much better for traders to sit on the fence for a while thinking things over, than to face the runaway train, blindly hoping that it will stop.

"Let the profits run, cut the losses short" is a common saying among traders. Its methodical implementation usually extends the trading life of most players. The gambler's approach, going for broke, generally ends in the gambler's own finale, the sad loss. Traders must have a systematic and steady approach to the market. Smaller, consistent profits tend to be preferable to huge P&L fluctuations.

Nobody is bigger than the market. At times, large players, naturally, will be able to have a significant impact on the market. But any artificial move will be very short-lived, regardless of how many billions of dollars have been sacrificed. The living example of this fact was the defeat of the central banks of the European Monetary System in September 1992 and the summer of 1993 in their attempt to prop up artificial ranges in foreign exchange. Because most players are generally small in size and scope, the individual impact will likely be smaller. Therefore, the challenge is not to *be* the market, but to *read* the market. Riding the wave is much more rewarding than being hit by it.

12 The Forward Currency Market

Foreign exchange players have diverse interests in the market, in terms of currencies and delivery dates. Whereas most volume occurs in the spot market, a very large segment of currency trades mature past the spot value date—the standard two business days. Foreign exchange trades that mature beyond the spot dates are known, collectively, as forward trades.

THE FORWARD FOREIGN CURRENCY MARKETPLACE

The forward currency market consists of two instruments: forward outright deals and swaps. Generally, this market includes only cash transactions. Therefore, currency futures contracts, although a special breed of forward outright transactions, are analyzed separately.

According to figures published by the Bank for International Settlements, the percentage share of the forward market was 57 percent in 1998. (See Figure 12.1.) Translated into U.S. dollars, out of an estimated daily gross turnover of US$1.49 trillion, the total forward market represents US$900 billion. (See Figure 12.2.)

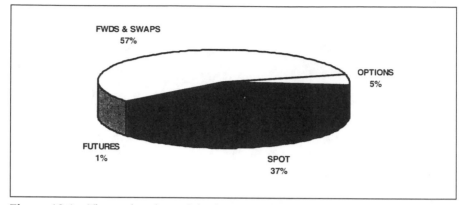

Figure 12.1. The market share of the foreign exchange instruments as of 1998. *(Source: the Bank for International Settlements)*

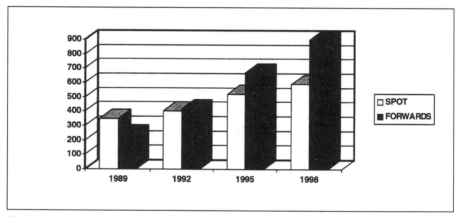

Figure 12.2. Spot volume versus forward volume. *(Source: Bridge Information Systems, Inc.)*

GENERAL CHARACTERISTICS OF THE FORWARD MARKET

In the forward market there is no norm with regard to the settlement dates, which range from 3 days to 3 years. Volume in currency swaps longer than one year tends to be light but, technically, there is no impediment to making these deals. Any date past the spot date and within the above range may be a forward settlement, provided that it is a valid business day for both currencies.

The forward markets are decentralized markets, with players around the world entering into a variety of deals either on a one-on-one basis or through brokers. In contrast, the currency futures market is a centralized market, in which all the deals are executed on trading floors provided by different exchanges. Whereas in the futures market only a handful of foreign currencies may be traded in multiples of standardized amounts, the forward markets are open to any currencies in any amount.

What is the difference between the forward outright and the swap market?

A *forward outright deal* is an individual trade that matures (in general) past the spot delivery date. Because its value date differs from the spot, intuitively, we must expect that the forward rate will also differ from the spot rate.

A *swap deal* is unusual among the rest of the foreign exchange instruments in the fact that it consists of two deals, or legs. All the other transactions consist of single deals. In its original form, a swap deal is a combination of a spot deal and a forward outright deal.

Before we approach these instruments in more detail, let's take a look at several technical aspects germane to forward pricing.

THE FORWARD PRICE

The forward price consists of two significant parts: the *spot exchange rate* and the *forward spread*. The forward spread is also known as the *forward points* or the *forward pips*. The forward spread is necessary for adjusting the spot rate for specific settlement dates different from the spot date. It holds, then, that the *maturity date* is another determining factor of the forward price.

THE SPOT RATE

The spot rate is the main building block. The forward price is derived from the spot price by adjusting the spot price with the forward spread, so it follows that both forward outright and swap deals are derivative instruments.

FORWARD SPREADS

Figure 12.3 presents major currencies' forward outright spreads on page 9375 on Telerate. On this page, the spot rates for some of the major currencies are followed by the forward spreads for several standard forward dates: spot/next (S/N), one week, one month, and so on up to one year.

```
[TELERATE - FORWARD CURRENCIES]                    PAGE   9375
             EUR/USD            USD/JPY          GBP/USD           AUD/USD
    INDEX

    SPT      1.0400-05         104.90-00        1.6208-18         0.6425-30
    O/N      1.28/    1.31    -1.77/   -1.27     75/   17475     0.11/    0.16
    T/N      1.29/    1.38    -4.47/   -4.42    0.18/    0.22    0.12/    0.17
    S/N      0.71/    0.72    -1.65/   -1.45    0.09/    0.12    0.15/    0.18
    1WK      4.73/    4.94   -10.83/  -10.73     0.6/     0.8    0.44/    0.49
    2WK                      -21.80/  -21.30        /
    3WK                      -32.60/  -32.10        /
    1MO      20.5/    22.7    -47.0/   -46.6     2.5/     3.9     1.5/     3.0
    2MO     49.20/   49.40  -107.80/ -107.40   13.75/   14.25    8.10/    8.40
    3MO      69.3/    69.7     -154/    -152    13.5/    16.5     9.8/    11.3
    4MO     89.00/   89.40  -199.75/ -198.75   13.50/   14.50   10.50/   11.00
    5MO    112.00/  112.50  -253.25/ -252.25   13.75/   14.75   10.60/   11.10
    6MO       129/    131     -301/    -297    13.5/    15.5    10.5/    14.5
    9MO    193.25/  194.25  -449.00/ -446.00   10.00/   12.00    6.30/    7.30
    1YR       254/    258     -600/    -595     0.5/     5.5     4.3/     6.8
```

Figure 12.3. Page 9375. *(Source: Telerate, Inc.)*

Just as in the case of the spot market, the left side of the quote is the bid side, and the right side is the offer side. Note, though, that the bid–offer relationship as just described only applies if the swap is executed in a foreign currency amount. If the swap is done in U.S. dollars, the right side of the forward quote becomes the bid and, conversely, the left side is the offer.

Example:
Your quotes are:
   USD/JPY spot = 117.96–06
   USD/JPY 3 month forward spread = 153.88 – 152.38

1. A customer sells and buys with you a ¥500 million (foreign currency amount) swap in 3 months. Therefore, you buy and sell ¥500 million swap at 153.88. Your prices are:

   118.06 for spot (because buying yen is equivalent to selling dollars), and

   116.521 in three months (because the forward spread is subtracted from the spot rate: 118.06 – 1.5388).

2. A customer sells and buys with you a USD/JPY 5 million (dollar amount) swap in 3 months. Therefore, you buy and sell USD/JPY (equivalent to selling and buying JPY) 5 million swap at 152.38 (forward spread). Your prices are:

117.96 for spot, and

116.436 for 3 months (because the forward spread is subtracted from the spot rate: 117.96 − 1.5238).

The typical misconception about forward prices is that they represent an expectation as to the direction of one currency in terms of another. Drawing on the previous example, the spot USD/JPY of 117.96 and the 3-month forward outright USD/JPY of 116.436 would suggest that the U.S. dollar is bound to be weaker in the future. This is false.

Certainly, any currency price, spot and forward, will always reflect the expectation of future price behavior. But this is not an expectation based on one currency being stronger or weaker than another. The forward spread is simply the result of the interest rate differential between the currencies traded, adjusted for the number of days until the maturity date. This market expectation of future changes in the interest rate differential is, however, essential for forward currency pricing.

Finally, the forward spreads may be influenced for specific periods or as a whole. Let's take an example of a situation in which only one of the forward rates for a standard period will be influenced. Let's assume that the real interest rates in a country have been low for a relatively long period of time, and the economy of that country has enjoyed low inflation. If that country's economic indicators that measure inflation, such as the Producer Price Index (PPI) or the Consumer Price Index (CPI), show that inflation has risen in two consecutive months, the market may expect that if inflation continues to rise for a third straight month, then the central bank of that country might increase the discount rate. Higher interest rates, of course, constitute the tool of choice for fighting inflation.

On the market expectation that the central bank will raise interest rates soon, the interest rate differential has a strong potential to increase for the one-month term, but this will have limited or no impact on the other standard settlement dates.

As one of the main factors in the pricing formula of forward spreads, changes in the spot rate will automatically trigger changes in the forward rates. The forward pricing method is presented in the section on interest rate differential later in this chapter.

INTRODUCTION TO THE TYPES OF FORWARD SPREADS

To calculate the 3-month forward outright USD/JPY rate, the forward spread was subtracted from the spot price. This type of spread is called *dis-*

count. If the forward spread is added to the spot price, it is called *premium.* On rare occasions, the forward spread is zero, and naturally the forward price will simply equal the spot price. This type of spread is known as *par.*

IDENTIFYING THE TYPES OF FORWARD SPREADS

Before learning how to calculate the forward spread, let's see how a player is able to identify a premium spread from a discount spread.

If the bid side (left side) of the forward outright spread is smaller than the offer side (right side), that specific spread is a premium, and it must be added to the spot price to obtain the forward price. For example, assume that the one-year forward spread in euro is 297–299 and the spot EUR/USD is 1.0542–45. Calculating the offer side, we get 1.0545 + 0.0299 = 1.0844.

Conversely, if the bid side of the forward outright spread is larger than the offer side, then it is a discount spread, and it will be deducted from the spot rate to calculate the forward outright price. For instance, assume that the one-year forward spread in Japanese yen is 634.00–630.00 and the spot USD/JPY is 117.96–06. Calculating the bid side we get 117.96 – 6.34 = 111.62.

Forward bid < Forward offer = Premium spread

Forward bid > Forward offer = Discount spread

Of course, the minus sign in front of the spread is also an accurate hint that you are facing a discount spread.

To better understand the importance of the spot exchange rate and consequently the significance of the spot value date, we discuss premium spreads, discount spreads, and at par. We focus on several diagrams and our examples are for currencies quoted in European terms.

PREMIUM SPREAD

A premium spread is a spread in which the interest rates in one foreign currency are higher in all periods than the U.S. interest rates. In such a market, as time progresses, prices go higher, starting from the spot level, rather like climbing a staircase. (See Figure 12.4.) Alternatively, it may be easier to visualize the forward dates and the behavior of the forward prices around the spot level on a -∞/+∞ axis, with zero being replaced by the spot level. In a premium market, the prices increase past the spot price. (See Figure 12.5.)

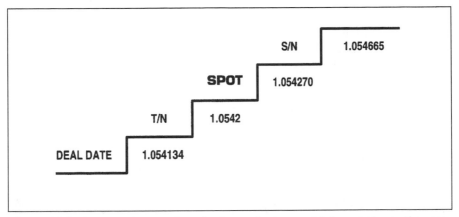

Figure 12.4. In a premium market, the forward prices are higher relative to the spot price, as time passes.

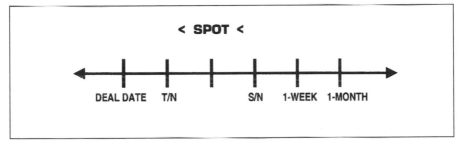

Figure 12.5. In a premium market, the forward prices are higher relative to the spot price, as time passes.

DISCOUNT SPREAD

The opposite is true for a discount market. The forward prices decrease relative to the spot exchange rate. (See Figure 12.6.) Again, it may be easier to visualize the behavior of the forward prices relative to the forward dates and around the spot level on a $+\infty/-\infty$ axis, with zero being replaced by the spot level. In a discount market, the prices decrease past the spot price. (See Figure 12.7.)

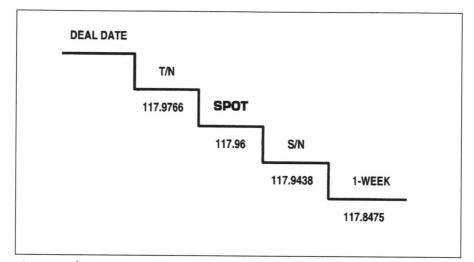

Figure 12.6. In a discount market, the forward prices are lower relative to the spot price, as time passes.

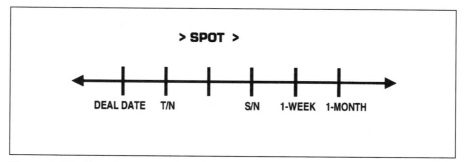

Figure 12.7. In a discount market, the forward prices are lower relative to the spot price, as time passes.

At Par

Assume that in USD/JPY, the spot price is 118.16 and the spot next (S/N) rate is − 0.0162–0.0161. Calculating the offer side, the forward price will equal:

$$118.16 - 0.0161 = 118.1439$$

METHODS OF CALCULATING THE FORWARD OUTRIGHT PRICES

Let's see now why the sum of 1.0542 (the bid of the EUR/USD spot price) and 67 (the bid of the 3-month EUR/USD forward spread) equals 1.0609. This is a common source of confusion when first approaching the forward currency markets.

By convention, traders refer to the last decimals as simply points or pips. To be mathematically correct, the 3-month EUR/USD forward spread should be displayed as 0.0067–0.00673, rather than 67–67.3. Traders, being pragmatic, cut through the less important details and focus only on the essential elements. They disregard the full forward spread format, but they don't err on their calculations.

One way to calculate the above forward price is:

$$1.0542 + 0.0067 = 1.0609$$

Now let's calculate the bid side of the 1-month EUR/USD forward price. The bid remains unchanged at 1.0542. The 1-month EUR/USD spread is 20.8–21.2. Because the bid is smaller than the offer, you will easily identify a premium spread and you will therefore add this spread to the spot rate.

In order to avoid any confusion caused by the decimal points in the forward spread, you may calculate the forward price another way. Drop the decimal point only in the spot price and add it to the forward spread, as in:

$$10542 + 20.8 = 10562.8$$

Return the decimal point to its rightful place to obtain the correct forward price:

$$10562.8 \Rightarrow 1.05628$$

Based on the foreign exchange rates you have seen so far, you may have gotten used to seeing four decimals, or two decimals in the case of the Japanese yen. There is no problem with having more decimals, and you do not have to round up the forward exchange rates to the perceived standard number of decimals.

Of course, both methods of calculation will reach the same result. Yet, if you are just starting, you may find one easier to visualize than the other.

Let's take another example and calculate the 1-year forward outright price of the USD/JPY. First, let's identify whether it is a premium or a discount spread, in order to know whether to add or subtract the 1-year forward spread from the spot price of 117.96.

The 1-year forward spread in USD/JPY is 634–630. The bid is larger than the offer, signaling a discount spread, so you must deduct. If we stick to the same side of the price, the bid side, then the 1-year forward price in USD/JPY looks like this:

$$117.96 - 6.34 = 111.62$$

Using a different term, 3 months, the forward price in USD/JPY is calculated as follows:

$$\text{Forward spread} = 153.88 - 152.38 = \text{discount}$$

$$\text{Spot price} = 117.96\text{–}118.06$$

$$\text{Bid side forward price } 11796 - 153.88 = 11642.12 \Rightarrow 116.4212$$

Now that you're able to identify all types of forward spreads, let's find out how they are calculated and what their relationship is to the interest rates.

THE INTEREST RATE DIFFERENTIAL

The interest rate differential is a determining factor in forward pricing. Single interest rates are not sufficient in foreign exchange, since any transaction automatically involves two currencies. Therefore, in order to be able to measure the change or the expectation of change in the future value of a currency in terms of another, two interest rates are necessary. Each of the eurocurrencies is quoted for different standard forward periods, similar to the periods in the forward currencies quotes.

Eurocurrencies provide an excellent tool for traders to calculate the forward spreads. The formula commonly used to determine the forward spread is:

$$\text{Forward spread} = S \times (E_f - E_\$) \times (t/360 \text{ or } 365) \times 100$$

where

S = spot

E_f = Euro foreign currency

$E_\$$ = Eurodollar

t = days to maturity

Notes:

1. If the interest rate differential between two currencies quoted in European terms $(E_f - E_\$)$ is positive, then the forward spread is

positive, which indicates that the spread is a premium. If the interest rate differential $(E_f - E_\$)$ is negative, then the forward spread is negative, which indicates that the spread is a discount. If the interest rate differential $(E_f - E_\$)$ is zero, then the spread is at par, and the spot exchange rate equals the forward exchange rate.

2. If the interest rate differential of one currency quoted in American terms and another currency quoted in European terms $(E_f - E_\$)$ is positive, then the forward spread is positive, which indicates that the spread is a discount. If the interest rate differential $(E_f - E_\$)$ is negative, then the forward spread is negative, which indicates that the spread is a premium. If the interest rate differential $(E_f - E_\$)$ is zero, then the spread is at par, and the spot exchange rate equals the forward exchange rate.

3. To annualize the forward spread, the number of days to maturity is divided by 360 days for most of the currencies and by 365 days for the Commonwealth currencies. This is a convention.

4. It is generally irrelevant whether the trader uses the bid, the offer, or an average of the spot rate to calculate the forward spread, because the object of swap trading is the forward spread itself, not the spot rate.

Example:
The 1-month spread in USD/CHF is calculated as follows:

$S = 1.5055$

Euroswiss $= 4^5/_8 - 4^3/_4$

Eurodollar $= 3^1/_{16} - 3^3/_{16}$

$t = 33$ days

Forward spread (bid) $= 1.5055 \times (4.6252 - 3.1875) \times$
$(33/360) \times 100 = 19.84$

Forward spread (offer) $= 1.5055 \times (4.75 - 3.0625) \times$
$(33/360) \times 100 = 23.29$

The forward spread thus calculated is marginally wider than the broker's price: 21–23. The tighter spread is the result of the fact that brokers have access to a larger pool of prices and consequently are able to optimize the prices.

Another method of obtaining forward spreads involves the individual calculation of the interest rates. The forward spreads are calculated as follows:

$$IR_f = S_f \times E_f \times (t/360 \text{ or } 365)$$
$$IR_\$ = S_\$ \times E_\$ \times (t/360)$$

where

IR_f = foreign interest rate

$IR_\$$ = U.S. interest rate

S_f = spot exchange rate in terms of the U.S. dollar

$S_\$$ = spot exchange rate in terms of itself

E_f = Euro foreign currency

$E_\$$ = Eurodollar

t = number of days until maturity

$$FR = (S_f + IR_f)/(S_\$ + IR_\$)$$

where

FR = forward rate

$$FS = FR - S_f$$

where

FS = forward spread

Example:

Using one of the previous examples:

E_f = Euroswiss = $4^5/_8 - 4^3/_4$

$E_\$$ = $3^1/_{16} - 3^3/_{16}$

t = 33 days (about one month)

S_f = 1.5055

$S_\$$ = 1

The bid is calculated as follows:

IR_f = 1.5055 × 0.04625 × (33/360) = .0064

$IR_\$$ = 1 × .031875 × (33/360) = .0029

FR = (1.5055 + .0064)/(1 + .0029) = 1.5075

FS = 1.5075 − 1.5055 = .20 or 20 forward pips

The offer is calculated as follows:

$IR_f = 1.5055 \times 0.0475 \times (33/360) = .0066$

$IR_\$ = 1 \times .030625 \times (33/360) = .0028$

$FR = (1.5055 + 1 .0066)/(1 + .0028) = 1.5079$

$FS = 1.5079 - 1.5055 = .24$ or 24 forward pips

This approach compares favorably with the original one.

Figure 12.8 presents a popular source of information in foreign exchange: pages 272 and 273 on Telerate. The pages display the major eurodeposit or eurocurrency rates: eurodollars and euroyen.

```
                                                      Mon Nov 01 09:39:06 1999
   Telerate
                                 Analytics/Pages
   11/01      09:31 NYC        [EURO DEPOSITS & FORWARDS]           PAGE    272
                                                            01/11 14:31 GMT
```

	DEPOSITS				FORWARDS AGAINST USD			
	SOURCE	CTR	RATE	GMT	SOURCE	CTR	RATE	GMT
O/N	ALLIED	DUB	2.70-2.80	11:38	O/N LEONIA	HEL	+0.7/	+0.9 07:07
T/N	ALLIED	DUB	2.70-2.80	11:38	T/N UBS WOR	ZUR	+0.76/	+0.81 13:25
1WK	DEUTSCHE	FFT	2.75-2.85	14:02	1WK UBS WOR	ZUR	+5.63/	+5.84 13:12
1MO	DEUTSCHE	FFT	2.78-2.84	14:02	1MO UBS WOR	ZUR	+24.2/	+24.6 14:20
2MO	DEUTSCHE	FFT	2.78-2.84	14:02	2MO UBS WOR	ZUR	+45.7/	+46.1 14:30
3MO	DEUTSCHE	FFT	2.83-2.89	14:02	3MO UBS WOR	ZUR	+73.7/	+74.0 14:27
6MO	UBS WOR	ZUR	3.32-3.45	13:07	6MO B N Z	WEL	+131/	+134 14:29
9MO	DEUTSCHE	FFT	3.48-3.54	14:02	9MO UBS WOR	ZUR	+199.7/	+200.7 14:29
1YR	RABOBANK	UTR	3.60 3.69	14:22	1YR UBS WOR	ZUR	+262.7/	+264.1 14:30
	EUR/USD				2YR UBS WOR	ZUR	+453.5/	+473.5 14:16
3721	BGL	LUX	1.0638 -48	14:31	3YR CHASE	LDN	+609/	+670 07:32
	EUR/GBP				4YR CHASE	LDN	+727/	+808 07:32
47389	I N G	AMS	0.6396 -02	14:30	5YR CHASE	LDN	+849/	+1000 07:32

```
                                                      Mon Nov 01 09:38:57 1999
   Telerate
                                 Analytics/Pages
   11/01      09:30 NYC     [JAPANESE YEN DEPOSITS AND FORWARDS]     PAGE 273
                                                            01/11 14:30 GMT
```

	DEPOSITS				FORWARDS AGAINST USD			
	SOURCE	CTR	RATE	GMT	SOURCE	CTR	RATE	GMT
O/N	INDOSUEZ	H K	0.02-0.13	08:44	O/N FUJI	TOK	-1.6/	-1.5 00:22
T/N	ABN AMRO	AMS	0.02-0.10	07:12	T/N SOC GEN	PAR	-3.07/	-3.02 14:17
1WK	INDOSUEZ	H K	0.01-0.12	00:31	1WK R B C	TOR	-12.4/	-12.1 12:48
1MO	INDOSUEZ	H K	0.09-0.21	00:31	1MO B N Z	WEL	-51/	-48 14:16
2MO	INDOSUEZ	H K	0.12-0.25	00:32	2MO CITI	N Y	-105.6/	-105.1 14:09
3MO	ABN AMRO	AMS	0.17-0.27	08:17	3MO B N Z	WEL	-156/	-153 14:15
6MO	INDOSUEZ	H K	0.09-0.21	00:32	6MO B N Z	WEL	-308/	-304 14:29
9MO	ABN AMRO	AMS	0.13-0.23	08:18	9MO B N Z	WEL	-452/	-446 14:20
1YR	ABN AMRO	AMS	0.13-0.23	08:18	1YR SOC GEN	PAR	-602.50/	-598.50 14:24
	USD/JPY				2YR FUJI	TOK	-1185/	-1165 07:46
44567	DRESDNER	FFT	104.12 -26	14:28	3YR FUJI	TOK	-1711/	-1681 07:52
	EUR/JPY				4YR FUJI	TOK	-2161/	-2121 07:52
47389	I N G	AMS	109.82 -88	14:30	5YR FUJI	TOK	-2555/	-2505 07:53

Figure 12.8. Pages 272 and 273. *(Source: Telerate, Inc.)*

So far, we have discussed two of the three determining factors in forward pricing: the interest rate differential and the spot exchange rate. Let's focus now on the last factor: the maturity date.

THE MATURITY DATES

Just as the spot exchange rate is the most important rate in foreign exchange, the spot value date is the most significant maturity date. All the other maturity dates are set up based on the spot date. Remember that the spot date means that the deal matures two business days from the day the deal was made (with the exception of the Canadian dollar). The two business days must be valid in both of the countries originating the currencies.

STANDARD FORWARD VALUE DATES

As you can see in Figure 12.3, there are several standard forward value dates. Any maturity date falling in one week, one month, one year, or a multiple of these periods is known as *standard maturity date* or *standard value date*. Other standard maturity dates are the *tomorrow/next* (*T/N*), which means that the value date is the next business day or one day prior to the spot date; and the *spot next* (*S/N*), which matures one business day past the spot date or in three business days. Finally, there is the *cash date*, when the deal date coincides with the maturity or delivery date.

In addition to the standard forward value dates, there are *odd maturity dates*. An odd maturity date is any valid day that is not a standard value date. This characteristic emphasizes both the liquidity and the flexibility of the overall forward markets. In contrast, the currency futures markets have only four delivery dates annually.

Let's take a look at Table 12.1 and discuss several characteristics of the value dates. As already mentioned, the forward dates are based on the spot dates. For instance, a customer who inquires about a 1-month forward outright price means one month from the spot date, not from the deal date. In the case of the monthly standard dates, the forward, or long, date is calculated as date-to-date. That is, if the current date is July 19 and the spot date falls on July 21, then the 1-month forward date should fall on August 21. Because August 21 falls on a weekend (or if it fell on a holiday), the delivery date will move ahead to the next immediate valid business day: August 23.

Table 12.1

Sunday	Monday	Tuesday	Wednesday	Thursday	July Friday	Saturday
				1	2	3
4	5	6	7	8	9	10
11	12	13	14	15	16	17
18	19	20	21	22	23	24
25	26	27	28	29	30	31

Sunday	Monday	Tuesday	Wednesday	Thursday	August Friday	Saturday
1	2	3	4	5	6	7
8	9	10	11	12	13	14
15	16	17	18	19	20	21
22	23	24	25	26	27	28
29	30	31				

END-OF-MONTH VALUE DATES

So far, it's all pretty straightforward. Let's change the scenario a little: The new current date is February 24. Referring to Table 12.2, what is the 1-month forward date? Tempting as the answer may be, the value date is not March 26. The reason is that the spot date falls on February 26, the last day of the month (in terms of business days). This means that the 1-month forward value date is March 31, the last business day in March. When the spot date falls on the last day of the month, then the 1-month forward date or any other monthly multiple falls, by convention, on the last day of a month as well. This exception is commonly observed in the market, so the trader or salesperson must remember it and make sure that the counterparty is aware of it. Through mistake or lack of knowledge, the *end-of-month–end-of-month rule* is sometimes not observed by both parties. This failure generally creates animosity among players and, at times, financial penalties.

What happens if, on January 27, a customer asks for a 1-month forward price? What will be the forward date? Since the spot falls on January 29, the delivery date must fall on the last business day of February, which is February 26.

Two observations are in order. First, unlike the standard monthly delivery dates, when the long date falls on the same day date as the spot but in a different month, and it will go forward to the next business day if the original long date is not a valid business date, the end-of-month–end-of-month rule allows the long date to move either forward or backward. In the previous example, the long date was moved backward. Conversely, if a one-month forward price is executed on February 24, the spot falls on February 26 and the long date will fall on March 31. In this case, the long date was moved forward.

Second, how can both January 29–February 26 and February 26–March 31 periods be called 1-month terms? After all, they do have different numbers of days and different prices, even assuming a similar interest rate differential and a constant spot exchange rate. Remember the forward pricing formula presented earlier in the chapter:

$$\text{Forward Spread} = S \times (E_f - E_\$) \times (t/360 \text{ or } 365) \times 100$$

where

S = spot exchange rate

E_f = Euro foreign currency

$E_\$$ = Eurodollar

$E_f - E_\$ = \Delta$ Euro

t = days to maturity

Although the traders discussed the forward deal in terms of one month, the calculation is always made in terms of days. None of the players is open to any undue risk or opportunity when asking for a monthly termed price rather than a price on a number of days, because, solely from this point of view, the number of days in a month is irrelevant.

Table 12.2.

Sunday	Monday	Tuesday	Wednesday	Thursday	January Friday	Saturday
					1	2
3	4	5	6	7	8	9
10	11	12	13	14	15	16
17	18	19	20	21	22	23
24	25	26	27	28	29	30
31						

Sunday	Monday	Tuesday	Wednesday	Thursday	February Friday	Saturday
	1	2	3	4	5	6
7	8	9	10	11	12	13
14	15	16	17	18	19	20
21	22	23	24	25	26	27
28						

Sunday	Monday	Tuesday	Wednesday	Thursday	March Friday	Saturday
	1	2	3	4	5	6
7	8	9	10	11	12	13
14	15	16	17	18	19	20
21	22	23	24	25	26	27
28	29	30	31			

FORWARD PRICING FOR ODD VALUE DATES (BROKEN DATES)

Forward pricing for odd value or broken dates is executed by using the standard formula. More caution must be exercised, however, as the trader may not have the same amount of information generally available for the standard dates.

Let's take an example.

Spot USD/CHF =1.5055–60, value January 5.

Six-month spread (185 days) = 78–82, value July 7.

Nine-month spread (274 days) = 87–93 value October 5.

What is the forward spread for August 8? The number of days, counted from the spot date, is 216.

The rates for Euroswiss and Eurodollars for 6 and 9 months are as follows:

Term	Forward spread	Euroswiss	Eurodollars
6 months (185 days)	263–266	$6^7/_{16}$–$6^9/_{16}$	$3^3/_8$–$3^1/_2$
9 months (274 days)	338–343	$6^3/_{16}$–$6^5/_{16}$	$3^9/_{16}$–$3^{11}/_{16}$

The period of 216 days may be broken down into 7 months and 3 days.

One option is to receive a broker's or a bank's reliable quote for 7 months forward spread. Things would become considerably easier, because the residual period is only 3 days.

An alternative is to simply calculate the daily forward points average between the 6 and 9 months forward spreads and adjust the forward price for the number of days in the odd date (216).

$$(338 - 263) \times (216 \text{ days} - 185 \text{ days}) / (274 \text{ days} - 185 \text{ days}) = 26 \text{ (bid side)}$$

$$263 + 26 = 289$$

$$(343 - 266) \times (216 \text{ days} - 185 \text{ days}) / (274 \text{ days} - 185 \text{ days}) = 27 \text{ (offer side)}$$

$$266 + 26 = 292$$

Therefore, a 216-day forward quote may be 289–293.

Convenient as it is, the method is not perfect. This approach assumes that the yield curve will remain linear, a rather risky assumption when the time span is so wide and so far in the future. In our specific example, the Eurodollar rates increase from one month to one year, with an increase of $3/16$ between six and nine months, whereas the Euromark decreases from one month to one year, with a drop of $4/16$ between six and nine months. The trader must look at the preceding periods for further indications and must consider the probability of any upcoming events that may have an impact on the interest rates during the period under consideration.

CURRENCY FORWARD OUTRIGHT DEALS

As it should be clear by now, a forward outright is a type of trade that matures sometime in the future, past the spot date. It is a derivative product (it is derived from the spot price and value date). Let's review its components and what they mean for the trader.

As we have previously shown, the forward outright price consists of the spot price and a forward spread, which is added to or subtracted from the spot price. Remember that while the spot market is very volatile, conceivably changing every second, the forward prices constitute a much slower market. The trader should take advantage of these features.

In a slow market, a trader looking for a forward outright price should simply inquire for an outright price in its original form. In a fast market, though, the execution should be different. Since the exchange risk is prevalent in the spot market, the spot part of the forward outright should be executed first. Only after the exchange risk is under control, or rather after dealing at the target spot exchange rate, should the forward spread be executed.

Quoting a forward outright price is slower than quoting a spot price, which may mean that the spot rate will move from the current level by the time the trader receives the full quote.

The forward rate adjustment may be executed with the same counterparty with which the spot deal was done, or it may be executed through a swap with either the same or a different counterparty.

Example:
Let's take the example of a 1-year forward outright deal in USD/CHF.

$$Spot\ price = 1.5055$$

$$Forward\ spread = 92\ premium$$

In a steady market, the trader may ask for the straight 1-year forward outright price of $1.5055 + .0092 = 1.5147$

In a fast market, the trader should just ask for and trade on the spot price, 1.5055, and later, either ask the same party for a quote in the 1-year forward spread, .0092, and execute the adjustment; or execute a swap for the CHF amount equivalent in size with the spot CHF that matures on the desired long date (1-year over spot) with the same or a different counterparty.

Either way, the same result will be achieved: 1.5147 value in one year.

Users of the forward outright deals are the common users of foreign exchange: commercial and investment banks, corporations, mutual funds, and high net-worth individuals.

Forward outrights are vulnerable to all major risks: market, interest rate, credit, and country.

In the previous example, we stripped the spot from the forward in order to avoid the adverse impact of exchange risk. This risk results mostly from the spot rate, with some additional risk generated by the impact of the spot rate on the forward spread.

The forward spread is linked to interest rate risk, and any change in the interest rate differential triggers a change in the forward spread.

Unlike currency futures, forward outright deals are exposed to credit risk in the same way that all the other cash products are exposed. Because they mature at a date past the spot value date, the longer the time exposures, the greater the default risk of the counterparty.

Finally, country risk is present in a fashion similar to the other FX instruments. Longer exposures until maturity increase the potential country risk.

CURRENCY SWAPS

A plain vanilla currency swap consists of the simultaneous buying and selling (or the other way around) of the same amount of the same currency with the same counterparty, such that the two legs of the transaction mature on different dates (one of the dates being the spot date) and are traded at different exchange rates (one of the exchange rates being the spot rate). (See Figure 12.9.)

Other currency swap versions have different amounts of the base currency being swapped, or the spot leg being replaced by another forward outright leg (forward-forward). An example of a forward-forward currency swap deal is buying and selling CHF 50,000,000 in 2 months against 4 months.

The currency swap transactions began in 1971, as a result of the transition from the fixed rates of the Bretton Woods Accord to the free-floating currencies. They evolved in the 1970s from the forward foreign exchange contracts (FFECs) and back-to-back/parallel loans (PLs).

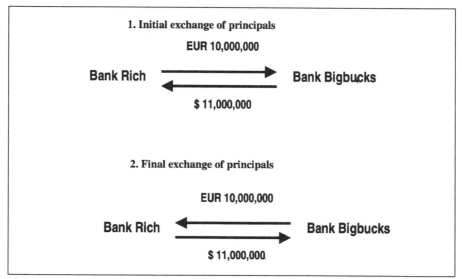

Figure 12.9. The mechanism of a currency swap.

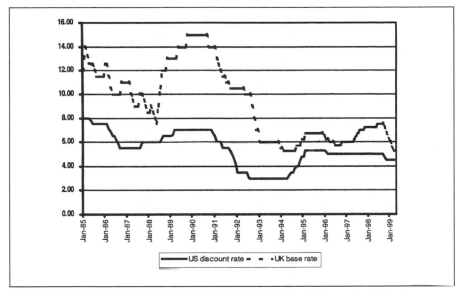

Figure 12.10. The interest rate differential between the U.S. and the U.K. discount rates.

Currency swaps have several applications:

1. *Taking advantage of current and expected changes in the interest rate differentials.* The difference between interest rates generates the forward points that traders deal. The expectations of change and the changes themselves are the focus of the currency forwards market. (See Figure 12.10.)

2. *Hedging.* Hedging is an important application of currency swaps, because their use eliminates exchange rate fluctuations. The counterparties are not exposed to exchange risk, because they buy and sell (or vice versa) the same amount of the same currency.

TRADING CURRENCY SWAPS

PRICING CURRENCY SWAPS: PREMIUM SPREAD

Example:

USD/CHF spot = 1.5060 – 65

6-month forward spread = 78 – 82 (premium)

On January 5, Bank Prima calls Bank Secunda for a U.S. dollar/Swiss franc 10,000,000 swap in 6 months. Bank Secunda quotes 78–82. In order to sell and buy U.S. dollars, Bank Prima takes the offer at 82.

Bank Secunda agrees and confirms the details as follows: "We buy and sell (B/S) US$10,000,000 against Swiss francs at 1.5060 against 1.5142 (because 1.5060 + .0082 = 1.5142) value January 7 against July 7." We assume that both the delivery dates are valid trading days.

To make a profit, Bank Secunda must sell and buy (S/B) US$10,000,000 against Swiss francs at a spread lower than 82—in a premium market. Several minutes later, Bank Secunda calls Bank Terza for a U.S. dollar/Swiss franc swap in 6 months in US$10,000,000. Bank Terza quotes 75–80. Bank Secunda takes the 80 bid. If the same spot rate is used (the spot rate is not important, provided that the market is not too volatile), the rates are 1.5060 and 1.5140, and the dates are identical.

Overall, Bank Secunda bought the forward spread at 80 (in the second transaction) and sold it at 82 (in the first transaction), making a 2 pips profit.

Table 12.3.

Deal Date	Type of Deal	Amount ($)	Rates	Amount (foreign currency)	Value date
Jan 5	Buy	$10,000,000	1.5060	CHF 15,060,000	Jan 7 (spot)
	Sell	$10,000,000	1.5142	CHF 15,142,000	Jul 7 (forward)
Total				CHF 82,000	
Jan 5	Sell	$10,000,000	1.5060	CHF 15,060,000	Jan 7 (spot)
	Buy	$10,000,000	1.5140	CHF 15,140,000	Jul 7 (forward)
Total				CHF – 80,000	
P&L (as of July 7) = CHF 15,142,000 – CHF 15,140,000 = CHF 2,000					

Bank Secunda made a nominal profit of CHF 2,000. The profit will only be realized 6 months from now, on July 7, when the final exchange between the two counterparties is executed.

However, when the future profit is discounted to the present value, the current P&L is lower. The present value is calculated as follows:

$$PV = \frac{\text{Amount at future value}}{[1 + (IR/100) \times (\text{Tenor}/360 \text{ or } 365)]}$$

where

PV = present value

IR = interest rate

Tenor = number of days

   Applied to our example:

   CHF 2,000/[1+(.04625 × 180/360)] = CHF 1,954.80

Assuming a revaluation rate of 1.5000 for the U.S. dollar/Swiss franc, the P&L in U.S. dollars is CHF 1,954.80/1.5000 = $1,303.20. The longer the period, the less the current profit will be. In addition, taxes will likely reduce the profit further.

PRICING CURRENCY SWAPS: DISCOUNT SPREAD

   Example:

   USD/JPY spot = 104.38–41

   6-month forward spread = 21.5 – 20.5(discount)

   On January 5, Bank Prima calls Bank Secunda for a U.S. dollar/Japanese yen 10,000,000 swap in 6 months. Bank Secunda quotes 21.5–20.5. To sell and buy (S/B) U.S. dollars [or buy and sell (B/S) Japanese yen], Bank Prima takes the offer at 20.5.

   Bank Secunda agrees and confirms the details as follows: "We buy and sell (B/S) US$10,000,000 against Japanese yen at 104.38 against 104.175 (because 104.38 − 20.5 = 104.175) value January 7 against July 7." We assume that both the delivery dates are valid trading days.

   To make a profit, Bank Secunda must sell and buy (S/B) US$10,000,000 at a higher spread. Several minutes later, Bank Secunda calls Bank Terza for a swap in 6 months in US$10,000,000 against Japanese yen. Bank Terza quotes 23–21. Bank Secunda takes the 21 offer. If the same spot rate is used (the spot rate is not important provided that the market is not too volatile), the rates are 104.38 and 104.17, and the dates are identical.

Table 12.4.

Deal date	Type of deal	Amount ($)	Rates	Amount (foreign currency)	Value date
Jan 5	Buy	$10,000,000	104.38	¥1,043,800,000	Jan 7 (spot)
	Sell	$10,000,000	104.175	¥1,041,750,000	Jul 7 (forward)
Total				− ¥2,050,000	
Jan 5	Sell	$10,000,000	104.38	¥1,043,800,000	Jan 7 (spot)
	Buy	$10,000,000	104.17	¥1,041,700,000	Jul 7 (forward)
Total				+ ¥2,100,000	
P&L (as of July 7) = ¥1,041,750,000 − ¥1,041,700,000 = ¥50,000					

Bank Secunda made a nominal profit of ¥50,000. Similar to the previous example, the profit will only be realized 6 months from now, on July 7, when the final exchange between the two counterparties is executed.

Discounted by the net present value, the current P&L is:

$$¥50,000/[1+(0.3125 \times 180/360) = ¥49,230.77$$

At a revaluation rate of 105.00 for the U.S. dollar/Japanese yen, the P&L in U.S. dollars is:

$$¥49,230.77/105.00 = \$468.86$$

Time and taxation will further reduce the amount of profit.

THE ROLLOVER OR TOM/NEXT SWAP

One of the most important concepts in the cash market is the *rollover* or *tomorrow/next* (*tom/next*, for short) *swap*. This swap is peculiar from several points of view. It is the only swap not designed for profit, although it will usually generate a small profit and loss. It is a swap designed for spot traders. Its main role is to change the old spot date to the current spot date.

Let's take an example to understand how using the rollover (or tomorrow/next swap) could have prevented a trader from getting into trouble.

Assume that on March 1, a spot trader buys USD/CHF 10,000,000 at 1.5000 value March 3 (with the standard spot date: two business days). Starting from a zero position in USD/CHF, the trader decides to keep this outstanding position until tomorrow. On March 2, the trader sells USD/CHF 10,000,000 at 1.5200, value March 4. Isn't this great? A nifty profit, and no position to reckon.

However, there is good news and bad news. The good news is that the profit is indeed there. The bad news is a little more complex. Actually, there is still a small position left over from the previous transaction. The position itself is not very risky, but it is confusing and, as a result, the trader almost gave out an uncovered check for several million Swiss francs. The gesture is penalized with a hefty compensation claim. Where did we go wrong? And how would using the rollover (tomorrow/ next swap) have prevented the error?

Let's take a more detailed look at the example.

Table 12.5.

Deal date	Amount bought	Exchange rate	Amount sold	Spot value date
March 1	USD 10,000,000	1.5000	CHF 15,000,000	March 3
March 2	CHF 15,200,000	1.5200	USD 10,000,000	March 4

The first spot deal executed was valued March 3, whereas the second was valued March 4. The two spot values are not identical. There is a one-day gap between the deals that results in a payment and receiving (P&R) problem.

The nostro accounts, which are the accounts kept by each bank or company for each foreign currency in the country of origin, have a positive, but close to zero, balance. On March 3, the trader in our example receives US$10,000,000 (because the trader bought this amount). This operation poses no problem. Receiving money has never been a problem. However, also on March 3, a reciprocal operation must take place. The trader must pay CHF 15,000,000 to the counterparty's nostro account in a Swiss bank or a Swiss branch of a foreign bank. But our trader's CHF nostro account on March 3 is, for all practical purposes, zero. The CHF payment cannot be executed, although the contract has been made. The payment can only be made a day later, on March 4, after our trader had sold the U.S. dollars, and consequently, bought CHF.

The problem of buying and selling US$10,000,000 at different rates can easily be solved simply by remembering that the nostro accounts are kept in the foreign currency. Therefore, the original position was equivalent to selling CHF 15,000,000. When taking profit on the next day, the trader should have bought 15,000,000, not 15,200,000, or sold US$10,000,000, because:

$$CHF\ 15,000,000/1.5200 = \$9,868,421.05,\ not\ \$10,000,000$$

Traders around the world solve payment problems by using the rollover (tomorrow/next swap). Technically, the T/N swap consists of the simultaneous closing of the original position, valuing the old spot value date, and reopening it in its identical form, save for the spot value date, which will be the current spot value date. Because the dates are different, it follows that the exchange rates are also different. The rates will be identical only in the rare case that the forward spread is at par. The rollover cost is generally very low.

From a trader's point of view, the tom/next swap will simply change, or roll over, the old spot value date to the new spot value date. In our example, the original spot value date, March 3, will be rolled over to March 4. This is important, because spot traders can only trade value spot, not any other values, be it tomorrow or any other date. In order for the trader to really close the position outstanding since the previous day, the value date must coincide with the current spot value date.

The T/N swap will not change the view of the trader in any way, or the original position or the profit and loss (P&L) figure. All it will do is enable the trader to deal currently with an outstanding position.

From the operations department's point of view, the tom/next swap will enable the company to make the payments stemming from the opening of any foreign exchange transaction.

The trader's expectation of the future behavior of the currency price or the total duration of a position until closing are irrelevant details to the back office. What is relevant is the capacity of the corporation to execute the due payments.

Let's take one last look at the details of the two spot deals, executed on consecutive days and maturing on different spot value dates.

Table 12.6.

Deal date	Amount bought	Exchange rate	Amount sold	Spot value date
March 1	USD 10,000,000	1.5000	CHF 15,000,000	March 3
March 2	CHF 15,200,000	1.5200	USD 10,000,000	March 4

To enable both the spot trader to correctly dispose of the overnight position and the back office to execute the P&R instructions, a T/N swap in Swiss franc must be executed. Assume the T/N forward spread to be −0.0001. The following table displays all the deals and their details pertinent to the scenario.

Table 12.7.

Type of deal	Deal date	Amount bought	Exchange rate	Amount sold	Spot value date	Total position (CHF)
Spot	March 1	USD 10,000,000	1.5000	(CHF 15,000,000)	March 3	(CHF 15,000,000)
Swap	March 2	CHF 15,000,000	1.5000	(USD 10,000,000)	March 3	CHF 15,000,000
(B/S)	March 2	USD 9,999,333.38	1.5001	(CHF 15,000,000)	March 4	(CHF 15,000,000)
Spot	March 2	CHF 15,200,000	1.5200	(USD 10,000,000)	March 4	CHF 200,000

Note: Details on T/N price calculations will follow in the next section of this chapter.

As of March 2, the trader is able to trade the original position, short CHF 15,000,000, value the current spot date: March 4. If, on the same day, the trader closes the position by buying CHF 15,000,000 at 1.5200, the total foreign currency position as of March 4 will be zero. But if the trader sells USD 10,000,000 at 1.5200, then the position will be positive CHF 200,000.

The T/N swap does not need to be made with the same bank with which the spot trade was executed, because it is a separate deal.

Why is this type of deal called *tomorrow/next*? The swap should theoretically be executed the day after the original spot deal, but the first leg of the swap will mature tomorrow (or the old spot value date) and the second will mature on the current value date (two business days). Therefore, the dates are *tomorrow* and the *next* business day.

In practice, the time of execution of this type of swap should be carefully linked to the ease or availability of trading. If it is difficult or expensive to execute the T/N swap on the next business day, simply leave an execution order on the original date of the spot deal. For instance, in the New York market it is easy to trade a T/N swap in Japanese yen during the entire business day following the spot deal. The opposite is generally true for the European currencies in the later part of the day.

In order to avoid any unpleasant consequences, it is advisable to send a leave order on the evening of the original spot trade day to a correspondent bank in the time zone of the country whose currency was traded. In this manner, a trader gains time in the morning, when the market tends to be busier, and the correspondent bank will have the opportunity to execute the T/N swap at a favorable rate.

In the European market, T/N swaps can be executed during the "normal" trading day, tomorrow, since the time zone overlaps with both the Asian and North American time zones.

CALCULATING THE T/N PRICE

Let's focus on the calculation of the T/N price. Please keep in mind that this swap is exceptional in terms of value dates. A plain vanilla swap will mature its short leg on the spot value date and the long leg on a specific forward date. The T/N swap will mature its short leg tomorrow and the long leg on the spot date. The exception in value dates extrapolates into an exception regarding the price structure.

Drawing on the previous example, let's use a spot rate of 1.5000 and a T/N spread of 1.5–1. You need both sides of the forward spread in order to identify whether it is a premium or a discount. Let's use the bid side of the T/N spread. Recall the method of identification of the spread:

Forward bid > forward offer ⇒ discount

Applying this rule for the T/N swap and knowing the price for the long leg, which is equivalent to the spot price, 1.6000, what will be the price of the short leg: 1.5001 or 1.4999?

The forward spread is certainly a discount. To better answer this apparently obvious question, please refer to Figure 12.6. As you can see, the T/N falls before the spot. T/N is one day away from the deal date, whereas the spot date is two days away. In the case of a discount forward market, that is equivalent to a higher T/N price. Therefore, the correct answer on the T/N exchange rate, which I am sure you have already arrived at, is 1.5001.

Conversely, if the T/N spread is at premium, then it will be subtracted from the spot price. For instance, if USD/JPY spot middle rate is 160.00 and the T/N forward spread is 2–3 (premium), the exchange rate for the short leg is 159.97 (if using the offer side of the forward spread).

COVERED INTEREST RATE ARBITRAGE

Another way of taking advantage of the forward market is *covered interest rate arbitrage*. Arbitrage is the risk-free type of trading whereby the same instrument is bought and sold in two different markets in order to cash in on the divergence between the two markets. This approach consists of borrowing currency A, exchanging it for currency B, investing currency B for the duration of the loan, and, after taking off the forward cover on maturity, showing a profit on the entire set of deals.

Theoretically, covered interest rate arbitrage seems like an attractive option. In reality, this type of trading can be difficult to implement because of possibly serious problems. One problem is that the major currencies operate at a high level of market efficiency. Neither can traders trade blindly in the more exotic currencies just to arbitrage, because the liquidity in those currencies is generally limited. Another problem is the impact on the balance sheet. From a corporate point of view, the balance sheet will be inflated due to the additional assets (the foreign currency denominated loans) and will suffer liabilities (the domestic deposits).

Despite these problems, many corporations and banks practice currency arbitrage.

EXAMPLE OF CURRENCY ARBITRAGE

Amount	= JPY 1,000,000,000
USD/JPY spot rate	= 104.40
USD/JPY 6 months forward spread	= 21.50–20
Time to maturity	= 180 days

Eurodollar 6 months rate	$= 3^{3}/_{8} - 3^{1}/_{2}$
Euroyen 6 months rate	$= 3 - 3^{1}/_{8}$

First step: Cost of deposit

$$\text{Cost 6 months (JPY)} = \text{JPY } 1{,}000{,}000{,}000 \times \left(\frac{3.125}{100}\right) \times \left(\frac{180 \text{ days}}{360 \text{ days}}\right)$$

$$= \text{JPY } 15{,}625{,}000$$

$$\text{Cost 6 months (USD)} = \frac{\text{JPY } 15{,}625{,}000}{(104.40 - .2150)} = \frac{\text{JPY } 15{,}625{,}000}{104.1850} =$$

$$= \text{USD } 149{,}973.60 \text{ (cost of deposit)}$$

Second step: Cost of swap

$$\frac{\text{JPY } 1{,}000{,}000{,}000}{\text{spot rate}} =$$

$$\frac{\text{JPY } 1{,}000{,}000{,}000}{104.40} = \text{USD } 9{,}578{,}544.06$$

$$\frac{\text{JPY } 1{,}000{,}000{,}000}{\text{forward outright rate}} =$$

$$\frac{\text{JPY } 1{,}000{,}000{,}000}{104.1850} = \text{USD } 9{,}598{,}310.70$$

Cost of swap = USD9,598,310.70 − USD9,578,544.06 = USD19,766.64

Total cost of trade = USD149,973.60 + USD19,766.64 = USD169,740.24

Cost of borrowing USD through JPY $= \left(\frac{\text{USD } 169{,}740.24}{\text{USD } 9{,}578{,}544.06}\right) \times \left(\frac{360}{180}\right) \times 100$

$$= 3.5442\%$$

3.5442% > 3.50%

From this example, we conclude that borrowing U.S. dollars through Japanese yen is more expensive than paying the offer side in eurodollars.

13 Currency Crosses

D espite international interest in the U.S. dollar and the consequent pricing of local currencies in terms of U.S. dollars, there is also a natural demand for pricing foreign currencies in terms of other currencies. At regional levels, commercial transactions between two neighboring countries may be conducted at the exchange rate between their own currencies, rather than going through the exchange rate against the U.S. dollar. At the international level, the pricing of one currency in terms of another may generate information unavailable in the standard quotes against the U.S. dollar. In this chapter you will learn the advantage of cross-currency trading, whether you trade the crosses or not.

THE CROSS FOREIGN CURRENCY MARKETPLACE

The U.S. dollar is the most actively traded currency worldwide. Currencies are generally quoted against the U.S. dollar. When currencies are traded against currencies other than the U.S. dollar, the prices are called *cross rates*. Therefore, a cross rate is a nondollar currency.

The most popular currency cross rates are euro/Japanese yen, euro/British pound, and euro/Swiss franc, which evolved from the traditional deutsche mark/Japanese yen, sterling/deutsche mark, and deutsche mark/Swiss franc cross rates after January 4, 1999.

ADVANTAGES OF CROSS-CURRENCY TRADING

Cross-currency trading has been growing significantly since the early 1980s. Although it shrank considerably in the aftermath of the euro introduction, the commercial demand for crosses remains high in the European market. A Swiss exporter to Germany who wants to repatriate profits will find it of little use to know the value of the Swiss franc and the euro in terms of the dollar. What the Swiss exporter needs to know is how many Swiss francs can be exchanged for the euros. The common misconception is that the Swiss franc is a stable currency. Spot dollar/Swiss franc traders are heavy users of the EUR/CHF. Because liquidity in the spot market for the U.S. dollar/Swiss franc is limited, they tend to cover in euro/dollars, negotiating these transactions through the cross. Yet, the cross is not "flat" by any means, as the currencies fluctuate against each other. This fluctuation is generally invisible in the exchange rates against the U.S. dollar. In terms of determining on the chart which currency is stronger, it is helpful to remember that a high value means the euro is stronger relative to the Swiss franc, and vice versa. (See Figure 13.1.)

Moreover, the German and Swiss economies have a high degree of correlation, which is reflected in their currencies as well. This is an important element for Swiss franc traders. Despite similarities, the Swiss franc market is less liquid than the euro market. Therefore, the Swiss franc traders are natural euro/Swiss franc users when they cannot trade this currency against the U.S. dollar.

Even when the economic relationships between two countries are not very close, the cross rates between their currencies may be significant. For instance, the most popular cross rate is the euro/Japanese yen rate. (See Figure 13.2.) Despite their gigantic economies, the euro zone and Japan do not currently have trade liaisons at par. However, this cross rate is very popular because the euro and the Japanese yen rates are the most traded currencies vis-à-vis the U.S. dollar. Economic internationalization has been an important factor in the growth of cross-currency volume. The opening of trading in Southeast Asia, Eastern Europe, and South America triggered a significant increase in cross trading. Although the regional currencies are under limited demand, the hard currencies prevalent in these areas are under increased demand. In addition, U.S. corporations have increased their level of sophistication in global management. Cross-currencies are used as an effective way of reducing financial risk, especially when a company must concomitantly trade several currencies. Instead, the company may now trade a single nondollar currency before profit repatriation.

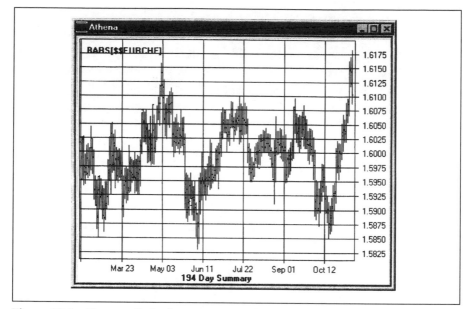

Figure 13.1. The euro/Swiss franc cross rate. *(Source: Bridge Information Systems, Inc.)*

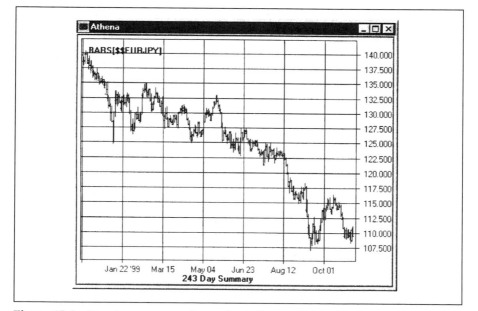

Figure 13.2. Euro/yen cross-rate fluctuations. *(Source: Bridge Information Systems, Inc.)*

Cross trading can also help traders avoid the wrath of the central banks' intervention. Although central banks do not generally intervene in the cross markets, the Bank of Japan intervened in June 1999 to buy euro/yen in order to rescue Japanese investors who had been caught in unprofitable euro-denominated investments.

From the technical analysis point of view, crosses are very important sources of information. The same technical rules naturally apply to the crosses: The market reacts on signals unavailable outside the cross charts. It is common to have a significant move in the euro that cannot be forecast off the euro/dollar chart. However, on the euro/Japanese yen or the euro/Swiss franc charts, technical points are available.

PRICE CALCULATION

Although a currency cross is a nondollar instrument, its calculation is based on currencies' rates in terms of U.S. dollars. For instance, the euro/Japanese yen cross is derived from the exchange rates of the euro/dollar and dollar/Japanese yen, known as *components*.

Cross rates are obtained by either dividing or multiplying two different currencies, or components. (See Figure 13.3.) To calculate the cross rates between the Japanese yen and the Swiss franc, the USD/JPY exchange rate is divided by the USD/CHF exchange rate. The currencies considered so far are all quoted in European terms, which means that the exchange rate displays the amount of foreign currency received in exchange for US$1.

	BID	OFFER
USD/CHF	1.5000	1.5010
USD/JPY	100.00	100.10
USD/CHF	1.5000	1.5010
USD/JPY	100.00	100.10
CHF/JPY	$\dfrac{100.00}{1.5010}$	$\dfrac{100.10}{1.5000}$
CHF/JPY	66.62	66.73

Figure 13.3. Diagram of cross-rate calculations for two currencies quoted in European terms.

If one of the components is a currency quoted in American terms, such as the euro and the British pound, while the other is in European terms, then the cross price is calculated by multiplying the components. An exchange rate quoted in American terms shows how many U.S. dollars will be received in exchange for one unit of foreign currency.

Example:

The average (between the bid and offer) rates of the major four currencies are:

USD/CHF = 1.5100

USD/JPY = 120.00

EUR/USD = 1.0700

GBP/USD =1.6200

The cross rates are calculated as follows:

CHF/JPY = (USD/JPY) / (USD/CHF) = 120.00 / 1.5100 = 79.47

EUR/JPY = (EUR/USD) $\times$ (USD/JPY) = 1.0700 $\times$ 120.00 = 128.40

EUR/GBP = (EUR/USD) / (GBP/USD) = 1.0700 / 1.6200 = 0.6605

These calculations are general approximations of the cross prices. To calculate the cross price thoroughly, a two-way (bid–offer) price is necessary.

In order to avoid any errors, it is easier, in the beginning, to start from the end result and work our way backward to the components.

Example:

As shown in Figure 13.3, the exchange rate for USD/CHF is 1.5000 – 1.5010 and the exchange rate for USD/JPY is 100.00 – 100.10. The task is to calculate the two-way price for the CHF/JPY cross rate.

In other words, our end result is a bid and an offer for the CHF/JPY cross.

A CHF/JPY bid means that you want to buy the CHF and sell the JPY. Buying the CHF is equivalent to selling the USD/CHF, and selling the JPY is the same as buying USD/JPY.

A CHF/JPY offer means that you want to sell the CHF and buy the JPY. Selling the CHF is equivalent to buying the USD/CHF, and buying the JPY is the same as selling USD/JPY.

Therefore, to calculate this type of cross, you must divide one offer by the other bid and vice versa, but never one bid by the other bid, or one offer by the other offer.

Applying our figures:

$$CHF/JPY\ BID = 66.62$$

and

$$CHF/JPY\ OFFER = 66.73$$

The CHF/JPY two-way price is therefore 66.62–66.73.

In reality, this approach, although correct, is not good enough. The spread between the bid and offer is, in this case, 11 pips, unacceptable by market standards. The spread should be 3 to 5 pips, such as 66.65–68, or 66.69–72. Therefore, the traders must skew the price depending on the market conditions.

If one of the components of the cross is quoted in American terms, the calculation is different. (See Figure 13.4.) First, the components are multiplied. Second, a bid is multiplied by the other bid, and an offer is multiplied by the other offer.

Example:

GBP/USD = 1.6000–1.6010   USD/CHF = 1.5000–1.5010

The GBP/CHF cross is calculated as follows:

GBP/CHF bid = 1.6000 × 1.5000 = 2.4000

GBP/CHF offer = 1.6010 × 1.5010 = 2.4031

The two-way GBP/CHF cross rate price is therefore 2.4000–2.4031

	BID	OFFER
GBP/USD	1.6000	1.6010
USD/CHF	1.5000	1.5010
GBP/USD	1.6000	1.6010
USD/CHF	1.5000	1.5010
GBP/CHF	1.6000 X 1.5000	1.6010 X 1.5010
GBP/CHF	2.4000	2.4031

Figure 13.4. Diagram of cross-rate calculations for a currency quoted in European terms and a currency quoted in American terms.

	BID	OFFER
EUR/USD	1.0500	1.0510
GBP/USD	1.6000	1.6010
EUR/USD	1.0500	1.0510
GBP/USD	1.6000	1.6010
EUR/GBP	$\dfrac{1.0500}{1.6010}$	$\dfrac{1.0510}{1.6000}$
EUR/GBP	0.6558	0.6569

Figure 13.5. Diagram of cross-rate calculations for two currencies quoted in American terms.

Finally, Figure 13.5 displays the calculations for two currencies in American terms. The exchange rate for EUR/USD is 1.0500–1.0510 and the exchange rate for GBP/USD is 1.6000–1.6010. The calculation of the two-way price for the EUR/GBP cross rate is as follows:

A EUR/GBP bid means that you want to buy the EUR and sell the GBP. Buying the EUR means buying the EUR/USD, and selling the GBP is the same as selling GBP/USD.

A EUR/GBP offer means that you want to sell the EUR and buy the GBP. Selling the EUR is equivalent to selling the EUR/USD, and buying the GBP is the same as buying GBP/USD.

Therefore, to calculate this type of cross, you must divide one offer by the other bid and vice versa.

Applying our figures:

$$\text{EUR/GBP BID} = 0.6558$$

and

$$\text{EUR/GBP OFFER} = 0.6569$$

The EUR/GBP two-way price is therefore 0.6558–0.6569.

RELATIVE STRENGTH
OF A CURRENCY

If the Canadian dollar/Japanese yen cross rises, its increase reflects the fact that the Canadian dollar is relatively stronger than the Japanese yen, and vice versa. What is the significance of this reading for the components?

CHF/JPY Trades Upward	CAD /JPY Trades Downward
Significance for the U.S. dollar:	Significance for the U.S. dollar:
CAD very strong, JPY strong	CAD strong, JPY very strong
CAD strong, JPY flat	CAD flat, JPY strong
CAD flat, JPY weak	CAD weak, JPY flat
CAD weak, JPY very weak	CAD very weak, JPY weak
CAD strong, JPY weak	CAD weak, JPY strong

Figure 13.6. The relative strength or weakness of one currency in terms of another on the cross has different readings for the components. Understanding these possibilities expands the trading options of a cross trader.

TRADING COMPONENTS

A cross trader is not limited to buying and selling specific currency crosses. By necessity, traders also leg-in or leg-out a cross. This means that they start or end their trading with a component, rather than always trading crosses. For instance, Swiss franc traders frequently get caught with unwanted positions in the interbank market. The optimal solution in the short run to weather a rapid unfavorable market move is to leg-in a EUR/CHF cross. When the market stabilizes, the trader can leg-out.

Another common scenario involves a trader caught in a losing cross position. Generally, a cross position makes a profit on only one of the components. Once it becomes clear which way the market is heading, the trader will leg-out the money-losing component, while keeping the profit-making component. This type of strategy can minimize a loss or generate a profit.

POSITION CALCULATION

Trading in crosses is executed in amounts of foreign currency rather than U.S. dollars, since no U.S. dollars are involved in the first place. The cross amounts are generally quoted in the first currency. This type of quoting is executed both in the case of crosses between European and American-quoted currencies: Canadian dollar (CAD) in the case of Canadian dollar/Japanese yen (CAD/JPY) or euro/Swiss franc (EUR/CHF). When one or both components are quoted in American terms, then it is the British pound (GBP) in the case of British pound/yen (GBP/JPY) or euro (EUR) for euro/sterling (EUR/GBP).

Therefore, if someone asks for a price in CAD/JPY 10 million, it is understood by both parties that the quote will be in CAD 10 million, not JPY 10 million. By the way, if the CAD/JPY cross is indeed quoted in CAD 10,000,000, what is the JPY amount? To answer this question, you need to know the cross exchange rate. Using a CAD/JPY rate of 81.58, for instance, the Japanese amount is ¥ 815,800,000:

$$CAD\ 10,000,000 \times 81.58 = ¥\ 815,800,000$$

When deciding to leg-out of this CAD/JPY cross position, the trader must know the U.S. dollar value of the components. If USD/CAD spot exchange rate is 1.5180, then the U.S. dollar amount against the Canadian dollar is $6,587,615.28:

$$CAD\ 10,000,000/1.5180 = \$6,587,615.28$$

How about the U.S. dollar amount against the Japanese yen? Since we have the cross rate, the USD/CAD rate, and the Japanese yen amount, we can easily calculate the U.S. dollar amount:

$$1.5180 \times 81.58 = 123.83844$$

$$¥815,800,000/123.83844 = \$6,587,615.28$$

There is not much reason to go through the calculations, though, because the U.S. dollar amounts are always virtually identical on both sides of any cross.

CALCULATION OF THE CROSS PROFIT AND LOSS

In the previous examples we used the CAD/JPY cross rate of 81.58 and the USD/CAD rate of 1.5180. Based on these rates, we were able to calculate the USD/JPY rate of 123.8384.

Let's assume that the trader:

- buys CAD 10,000,000 at 81.58, and
- sells CAD 10,000,000 at 81.68.

Because the trader bought low and sold high, we know that the deals generated a profit. To calculate the cross P&L, several methods may be employed.

Example:
The first method consists of translating the CAD/JPY rates into USD/JPY rates and then calculating the profit and loss by using the standard formula for the USD/JPY spot exchange rates.

$$81.58 \times 1.5180 = 123.8384$$

$$81.68 \times 1.5180 = 123.9902$$

$$CAD\ 10,000,000/1.5180 = \$\ 6,587,615.28$$

Assuming a closing/revaluation price of 124.00, the P&L can be calculated as follows:

P&L = (123.9902 – 123.8384) × \$6,587,615.28 /124.00 = \$ 8,064.52

Please notice that the entire profit was calculated for the Japanese yen. In Canadian dollars there was no P&L because the same CAD amount was bought and sold at the same rate.

The second method is a little faster, because it involves only the cross rates, the cross amount, and the closing/revaluation rate for the Japanese yen:

P&L = (81.68 – 81.53) * CAD 10,000,000/124.00 = \$ 8,064.52

The same methods are applied for a higher number of cross deals.

Example:
A trader executes the following cross deals:

Buy	At	Sell	At
CAD 3,000,000	81.45	CAD 10,000,000	82.00
CAD 5,000,000	81.50	CAD 10,000,000	81.90
CAD 2,000,000	81.40		
CAD 10,000,000	81.70		

The first step in calculating the P&L is averaging the buying and the selling exchange rates.

Buy	At	Sell	At
CAD	3,000,000 × 81.45 = ¥ 244,350,000	CAD 10,000,000 × 82.00 = ¥ 820,000,000	
CAD	5,000,000 × 81.50 = ¥ 407,500,000	CAD 10,000,000 × 81.90 = ¥ 819,000,000	
CAD	2,000,000 × 81.40 = ¥ 162,800,000		
CAD	10,000,000 × 81.70 = ¥ 817,000,000		
Total	CAD 20,000,000 ¥1,631,650,000	CAD 20,000,000 ¥1,639,000,000	

Buying exchange rate	Selling exchange rate
¥1,631,650,000 / CAD 20,000,000 = 81.5825	¥1,639,000,000 / CAD 20,000,000 = 81.95

The second step is calculating the P&L. Using the same revaluation rate in USD/JPY as in the previous example, the P&L is calculated as follows:

$$(81.95 - 81.5825) \times CAD20,000,000 / 124.00 = \$59,274.19$$

Currency cross-trading continues to be a popular instrument in foreign exchange. Volume in the nondollar currencies is still small, and crosses do not represent serious competition to the U.S. dollar.

The importance of crosses is enhanced nowadays by the unprecedented internationalization of business and risk management. As crosses are used increasingly by a variety of players, the foreign exchange markets will benefit.

14 Currency Futures

Currency futures are specific types of forward outright deals. Because they are derived from the spot price, they are derivative instruments. (See Figure 14.1.) They are specific with regard to the expiration date and the size of the trade amount. Whereas, generally, forward outright deals—those that mature past the spot delivery date—will mature on any valid date in the two countries whose currencies are being traded, standardized amounts of foreign currency futures mature only on the third Wednesday of March, June, September, and December.

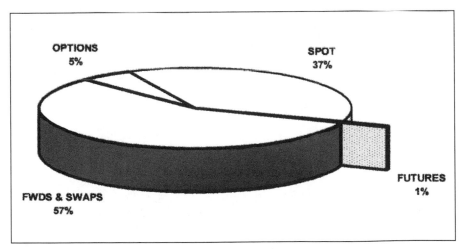

Figure 14.1. The market share of the foreign exchange instruments.

THE CURRENCY FUTURES MARKETPLACE

Though currency futures trading is relatively new, commodity futures trading goes back a long time. The Chicago Mercantile Exchange (CME), for instance, was established in 1919, succeeding the Butter and Egg Board, which had been established in 1898. It is on regulated exchanges such as the CME that currency futures are traded.

Currency futures are traded on regulated exchanges similar to the stock markets. The largest currency futures markets are in the United States and the largest of these American markets is the International Monetary Market (IMM) division of the Chicago Mercantile Exchange.

Foreign currencies futures trading began on May 16, 1972. The Exchange consists of three divisions:

1. The International Monetary Market (IMM), for currency and interest rate futures and options, with 1287 members.
2. The Chicago Mercantile Exchange (CME), for agricultural commodities, with 626 members.
3. The Index and Option Market (IOM), established in 1982, for equity-related futures and options, with 812 members.

THE INTERNATIONAL MONETARY MARKET

The trading success of currency futures since 1972 triggered the introduction of options on deutsche mark futures on the IMM in 1984; on British pound and Swiss franc futures in 1985; and on Japanese yen, Canadian dollar, and ECU futures in 1986. By 1992, the IMM had also introduced its first nondollar futures and options: the deutsche mark/Japanese yen cross contracts.

Besides the IMM, one can trade currency futures markets on a much smaller scale on FINEX in New York City.

FINEX
FINEX is part of the New York Cotton Exchange (NYCE), the oldest futures exchange in New York (founded in 1870). The exchange lists futures on euro crosses, other crosses, and the USDX, a basket of ten currencies: deutsche mark, Japanese yen, French franc, British pound, Canadian dollar, Italian lira, Dutch guilder, Belgian franc, Swedish krona, and Swiss franc. The USDX is a unique contract that offers the investor the opportunity to

trade the dollar broadly, rather than against a specific currency. The individual currencies that are part of the euro will be replaced by it.

The size of the USDX contract is $1,000 times the U.S. Dollar Index. The size of the U.S. Index varies continuously, as the U.S. dollar fluctuates against the basket currencies. It has the same maturity dates as the IMM and PHLX contracts: the third Wednesday in March, June, September, and December.

The ticker symbol is DX. The minimum price quotation is .01 of a U.S. Dollar Index, which is equivalent to $10.00.

FINEX offers the following crosses:

Contract	Contract size	Symbol
• Euro/Japanese yen	100,000 euro	EJ
• Euro/Swedish krona	100,000 euro	RK
• Euro/Swiss franc	100,000 euro	RZ
• Euro/British pound	100,000 euro	GB
• Euro/Norwegian krone	100,000 euro	OL
• Euro/Canadian dollar	100,000 euro	EP
• Australian dollar/NZ dollar	200,000 A. dollars	AR
• British pound/Japanese yen	125,000 British pound	SY
• British pound/Swiss franc	125,000 British pound	SS
• Swiss franc/ Japanese yen	2000,000 Swiss franc	ZY

CHARACTERISTICS OF CURRENCY FUTURES

Let's take a look now at the characteristics of currency futures that make them attractive.

First, a futures market provides certain advantages to the trading of futures and options on futures:

- It is open to all market participants, individuals included. This is different from the spot market, which is virtually closed to individuals—except high net-worth individuals—because of the size of the currency amounts traded.
- It is a central market, just as efficient as the cash market, and whereas the cash market is a very decentralized market, futures trading takes place under one roof. The "open" trading interaction

on the floor is very helpful to traders, who interact physically in the trading arena.

- It eliminates the credit risk because the Chicago Mercantile Exchange Clearinghouse acts as the buyer for every seller, and vice versa. In turn, the Clearinghouse minimizes its own exposure by requiring traders who maintain a nonprofitable position to post margins equal in size to their losses.

What a futures market does not do is guarantee that the currency will trade at a specific price at any future time. For example, if the British pound futures' settlement price on August 3 for expiration in September is 1.6000, it doesn't suggest or guarantee a price of 1.6000 for the September expiration date. Therefore, one should be aware that the price simply reflects the market expectations at a certain time regarding the future price of a specific currency.

Second, currency futures provide several benefits for traders:

- Because futures are special types of forward outright contracts, corporations can use them for hedging purposes.

- Although the futures and spot markets trade closely together, certain divergences between the two occur, generating arbitraging opportunities.

- Gaps, volume, and open interest are significant technical analysis tools solely available in the futures market. Yet their significance extrapolates to the spot market as well.

- In the second part of the trading day in the United States, liquidity may suffer in the Swiss franc or the British pound. The futures prices are used in this instance for approximating the spot prices, providing "price discovery" when the spot market cannot provide a price, although the practicality of this characteristic is limited because the futures transactions might have occurred on light volume, commonly too little to satisfy the demand in the spot market.

Because of these benefits, currency futures trading volume has steadily attracted a large variety of players.

THE LOOK OF CURRENCY FUTURES

Currency futures look different relative to the cash rates we have seen so far. In addition to the euro and the British pound, all other quotes on the

IMM are in American terms, not European. In the cash market, however, many of the exchange rates are quoted in European terms. The price difference between the futures and the cash quotes occurs because a futures contract is a forward outright, not a spot. The difference in the look of Telerate quotes—no dot between 1 and the rest of the quote—is generated by a technicality: There is not enough space on the monitor screen.

To calculate the futures prices for the rest of the currencies, you simply get the inverse of the outright price of the currency quoted in European terms. The outright price, as you recall, is calculated by adding or subtracting the forward pips to or from the spot price:

Currency future price = 1/(Spot price in European terms +/– forward spread)

Example:
If the spot USD/CHF price is 1.5100 and the IMM discount spread is 0.0080, then the IMM dated USD/CHF forward outright will be

$$1.5100 \quad 0.0080 - 1.5020, \text{ in European terms,}$$

and

$$1/1.5020 = 0.6658, \text{ in American terms.}$$

Because futures are forward outright contracts and the forward prices are generally slow movers, the elimination of the forward spreads will transform the futures contracts into spot contracts. This is important in order to compare the two types of contracts, and it is important to the traders for hedging, arbitrage, and price discovery.

Figure 14.2 shows the convergence between the futures and spot prices.

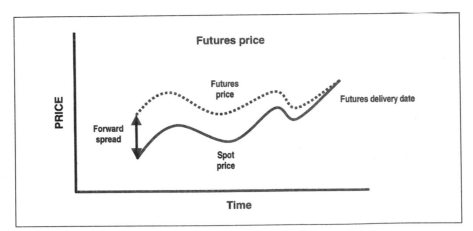

Figure 14.2. Diagram of the convergence between the futures and the spot prices.

Forward Outright Price Calculation

Calculate the forward outright pips (or spread) as follows:

$$FP= S \times (E_{fc} - E_\$) \times (t/360*)$$

where

FP = forward outright pips

S = spot price

$E_\$$ = Eurodollar rate

E_{fc} = Eurocurrency rate

t = days to delivery

The forward outright price is calculated as:

$$FWD\ PRICE=S+FP$$

Example:

USD/CAD spot = 1.5000

Eurodollar 2 month = 5.20%

Eurocanada 2 month = 4.60%

T = 60 days

FP = $1.5000 \times (0.046 - 0.052\ ) \times (60/360) = -0.001$

FWD price = $1.5000 - 0.001 = 1.4990$ (in European terms)

The future price or the forward outright price thus obtained and expressed in American terms is then:

$1/1.4990 = 0.6671$

FUTURES MARKET AND CASH MARKET: COMPARISONS

Let's see how the futures market (FM) compares to the cash interbank market (CM).

Market Environment

- *FM:* Trading takes place in a centralized market, by open outcry of prices and amounts, through floor brokers.

  CM: Trading is completely decentralized, being executed generally through dealing systems (interbank) and phones (with brokers).

- *FM:* The monitor shows only real prices already traded on the floor.

  CM: The monitor shows only suggested prices.

Market Participants

- *FM:* Players consist of commercial banks, investment banks, corporations, financial institutions, and individual speculators.

  CM: By and large, the participants are commercial and investment banks, along with large corporations; individuals and smaller corporations generally have limited participation.

- *FM:* Counterparty is the exchange.

  CM: The counterparties know their identities, either before the trade (dealing systems) or after the trade (brokers' market).

Quoting Style

- *FM:* Players make one-sided prices.

  CM: Players make and request two-way prices.

- *FM:* Trading is executed in foreign currency amounts only.

  CM: Generally, foreign currencies are quoted against the U.S. dollar, except for crosses and small foreign currency fixed amounts.

- *FM:* Futures are traded in multiples of fixed amounts of foreign currencies, known as contracts.

  CM: Generally, the trading unit is $1,000,000, and the unofficial standard is $10,000,000; crosses are also quoted in million units of foreign currencies; any odd amounts in any currency may be traded.

- *FM:* Prices are quoted in American terms.

  CM: Prices are quoted in both European and American terms.

Settlement Dates

- *FM:* The maturity dates are standardized in order to maximize liquidity: March, June, September, and December.

  CM: The settlement dates for spot and forward are spread widely, depending on the agreement between buyers and sellers.

- *FM:* Less than 1 percent of the trades result in physical delivery.

  CM: All trades result in physical delivery.

- *FM:* Settlements are made daily through the Exchange's clearing-house.

  CM: Settlements occur in the spot market two days past the original transaction (except the Canadian dollar, which matures only one day later) or on an agreed forward date.

- *FM:* Futures may be quoted up to 12 months in advance.

  CM: The long dates are open, as maturities may go well over 3 years.

Trading Costs

- *FM:* Initial and variation margins are required for all players.

  CM: Margins are not required.

- *FM:* Commissions are required on a single, round-turn basis.

  CM: The buyer and seller in the brokers' market pay commissions equally; there are no commissions in the direct market.

Volume

- *FM:* Volume is only a fraction of the cash market.

  CM: Out of the $1.5 trillion traded daily, most of the volume is traded in the spot, forward outright, and swap.

MARGINS

Margin is the amount of money or collateral deposited by a customer with the broker, by a broker with the clearing member, or by a clearing member with the clearinghouse in order to insure the broker or clearinghouse against loss on outstanding futures positions.

There are two types of margin: initiation and variation or maintenance. *Initiation margin*, which is covered via liquid government instruments such as T-bills, entitles a trader or firm to trade currency futures. The trader's daily loss cannot exceed the size of this margin.

Variation or *maintenance margin* must fully cover any unrealized loss and must be posted in cash by any trader holding an overnight position with a negative P&L. It must be kept on deposit at all times.

Margins are applied differently to each currency contract and, within each currency, separately to speculative and hedging contracts.

Example:

As of August 24, 1993, some of the initiation margins were as follows:

	BP	CD	DM	SF	JY
Speculative	$ 2295	$ 810	$ 1350	$ 1755	$ 2970
Hedging	$ 1700	$ 600	$ 1000	$ 1300	$ 2200

The margins posted are interest bearing.

CONTRACT SIZE

The size of a contract in the futures market differs among currencies. The specific amounts for the major currencies contracts are:

Currency	Symbol Chicago	Contract Size
Euro	EC	125,000
Swiss franc	SF	125,000
Japanese yen	JY	12,500,000
British pound	BP	62,500
Canadian dollar	CD	100,000
Australian dollar	AD	100,000
New Zealand dollar	NE	100,000
Brazilian real	BR	100,000
Mexican peso	MP	500,000
Russian ruble	RU	500,000
South African rand	RA	500,000

Price information on foreign currencies futures is available daily in the major newspapers.

FLOOR TRADING

There are two types of traders who deal futures on the floor: floor traders, or locals, and floor brokers. *Floor traders* are exchange members who execute their own trades by being physically present in the pit, which is the place for futures trading. *Floor brokers* are individuals on the exchange floor engaged in executing orders for another person. They may also trade for their own accounts, but their primary responsibility is executing the customers' orders first. Brokers are licensed by the federal government.

CME enforces strict rules and trading activity is monitored by a computerized surveillance system.

To identify the traders on the floor, the members don trading jackets in the colors of the firm they represent. They wear colorful identification badges: green for IMM, blue for IOM, and gold for CME. For further ease of identification, each badge also sports a unique set of initials (handle), not necessarily corresponding with the trader's name.

On the CME, up to 4300 members may trade at any given time. The exact number varies. This total number of people on the floor consists of brokers, traders, runners, supervisors, pit observers, and others.

The trading floor itself is divided into four major quadrants: currencies, interest rates, equity, and agricultural (in clockwise order). Within each quadrant are trading pits for the major financial instruments. Each of the four major currency futures is traded in individual pits. The others share trading pits. The quadrants are divided by work stations. Large electronic displays continuously show the price activity of the futures traded on the exchanges.

The players on the floor attempt to communicate with each other via lively primal screams, better known as *open outcry*. This method is mercifully supplemented by hand signals, when hearing is temporarily overpowered. Executing the graceful hand signals may be taxing even for professional mimes.

TRADING HOURS

Whereas the cash market trades virtually around the clock, the futures markets trade within certain times. For instance, Chicago IMM trades between 7:20 AM and 2 PM CST, except for the days prior to CME holidays and bank holidays when the Exchange is open. On these days trading ends at 12 noon CST.

The trading hours in the futures market have an important bearing on the cash market trading hours. The "unofficially official" trading hours in the New York cash market are 8:30 AM to 3 PM EDT.

Banks do not have an obligation to quote exchange rates outside these hours. The IMM starts trading at 8:20 AM EDT because the most important economic data is released in the United States at 8:30 AM EDT. Therefore, futures traders have 10 minutes to make last-minute adjustments in their positions.

MINIMUM PRICE CHANGE

Currency futures prices change in increments of 1 pip, with the exception of the British pound price, which moves in increments of 2 pips.

Value of 1 Pip

Every time a currency futures contract moves up or down, it generates a change in profit and loss (P&L) equal to the value of 1 pip.

The values of 1 pip differ among currencies:

- For EC, SF, and JY, a pip is worth $12.50.
- For BP, a pip is valued at $6.25.
- For CD and AD, one pip is priced at $10.00.

For traders outside the exchange, the prices are available from on-line monitors. The most popular pages are found on Bridge, Telerate, Reuters, and Bloomberg. Telerate presents the currency futures on composite pages, while Reuters and Bloomberg display currency futures on individual pages. The information is otherwise similar.

Let's take a look at page 914 from Telerate (in Figure 14.3) and sort out the information. This page displays the futures of the four major cur-

	TIME	NET	LAST	PREV1	PREV2	LOW	HIGH	VOL	OPEN	CLOSE
DEUTSCHE MARK IMM										
SEP 93	0854 -	66	14934	A14936	14940	14912	15018	389	14980	15000
DEC 93	0852 -	68	A14850	14874	14850	14850	14920	105	14918	14918
MAR 94	0848		A14800	A14810	A14820					14866
BRITISH POUND IMM										
SEP 93	0854 -	21	5813	5814	5815	5807	5852	990	5830	5834
DEC 93	0854 -	14	A5768	A5769	A5770	5765	5805	140	5765	5787
MAR 94	0844 -	8	5740	5745	B5600	5745	5748	3	5745	5756
SWISS FRANC IMM										
SEP 93	0854 -	57	6628	6629	6630	6628	6690	501	6675	6685
DEC 93	0853 -	37	A6615	A6618	A6620	6625	6650	9	42-48	6668
MAR 94	0851		A6610	A6620	A6630					6661
JAPANESE YEN IMM										
SEP 93	0854 -	9	9575	9576	A9577	9555	9607	586	9575	9584
DEC 93	0841 -	2	9590	9588	A9589	9575	9594	13	80-85	9592
MAR 94	0806									9614

Telerate MATRIX   9:54 EOT   TERMINAL

[TELERATE FUTURES SERVICE]   PAGE 914

Figure 14.3. The futures market for the major currencies—deutsche mark, Japanese yen, British pound, and Swiss franc—on page 914 as shown by Telerate. *(Source: Telerate, Inc.)*

rencies, in the following order: the British pound, the deutsche mark, the Swiss franc, and the Japanese yen.

- The first column shows the closest expiration dates to the current date, with the earliest contract at the top.
- The second column shows Chicago (Central) time.
- The third column, labeled NET, reflects the price change between the previous day's settlement and the latest available price.
- The fourth column, LAST, shows the latest price actually traded in the market. This is different from the monitor prices in the cash market, which are only suggested prices. When the price is preceded by the letter S, that is the current day's settlement price. The letter *A* stands for asked price, or the offered price; and *B* for bid price. When *A* or *B* is posted, it indicates that only a one-sided price had been available (offer or bid), prior to being traded. The letter *R* stands for revised price and is used to indicate a change the exchange may make to adjust a price posting error.
- The fifth and sixth columns show the previous two prices traded, in order to indicate the very short-term price behavior. The exchange posts seven previous prices on the floor.
- The seventh and eighth columns display the high and the low prices of the day. The trading range is common to the entire futures market. This is different from the cash market situation, in which traders generally have close but dissimilar daily ranges.
- The ninth column shows the currency futures trading volume.
- The tenth column shows the opening price. This price is derived from the cash forward outright price as of 7:20 Central Standard Time (CST), the same way we calculated the futures example before.
- The last—eleventh—column is labeled CLOSE and it may create confusion in the beginning. The closing price posted in this column always reflects the settlement price of the previous business day. The current day's settlement is always posted in the LAST column—the fourth column— with an *S* in front of it. The settlement price is common to all the parties involved, unlike the cash market situation. Its importance is based on the margin, which has to be posted by the traders holding overnight positions who have a negative P&L. The NET column is therefore a convenient feature for monitoring one's position and profitability.

MARK-TO-MARKET

Mark-to-market is a daily cash flow system used by the U.S. futures exchanges to maintain a minimum level of margin equity for a specific currency future or option, by calculating the profit and loss at the end of each trading day, in each contract position resulting from the price fluctuation.

The calculation of the profit and loss (P&L) for currency futures is executed as follows:

$$\text{P\&L futures} = (SP - BP) \times K \times \$12.50*$$

where

SP = average selling price

BP = average buying price

K = Number of Contracts Traded

> *Example:*
> You sold 100 Sep EC contracts at 10700 and 100 Sep EC contracts at 10780. You closed your position by buying back 200 Sep EC contracts at 10850. Let's calculate your P&L.
>
> $$\text{P\&L} = (10850 - 10740\ ) \times 200 \times \$12.50 = \$275.000$$
>
> Nice profit.

ARBITRAGE

Arbitrage is the risk-free type of trading in which the same instrument is bought and sold simultaneously in two different markets in order to cash in on the divergence between these markets. Let's take a look at the arbitrage opportunities in the futures market.

The futures market activity closely resembles the spot market activity. There is, of course, a good reason for this. Futures are forward outrights, after all. The forward market moves rather slowly and the forward pips, the spread, can easily be stripped. What you are left with is the spot price, as derived from the futures price. Therefore, the prices should move in tandem. They do that for most of the time, but there are some rare exceptions, and the arbitrageurs scramble to bank on these opportunities.

---

*Value of 1 pip for euro, yen, and Swiss franc.

A Trader's Point of View

How and when do these situations occur? In terms of volume, the futures market is only a fraction, relative to the spot market. Consequently, it is easier to "move the market." Just imagine extending two rubber bands: a thin one and a thick one—about 37 times thicker. Which one can you extend easier? (Bodybuilders need not apply.)

Timing, as usual, is very important. Arbitrage opportunities occur when the market is volatile. It is almost impossible to spot a price divergence between the cash and futures in a normally busy market. Because currency futures are less liquid, daily ranges—the number of pips between the low and the high of the day—tend to overshoot during a fast market (or overextend the thinner rubber band). It's arbitrage time.

Arbitraging sounds pretty easy. Doesn't everybody like getting involved in a riskless operation that is profitable? Well, there is more exchange risk than meets the eye, especially for a type of deal that is supposed to be riskless.

Whereas the range is wider for foreign currencies than for the spot currencies, liquidity is more limited. Traders may find it difficult to match the futures amounts with the spot amounts. It is much easier to execute an order on the spot side. In addition, translating the cash amounts, generally quoted against the U.S. dollar, to numbers of standardized foreign currency contracts adds to the difficulty of the task.

EXCHANGE FOR PHYSICAL (EFP)

Currency futures are, as we remember from the definition, forward outright deals, with several special characteristics. This is a very basic but useful issue to recall. Also, as we know by now, futures are traded on centralized markets that operate about eight hours per day. What happens if traders want to trade outside these hours, but lack access to GLOBEX, or their venue lacks the required depth of trading? A popular solution is the *exchange for physical* (*EFP*).

EFPs consist of deals executed in the cash market, outside the exchanges, for amounts equivalent to the currency futures amount, on forward outright prices valued for the futures' expiration. Commercial and investment banks generally quote EFPs even during regular trading hours.

EFPs differ from the regular forward outright deals not only from the point of view of the standardized amounts and expiration dates, but also from the point of view of the paying and receiving instructions (P&R). The trader asking for and trading the EFPs must instruct the market maker to make the payments to the appropriate currency futures broker on the exchange, not to the regular nostro accounts. Unlike a cash forward outright deal, an EFP has the same credit risk coverage as a currency future contract. Therefore, EFPs are the instrument of choice for credit-conscious players.

Moreover, if there is a time difference between the futures and EFP positions, the futures positions will be subject to the margin requirements, even if the positions are overall square. Because EFPs may be traded parallel to currency futures, arbitrage opportunities are theoretically possible. In reality, the costs of transactions and the tight market correlation minimize these opportunities.

CURRENT DIRECTIONS IN THE FUTURES MARKETS

GLOBEX

The future direction of the currency futures markets will be influenced by the ongoing performance of GLOBEX. GLOBEX is an electronic trading system created through a joint venture of the Chicago Mercantile Exchange (CME), the Chicago Board of Trade (CBT), and Reuters PLC. The system was conceived in 1987 as an after-hours trading system, geared toward global futures trading. The system, with terminals in Chicago and New York, was launched on June 25, 1992.

GLOBEX is designed to be used between 6 PM and 6 AM CST, Sunday through Thursday. The system is also designed to allow Far Eastern and European traders to trade futures contracts after the normal business hours in the United States.

The reception has been less enthusiastic than expected. Despite the trading advantages and state-of-the-art technology, the system has been primarily used by domestic players immediately after hours for "clean-up" purposes. Traders who are left with unwanted positions from the regular trading hours tend to square off their positions through GLOBEX. As the transition from the open outcry trading style to quiet computer trading settles, traders are likely to increase their use of GLOBEX.

CHANGES IN TRADING HABITS

Some decline in the currency futures trading volume was registered. The lack of interest can be traced to a number of large corporations that consider the hedging process too cumbersome, and to losses inflicted on smaller investors as a result of the unusually volatile conditions in September 1992.

To counterbalance this trend, several proposals are under consideration. They include increasing the size of the contract and establishing a rule for big order execution geared to trading large amounts only among institutions.

OTHER PRODUCTS

In addition to the cross futures contracts, the Board of Governors of the Chicago Mercantile Exchange approved the trading of two new instruments called *rolling spot contracts* and *all-or-nothing contracts*. These currency products are designed to duplicate more interbank currency market instruments, and are generally used by commercial and investment banks only.

In the spot market, the overnight positions must be "rolled over" in terms of the value date, which is two business days (except for the Canadian dollar). As this operation may be cumbersome as far as the execution and the accounting are concerned, CME offers an alternative that will automatically roll over the position to the next business day. The product minimizes the accounting required and does not generate delivery of currency. The trades are guaranteed by the exchange, so the credit risk is minimized.

The first rolling spot contract was offered in the British pound, in the size of BP 250,000, four times the size of the BP future. The larger size is necessary because the amount being rolled over in the cash market tends to be larger. Rolling spot contracts will be offered for all the currency futures contracts traded on the IMM. Traders should be aware of the fixed amount of the currency futures contract vis-à-vis the amount needed to roll over.

REGULATION IN THE UNITED STATES

The Commodity Futures Trading Commission (CFTC) was created by Congress in 1974 as an independent agency with a mandate to regulate commodity futures and options markets in the United States. The mandate was renewed in 1978, 1982, and 1986.

The CFTC's responsibilities are to:

- Ensure the economic utility of futures markets, via competitiveness and efficiency.
- Ensure the integrity of these markets.

- Protect the participants against manipulation, fraud, and abusive practices.

The Commission, based in Washington, D.C., regulates the activities of 285 commodity brokerage firms; 48,211 salespeople; 8017 floor brokers; 1325 commodity pool operators (CPOs); 2733 commodity trading advisers (CTAs); and 1486 introducing brokers (IBs).

The CFTC reviews the terms and conditions of proposed futures contracts and registers them through the National Futures Association (NFA). NFA is a self-regulatory organization that consists of futures commission merchants (FCMs), commodity pool operators (CPOs), commodity trading advisers (CTAs), introducing brokers (IBs), leverage transaction merchants (LTMs), commodity exchanges, commercial firms, and banks. It is responsible for certain aspects of the regulation of futures commission merchants (FCMs), commodity pool operators (CPOs), commodity trading advisers (CTAs), introducing brokers (IBs), and leverage transaction merchants (LTMs), focusing primarily on the qualifications and proficiency, financial conditions, retail sales practices, and business conduct of these futures professionals.

CONCLUSION

The establishment of the International Monetary Market by the Chicago Mercantile Exchange in 1972 was an innovative step in the long history of the commodity futures markets. Foreign currency futures offer an alternative to the cash market and a mechanism for hedging. The IMM also opened the market to smaller investors. The IMM was beneficial to the CME as a whole, as it contributed to the overall growth of the futures industry.

The Exchange has been positioning itself for technological steps in the markets. GLOBEX provides a splendid computerized trading environment. Although its use has been hampered by the human need to adjust to changes, the trading system is strategically placed to answer the trading requirements of the twenty-first century.

15 Currency Options

A *currency option* is a contract between a buyer and a seller that gives the buyer the right, but not the obligation, to trade a specific amount of currency at a predetermined price and within a predetermined period of time, regardless of the market price of the currency; and gives the seller, or *writer*, the obligation to deliver the currency under the predetermined terms, if and when the buyer wants to exercise the option.

Currency options are unique trading instruments, equally fit for speculation and hedging. Options allow for a comprehensive customization of each individual strategy, a quality of vital importance for the sophisticated investor. More factors affect the option price relative to the prices of other foreign currency instruments. Unlike spot or forwards, both high and low volatility may generate a profit in the options market. For some, options are a cheaper vehicle for currency trading. For others, options mean added security and exact stop-loss order execution.

This chapter's presentation of the fundamentals of options will enable you to select the most advantageous characteristics for your own trading strategy.

THE CURRENCY OPTIONS MARKETPLACE

Currency options constitute the fastest-growing segment of the foreign exchange market. As of April 1998, options represented 5 percent of the foreign exchange market. (See Figure 15.1.) The biggest options trading center is the United States, followed by the United Kingdom and Japan.

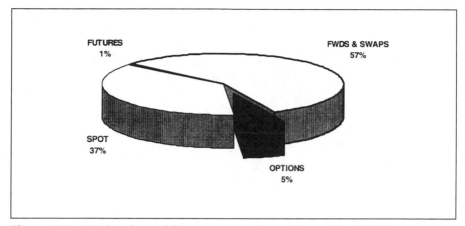

Figure 15.1. Market share of the currency options. *(Source: The Bank for International Settlements)*

Options prices are based on, or derived from, the cash instruments. Therefore, an option is a derivative instrument. Options are usually mentioned vis-à-vis insurance and hedging strategies. Often, however, traders have misconceptions regarding both the difficulty and simplicity of using options. There are also misconceptions regarding the capabilities of options. This chapter presents a balanced look at what options are and how they can be of help to you.

BENEFITS OF TRADING OPTIONS

There must be some important advantages to options; otherwise it would be impossible to justify the rush to trade them all around the world. Once you see what they are, you can then decide whether options make sense to you and, if so, how you can profitably take advantage of them.

TRADE, DO NOT GAMBLE

Let's assume for a moment that you, along with the rest of the market, expect some important news, perhaps the release of economic data or the approach of a significant chart point. It is just one of those "make it or break it" situations. Let's continue to assume, rather safely, that you would rather make it than break it.

The currency is likely to become very volatile after the fact. But if you wait until the information is becoming available, you may find it difficult to join the consequent fast market. In the cash market, you will likely face the choice of either waiting longer than you want to, or gambling and taking a 50–50 chance, plunging in either way and hoping for the best. Of course, hope hasn't so far proven itself to be one of the leading money management theories. And gambling is conducted in institutions better equipped for that type of activity.

The answer to this kind of trading dilemma is options. Unlike in the cash market, you can buy both a call and a put, in an option strategy called a straddle, and you can realize a profit regardless of the direction of the market.

FLAT MARKET

There are few worse scenarios for currency traders than a relatively flat market. A quiet market is difficult to bear, especially when traders are flexible enough to consider as a "good" factor both a positive and a negative piece of information for the economy. That is because "good" refers to the capacity of a factor to create volatility in the market. Reality is that slow trading periods do occur. Again, the solution to the problem is options trading.

In a flat market, a trader may sell, or write, options. Because the writer of the option will receive a premium, or the price of the option, from the buyer of the option, this becomes good old-fashioned trading income.

Traders who expect the currency to rise buy call options from sellers, or writers. Those who expect the currency to ease buy puts from sellers, or writers. Writers either have an opposite expectation from buyers or expect a relatively stable market.

LIQUID MARKET

Once, when a group of students was asked why they would trade currency options instead of cash instruments, one of the answers stood out: "Because they are there." It is absolutely true, at least in terms of liquidity: The market is out there, both for cash and currency futures. The options markets are deep and there are many counterparties ready and willing to intellectually duel with you on the direction or volatility of the market. Liquidity is a sine qua non condition for a successful market, and currency options markets are generally deep.

INSURANCE

It is important to understand that trading options will not necessarily provide you with any financial insurance. Traders who buy options should realize that they are not securing insurance per se, but insurance in the sense of simply knowing how much they can lose if the market performs differently from their forecast.

However, if trading options means selling, or writing, options, the insurance aspect completely and fully disappears, other things being equal. If the market makes an adverse move, the writer has no protection from the option.

Of course, things are not so terrible for the writer, who will be paid the premium; this offers a limited buffer against the adverse move. In addition, the option writer can always hedge or cover the short position.

HEDGING

At one time, the usual hedging methods for corporations revolved around swaps, forward outright contracts, and futures. However, for some time, currency hedging has become an important tool for corporations, and currency options are increasingly becoming vital tools in this process.

One advantage is that buyers know the maximum loss that they might suffer. This feature is important, as management is able to consider real costs, not expectations, when hedging is considered. Also, with the continuous overall growth of foreign exchange markets, the increased currency volatility, and the more general internationalization of trade, corporate treasurers have been presented with higher obstacles to clear. Currency options have the advantage of offering more comprehensive hedging possibilities, due to their capacity for customization.

RANGING THE EXCHANGE RISK

Not all corporations are willing to hedge the entire currency position. Some players fix either the upside or the downside risk, and these single-side risks may be fixed through basic options. Limiting the risk—and profitability—on both sides may be achieved through an option known as a *fence*. The ability to fix, or *range*, one or both sides of the exchange risk constitutes a major advantage of trading options. (Options strategies are discussed in Chapter 16.)

WHERE CURRENCY OPTIONS ARE TRADED

In the currency markets, options are available on either cash or futures. It follows, then, that they are traded either *over-the-counter* (*OTC*) or on the centralized futures markets.

The Over-the-Counter Market

The majority of currency options, around 81 percent, are traded over-the-counter. (See Figure 15.2.) The over-the-counter market is similar to the spot or swap market. Corporations may call banks and banks will trade with each other either directly or in the brokers' market. This type of dealing allows for maximum flexibility: any amount, any currency, any odd expiration date, any time. The currency amounts may be even or odd. The amounts may be quoted in either U.S. dollars or foreign currencies.

Any currency may be traded as an option, not only the ones available as futures contracts. Therefore, traders may quote on any exotic currency, as required, including any cross currencies. The expiration date may be quoted anywhere from several hours to several years, although the bulk of dates are concentrated around the even dates—one week, one month, two months, and so on. The cash market never closes, so options may be traded literally around the clock.

Customization doesn't come free. Credit and country risk are important factors in the decision-making process.

Options on Currency Futures

In the United States, three exchanges offer option contracts on currency futures: the Chicago Mercantile Exchange (CME), the Philadelphia Stock Exchange (PHLX), and the New York FINEX.

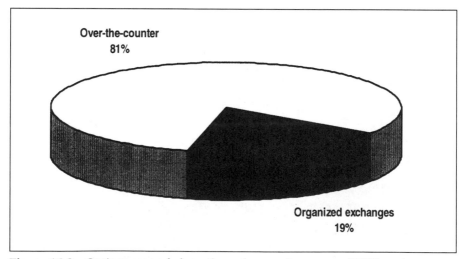

Figure 15.2. Options are traded mostly on the over-the-counter (OTC) market. *(Source: The Bank for International Settlements)*

Commodity Size	Months	Codes Clr/Tick	Minimum Fluctuation In Price	Strike Price Interval/Notes
Australian Dollar	Mar, Jun, Sep, Dec	AD / AD	0.0001	
100,000 Australian Dollars			(1 pt.)	
Australian Dollar	Quarterly, Serial Months & Weekly Expiration Options	AD / KA Calls	0.0001	$ / AD
Options		AD / JA Puts	(1 pt.)	$0.01 intervals e.g. $0.76, $0.77 plus .005 intervals for the first 7 listed expirations e.g. $0.775, $0.780.
		Weekly Exp. Options: 1AC / 5AC Calls 1AP / 5AP Puts	($10.00)	
			Weekly options.	
Brazilian Real	All 12 calendar months and weekly expiration options.	BRC / Calls	0.0001	$ / BR
Options		BRP / Puts	(1 pt.)	0.01 intervals e.g. 1.0600, 1.0700, 1.0800 and for the first 7 listed expirations only additional strikes at $0.005 intervals e.g. $1.08500, $1.09000.
			($10.00 / pt.)	
		Weekly Exp. Options: 1RC / 5RC Calls 1RP / 5RP Puts	($10.00) cab − $5.00	
			Weekly options.	
British Pound 62,500 British Pounds	Mar, Jun, Sep, Dec	BP / BP	0.0002 (2 pt.)	
British Pound	Quarterly, Serial Months & Weekly Expiration Options	BP / CP Calls	0.0002	$ / BP
Options		BP / PP Puts	(2 pt.)	$0.020 intervals e.g. $1.440, $1.460, $1.480, etc. plus strikes at $0.01 intervals for the first 7 listed expirations e.g. 1.43, 1.44, 1.45, etc.
			($6.25 / pt)	
		Weekly Exp. Options: 1BC / 5BC Calls 1BP / 5BP Puts	($12.50) cab = $6.25	
	GLOBEX:			
Canadian Dollar 100,000 Canadian Dollars	Mar, Jun, Sep, Dec	C1 / CD	0.0001 (1 pt.)	
Canadian Dollar	Quarterly, Serial Months & Weekly Expiration Options	C1 / CV Calls	0.0001	$ / CD
Options		C1 / PV Puts	(1 pt.) ($10.00 / pt.)	$0.005 intervals e.g. $0.800, $0.805.
		Weekly Exp. Options: 1CC / 5CC Calls 1CP / 5CP Puts	($10.00) cab = $5.00	
	GLOBEX: One Quarterly & Two Serial Months		0.00005 (1/2 pt.)	

Figure 15.3. Contract specifications of options on currency futures on the Chicago Mercantile Exchange. *(Source: CME)*

Commodity Size	Months	Codes Clr/Tick	Minimum Fluctuation In Price	Strike Price Interval/Notes
Deutsche Mark 125,000 Deutsche Marks	Mar, Jun, Sep, Dec	D1 / DM	0.0001 (1 pt)	
Deutsche Mark	Quarterly, Serial Months & Weekly Expiration Options	D1 / CM Calls	0.0001	$ / DM
Options		D1 / PM Puts	(1 pt.) ($12.50 / pt.)	$0.01 intervals e.g. $0.63, $0.64 plus $0.005 intervals for first 7 listed expirations e.g. $0.635, $0.640.
	GLOBEX: One Quarterly & Two Serial Months	Weekly Exp. Options: 1DC / 5DC Calls 1DP / 5DP Puts	($12.50) cab = $6.25 0.00005 (1/2 pt.)	
Euro FX Unit 125,000 x Euro	Mar, Jun, Sep, Dec	EC / EC	0.0001 (1 pt.)	
Euro FX Unit	Quarterly, Serial Months & Weekly Expiration Options	EC / EC Calls	0.0001	$0.01 per ECU, e.g., $1.0500, $1.0600, $1.0700, etc.
Options		EC / EC Puts	(1 pt.) ($12.50 / pt.)	and for the first 7 listed option expirations only, additional strike prices at intervals of $.005, e.g., $1.055, $1.065, $1.075, etc.
	GLOBEX: March Quarterly Cycle	Weekly Exp. Options: 1X /2X / 3X/ 4X / 5X	($12.50) cab=$6.25	
French Francs 500,000 French Francs	Mar, Jun, Sep, Dec	FR / FR	0.00002 (2 pt.)	See note
French Francs	Quarterly, Serial Months & Weekly Expiration Options	FR / IF Calls	0.00002	US$ per French Franc 0.00250 intervals e.g. 0.18000, 0.18250, 0.18500.
Options		FR /IF Puts	(2 pt.) (5.00 / pt.)	See note
		Weekly Exp. Options: 1L / 5L Calls 1L / 5L2 Puts	($10:00) cab = $5.00	**
Japanese Yen 12,500,000 Japanese Yen	Mar, Jun, Sep, Dec	J1 / JY	0.000001 (1 pt.)	
Japanese Yen	Quarterly, Serial Months & Weekly Expiration Options	J1 / CJ Calls	0.000001	$ / JY
Options		J1 / PJ Puts	(1 pt.) ($12:50 / pt.)	$0.0001 intervals e.g. $0.0072, $0.0071 plus $0.00005 intervals for the first 7 listed expirations, e.g. $0.00725, $0.00730.

Figure 15.3. (*Continued*)

Commodity Size	Months	Codes Clr/Tick	Minimum Fluctuation In Price	Strike Price Interval/Notes
Japanese yen (*cont.*)	GLOBEX:	Weekly Exp. Options: 1JC / 5JC Calls 1JP / 5JP Puts	($12:50) cab - $6.25	
		One Quarterly & Two Serial Months		0.0000005 (1/2 pt.)
Mexican Peso 500,000 New Mexican Pesos	Mar, Jun, Sep, Dec	MP / MP	0.000025 (2½ pts.)	N/A
Mexican Peso	Quarterly, Serial Months & Weekly Expiration Options	MPC / Calls	0.000025	$ / MP
Options		MPP / Puts	(2½ pts.) ($5.00 / pt.)	$0.01 intervals e.g. $0.12, $0.13, $0.14, etc.
		Weekly Exp. Options: 1MC / 5MC Calls 1MP / 5MP Puts	($12.50) cab = $6.25	
New Zealand Dollar 100,000 New Zealand Dollars	Mar, Jun, Sep, Dec	NE / NE	0.0001 (1 pt.)	
New Zealand Dollar	Quarterly, Serial Months & Weekly Expiration Options	NE / NE Calls	0.0001	$0.01 per New Zealand Dollar, e.g., $0.70, $0.71, $0.72, etc. and for the first 7 listed options expirations only, additional strikes at intervals of $0.005, e.g., $0.705, $0.715, $0.725, etc.
Options		NE / NE Puts	(1 pt.) ($10.00 / pt.)	
		Weekly Exp. Options: 1ZC / 5ZC Calls 1ZP / 5ZP Puts	($10.00) cab = $5.00	
Russian Ruble 500,000 Russian Rubles	Mar, Jun, Sep, Dec	RU/RU	0.000025 (2½ pts.)	
Russian Ruble	Quarterly, Serial Months & Weekly Expiration Options	RU/RU Calls	0.000025	$0.005 per Russian Ruble, e.g., $.165, $.175, $.185, etc.
Options		RU / RU Puts	(2½ pts.) ($5.00 / pt.)	
	Mar, Jun, Sep, Oct, Nov, Dec	Weekly Exp. Options: 1U,2U,3U 4U,5U	($12.50) cab=$6.25	
South African Rand 500,000 South African Rand	All 12 calendar months.	RA / RA	0.000025 (2½ pts.)	N/A
South African Rand	All 12 Calendar Months & Weekly Expiration Options	RA / RA Calls	0.000025	$/RA at intervals of $0.00500, e.g., $0.21500, $0.22000, $0.22500, etc. and for the first 7 listed options expirations only, additional strikes at intervals of $0.00250, e.g., $0.21750, $0.22250, $0.22750, etc.
Options		RA / RA Puts	(2½ pts.) ($5.00 / pt.)	
		Weekly Exp. Options: 1NC / 5NC Calls 1NP / 5NP Puts	($12.50) cab = $6.25	

Figure 15.3. (*Continued*)

Commodity Size	Months	Codes Clr/Tick	Minimum Fluctuation In Price	Strike Price Interval/Notes
Swiss Franc 125,000 Swiss Francs	Mar, Jun, Sep, Dec GLOBEX:(	E1 / SF	0.0001 (1 pt.) $12.50 / pt.)	
Swiss Franc	Quarterly, Serial Months & Weekly Expiration Options	E1 / SF Calls	0.0001	$ / SF $0.01
Options		E1 / PF Puts	(1 pt.) ($12.50 / pt.)	e.g. $0.72, $0.73 plus $0.005 intervals for the first 4 listed expirations e.g. $0.725, $0.730.
	GLOBEX:	Weekly Exp. Options: 1SC / 5SC Calls 1SP / 5SP Puts	($12.50) 0.00005 (1/2 pt.)	

Figure 15.3. (*Continued*)

Options on deutsche mark futures were introduced on the Chicago IMM in 1984 by the Chicago Mercantile Exchange's Index and Option Market (IOM). In 1985, options on British pound and Swiss franc futures were added. Since 1987, options on Japanese yen, Canadian dollar, French franc, and Australian dollar have been introduced as well.

The introduction of the euro in 1999 was followed by the prompt introduction of options on euro futures. At the time of this writing, the futures markets were still trading options on legacy currencies, such as deutsche mark.

Trading options on futures on either the Chicago (see Figure 15.3) or Philadelphia (see Figure 15.4) centralized markets minimizes credit and country risk, as the clearinghouse takes the opposite side on every deal. Therefore, a trader buys from or sells to the exchange, not another trader. This way, traders can focus on dealing, rather than on securing credit lines with the other participants. However, traders must be aware of the limitations generated by the reduced number of currencies available to trade and by the standardization of currency contract sizes and expiration dates.

Trading an option on currency futures will entitle the buyer to the right, but not the obligation, to take physical possession of the currency future. Unlike the currency futures, buying currency options does not require an initiation margin. The option premium, or price, paid by the buyer to the seller, or writer, reflects the buyer's total risk.

However, upon taking physical possession of the currency future by exercising the option, a trader will have to deposit a margin.

	Australian Dollar	British Pound	Canadian Dollar	Deutsche Mark	Euro
TICKER SYMBOLS					
(American/European)					
Mid-month Options	XAD/CAD	XBP/CBP	XCD/CCD	XDM/CDM	XEU/ECU
Half-point Strike	XAZ/CAZ	n.a/n.a	n.a/n.a	XDZ/CDZ	n.a./n.a.
(Three near-term months only)					
Month-end Options	ADW/EDA	BPW/EPO	CDW/ECD	DMW/EDM	XEW/ECW
Half-point Strike	AZW/EAW	n.a/n.a	n.a/n.a	DMZ/EDZ	n.a./n.a.
Long-term Options					
13 to 24 Months	n.a	n.a/YPX	n.a	n.a/YDM	n.a
CONTRACT SIZE	50,000	31,250	50,000	62,500	62,500
POSITION & EXERCISE					
LIMITS	200,000	200,000	200,000	200,000	200,000
BASE CURRENCY	USD	USD	USD	USD	USD
UNDERLYING CURRENCY	AUD	GBP	CAD	DEM	EURO
EXERCISE PRICE INTERVALS					
Three Nearest Months	1¢	1¢.	5¢.	5¢	2¢
6, 9 and 12 Months	1¢	2¢.	5¢	1¢	2¢
Over 12 Months	n.a.	4¢	n.a.	2¢	n.a.
PREMIUM QUOTATIONS	Cents per unit	Cents per unit	Cents per unit	Cents per unit	Cents per unit
MINIMUM PREMIUM	$.(00)01	$.(00)01	$.(00)01	$.(00)01	$.(00)01
CHANGE	per unit	per unit	per unit	per unit	per unit
	= $5.00	= $3.125	= $5.00	= $6.25	= $6.25
MARGIN	USD	USD	USD	USD	USD

	French Franc	Japanese Yen	Swiss Franc	Deutsche Mark/ Japanese Yen	British Pound/ Deutsche Mark
TICKER SYMBOLS					
(American/European)					
Mid-Month Options	XFF/CFF	XJY/CJY	XSF/CSF	n.a/MYX	n.a/PMX
Half-point Strike	n.a/n.a	XJZ/CJZ	XSZ/CSZ	n.a/MYZ	n.a/n.a
(Three near-term months only)					
Month-end Options	FFW/EFF	JYW/EJY	SFW/ESW	n.a/MYW	n.a/PMW
High-point Strike	n.a/n.a	JYZ/EJZ	SFZ/ESZ	n.a/MXZ	n.a/n.a
Long-term Options					
13 to 24 Months	n.a/YFF	n.a/YJY	n.a	n.a	n.a
CONTRACT SIZE	250,000	6,250,000	62,500	62,500 DM	31,250 BP
POSITION & EXERCISE LIMITS	200,000	200,000	200,000	200,000	200,000
BASE CURRENCY	USD	USD	USD	JPY	DEM
UNDERLYING CURRENCY	FRF	JPY	CHF	DEM	GBP
EXERCISE PRICE INTERVALS					
Three Nearest Months	.25¢	.005¢	.5¢	.5 JY	.02 DM
6, 9 and 12 Months	.25¢	.01¢	1¢	1 JY	.02 DM
Over 12 Months	.50¢	.02¢	n.a.	n.a.	n.a.

Figure 15.4. Contract specifications on standardized options on the Philadelphia Stock Exchange. *(Source: Philadelphia Stock Exchange)*

	French Franc	Japanese Yen	Swiss Franc	Deutsche Mark/ Japanese Yen	British Pound/ Deutsche Mark
PREMIUM QUOTATIONS	Tenths of a cent per unit	Hundredths of a cent per unit	Cents per unit	Japanese yen	Deutsche mark per BP
MINIMUM PREMIUM CHANGE	$.(000)02 per unit = $5.00	$.(0000)01 per unit = $6.25	$.(00)01 per unit = $6.25	.01 JY per unit = 625 JY	.0002 DM per unit = 6.25 DM
MARGIN	USD	USD	USD	USD or JY	USD or DM

Expiration Months

Mid-month Options: March, June, September, and December + two near-term months

Month-end Options: Three nearest months

Long-term Options: 18 and 24 months (June and December)

Expiration Date/Last Trading Day

Providing it is a business day, otherwise the day immediately prior:

Mid-month Options: Friday before the third Wednesday of expiring month

Month-end Options: Last Friday of the month

Long-term Options: Friday before the third Wednesday of expiring month

Expiration Settlement Date

Mid-month Options: Third Thursday of expiring month, except for March, June, September, and December expirations, which are the third Wednesday

Month-end Options: Thursday following the last Friday of the month

Long-term Options: Third Thursday of expiration month, except for March, June, September, and December expirations, which are the third Wednesday

Exercise Style

Mid-month Options:

Dollar Based: American and European

Cross Rates: European

Month-End Options:

Dollar Based: American and European

Cross Rates: European

Long-term Options: European

Trading Hours:

2:30 AM to 2:30 PM Philadelphia time, Monday through Friday.

Trading hours for Canadian dollar are 7 AM to 2:30 PM Philadelphia time, Monday through Friday.

Issuer and Guarantor:

The Options Clearing Corporation (OCC)

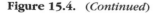

Figure 15.4. *(Continued)*

THE U.S. DOLLAR INDEX

FINEX, a division of the New York Cotton Exchange, offers a centralized market for trading options on the U.S. Dollar Index. This index, which consists of the weighted average of the prices of ten foreign currencies against the U.S. dollar, provides the same general indication of the international value of the U.S. dollar that the Dow Jones Industrial Average provides of the value of the U.S. stock market.

The ten countries have advanced foreign exchange markets and close economic relations with the United States. The currencies, the formula, and the weights used to calculate the USDX are identical to those used by the Federal Reserve Board to calculate its own trade-weighted dollar index.

Here are the details for the spot USDX:

Currency	Base Rate	Weight (%)
Deutsche mark	35.548	20.8
Japanese yen	0.3819	13.6
French franc	22.191	13.1
British pound	247.24	11.9
Canadian dollar	100.33	9.1
Italian lire	0.176	9.0
Dutch guilder	34.834	8.3
Belgian franc	2.5377	6.4
Swedish krona	22.582	4.2
Swiss franc	31.084	3.6

Upon the cessation of the European legacy currencies in 2002, the combined weight of the deutsche mark, French franc, Italian lire, Dutch guilder, and Belgian franc will be replaced by equivalent weight of the euro. The weights to be used are:

1 EUR = 1.95583 DEM
1 EUR = 6.55957 FRF
1 EUR = 1936.27 ITL
1 EUR = 2.20371 NLG
1 EUR = 40.3399 BEF

The spot USDX is calculated as the geometric trade-weighted average of the changes of the ten major currencies relative to the base period of March 1973, rounded to two decimal points.

Multiplier = (Base rate/Spot rate)Currency weight

where

Base rate = exchange rate in the base period (March 1973) in American terms

Spot rate = current spot rate in American terms

Currency weight = weight assigned to each currency, based on the respective country's relative share of world trade.

The futures contract (symbol is DX) size is $1,000 times the U.S. Dollar Index. FINEX offers options (symbol DO) on USDX futures.

In addition to options on the U.S. Dollar Index, FINEX provides options on the following currency pairs:

- Euro/Japanese yen
- Euro/Swedish krona
- Euro/Swiss franc
- Euro/British pound
- Euro/Norwegian krone
- Euro/Canadian dollar
- Australian dollar/NZ dollar
- Australian dollar/Japanese yen
- British pound/Japanese yen
- British pound/Swiss franc
- Swiss franc/Japanese yen

PREMIUM

Premium is the price of the option paid by the buyer to the seller. It is usually paid at the time of the trade, but it may also be paid at the expiration date. Premium may be quoted in points or in percentages and may be expressed in four different ways:

1. Percentage in U.S. dollars.

If both the unit of account and the premium are quoted in the same currency, then the price will be quoted in the OTC market as a percentage of the U.S. dollar amount through the strike or exercise price—the price at which the underlying currency will be delivered upon exercise.

Example:

Buy a June 5 Swiss franc call struck at CHF 1.50 for 4 percent.

If the amount is CHF 3,000,000, then the premium will be:

$$CHF\ 3,000,000\ /\ CHF\ 1.50 = \$2,000,000$$
$$\$2,000,000 \times 4\ percent = \$80,000$$

2. In U.S. dollars where the option quotes are made in foreign currency per U.S. dollar (European terms) in the OTC market.

Example:

Buy a June 5 Swiss franc call struck at CHF 1.50 for $ .027. If the amount is CHF 3,000,000, then the premium will be:

$$CHF\ 3,000,000 \times \$\ .027 = \$81,000$$

3. In U.S. dollars where the option quotes are made in U.S. dollar per foreign currency unit (American terms) on the futures market.

Example:

A quotation of .88 would represent $.0088 per SF. The option premium would be $550 (62,500 SF * $.0088) on the Philadelphia Stock Exchange.

4. In foreign currency.

Example:

A quotation of .60 in a SF/JY contract would be .6 yen per Swiss franc on the Philadelphia Stock Exchange. The premium would be 37,500 JY (.6 JY * 62,500 SF).

THEORETICAL MODELS: FACTORS DETERMINING OPTION PRICE

Seven major factors have an impact on the option price:

1. Price of the currency.

2. Strike (exercise) price.

3. Volatility of the currency.

4. Expiration date.

5. Interest rate differential.

6. Call or put.

7. American or European option style.

In the next seven sections, we examine these factors in detail and provide numerous figures and examples to illustrate their impact on option prices.

PRICE OF THE CURRENCY

The currency price is the central building block, as all the other factors are compared and analyzed against it. It is the currency price behavior that both generates the need for options and impacts on the profitability of options.

The impact of the currency price on the option premium is measured by delta, the first of the Greek letters used to describe aspects of the theoretical pricing models in this discussion of factors determining the option price.

Delta

Delta, or commonly Δ, is the first derivative of the option-pricing model. Delta may be viewed from three angles.

1. Generally, delta is understood to be the *change* of the currency option price relative to a change in the currency price. For instance, an option with a delta of .5 is expected to move at one half the rate of change of the currency price. Therefore, if the price of a currency goes up 10 percent, then the price of an option on that particular currency is expected to rise by 5 percent.

2. Delta may also be perceived by futures traders to be the *hedge ratio* between the option contracts and the currency futures contracts necessary to establish a neutral hedge. Therefore, an option with a delta of .5 will need two option contracts for each of the currency futures contracts.

3. Finally, delta may be called the *theoretical* or *equivalent share position*. In this case, delta is the number of currency futures contracts by which a call buyer is long or a put buyer is short. If we use the same example of the delta of .5, then the buyer of the put option is short half a currency futures contract.

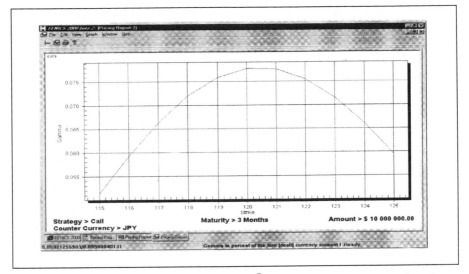

Figure 15.5. Graph of delta. *(Source: FENICS® Software.* © *by Inventure America Inc. All rights reserved.)*

The value of delta ranges between 0 and 1. Figure 15.5 presents a graph of delta.

Dynamic Hedging

The relationship between the price of the currency and the premium of the option on that specific currency is intrinsically dynamic. To keep this relationship constant, the position must be *delta hedged*. Because the hedge must be adjusted continuously, this process is known as *dynamic hedging*. The failure to implement dynamic hedging adds market risk to the position.

Applying this method in practice may be a taxing undertaking. When volatility significantly exceeds a trader's forecast, the cost of dynamic hedging may be very high. In addition, the hedge does not provide comprehensive protection during high volatility—crisis—situations, in which the currency prices gap. *Price gapping* occurs when prices jump from one level to another, rather than moving continuously to the sequential price. For instance, if the price is 1.6000, then the next price on the upside in a regular market should be 1.6001 and then 1.6002. In a gapping market, the next price after 1.6000 may be 1.6050, allowing traders no room for adjusting their positions.

Traders may be unable to secure prices in the spot, forward outright, or futures market, temporarily leaving the position delta unhedged. In order to avoid the high cost of hedging and the risk of unusually high volatility, traders may hedge their original options positions with other options. This method of risk neutralization is called *gamma* or *vega hedging*.

Gamma

Gamma (Γ) is also known·as the *curvature of the option*. (See Figure 15.6.) It is the second derivative of the option-pricing model and is the rate of change of an option's delta, or the sensitivity of the delta. For instance, an option with delta = .5 and gamma = .05 is expected to have a delta = .55 if the currency rises by 1 point, or a delta = .45 if the currency decreases by 1 point. Gamma ranges between 0 percent and 100 percent. The higher the gamma, the higher the sensitivity of the delta. It may therefore be useful to think of gamma as the acceleration of the option relative to the movement of the currency.

A Trader's Point of View

- Gamma is at its highest for short-dated at-the-money options.
- Options buyers like high gamma options because of the advantageous leverage.
- Writers of high gamma options are taking high risk due to potentially great fluctuations in the premium caused by relatively small swerves in the spot rate.

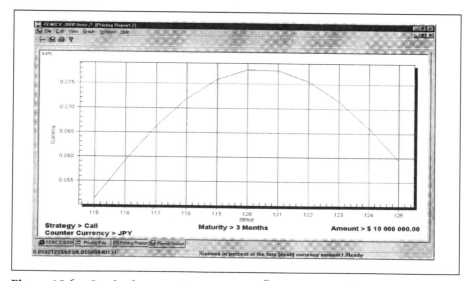

Figure 15.6. Graph of gamma.*(Source: FENICS® Software. © by Inventure America Inc. All rights reserved.)*

STRIKE OR EXERCISE PRICE

What does it mean to say that the buyer has the right to "exercise" his or her option at a predetermined price? *Exercising* refers to the process in which a buyer converts the option into a currency position. In the case of a call, exercising will create a long currency position, whereas in the case of a put, the buyer will have a short currency position.

The *exercise* or *strike price*, then, is simply the price at which the underlying currency will be delivered upon exercise. How does it relate to the currency price?

In-the-Money

A call that has a present currency price higher than the strike price is called in-the-money or ITM. (See Figure 15.7.) A put that has the present currency price lower than the strike price is called in-the-money or ITM. (See Figure 15.8.)

In-the-money currency options are the most expensive, since the strike price is better than the current price of the underlying currency, and the currency must move only moderately in order to generate a profit.

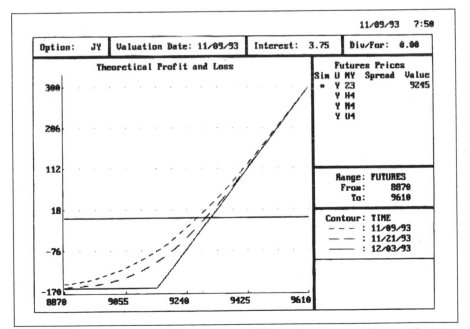

Figure 15.7. Diagram of a call in-the-money (ITM) on Japanese yen futures. *(Source: FutureSource)*

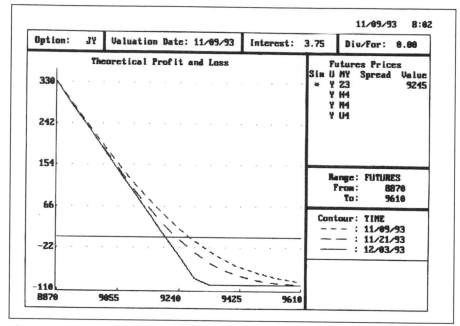

Figure 15.8. Diagram of a put in-the-money (ITM) on Japanese yen futures. *(Source: FutureSource)*

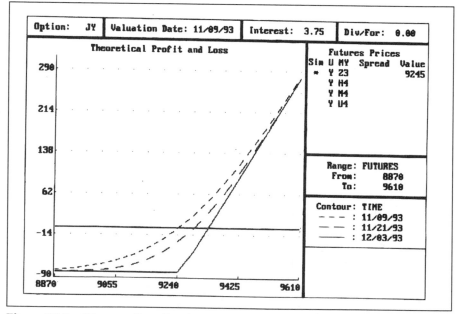

Figure 15.9. Diagram of a call at-the-money (ATM) on Japanese yen futures. *(Source: FutureSource)*

Example:

Option	Underlying Price	In-the-money	By
EUR Mar 1.0700 call	1.0800	Yes	100

Underlying price > Strike price, by 1.0800 - 1.0700 = .0100, or 100 pips in-the-money

EUR Mar 1.0800 put	1.0700	Yes	100

Underlying price < Strike price, by 1.0800 - 1.0700 = .0100, or 100 pips in-the-money

At-the-Money

If the present currency price is approximately equal to the strike price, the option is at-the-money or ATM. (See Figures 15.9 and 15.10.) These currency options have less expensive premiums, as the strike price is close or identical to the current price of the underlying currency.

Example:

Option	Underlying Price	At-the-money	By
CHF Sep	69 call	69.00	Yes 0
CHF Sep	69 put	69.00	Yes 0

Underlying price = Strike price

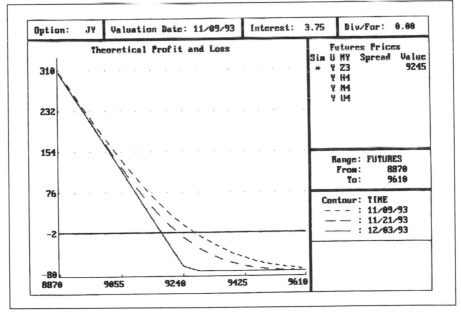

Figure 15.10. Diagram of a put at-the-money (ATM) on Japanese yen futures. *(Source: FutureSource)*

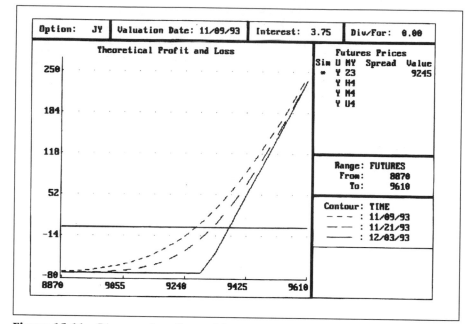

Figure 15.11. Diagram of a call out-of-the-money (OTM) on Japanese yen futures. *(Source: FutureSource)*

Out-of-the-Money

A call that has the present currency price lower than the strike price is called out-of-the-money or OTM. (See Figure 15.11.) A put that has the present currency price higher than the strike price is called out-of-the-money or OTM. (See Figure 15.12.)

Example:

Option	Underlying Price	Out-the-money	By
GBP Dec 150 call	147.50	Yes	250

Underlying price < Strike price, by 147.50 − 150 = 2.50, or 250 pips

Option	Underlying Price	Out-the-money	By
GBP Dec 145 put	147.50	Yes	250

Underlying price > Strike price, by 147.50 − 145 = 2.50, or 250 pips

The premiums for OTM options are the cheapest, since the strike price is worse than the current price of the underlying currency. Therefore, the currency must make a substantial move in order to generate a good profit.

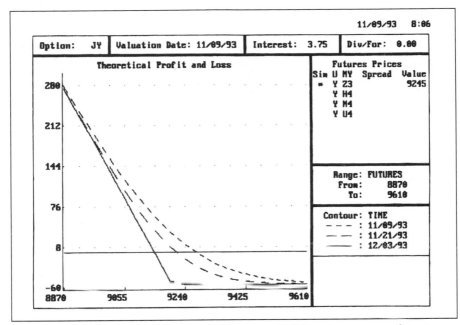

Figure 15.12. Diagram of a put out-of-the-money (OTM) on Japanese yen futures. *(Source: FutureSource)*

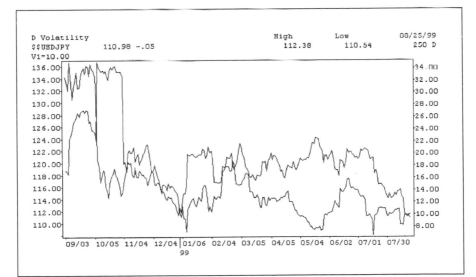

Figure 15.13. Historical price volatility of the Japanese yen. *(Source: Bridge Information Systems, Inc.)*

Intrinsic Value

Intrinsic value is the amount by which an option is in-the-money. In the case of a call, the intrinsic value equals the difference between the underlying currency price and the strike price.

Example:

$$IV_{call} = PCP - SP$$

where

IV_{call} = intrinsic value of a call

CP = present currency price

SP = strike price

In the case of a put, the intrinsic value equals the difference between the strike price and the present currency price, when beneficial.

Example:

$$Iv_{put} = SP - PCP$$

where

IV_{put} = intrinsic value of a put

SP = strike price

PCP = present currency price

It follows, then, that out-of-the-money options do not have any intrinsic value.

Extrinsic Value or Time Value

The extrinsic or time value (also known as the time premium) consists of the difference between the option premium and its intrinsic value. Since out-of-the-money options do not have any intrinsic value, these options' premium equals only the time value.

Example:

$$TV = P - IV$$

where

TV = time value

P = premium

IV = intrinsic value

In this example, you can identify each option's premium, intrinsic value, and time (extrinsic) value, based on the currency option, currency price, and option price:

Example:

Currency Option	Present Currency Price	Option Premium	Intrinsic Value	Time Value
EUR Jun 1.10 call	1.0400	0.25	0	0.25
CAD Sep 60 put	59.86	1.59	0.14	1.45
CHF Mar 69 call	72.29	3.48	3.29	0.19
JPY Dec 89 put	89.00	1.50	0	1.50

VOLATILITY OF THE CURRENCY

Volatility is the degree to which the price of currency tends to fluctuate within a certain period of time. Free-floating currencies, such as the euro or the Japanese yen, tend to be volatile against the U.S. dollar. (See Figure 15.13.)

The volatility of a pegged currency, such as the Argentine peso, is nearly 0 versus the currency against which it is pegged, in this case the dollar.

Sometimes a currency not officially pegged is quasipegged and, as a result, its volatility is low. The Saudi riyal, for instance, is quasipegged to

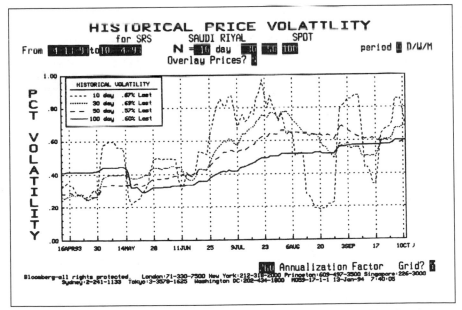

Figure 15.14. Historical price volatility of the Saudi riyal. *(Source: Bloomberg)*

the U.S. dollar at the rate of 3.75 and its historical volatility vis-à-vis the U.S. dollar is very low. (See Figure 15.14.)

Volatility is a key factor in option pricing. Unfortunately, measuring volatility is a rather strenuous effort.

Example:

$$V^2 = \frac{\sum_{i-1}(P_i - P)}{n - 1}$$

where

V = volatility

n = number of observations

P_i = daily price

P = average price of all P_i

In probability theory, the bell-shaped curve, known as the normal distribution curve, can be measured in terms of its mean, or the height of the curve, and its standard deviation (σ), or the speed at which the curve spreads out. (See Figure 15.15.) The standard deviation helps us measure the probability that a random event will occur. Traders use the standard deviation to measure the exact likelihood of a currency level's occurring within a certain range:

1 σ takes in 68.3 percent of all the possible outcomes (or 2/3).

2 σ takes in 95.4 percent of all the possible outcomes (or 19/20).

3 σ takes in 99.7 percent of all the possible outcomes (or 369/370).

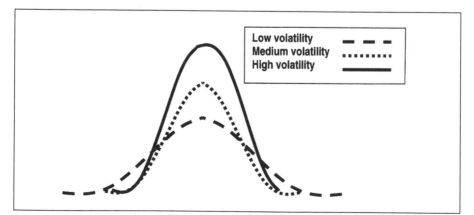

Figure 15.15. The normal distribution curve.

How does this apply to a foreign exchange rate? If USD/CAD is trading today at 1.6200 and has a volatility of 12 percent, then a standard deviation price change of one over a year's time would be:

$$1.6200 \times 12 \text{ percent} = 0.1944$$

So, one year from now, we expect the USD/CAD to trade between:

1.4256 and 1.8144 (1.6200 +/− 0.1944) for 2/3 of the time.

1.2312 and 2.0088 (1.6200 +/− 0.1944) for 19/20 of the time.

1.0368 and 2.2032 (1.6200 +/− 0.1944) for 369/370 of the time.

Only rarely do traders concern themselves with the price movement in a year's time, so it may help to calculate the standard deviation in shorter periods of time.

To change a volatility number from a yearly standard deviation to a weekly standard deviation:

$$\sqrt{52} = 7.2$$

To change a volatility number from a yearly standard deviation to a daily standard deviation

$$\sqrt{256} = 16$$

Example:
A JPY Sep futures contract trades at 89.90 and has an annual volatility of 14 percent; it will have a weekly standard deviation of

$$(89.90 \times .14) / 7.2 = 1.75$$

and a daily standard deviation of:

$$(89.90 \times .14) / 16 = 0.79$$

There are basically two ways to consider volatility. The first is to calculate the standard deviation in a series of rates of changes of spot currency prices that occurred in the past. This is the *historical volatility*. A trader can, therefore, measure the volatility over any time frame: the last 10 days, 30 days, 90 days, or any other period. The second method of measuring volatility is to consider the premiums currently trading in the market, such as OTC or on the Chicago IMM, and calculate the figure, based on the level of the option premium. This approach is called the *implied volatility*.

Comparing the two types of volatility, you will see that, despite a certain degree of correlation, significant differences do exist. These differences emphasize the difficulty of gauging volatility.

Vega

Vega gauges volatility impact on the option premium. Vega (ς) is the sensitivity of the theoretical value of an option to a change in volatility. (See Figure 15.16.) For instance, a vega of .2 will generate a .2 percent increase in the premium for each percentage increase in the volatility estimate, and a .2 percent decrease in the premium for each percentage decrease in the volatility estimate.

A Trader's Point of View

- Changes in volatility have a maximum dollar impact on at-the-money options and a maximum percentage impact on out-of-the-money options.

- An increase in volatility causes delta to converge toward .5, whereas a volatility decrease causes delta to diverge from .5.

- The impact of a change in volatility is more significant for a long-term option than for a short-term option.

EXPIRATION DATE

The option is traded for a predetermined period of time, and when this time expires, there is a delivery date known as the *expiration date*. A buyer who

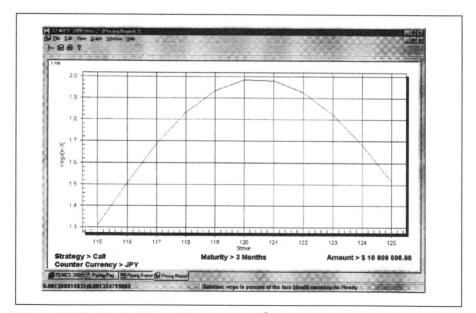

Figure 15.16. Graph of vega. *(Source: FENICS® Software. © by Inventure America Inc. All rights reserved.)*

intends to exercise the option must inform the writer on or before expiration. The buyer's failure to inform the writer about exercising the option frees the writer of any legal obligation. However, some exercise is automatic if an option is in-the-money at expiration. An option cannot be exercised past the expiration date.

The writer must be available to be contacted when the option is due to expire.

A Trader's Point of View

Time is an important factor in an option's pricing. The decrease in the time to expiration has a similar impact on the delta, gamma, theta (discussed next), vega, and theoretical value as a decrease in volatility.

Theta

Theta (T), also known as time decay, occurs as the very slow or nonexistent movement of the currency triggers losses in the option's theoretical value. (See Figure 15.17.)

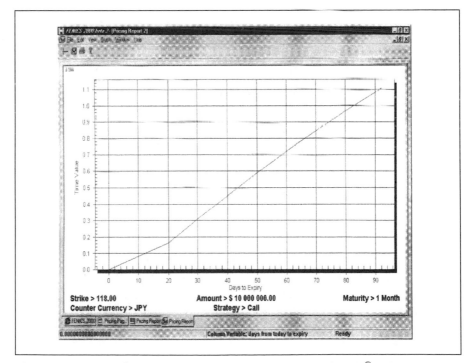

Figure 15.17. Graph of theta on a reversed order. *(Source: FENICS® Software. © by Inventure America Inc. All rights reserved.)*

For instance, a theta of .02 will generate a loss of 0.02 in the premium for each day that the currency price is flat. Intrinsic value is not affected by time, but extrinsic value is. Time decay accelerates as the option approaches expiration, since the number of possible outcomes is continuously reduced as the time passes.

Time has its maximum impact on at-the-money options and its minimum effect on in-the-money options. Time's effect on out-of-the-money options occurs somewhere within that range.

A Trader's Point of View

Theta is always more significant for a short-term at-the-money option than for a long-term at-the-money option.

The table presented here shows the relations among the foreign currency, type of option, and delta (hedge ratio), gamma (curvature), theta (time decay), and vega (volatility) positions.

Position	Delta (Δ)	Gamma (Γ)	Theta (T)	Vega (ς)
Long currency	+	0	0	0
Short currency	−	0	0	0
Long calls	+	+	−	+
Short calls	−	−	+	−
Long puts	−	+	−	+
Short puts	+	−	+	−

INTEREST RATE DIFFERENTIAL

Unlike other financial markets, in foreign exchange a single interest rate is insufficient for the decision makers. Every exchange rate means the simultaneous buying of one currency in terms of another.

In options trading, the premium of a call on a foreign currency increases when the U.S. interest rate increases relative to the foreign interest rate, all else being equal. This occurs either when U.S. interest rates rise and foreign interest rates are stable, or when U.S. interest rates are stable but foreign interest rates fall.

The opposite is true in the case of a foreign currency put buying. The option premium increases when U.S. interest rates decrease relative to foreign interest rates, or when foreign interest rates increase vis-à-vis American ones.

Generally, the interest rate used is the risk-free rate (r) of government instruments, such as T-bills.

Interest rates are important for options pricing for two reasons. First, the pricing formula includes the forward price, which is calculated on the differential between domestic and foreign interest rates. Second, the premium of an option must be discounted back to the present value by a risk-free interest rate.

Premium is the expected value of the option at expiration. Because the premium is paid up front, its value is discounted through the present value formula:

$$\text{Premium} = \text{Expected value} / [1 + IR \text{ (number of days}/365)]$$

Interest rate parity is known among traders as the *cost of carry*, where the forward price is determined by the cost of borrowing money in order to hold the position. For example, the 1-year forward price of EUR/USD is determined by the spot EUR/USD 1.1000 and the 1-year interest rate differential: 1.1060. If the quoted prices differ, the arbitrageurs will cash in on the opportunity.

A Trader's Point of View

The impact of interest rates on the theoretical value of options is more significant on deep in-the-money options.

CALL OR PUT

Currency Call

A *call* is a contract between the buyer and the seller, which holds that:

- The buyer has the right, but not the obligation, to buy a specific quantity of a currency at a predetermined price and within a predetermined period of time, regardless of the market price of the currency.

- The writer assumes the obligation to deliver the specific quantity of a currency at a predetermined price and within a predetermined period of time, regardless of the market price of the currency, if the buyer wants to exercise the call option.

A call option is traded because the buyer believes that the underlying currency will rise above a certain price, whereas the seller expects that the currency will either remain stable or move lower.

Currency Put

Conversely, a *put* is a contract between the buyer and the seller, which holds that:

- The buyer has the right, but not the obligation, to sell a specific quantity of a currency at a predetermined price and within a pre-determined period of time, regardless of the market price of the currency.

- The writer assumes the obligation to take delivery of the specific quantity of a currency at a predetermined price and within a pre-determined period of time, regardless of the market price of the currency, if the buyer wants to exercise the put option.

In the case of the put, the buyer expects the underlying currency to weaken to or below a specific level, while the seller believes the currency will rise, or simply trade the range.

Perhaps it is a good time to emphasize that the seller of a call is not the same as the buyer of the put. As we go along, it will become more apparent why this distinction is significant.

AMERICAN OR EUROPEAN OPTION STYLE

The exercise of an option may occur on or prior to expiry. Depending on when exercising may occur, there are two types of options: American and European style. The *American style option* may be exercised on any valid business date throughout the life of the option. The *European style currency option* may only be exercised on the expiry date.

Early Exercise of American Style Options

Generally speaking, American options are not exercised prior to expiry but there are exceptions. These occur when an option is deep in the money, when the option is approaching the expiration date and has no extrinsic value, and with call options on high-interest currencies or put options on low-interest currencies.

The logic behind the exercise of an American style option is that a high-interest currency is likely to depreciate against the U.S. dollar, and vice versa.

The additional opportunities offered by American style options translate into a higher cost, or premium. However, one should keep in mind that early exercise is usually not beneficial.

Advantageous Early Exercising Scenarios

- Bid–offer spreads in the market may make it too expensive to sell the option and trade forward outrights.
- If the option shifts deeply into the money, the interest rate differential gained by early exercise may exceed the value of the option.
- If the option amount is small or the expiration is close and the option value only consists of the intrinsic value, it may be better to use the early exercise.

OPTION PRICING

Due to the complexity of its determining factors, option pricing is difficult. In the absence of option pricing models, option trading is nothing but inefficient gambling. The flurry of options on equities in the 1920s had an accelerating impact on the stock market crash of 1929.

THE BLACK-SCHOLES FORMULA

The pioneering efforts of several researchers have been vital for option pricing. In 1972, professors Myron Scholes and Fischer Black published in the *Journal of Political Economy* a method of calculating the fair price, or premium, for a European style call option on stocks. The method became known around the world as the *Black-Scholes model*. The Black-Scholes fair value model holds that a stock and the call option on that particular stock are comparable investments; thus, buying the stock and selling the option on the stock as a hedge may create a riskless portfolio. The movement of the price of the option will reflect the movement of the price of the stock, but not necessarily by the same amplitude. Therefore, it is necessary to hold only the amount of stock that will duplicate the movement of the price of the option.

$$C = SN(d_1) - E / e^{\rho t} N(d_2)$$

and

$$d_1 = [\ln (S/E) + (\rho + .5\sigma^2) \, t] / \sigma \sqrt{t}$$

$$d_2 = d_1 - \sigma \sqrt{t}$$

where

S = spot exchange rate

E = exercise or strike price

$e = 2.71828$

t = time till expiration

σ = standard deviation of the continuously compounded annual rate of change of the exchange rate

ρ = risk-free rate (T-bills)

ln = the natural logarithm

$N(d)$ = probability that a deviation less than d will occur in a normal distribution with a mean of zero and a standard deviation of 1

The Black-Scholes option pricing model holds, in its original form, several theoretical assumptions, which may diverge from the realities of the financial world. Among those assumptions are:

- constant interest rates,
- constant and known volatility,
- no transaction or taxation costs,
- no dividends,
- no early exercise, and
- continuous trading.

One serious problem that the model in its original form is unable to answer is the expectation of "normal" or continuous trading behavior of the foreign exchange market. Despite its efficient structure, the foreign exchange market has been affected by a long series of unexpected factors that disrupted the daily continuity of trading. These factors ranged from political crises, such as the "kidnapping" of Mikhail Gorbachev, then Soviet President, in 1991; to the currency crisis on the European Monetary System in 1993; and to the 11.8 yen dollar/yen collapse in October 1998, when a leading hedge fund was forced to liquidate positions. The log-normal distribution is unable to include these types of aberrations.

Robert Merton, who adapted several other assumptions made by the Black-Scholes model, such as no dividends and constant interest rates, relaxed the assumption of market continuity in 1973.

Another weakness is the relationship between spot and forward prices. Despite attempts to make the forward price something more than a "guesstimate," extraneous forces may affect the forward price. Therefore, the option pricing model tends to underprice out-of-the-money currency options.

The original Black-Scholes formula can be applied only to European call options. However, there is a relationship between a call option and a put option established through the forward market. This is called the *put-call-forward exchange parity (PCFP) theory.*

$$C - P = (F - E) / (1 + r)^t$$

where:

C = call

P = put

F = forward price

E = exercise price

r = interest rate

The idea is that the option of buying the domestic currency with a foreign currency at a certain price x is equivalent to the option of selling the foreign currency with the domestic currency at the same price x. Therefore, the call option in the domestic currency becomes the put option in the other, and vice versa.

Another pricing model, introduced by Cox, Ross, and Rubinstein in 1979, was meant to apply to the early exercise provision of American style options. As it assumes that early exercise will occur only if the advantage of holding the currency exceeds the time value of the option, their binomial method evaluated the call premium by estimating the probability of early exercise for each successive day. The theoretical premium is compared to the holding cost of the cash hedge position until the option's time value is worth less than the forward points of the currency hedge when the option should be exercised.

The practical applications of the Cox-Ross-Rubinstein model are tedious, and the binomial pricing models must compromise on the number of trials.

In 1983, Mark Garman and Steven Kohlhagen expanded the Black-Scholes model to foreign exchange by using the interest rate differential (the difference between two interest rates) rather than a single interest rate, and consequently allowing for the currency forward to be traded at either premium or discount.

Also in 1983, Orlin Grabbe provided a different adaptation of the Black-Scholes model to foreign exchange. Bodurtha and Courtadon proposed another foreign exchange option pricing model in 1987.

The Black-Scholes formula was adjusted for foreign exchange as follows:

$$C = e^{-r_f t} SN(d) - Ee^{-r_d t} N(d - \sigma \sqrt{t})$$

and

$$d = [\ln(S/E) + (r_d - r_f + \sigma^2/2)\, t] / \sigma \sqrt{t}$$

where

S = spot exchange rate

E = exercise or strike price

e = 2.71828

t = time till expiration

σ = standard deviation of the continuously compounded annual rate of change of the exchange rate

r_d = domestic interest rate

r_f = foreign interest rate

$\ln$ = the natural logarithm

$N(d)$ = probability that a deviation less than d will occur in a normal distribution with a mean of zero and a standard deviation of 1

16 Major Option Strategies on Currencies

S ome basic considerations prior to deciding on the best option trading strategy for you are:

- Do you expect the currency to strengthen, weaken, or stay relatively stable?
- Do you expect high or low volatility?
- Why are you choosing to trade an option over a spot, a forward outright, or a futures contract?

This chapter describes the comprehensive gamut of choices available in option trading, in detail and with numerous examples and illustrations. We start with the simple and move to options with the complexity and flexibility that have characterized option trading and turned it into a fast-growing market.

BASIC STRATEGIES

BUYING A CALL OPTION

The buyer of a euro call option acquires the right, but not the obligation, to buy a certain amount of euro at a certain price, on or before a specified value date. The buyer expects the euro to rise (whereas the seller expects the currency to remain stable or ease). The maximum risk the buyer may incur is the premium paid to the seller, or writer, of the option. The maximum benefit is theoretically unlimited but it is not known, as it is impossible to know how the euro will perform. A simple rise in the price of the euro will not guarantee a profit for the buyer, because the rise must be enough to cover the premium before any profit is earned. (See Figure 16.1.)

The premium is the highest for the deep ITM calls and the lowest for deep OTM calls. With an OTM call option, the buyer encounters the smallest financial risk, while having the best leverage. *Leverage* refers to the expected return on investment, the potential profit generated by the buyer's investment.

Of course, OTM options in general, and OTM calls specifically, stand the least chance of performing profitably because, for them to be profitable, the currency needs to make a substantial price move.

BUYING A SYNTHETIC CALL OPTION

Synthetic options rarely generate arbitrage opportunities, but help one better understand the intricacies of the market. A trader can easily shift from a

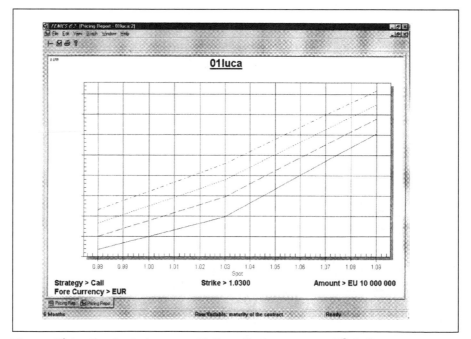

Figure 16.1. Graph of a long euro/dollar call. *(Source: FENICS® Software © 1999 by Inventure America Inc. All rights reserved.)*

long call position to a long put position, or a from a short call position to a short put position. However, the trader cannot turn a long call position into a short put position or a short call position into a long put position.

A *synthetic call option* consists of a combination of a long currency call and a long currency put. (See Figure 16.2.) The same characteristics of the long call apply.

SELLING A CALL OPTION

Selling a call option is equivalent to writing a naked call on an amount of currency that the writer does not own. In return for the premium, the writer will be ready to sell the predetermined amount of euro at the predetermined exercise, or strike, price if and when the buyer chooses to do so, on or before expiration. (See Figure 16.3.)

The maximum benefit for the seller is the premium received from the buyer. The maximum risk for the seller is unlimited and unknown. The only financial buffer against loss is the premium. But even if the currency rises, the seller will not lose as long as the currency advancement does not exceed the amount of the premium.

The break-even point (BEP) is calculated as the sum of the exercise price and the premium.

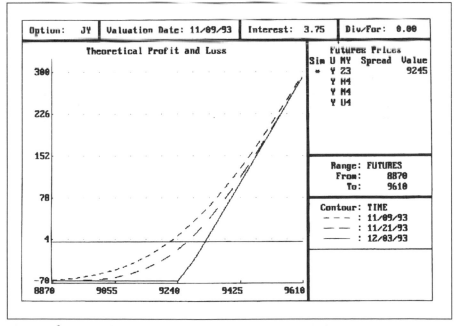

Figure 16.2. Graph of a long synthetic call on Japanese yen futures. *(Courtesy of FutureSource)*

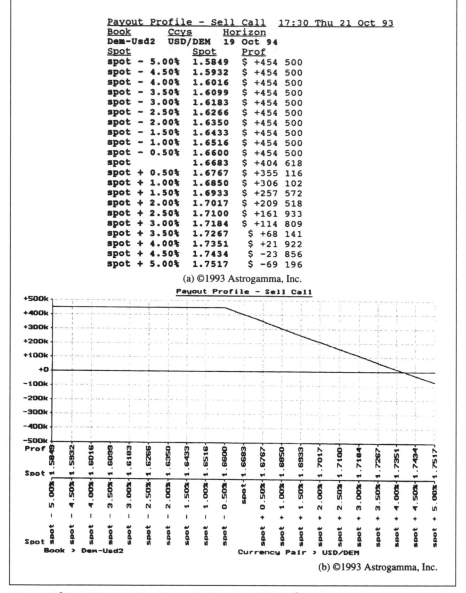

Figure 16.3. Diagram of a short call. *(Source: FENICS® Software © 1999 by Inventure America Inc. All rights reserved.)*

$$\text{BEP (call selling)} = S + P$$

where

S = exercise or strike price

P = premium

A Trader's Point of View

Generally, near-term call options are more desirable to write, as there is less time available for a wide price swing in currency.

A sharp rally in the price of the currency immediately following the writing of the option will generate the largest loss, given the fact that there is no time premium amortization.

In order to avoid or minimize the negative impact of a currency advance, the writer should use a stop-loss order or liquidate the position.

BUYING A PUT OPTION

The buyer of a yen put option acquires the right, but not the obligation, to sell a certain amount of yen at a certain price, on or before a specified value date. The buyer expects the yen to ease (whereas the seller expects the currency to remain stable or rise).

The maximum risk the buyer may incur is the premium paid to the seller of the option. The maximum benefit is theoretically unlimited but it is not known, as it is impossible to know how the yen will perform. A simple fall in the price of yen will not guarantee a profit for the buyer because the currency must fall low enough to cover the premium before any profit is earned. (See Figure 16.4.)

The premium is highest for deep ITM calls and lowest for deep OTM calls. With an OTM call option, the buyer encounters the smallest financial risk, while having the best leverage. Of course, OTM options in general, and OTM calls specifically, stand the least chance of performing profitably, because for them to be profitable, the currency needs to make a substantial price move.

BUYING A SYNTHETIC PUT OPTION

A *synthetic put option* consists of a combination of short currency and a long currency call. (See Figure 16.5.) The same characteristics of the long put apply.

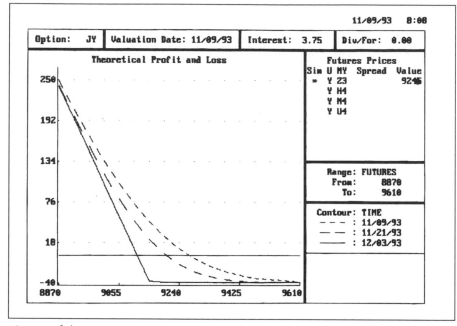

Figure 16.4. Graph of a long put on Japanese yen futures. *(Source: FutureSource)*

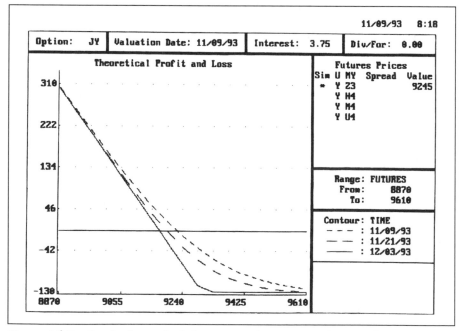

Figure 16.5. Graph of a synthetic long put on Japanese yen futures. *(Source: FutureSource)*

SELLING A PUT OPTION

A trader who expects a specific currency to rise or to remain relatively stable for the life of the option sells a currency put option for a premium. The trader selling the put option is known as the writer. In return for the premium, the writer will be ready to buy the predetermined amount of euro at the predetermined exercise, or strike, price, if and when the buyer chooses to do so, on or before expiration. (See Figure 16.6.)

The maximum benefit for the seller is the premium received from the buyer. This means that the seller needs the price of the currency to stay at any level above the strike price of the put option. The maximum risk for the seller is unlimited, and the only financial buffer against loss is the premium.

The break-even point (BEP) is calculated as the difference between the exercise price and the premium.

$$BEP \text{ (put selling)} = S - P$$

where

S = exercise or strike price

P = premium

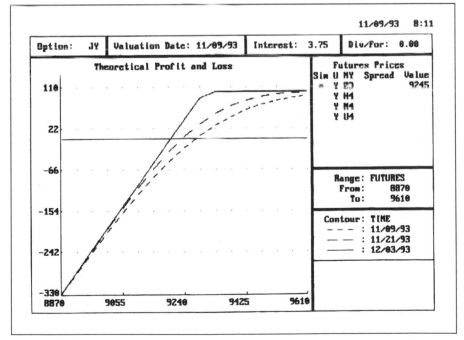

Figure 16.6. Graph of a short put on Japanese yen futures. *(Source: FutureSource)*

A Trader's Point of View

In addition to gaining the premium income, traders also write put options in order to acquire a currency below the current market price.

If the currency price trades below the exercise price, the put will be exercised. However, the exercise is likely to occur only if the option is in-the-money and near-term.

In order to avoid or minimize a loss, the put writer can leave a stop-loss order or buy a put identical to the one originally written.

COMPOUND STRATEGIES

Two of the major problems in foreign exchange—at least for cash traders—are solved by options.

The first problem occurs when the market is very quiet and currency prices are relatively stable. The lack of volatility generally results in lack of profitability. The way out? Options writing.

The second problem appears when traders have certain expectations about a rise in volatility, but lack the confidence to take a view on the direction of the market. We have already talked about the opportunities provided by trading individual calls and puts. Now we can move a step further and combine these classes of options in search of better profits and hedges. These compound strategies are also known as *currency spreads*.

CURRENCY SPREADS

A *spread* is a long currency option and an offsetting short currency option, generally in the same currency. If the spread is executed in two different currencies, then the spread is called an intermarket spread.

We discuss two types of spreads. The first is the non-ratio, or regular, spread, which is a compound option strategy in which the number of long options is the same as the number of short options. The second is the ratio spread, in which the number of long options is different from the number of short options.

NON-RATIO (REGULAR) SPREADS

Under the combinations that pair equal numbers of long and short options, we present the following spreads:

1. Straddles
2. Strangles

3. Vertical

4. Calendar

5. Box

6. Butterfly

7. Condor

8. Combination

Straddles (Buying)

Many times, traders are faced with the specter of the release of certain economic data, the expectation of a central bank changing the discount rate, or expectations about the breakout of a currency through a special chart level. Traders are confident about a sudden release of energy in the price of a currency and in its volatility, but not quite sure about the direction of the move. Certainly, these traders would like to soar on the news, not be burled.

Long Straddle. A popular choice among option traders in this situation, a quiet market before the big storm, is buying a straddle. A long straddle consists of a long call and a long put on the same currency, at the same strike price and with the same expiration dates. (See Figure 16.7.) The

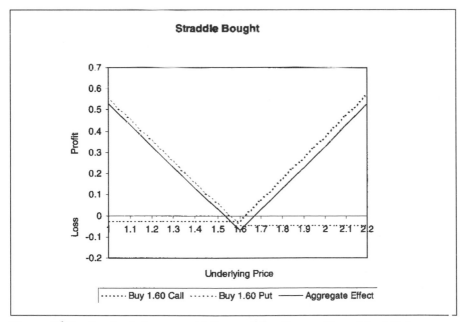

Figure 16.7. Graph of a long euro/dollar straddle. *(Source: Spreadsheet Link, Limited)*

buyer pays a premium on the call and a premium on the put in order to have the right, but not the obligation, to buy or to sell a predetermined amount of foreign currency on or before expiration, at a predetermined price.

The buyer enters a long straddle position in anticipation of a sharp increase in volatility, in effect buying volatility. In order to make a profit, the currency must swing high or low enough to cover investment costs, but once the cost of the premiums is cleared, the profit is theoretically unlimited.

The maximum loss for the buyer is the sum of the premiums. Naturally, the buyer does not have to wait to physically lose the entire investment, as the position can be sold.

Of course, when the price of the currency rises, the value of the call rises, while the value of the put declines. The opposite is true if the value of the currency declines.

The upside break-even point is the sum of the strike price and the premium on the straddle (which is simply the premiums on the individual call and put):

$$\text{BEP (upside)} = S + P$$

where

S = exercise or strike price

P = premium

The downside break-even point is the difference between the strike price and the premium on the straddle (which is simply the compound premium on the individual call and put):

$$\text{BEP (downside)} = S - P$$

Straddles (Selling)
Short Straddle. A short straddle consists of a short call and a short put on the same currency, at the same strike price and with the same expiration dates. (See Figure 16.8.) The writer expects the currency to be relatively stable. In effect, the writer sells volatility.

The maximum profit consists of the combined premium of the two individual options. The loss occurs when the level of the premium is exceeded by the currency swing; then the loss is unlimited.

Strangles (Selling)
A strangle is nothing but a straddle with a twist. The twist consists of disregarding the condition in the definition of the straddle that both options have the same strike price.

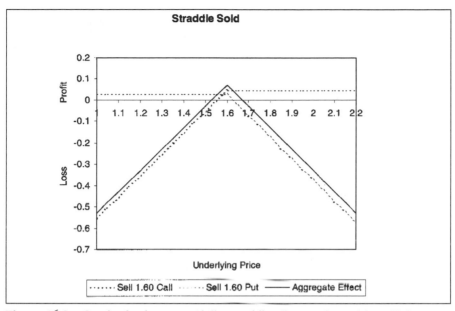

Figure 16.8. Graph of a short euro/dollar straddle. *(Source: Spreadsheet Link, Limited)*

Strangles (Buying)

Long Strangle. A long strangle consists of a long call and a long put on the same currency, at different strike prices, but with the same expiration dates. (See Figure 16.9.) In order to minimize the risk, traders generally buy out-of-the money options. Exactly as in the case of the straddle, the buyer pays a premium on the call and a premium on the put in order to have the right, but not the obligation, to buy or to sell a predetermined amount of foreign currency on or before expiration, at a predetermined price.

The buyer enters a long strangle strategy in anticipation of a sharp increase in volatility, buying volatility. In order to make a profit, the currency must swing high or low enough to cover the investment costs, but once the cost of the premiums is cleared, the profit is theoretically unlimited.

The maximum loss for the buyer is the sum of the premiums. Naturally, the buyer does not have to wait to physically lose the entire investment, as the position can be sold.

Of course, when the price of the currency rises, the value of the call rises, while the value of the put declines. The opposite is true if the value of the currency declines.

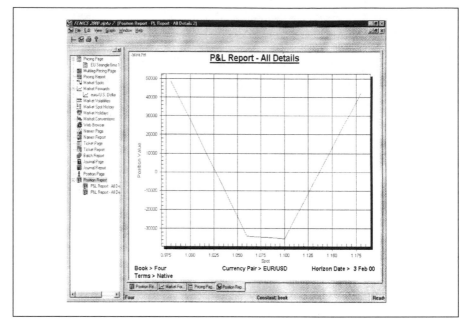

Figure 16.9. Graph of a long euro/dollar strangle. *(Source: FENICS® Software ©
1999 by Inventure America Inc. All rights reserved.)*

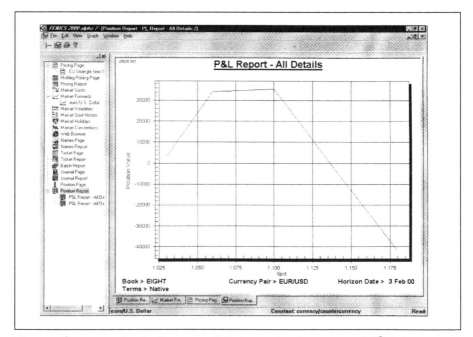

Figure 16.10. Graph of a short euro/dollar strangle. *(Source: FENICS® Software ©
1999 by Inventure America Inc. All rights reserved.)*

Short Strangle (Selling). A short strangle consists of a short call and a short put on the same currency, with the same expiration dates, but with different strike prices. (See Figure 16.10.) The writer expects the currency to be relatively stable. In effect, the writer sells volatility. The maximum profit consists of the combined premium of the two individual options. The loss occurs when the level of the premium is exceeded by the currency swing, and then the loss is unlimited.

Vertical Spreads

A vertical spread consists of a strategy with two similar options (i.e., calls or puts), one being bought and the other sold, on the same currency with the same expiration date, but with different strike prices.

There are several types of vertical spreads:

- Vertical bull call spreads
- Vertical bull put spreads
- Vertical bear put spreads
- Vertical bear call spreads

Vertical Bull Spreads. A vertical bull spread is an option combination whose theoretical value will rise to a predetermined maximum profit if the price of the underlying currency rises, and whose maximum loss is also predetermined.

A *vertical bull call spread* is a compound strategy of two options with a common expiration date, when one option is a long call with a lower strike price and the other is a short call with a higher strike price. (See Figure 16.11) This strategy offers a less risky alternative to buying a naked call.

The buyer's maximum profit consists of the dollar difference between the two strike prices, minus the total premium paid. The break-even point is calculated as the sum of the lower strike price and the total premium. The maximum loss is limited to the premium paid for the two options.

A *vertical bull put spread* is a compound strategy of two options with a common expiration date, when one option is a long put with a lower strike price and the other is a short put with a higher strike price. (See Figure 16.12.) This strategy is less bullish than a long call.

The buyer's maximum profit consists of the net premium for the two options (one paid, the other received). The break-even point is calculated as the difference between the higher strike price and the net premium received. The maximum loss is limited to the dollar difference between the two strike prices, minus the total premium received.

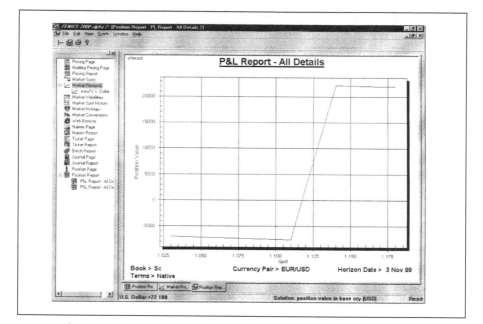

Figure 16.11. Graph of a vertical bull call spread. *(Source: FENICS® Software ©
1999 by Inventure America Inc. All rights reserved.)*

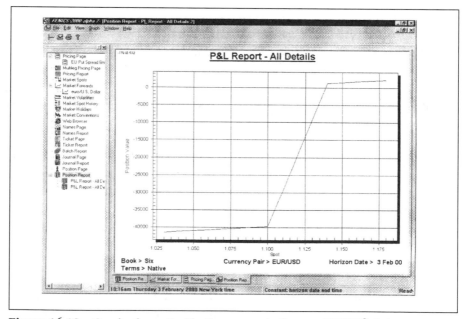

Figure 16.12. Graph of a vertical bull put spread. *(Source: FENICS® Software ©
1999 by Inventure America Inc. All rights reserved.)*

Vertical Bear Spreads. A vertical bear spread is an option combination whose theoretical value will decline to a predetermined maximum profit if the price of the underlying currency declines and whose maximum loss is also predetermined.

A *vertical bear put spread* is a compound strategy of two options with a common expiration date, when one option is a long put with a higher strike price and the other is a short put with a lower strike price. (See Figure 16.13.) This strategy offers a less risky alternative to buying a naked put.

The buyer's maximum profit consists of the dollar difference between the two strike prices, minus the total premium paid. The break-even point is calculated as the difference between the higher strike price and the total premium. The maximum loss is limited to the premium paid for the two options.

A *vertical bear call spread* is a compound strategy of two options with a common expiration date, when one option is a short call with a lower strike price and the other is a long call with a higher strike price. (See Figure 16.14.) This strategy offers a less risky alternative to writing a naked call.

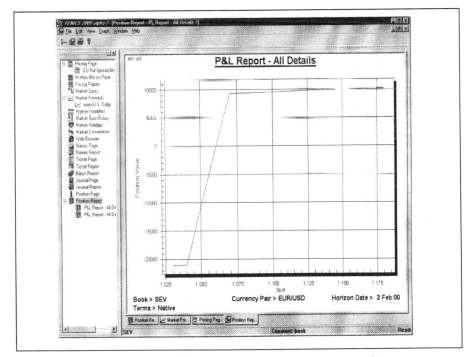

Figure 16.13. Graph of a vertical bear put spread. *(Source: FENICS® Software © 1999 by Inventure America Inc. All rights reserved.)*

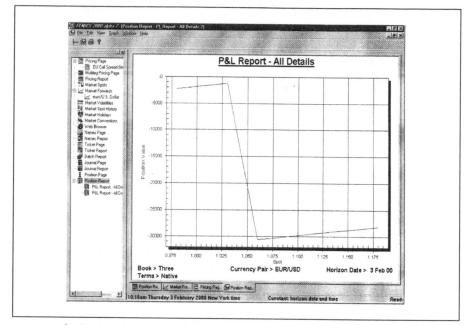

Figure 16.14. Graph of a vertical bear call spread. *(Source: FENICS® Software ©*
1999 by Inventure America Inc. All rights reserved.)

The seller's maximum profit is limited to the premium paid for the
two options. The break-even point is calculated as the sum of the lower
strike price and the total premium. The maximum loss consists of the dollar
difference between the two strike prices, minus the total premium received.

Calendar Spreads

There are three types of calendar spreads, also called time and horizontal
spreads: calendar spreads, calendar combinations, and calendar straddles.

A *calendar spread* is a combination of two similar types of options,
either calls or puts, with the same strike price but different expiration dates.
The dissimilarity between the expiration dates allows this type of spread to
capitalize on both the impact of the time decay and the interest rate differentials.

Calendar spreads are very complex in terms of both trading and P&L
calculation. P&L can only be estimated. The maximum profit will be
achieved if the implied volatility of the currency is higher, while the interest rate differential is narrower. The maximum loss is estimated to be the
net premium, assuming that both the volatility and the interest rate differential remain stable.

Offshoots of the calendar spreads are calendar combinations. A *calendar combination* consists of the simultaneous call calendar spread and put calendar spread, in which the strike price of the calls is higher than the strike price of the puts.

Another offshoot is the calendar straddle. The *calendar straddle* consists of simultaneous buying of a longer-term straddle and a near-term straddle with a common strike price.

Box Spreads

A *box spread* consists of four options with a common expiration date: a long call and a short put at one strike price and a long put and a short call at a different strike price.

Butterfly Spreads

A *butterfly spread* consists of a combination of a bull spread and a bear spread, using either calls or puts. Therefore, in the general form, the spread may consist of either:

- four same-type options with a common expiration date, as follows: two long identical options, one short option with an immediately lower strike price, and one short option with an immediately higher strike price; or

- four same-type options with a common expiration date as follows: two short identical options, one long option with an immediately lower strike price, and one long option with an immediately higher strike price.

Usually a butterfly spread is set up with long-term options. The maximum profit for a long butterfly occurs when the price of the currency reaches the level of the middle strike price at expiration. (See Figure 16.15.) The upside break-even point is the difference between the highest strike price and the net debit. The downside break-even point is the sum of the lowest strike price and the net debit. The maximum loss equals the premium paid.

The maximum profit for a short butterfly equals the premium paid, and occurs when the currency price trades outside the extreme strike prices at expiration. (See Figure 16.16.) The upside break-even point is the difference between the highest strike price and the net credit. The downside break-even point is the sum of the lowest strike price and the net credit. The maximum loss occurs when the price of the currency reaches the level of the middle strike price at expiration.

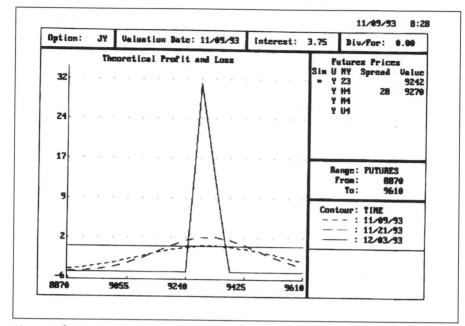

Figure 16.15. Graph of a long butterfly on Japanese yen futures. *(Source: FutureSource)*

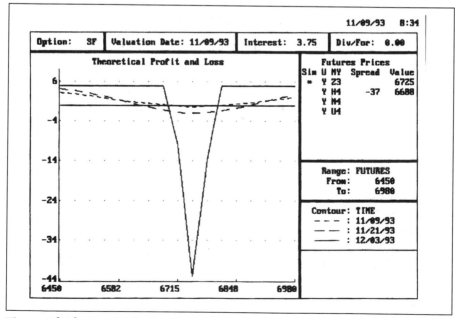

Figure 16.16. Graph of a short butterfly on Swiss franc futures. *(Source: FutureSource)*

Condor Spread
A *condor spread* consists of either:

- same-type options with a common expiration date, as follows: two long options with consecutive strike prices, one short option with an immediately lower strike price, and one short option with an immediately higher strike price; or

- same-type options with a common expiration date, as follows: two short options with consecutive strike prices, one long option with an immediately lower strike price, and one long option with an immediately higher strike price. (See Figures 16.17 and 16.18.)

Combination Spreads or Synthetic Futures
A *combination spread* (*synthetic future*) consists of a long call and a short put, or a long put and a short call, with a common expiration date.

RATIO SPREADS

A *ratio spread* is a spread in which the number of long options is different from the number of short options. Therefore, there is a certain ratio between the long and short options.

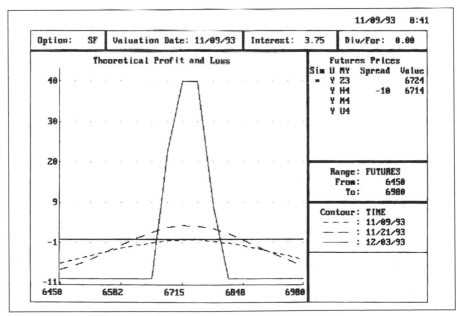

Figure 16.17.   Graph of a long condor on Swiss franc futures. *(Source: FutureSource)*

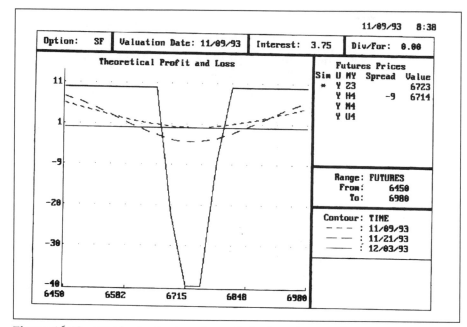

Figure 16.18. Graph of a short condor on Swiss franc futures. *(Source: FutureSource)*

The compound strategies discussed in the non-ratio spread section— the straddles and the strangles—have a one-on-one ratio in their original form. But, by convention, the one-on-one ratio is not considered a ratio. In terms of these compound strategies, they may be truly "ratioed" by chang- ing the number of one of the option classes.

The most popular ratio spreads are:

1. Ratio calls
2. Ratio puts
3. Call ratio backspreads
4. Put ratio backspreads
5. Diagonal ratios
6. Christmas trees

Before presenting these ratio spreads, I would like to introduce the concept of neutral spread, which is useful in understanding other types of spreads. A *neutral spread*, or a *delta-neutral spread*, consists of a long op- tion position and a short option position that have their respective total delta positions relatively equal. This being established, we can move along.

RATIO CALL SPREAD

A *ratio call spread* consists of a number of long calls with lower strike prices and a larger number of short calls with higher strike prices. (See Figure 16.19.) This type of combination is generally delta neutral.

The maximum profit is realized when the currency price is at the higher strike price.

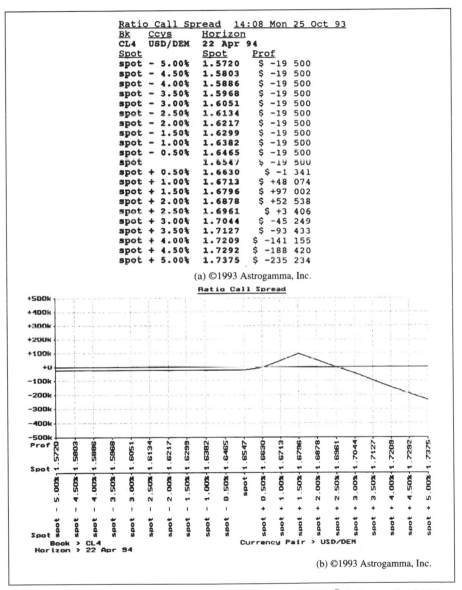

```
            Ratio Call Spread    14:08 Mon 25 Oct 93
            Bk    Ccys        Horizon
            CL4   USD/DEM      22 Apr 94
            Spot               Spot      Prof
            spot - 5.00%       1.5720    $ -19 500
            spot - 4.50%       1.5803    $ -19 500
            spot - 4.00%       1.5886    $ -19 500
            spot - 3.50%       1.5968    $ -19 500
            spot - 3.00%       1.6051    $ -19 500
            spot - 2.50%       1.6134    $ -19 500
            spot - 2.00%       1.6217    $ -19 500
            spot - 1.50%       1.6299    $ -19 500
            spot - 1.00%       1.6382    $ -19 500
            spot - 0.50%       1.6465    $ -19 500
            spot               1.6547    $ -19 500
            spot + 0.50%       1.6630     $ -1 341
            spot + 1.00%       1.6713     $ +48 074
            spot + 1.50%       1.6796     $ +97 002
            spot + 2.00%       1.6878     $ +52 538
            spot + 2.50%       1.6961      $ +3 406
            spot + 3.00%       1.7044     $ -45 249
            spot + 3.50%       1.7127     $ -93 433
            spot + 4.00%       1.7209    $ -141 155
            spot + 4.50%       1.7292    $ -188 420
            spot + 5.00%       1.7375    $ -235 234
```

(a) ©1993 Astrogamma, Inc.

(b) ©1993 Astrogamma, Inc.

Figure 16.19. Diagram of a ratio call spread. *(Source: FENICS® Software © 1999 by Inventure America Inc. All rights reserved.)*

This combination has two break-even points. The downside break-even point consists of the sum of the lower strike price and the debit, divided by the number of long calls. The upside break-even point consists of the sum of the higher strike price and the maximum profit potential, divided by the number of naked calls.

The maximum downside risk is the net premium, and the upside risk is unlimited.

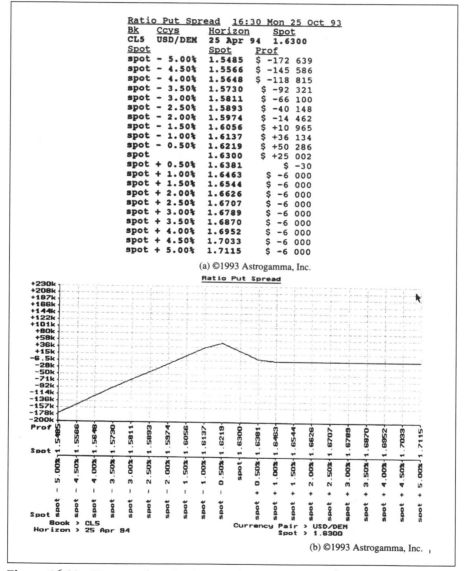

Ratio Put Spread   16:30 Mon 25 Oct 93

Bk	Ccys	Horizon	Spot
CL5	USD/DEM	25 Apr 94	1.6300

Spot	Spot	Prof
spot - 5.00%	1.5485	$ -172 639
spot - 4.50%	1.5566	$ -145 586
spot - 4.00%	1.5648	$ -118 815
spot - 3.50%	1.5730	$ -92 321
spot - 3.00%	1.5811	$ -66 100
spot - 2.50%	1.5893	$ -40 148
spot - 2.00%	1.5974	$ -14 462
spot - 1.50%	1.6056	$ +10 965
spot - 1.00%	1.6137	$ +36 134
spot - 0.50%	1.6219	$ +50 286
spot	1.6300	$ +25 002
spot + 0.50%	1.6381	$ -30
spot + 1.00%	1.6463	$ -6 000
spot + 1.50%	1.6544	$ -6 000
spot + 2.00%	1.6626	$ -6 000
spot + 2.50%	1.6707	$ -6 000
spot + 3.00%	1.6789	$ -6 000
spot + 3.50%	1.6870	$ -6 000
spot + 4.00%	1.6952	$ -6 000
spot + 4.50%	1.7033	$ -6 000
spot + 5.00%	1.7115	$ -6 000

(a) ©1993 Astrogamma, Inc.

(b) ©1993 Astrogamma, Inc.

Figure 16.20. Diagram of a ratio put spread. *(Source: FENICS® Software © 1999 by Inventure America Inc. All rights reserved.)*

RATIO PUT SPREAD

A *ratio put spread* consists of a number of long puts with higher strike prices and a larger number of short puts with lower strike prices. (See Figure 16.20.) This ratio spread is generally designed as delta-neutral.

The maximum profit is realized when the currency price is at the lower strike price.

This combination has two break-even points. The downside break-even point consists of the difference between the lower strike price and the maximum profit potential, divided by the number of naked puts. The upside break-even point consists of the difference between the higher strike price and the debit, divided by the number of long puts.

The maximum downside risk is unlimited, and the upside risk is the net premium.

CALL RATIO BACKSPREAD

A *call ratio backspread* consists of short calls with a lower strike price and more long calls with higher strike prices. This spread is usually established as a delta-neutral ratio spread. It benefits from a price movement in either direction, but it is essentially a bullish position.

The maximum upside profit potential is unlimited and the downside profit potential consists of the total premium received. The maximum loss potential occurs when the currency price reaches the higher strike price at expiration.

PUT RATIO BACKSPREAD

A *put ratio backspread* consists of short puts with a higher strike price and more long puts with lower strike prices. (See Figure 16.21.) This spread is usually established as a delta-neutral ratio spread. It benefits from a price movement in either direction, but it is essentially a bearish position.

The maximum upside profit potential consists of the total premium received, and the downside profit potential is unlimited. The maximum loss potential occurs when the currency price reaches the lower strike price at expiration.

CHRISTMAS TREE SPREAD

A *Christmas tree spread* consists of several short options at two or more strike prices.

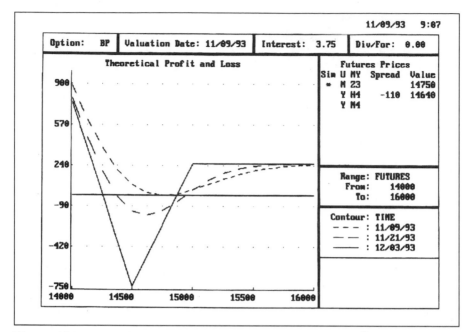

Figure 16.21. Diagram of a put ratio backspread. *(Source: FENICS® Software ©*
1999 by Inventure America Inc. All rights reserved.)

Diagonal Spread

A *diagonal spread* consists of several same-type options, such that the long
side and the short side have different strike prices and different expirations.

SPREADS WITH BOTH OPTIONS
AND CURRENCY

The currency spreads and combinations we have presented so far have
been composed of currency options only. In addition to options, three
spreads also consist of the underlying currency, whether cash or futures:

1. covered long,
2. covered short, and
3. fence.

Covered Long

A *covered long* involves selling a call against a long currency position. This strategy was designed to enhance the profitability of currency

trading in a quiet market, via the option's premium (see Figure 16.20). A covered long is synonymous to a short put.

COVERED SHORT

A *covered short* involves shorting a put against a short currency position. This strategy was designed to enhance the profitability of currency trading in a quiet market, via the option's premium. A covered short is synonymous to a short call.

FENCE

Fences have become strategies of choice among corporations due to their insurance features, acquired at minimum or no cost. The idea behind the strategy is that the security against a loss is purchased at the cost of limiting the unlimited profitability offered by an individual option. (See Figure 16.22.) The price in dollars and cents may be low, but is it worth giving up the unlimited profit potential of a currency swing?

The trade-off is not too bad, because the profit potential can be unlimited only in theory. In the real trading world, most currencies tend to have limited price activity. Therefore, a well-planned fence not only provides much-needed insurance against unfavorable currency activity at a low price, but also allows the buyer to take advantage of the trading range.

A fence consists of either:

* a long currency position, a long out-of-the-money put, and a short out-of-the-money call, when the options have the same expiration date (this strategy is also known as *risk conversion*); or

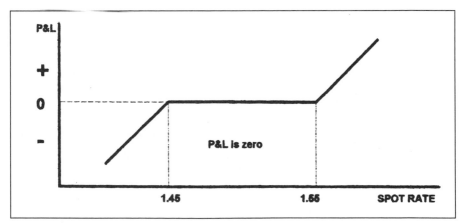

Figure 16.22. Diagram of a fence compound strategy.

- a short currency position, a short out-of-the-money put, and a long out-of-the-money call, when the options have the same expiration date (this strategy is also known as *risk reversal*).

As an example, a buyer who wants to avoid the risk of a currency upswing at a reduced price can purchase a call and also write a put on the specific currency.

For instance, let's assume that the spot GBP/USD trades at 1.50, and the trader buys a $1.45 6-month GBP call and sells a $1.55 put, where the premium paid (for the call) and the premium received (for the put) are identical. The P&L for the life of the options (6 months, in this example) will be zero if the GBP/USD spot trades between 1.45 and 1.55 for the period. Because the option cost is zero, the break-even point is the strike price.

The downside of the fence strategy is that the maximum loss is unlimited. Should the trader want to limit the potential loss, an additional option should be bought.

EXOTIC OPTIONS*

The range of options strategies is continuously expanding to better encompass the diversity of needs in the financial arena. A study of the exotic options developed by Astrogamma is presented here.

BARRIER OPTIONS

Barrier options are also known as *trigger options, cutoff options, cutout options, stop options, down/up-and-outs/ins, knockups*, etc. They are very similar to European style vanilla options, except that a second strike price—the trigger—is specified and, when reached in the market, automatically causes the option to be "inspired" in *knockin options* (see Figure 16.23) or expired in *knockout options* (see Figure 16.24).

With knockouts, the trader buys a vanilla option that goes away if the trigger is reached. With knockins, the trader is buying a vanilla option that does not exist until the trigger is reached. The determination as to when the trigger is hit can be based on the spot currency rate (spot style) or the forward currency underlying the option (forward style).

---

*Excerpted from the FENICS® FX options trading software Help pages. (© 1993 Astrogamma, Inc. Reproduced with permission.)

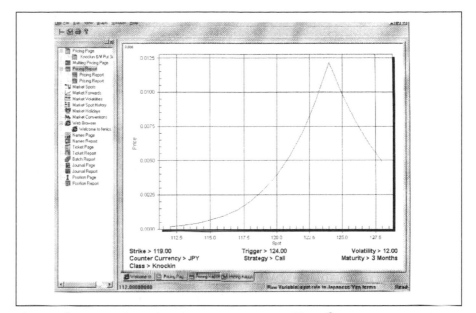

Figure 16.23. Graph of a knockin option. *(Source: FENICS® Software © 1999 by Inventure America Inc. All rights reserved.)*

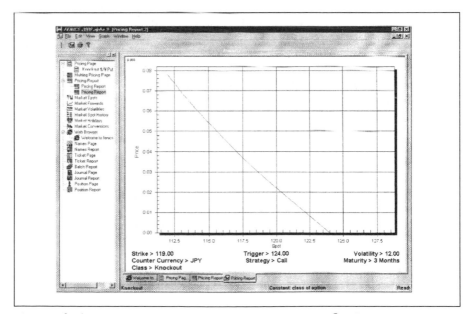

Figure 16.24. Graph of a knockout option. *(Source: FENICS® Software © 1999 by Inventure America Inc. All rights reserved.)*

In standard knockouts and knockins, the bias of the trigger is opposite to that of the underlying vanilla option. In other words, as the likelihood of being triggered increases, the option is losing intrinsic value or becoming more out-of-the-money.

There is also another set of variants, known as *reverse knockouts* and *reverse knockins*, in which the likelihood of being triggered increases as the option's intrinsic value increases. These are often referred to as in-the-money knockouts and knockins, because the trigger must be in-the-money with respect to the strike in order for the option to have any value at all (reverse knockout), or to be any different from a vanilla option (reverse knockin).

Any option that is triggered when it has intrinsic value is virtually impossible to hedge near the trigger, so the reverse varieties are very rare.

KNOCKOUTS FOR CORPORATE HEDGING

From a corporate standpoint, normal knockouts are the most appealing of the barrier types. Assuming that a corporate customer is buying the underlying vanilla option for hedging purposes, it is clear that, when the trigger is reached, FX rates have moved his or her way, and the protection of the option may no longer be needed.

For example, consider a corporate customer who is long British pounds against U.S. dollars, value three months from now. Assume that cable is now 1.5500 and that the customer's level of pain on the downside is 1.5000. The corporate customer could buy a knockout put (an up-and-out) with a strike price of 1.5000 and a trigger at 1.6000. If sterling reaches 1.6000 prior to expiration, the customer will sell the pounds there, as the option's protection is not needed any more. Otherwise, the corporate customer either exercises the 1.5000 put or lets it expire out-of-the-money on expiration day.

The advantage of a knockout option in comparison with a pair of orders (a take-profit at 1.6000 and a stop-loss at 1.5000) is that the British pound can drop below 1.5000 without having the customer stopped out, with a possible gain if it recovers. The advantage of a knockout option in comparison with a risk reversal (whereby the customer would sell a 1.6000 call instead of leaving a sell order there) is that the position is closed as soon as 1.6000 is reached. There is no chance that the customer will have to let the 1.6000 bids go untouched because of a need for a long position in sterling to cover the short option, then watch helplessly as cable drops below 1.6000 again.

The disadvantage of a knockout option, in comparison with both the pair of orders and the pair of options, is that it costs money, but not as much as the 1.5000 put would cost by itself. How much cheaper the knock-out option is than the corresponding normal option depends entirely on how far away the trigger is from the current market. If the trigger is set very close, the knockout option is very cheap, because the likelihood of the trigger being reached before expiration is very great. Conversely, if the trigger is very far away from the current market, the savings are minimal.

The corporate hedging rationale for the remaining types of barrier options is not so clear, particularly for reverses, which get knocked in or out when the option has intrinsic value. Reverse knockins seem appealing, until one realizes that the trigger has to be so far in-the-money to realize meaningful costs savings that the risk of the option never knocking in is too great to bear.

HEDGING A POSITION IN BARRIER OPTIONS

There is an almost perfect static hedge for a forward knockout option. Let's say that the trader sold a knockout call. To cover the position, the trader buys a vanilla call with the same strike and maturity against it. Then, the trader sells a put with the same maturity struck so that when the forward reaches the trigger, the call bought and the put sold are worth the same.

The idea is that the call covers the vanilla part of the knockout exactly, the put compensates for the difference in premium, and, if the knockout expires early, the trader unwinds the two hedge options at flat.

For forward knockout options, the strike price of this put is a constant over the life of the option. The formula for forward knockouts is:

$$\text{Forward knockout option strike price} = \text{Trigger}^2 / \text{Strike}$$

Therefore, the trigger is the geometric average of the strike and the hedge strike, which comes in handy when forward = trigger.

To be a perfect hedge, the hedge option should be executed in a ratio of strike/trigger for calls and trigger/strike for puts. This ratio is usually very close to 1:1.

For spot knockouts, the hedge strike unfortunately drifts. If using this hedging method, the trader will still have the residual risk up to the swap points between the spot and the forward. It still is a darn good hedge, though.

The static hedge for a knockin option follows directly from that for the knockout. It is easy to demonstrate that buying both a knockout and knockin with the same specifications is the same as buying a vanilla option: If the trigger is never reached, the trader owns the vanilla option from the knockout. If the trigger is reached, the trader owns the vanilla option from the knockin. Either way, the trader owns the vanilla option. The following formula holds for reverse knocks, as well:

$$\text{Knockout} + \text{Knockin} = \text{Vanilla}$$

From this discussion, we know that:

(1) Knockout call = Vanilla call (at strike) − Vanilla put (at hedge strike)

(2) Knockin call = Vanilla call − Knockout call

Therefore, substituting from (1):

(3) Knockin call = Vanilla call − (Vanilla call − Vanilla put) = Vanilla put

It's a little hard to believe, but the perfect static hedge for a forward knockin call is simply a vanilla put at the same hedge strike and in the same ratio as for the knockout call. Thinking through the logic of this position makes it clear why this is the case.

The trader buys a knockin call and hedges it by selling a vanilla put struck so that when the forward reaches the trigger, the call bought and the put sold are worth the same. When the knockin is triggered, the trader is long a call and short a put with the same value (a classic risk reversal), and unwinds it at flat.

The same conditions apply to hedging spot knockins, but it is a more dynamic hedge because the trader does not know where the forward will be when spot reaches the trigger. It is still a great hedge.

There is no similarly simple hedging strategy for reverses, or for any option that gets triggered when the underlying vanilla has intrinsic value. They become virtually impossible to hedge around the trigger, especially near expiration, because on one side of the trigger they are worthless and on the other side they are worth intrinsic value, which may be substantial if the trigger is deep in-the-money with respect to strike. This "on-off" feature is much more complicated to hedge than, for example, a vanilla option at expiration.

BARRIERS II

As the preceding discussion makes clear, barrier options have "imbedded" options, in the form of the trigger, that turn traditional notions of risk management on their heads. It's useful to point out a few of the important differences from normal options that the trader should be aware of when dealing barriers.

The most noticeable difference between knockouts and vanilla options is the delta, which is much higher for the knockout than for the vanilla, at least for knockouts with sensible triggers. It's easy to point to the replicating strategy and conclude that, when the trader is long a knockout, the trader is really long a risk reversal with the underlying vanilla as one leg, so the delta of the knockout is obviously higher.

But the real reason is even simpler and more intuitively appealing than that. When the knockout gets triggered, the vanilla underlying it still has time value, but as you move away from the trigger, the knockout starts to behave more like the vanilla, until the two are indistinguishable. Obviously, if the knockout loses its value more quickly as you near the trigger, the knockout is more sensitive to movements in spot across the entire range of spot movements, which means its delta must be higher.

High knockout deltas start to seem like an easy concept to grasp when you consider what happens to knockins: Knockin calls have *negative* deltas and knockin puts have *positive* deltas. Once again, this isn't hard to understand when you look at the replicating strategy, but it also makes intuitive sense.

Take the example of a USD/CAD knockin USD call (a down-and-in) with a strike of 1.5000 and a trigger of 1.4000. As spot moves toward 1.5000, the underlying vanilla is gaining intrinsic value, but the likelihood that the trader will ever have a vanilla option to exercise (i.e., the chance of the option being knocked in) is diminishing, so the knockin USD call is worth less and less. On the other hand, as spot moves to 1.4000, it is becoming more and more likely that you will own a valuable vanilla option, so the value of the knockin is increasing. As soon as the call is knocked in, its delta becomes positive. Thus, even though it is a call, the knockin loses value when spot rises (away from the trigger) and gains value when spot falls—negative delta.

Because the deltas of standard knockouts and knockins are discontinuous through the trigger, the trader must be prepared to unwind the delta hedge for the knockout, or to flip the direction of the delta hedge for the knockin, using an order. Similarly, if the trader has hedged the knock with the replicating strategy, the hedge position will need to be delta-hedged when the offsetting barrier option is triggered.

The most striking feature about the reverse knockouts is their prices, which seem disconcertingly low, unless the trigger is very far in the money. This is because they have the same likelihood of expiring worthless as a vanilla option; their upside is not only limited but disappears completely if the trigger is reached.

Let's take the example of a USD/CAD reverse knockout USD call (an up-and-out) with a strike of 1.5300 and a trigger of 1.5500. Despite the fact that the option could end up with as much as 200 points of intrinsic value, it is virtually worthless, regardless of where the spot is. The reason is that any time it gets intrinsic value, the likelihood of expiring worthless increases. This is in contrast to a straight vanilla or knockout call, which has unlimited upside, or a 1.5300:1.5500 USD call spread, which also has 200 points of intrinsic value but doesn't lose that value when spot goes above 1.5500.

For the same reasons, long positions in the typical reverse knockout have negative vega. By contrast, the values of reverse knockins are virtually indistinguishable from vanilla options unless the trigger is in-the-money. The deltas of reverse knocks become very unstable near the trigger, especially when approaching expiration. (See Figures 16.25 and 16.26.)

OPTIMAL OPTIONS

Previously known as *lookback options*, *optimal options* refer to the most favorable rate of the underlying currency that existed (from the holder's perspective) during the life of the option. This rate becomes the strike in the case of optimal strike options; or it becomes the underlying, determin-

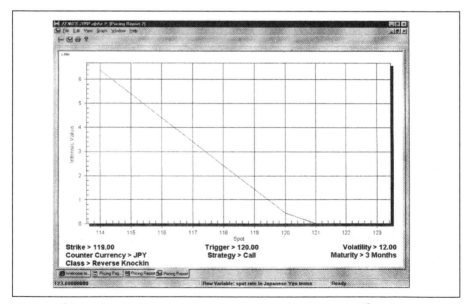

Figure 16.25. Graph of a reverse knockin option. *(Source: FENICS® Software © 1999 by Inventure America Inc. All rights reserved.)*

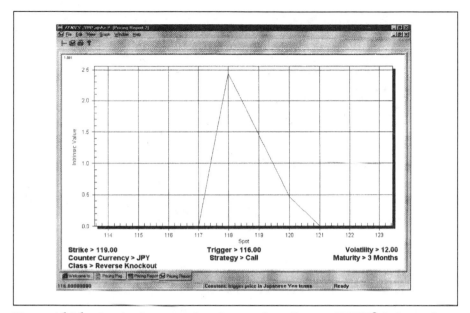

Figure 16.26. Graph of a reverse knockout option. *(Source: FENICS® Software © 1999 by Inventure America Inc. All rights reserved.)*

ing the intrinsic value when compared to a predetermined fixed strike in the case of optimal rate options. Optimals can be based on the spot rate (spot style) or the forward rate (forward style).

The highest underlying rate achieved during the option's life would become the strike of an optional strike put option and the underlying rate of an optimal rate call option. Conversely, the lowest underlying rate achieved during the option's life would become the strike of an optional strike call and the rate of an optimal rate put option.

Because these options allow the holder to transact at the most favorable rate that existed during the life of the option, they are very expensive—almost twice the premium of the at-the-money options.

OPTIMALS FOR CORPORATE HEDGING

Despite their high price, optimal options are still good hedging vehicles when the trader expects more volatility than the market does. Optimals can be hedged quite well with straddles.

RISK MANAGEMENT ASPECTS OF BARRIER OPTIONS

When looking at the price and volatility sensitivity of optimal strike options, it helps to remember that they can be replicated with straddles.

Optimal strike options have virtually no spot sensitivity, but plenty of gamma, vega, and time decay.

AVERAGE OPTIONS

Average options refer to the average rate of the underlying currency that existed during the life of the option. This rate becomes the strike in the case of the average strike options; or it becomes the underlying, determining the intrinsic value when compared to a predetermined fixed strike, in the case of average rate options. Average options can be based on the spot rate (spot style) or the forward underlying the option (forward style). The average can be calculated arithmetically or geometrically, and the rates can be tabulated with a variety of frequencies. (See Figure 16.27.)

AVERAGES FOR CORPORATE HEDGING

The appeal of average options for corporate hedging is obvious. In theory, the goal of a corporation in hedging its foreign exchange exposure is to minimize the P&L impact of foreign exchange rate fluctuations. While transacting at the average rate for a given period is not sufficient to achieve

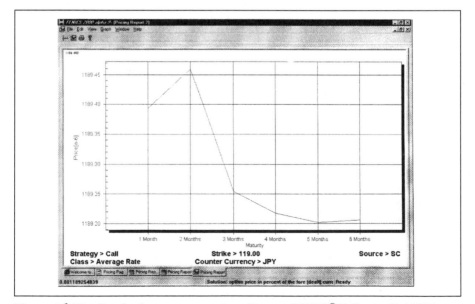

Figure 16.27. Graph of an average option. *(Source: FENICS® Software © 1999 by Inventure America Inc. All rights reserved.)*

this goal, it does help avoid the uncertainties that go along with trying to second-guess the market, and it provides a reasonable measure of downside protection at about half the cost of vanilla options.

Vanilla options are also tremendously valuable in hedging nontransactional (portfolio) exposures, such as interest in a foreign subsidiary or other offshore investments. As static hedges, average rate options may be attractive because they tend to hold their intrinsic value and are not so dependent on where the spot is at expiration.

HEDGING A POSITION IN AVERAGE OPTIONS

Although the most complicated exotic options to price and manage, average options are more like vanilla options than the other exotics when it comes to hedging.

RISK MANAGEMENT ASPECTS OF AVERAGE OPTIONS

Average options are much less susceptible to market volatility than vanilla options and, therefore, somewhat cheaper. Otherwise, the differences between the two classes of average options become more pronounced, and their relationship to vanilla options becomes muddled.

CONCLUSION

Given a choice, foreign exchange traders will not trade currency options when they are confident about the direction of the market. Dollar per dollar, the profit is lower when trading options vis-à-vis spot, forwards, or futures, simply because of the premium involved.

The reverse of the scenario, though, is that at times traders cannot forecast the direction of the market prior to certain events, but expect high volatility. In this case, the best choice is to trade options.

Lack of activity in the currency market signals another opportunity for trading options. Unlike any of the other instruments, options selling, or writing, enables a trader to produce in an otherwise unprofitable environment.

By using options, corporations are able to customize sophisticated strategies for a variety of purposes, such as hedging or insurance. Options trading also allows advanced strategies to be achieved at relatively low cost.

There are certain costs attached to options trading. These costs are pertinent to the adequate capitalization for delta (or gamma or vega) hedging and research costs.

Finally, options trading expands and improves the range of risk management tools. This is a vital feature in a market trading an average daily volume of $1.4 trillion.

NEW DIRECTIONS IN OPTIONS TRADING

Currently, the options share of the currency market is estimated at 5 percent (1993). The increased complexity of the world economic and political environment will fuel the growth of options trading in the twenty-first century. More and more corporations around the world are getting involved in options trading for hedging, risk management, and speculation purposes.

The crises on the European Monetary System in September 1992 and July 1993 and the dollar/yen meltdown of October 1998 are perfect examples of real-life scenarios that may be disastrous for unprotected financial entities. Premiums skyrocket due to unprecedented volatility and the specific needs of various corporations.

The new currency players from emerging economies are increasing their trading efforts around the world. Since 1989, these players have started to become more involved in foreign exchange in general and options trading in particular. From South America to Southeast Asia to Eastern Europe, the demand for derivatives has become substantial.

The options market will also increase due to continuous instrument innovations. In response to diverse international demand, options strategies are continuously being developed. In addition, technological breakthroughs in hardware and software have been pillars for both increased trading sophistication and affordability.

While players around the world are by and large indifferent to the risks germane to options trading, central banks and even governments are less confident. The specter of mismanaged risks, from market to credit, fosters an ongoing concern.

17 Economic Fundamentals

F orecasting is based on two essential types of analysis: fundamental, discussed in detail in Chapters 17 and 18; and technical, the chart study of past behavior of commodity prices, discussed in Chapters 19 through 28. What are the fundamentals? As the name indicates, they refer to factors that either show the fundamental state of the economy or fundamentally alter the outlook of one economy relative to the world economy. This chapter focuses on the theoretical models of exchange rate determination and on the major economic factors and their likelihood of affecting the foreign exchange rates.

ECONOMIC FUNDAMENTALS

Any news that has a direct or indirect bearing on the economy may be considered fundamental. The news may refer to changes in the economy, changes in interest rates, political elections, coup d'ètats, or natural disasters. It's a busy, busy world.

In order to navigate through the large, complex, and changing universe of fundamentals, they may be classified into four categories: economic factors, financial factors, political factors, and crises. A rough comparison of these categories provides us with a simple but very important finding: By and large, economic factors differ from the other three factors in terms of the certainty of their release. The dates and times of economic data release are known well in advance, at least among the industrialized nations. (See Figures 17.1 and 17.2).

```
--------------------------Tuesday, Aug 10--------------------------------
                               Asia

    Hong Kong: Jun trade data classified by country/territory and commodity at
1615
    Hong Kong: HKMA tender for Exchange Fund Bills at 1100 Singapore: September
tender result of the Certificate of Entitlement to own a Vehicle in Singapore.
This reflects consumer sentiment. (Previous: August COE up S $2,276 to $45,876
for the medium-sized car category).
    Singapore: September tender result of the Certificate of Entitlement to own
a Vehicle in Singapore. This reflects consumer sentiment. (Previous: August COE
up S $2,276 to $45,876 for the medium-sized car category).
    Indonesia: Weekly data on foreign reserves and net domestic assets.
    Japan: Prelim net fund inflow for Jul at 0850 (Previous: Jun 2.2 trln yen
outflow)
    Japan: Prelim net buying of overseas bonds for Jul at 0850 (Previous: Jun
1.5 trln yen
    Japan: Prelim net overseas buying of Japan bonds for Jul at 0850
(Previous: Jun -1.5 trln yen)
    Japan: Prelim net overseas buying of Japan stocks for Jul at 0850
(Previous: Jun 1.1 trln yen)
    Japan: Bank loans (BOJ) for Jul at 0850 (Previous: Jun -5.7% on year)
    Japan: Net deposits-plus-CDs (BOJ) for Jul at 0850 (Previous: Jun 3.0%
on year)
    Japan: Key machinery orders (EPA) for Jun at 1400 (Previous: May 3.8% on
month)
    Japan: Public works starts (MOC) for Jun at 1400 (Previous: May 2.6% on
month)
    Japan: Private civil engineering starts for Jun at 1400 (MOC) (Previous:
May -9.0% on year)
    Japan: Monthly economic report (EPA) after economic ministers meeting:

                               Europe

    --0730 Sweden: Central government borrowing requirement and financing
    --0800 France: IEA Oil Market Report
    --0830 UK: Acquisitions and mergers by UK companies
    --After 1500 Italy: Treasury announces types of medium- and long-term bonds
it will offer at auction
    --Brussels: Euro-zone June unemployment
    --Belgium: Belgium weekly Treasury-bill auction

                               Americas

    --0900 ET: Bank of Tokyo-Mitsubishi/Schroder Wertheim weekly US chain
store sales for week ended Aug 7; (week ended Jul 31: +0.1%)
    --1000 ET: Jun Richmond Fed business conditions survey
    --1035 ET: Redbook weekly survey of US retail sales (Previous: final
week of Jul -0.1% from Jun)
    --1330 ET: Treasury auctions $15.0 bln in 5-year notes (Previous:
accepted rate 5.367%)
    --1600 ET: American Petroleum Institute's weekly US oil statistics
for week ended Jul 30
```

Figure 17.1. The global calendar of economic data is available on Story 1069. *(Source: Bridge Information Systems, Inc.)*

```
---------------------- Monday, Aug 16 ------------------------

    --1300 ET: Aug National Association of Home Builders' survey of housing
market index for new single-family home sales (Jul: 74)
    --1330 ET: Treasury auctions 13- & 26-week bills

---------------------- Tuesday, Aug 17 ----------------------

    --0830 ET: Jul housing starts (Jun: Starts -5.6% at 1.571-mln-unit
rate, Permits +3.1% to 1.641-mln rate; Forecast: Starts 1.600-mln rate,
Permits 1.600-mln rate)
    --0830 ET: Jul consumer price index (Jun: unchanged, core rate +0.1%;
Forecast +0.3%, core +0.1%)
    --0900 ET: Bank of Tokyo-Mitsubishi/Schroder Wertheim weekly US chain
store sales for week ended Aug 14
    --0915 ET: Jul industrial production/capacity utilization (Jun:
industrial production +0.2%, capacity utilization 80.3%; Forecast: production
+0 5%, capacity utilization 80.5%)
    --1000 ET: Jul real earnings (Jun: +0.7%)
    --1035 ET: Redbook weekly survey of US retail sales
    --1330 ET: Treasury auctions 52-week bills (Previous: accepted rate
4.710%)
```

Figure 17.2. The calendar of U.S. economic data is available on Story 55. *(Source: Bridge Information Systems, Inc.)*

Political factors vary greatly in terms of the certainty of their dates and times of occurrence. For instance, the time of presidential elections in some countries is known long in advance, such as every four years in the United States. In other countries, like Italy, where governments are less stable, the timing of parliamentary elections cannot be forecast in advance. Moreover, the rapid fall of the Soviet Empire was unforeseen by anybody, fundamentally oriented or not.

With financial factors, timing remains a mystery. Discount rates are changed by central banks, and this activity is surrounded by secrecy, despite the fact that the markets closely watch the central banks' activities and try to forecast the timing of their moves. However, central banks only change their rates during scheduled meetings.

A crisis may or may not be an important factor, depending on the predictability of the crisis. The impact on foreign exchange of the allied forces' military response to the Iraqi aggression against Kuwait in 1991 was minimal, whereas the "kidnapping" of Mikhail Gorbachev, then president of the Soviet Union, had a sharp effect on the foreign exchange markets.

THEORIES OF EXCHANGE RATE DETERMINATION

After spending a long and fruitful life within the Bretton Woods Accord cocoon, currencies around the world were allowed at last, in 1971, more freedom to move against each other, to find their own equilibrium levels, and to take the pressure off governments and central banks in terms of keeping a country's money within the prescribed ranges. Few imagined at the time that, after 27 years of virtual standstill, currencies could exhibit volatile behavior under international conditions of relative peace and prosperity. As you can see from Figure 17.3, the U.S. dollar has displayed "roller coaster" behavior since 1973, the true start of currency free-floating.

Attempting to understand why currencies move so much is difficult. Many attempts have been made to learn the factors determining the volatility of the foreign exchange market. In this section, the three most significant theories of exchange rate determination are discussed. The three models are traditional theories, modern monetary theories on short-term exchange rate volatility, and synthesis of traditional and modern monetary views.

The traditional theories consist of the purchasing power parity (PPP) and the theory of elasticities.

Figure 17.3. The monthly sterling/dollar chart. *(Source: Bridge Information Systems, Inc.)*

PURCHASING POWER PARITY

The oldest and still the most popular of the theories is the purchasing power parity. *Purchasing power parity* was developed in 1556 by Martin de Azpilcueta Navarro. The theory states that the price of a good in one country should equal the price of the same good in another country, exchanged at the current rate—the law of one price.

For example, if the foreign currency (such as the JPY against the USD in 1985 at about 240) is undervalued, the purchasing power of the domestic currency (USD) is higher abroad. As the flow of USD moves abroad, domestic prices fall and foreign prices rise as the domestic demand rises, or the foreign currency rises until the two currencies reach parity.

$$P_d = S \times P_f$$

where

P_d – domestic price of product A

S = spot exchange rate

P_f = foreign price of product A

There are two versions of the purchasing power parity theory: the absolute version and the relative version.

The PPP Absolute Version

Under the *absolute version*, the exchange rate simply equals the ratio of the two countries' general price levels, which is the weighted average of all goods produced in a country.

However, this version quickly comes under fire. First, which two countries produce or consume the same goods? None. Even if we examine the previous two German states or the still split Korea, countries that have the same culture, language, and idiosyncrasies despite their political divisions, we would be hard-pressed to find similar production and consumption.

The typical PPP example publicized on a yearly basis is the price of a hamburger around the world. Now, tasty as they may be, hamburgers are much less popular outside the United States than they are here. In addition, hamburgers are targeted differently in other countries. Whereas in the United States hamburgers are generally considered an inexpensive yet satisfying fast food, in Tokyo or Paris they are part of a chic type of meal, and in Moscow they are rather expensive imports. There are also cultures in which beef is not consumed.

Second, the absolute version assumes that transportation costs and trade barriers are insignificant. In reality, transportation costs are significant and dissimilar around the world. Trade barriers are still alive and well, sometimes obvious and sometimes hidden, and they influence costs and goods distribution.

Finally, this version disregards the importance of brand names. With many commodities, such as soybeans, price is likely to be the main factor. Cars, however, are chosen not only based on the best price for the same type of car, but also on the basis of the name. After all, as one might say in California, "You are what you drive." Even with some commodities, brand names are important. Coffee is not just coffee, but java or espresso or vanilla flavor. Orange juice, as well, comes under different brand names. These cases show what happens to the absolute version of the purchasing power parity in the real world, where the theory fails.

The PPP Relative Version
In order to eliminate some of these problems, the purchasing power parity theory was designed in a different form—the relative version. Under the *relative version*, the percentage change in the exchange rate from a given base period must equal the difference between the percentage change in the domestic price level and the percentage change in the foreign price level.

For instance, since U.S. prices rose by 6 percent and German prices rose by 2.4 percent between 1985 and 1989, the U.S. dollar should have risen by 3.6 percent. However, although the prices in the two countries did increase by approximately those percentages, the U.S. dollar fell about 50 percent.

Obviously, the relative version of the PPP is not free of problems. First, it is difficult or arbitrary to define the base period. Second, trade restrictions remain a real and thorny issue, just as with the absolute version. Third, different price index weighting and the inclusion of different products in the indexes make the comparison difficult. Finally, in the long term, countries' internal price ratios may change, causing the exchange rate to move away from the relative PPP.

In conclusion, the spot exchange rate moves independently of relative domestic and foreign prices. In the short run, the exchange rate is influenced by financial market conditions, not by commodity market conditions.

Despite these problems, the theory behind the Plaza Accord of September 1985 and the subsequent Louvre Accord in February 1987, in which the G-3 countries decided to devaluate the U.S. dollar relative to the European and Japanese currencies, was purchasing power parity.

How successful was the implementation of the theory in reality? In qualifying the success of the application of this theory, the problems germane to each of the versions must be emphasized.

Trade barriers, which have negatively affected the ability of the devalued U.S. dollar to achieve a more balanced international trade, are still a major problem. Despite the internationalization of both industries and consumption, countries still do not have common production or consumption. Brand names continue to maintain their importance. Satisfied consumers are loyal consumers, and it is difficult to convince them to switch brands. The trade deficit between the U.S. and Japan carved new records going into the twenty-first century.

Therefore, price by itself generally fails to be the trigger in consumers' minds. It is value, or the perception of value, and the propensity to spend that will sway value-oriented shoppers. These are just some of the reasons the purchasing power parity theory failed to achieve the original goals of the Plaza Accord of 1985.

The J Curve

The application of the purchasing power parity, in reality, creates the J curve effect. The *J curve* theory holds that the devaluation of a currency will trigger export gains in the long term, rather than the short term. The reasons behind this theory are linked to previous contracts, existing inventories, and behavior modification.

THEORY OF ELASTICITIES

The *theory of elasticities* was popular in the post–World War II era, when it determined the balance of trade's response to a change in the exchange rate. Later, this theory was modified to examine the exchange rate's response to a disturbance in the trade balance.

The theory of elasticities holds that the exchange rate is simply the price of foreign exchange that maintains the balance of payments in equilibrium. In other words, the degree to which the exchange rate responds to a change in the trade balance depends entirely on the elasticity of demand to a change in price.

Therefore, if demand is price inelastic, then a decline in imports and a rise in exports is small. Consequently, the exchange rate must rise steeply to eliminate the payment deficit. On the other hand, if demand is price elastic, then the decline in imports and the rise in exports are large. Therefore, the exchange rates need little adjustment.

For instance, if the imports of country A are strong, then the trade balance is weak. Consequently, the exchange rate rises, leading to the growth of country A's exports, and triggers in turn a rise in its domestic income, along with a decrease in its foreign income.

Whereas a rise in the domestic income (in country A) will trigger an increase in the domestic consumption of both domestic and foreign goods and, therefore, more demand for foreign currencies, a decrease in the foreign income (in country B) will trigger a decrease in the domestic consumption of both country B's domestic and foreign goods, and therefore less demand for its own currency.

The elasticities approach is not problem-free, either. First, in the short term, the exchange rate is more inelastic than it is in the long term. Because the spot market focuses on the short term, the lack of elasticity will impact the exchange rate. Second, additional exchange rate variables arise continuously, changing the rules of the game.

The volatility of the spot exchange rate is influenced to a large extent by short-term variables not anticipated during the Bretton Woods Accord era. Despite the shortcomings, the traditional views on exchange rate determination still tend to explain the long-term behavior of foreign currencies.

The Fisher Effect

The *Fisher effect* holds that the nominal interest rate consists of the real interest rate plus the expected rate of inflation.

$$I_n = I_r + I_e$$

where

I_n = nominal interest rate

I_r = real interest rate

I_e = expected rate of inflation

Therefore, for countries with identical real interest rates, their nominal interest rates will differ with respect to their individual expected rates of inflation.

The International Fisher Effect

The *international Fisher effect* holds that investors will keep assets denominated in depreciating currencies only to the extent that the interest rates are sufficiently high to balance the expected currency losses.

This is a very important point, not only for investors but also for the governments of countries with currencies expected to depreciate. In order to attract investments to such countries, it is vital that interest rates exceed expected losses on foreign exchange.

MODERN MONETARY THEORIES ON SHORT-TERM EXCHANGE RATE VOLATILITY

The modern monetary theories on short-term exchange rate volatility take into consideration the short-term capital markets' role and the long-term impact of the commodity markets on foreign exchange. These theories hold that the divergence between the exchange rate and the purchasing power parity is due to the supply and demand for financial assets and the international capability.

One of the modern monetary theories states that exchange rate volatility is triggered by a one-time domestic money supply increase, because this is assumed to raise expectations of higher future monetary growth.

The purchasing power parity theory is extended to include the capital markets. If, in both countries whose currencies are exchanged, the demand for money is determined by the level of domestic income and domestic interest rates, then a higher income increases demand for transactions balances while a higher interest rate increases the opportunity cost of holding money, reducing the demand for money.

Under absolute PPP, the spot exchange rate equaled the ratio of the domestic price level to the foreign price level. Therefore, the two countries' relative money supply, relative interest rates, and relative real incomes determine the spot exchange rate.

Under a second approach, the exchange rate adjusts instantaneously to maintain continuous interest rate parity, but only in the long run to maintain PPP.

Volatility occurs because the commodity markets adjust more slowly than the financial markets. This version is known as the dynamic monetary approach.

The Portfolio-Balance Approach

Whereas in previous examples it was assumed that international financial assets were interchangeable, the portfolio-balance approach holds the opposite. Due to the differences between international assets, investors, likely to focus on only a group of financial assets, will have to purchase the specific currency or currencies. Therefore, the portfolio-balance approach holds that currency demand is triggered by the demand for financial assets, rather than the demand for the currency per se.

SYNTHESIS OF TRADITIONAL AND MODERN MONETARY VIEWS

In order to better suit the previous theories to the realities of the market, some of the more stringent conditions were adjusted into a synthesis of the traditional and modern monetary theories.

A short-term capital outflow induced by a monetary shock creates a payments imbalance that requires an exchange rate change to maintain balance of payments equilibrium. Speculative forces, commodity markets disturbances, and the existence of short-term capital mobility trigger the exchange rate volatility. The degree of change in the exchange rate is a function of consumers' elasticity of demand.

Because the financial markets adjust faster than the commodities markets, the exchange rate tends to be affected in the short term by capital market changes, and in the long term by commodities changes.

ECONOMIC INDICATORS

Economic indicators are the bread and butter of the fundamental factors. Unlike other factors, they occur in a steady stream, at certain times, and a little more often than changes in interest rates, governments, or underground activity along the San Andreas Fault in California.

Knowing the date and time of release of economic indicators is very important to the foreign exchange trader. (See Figure 17.4.) Based on this information, a trader is able to enter, exit, or adjust a foreign exchange position. Eyes glued to the monitor screens, traders around the world act on the economic data.

However, though this information is important, the information alone is not sufficient. It is the skill of the forecaster and trader in using the information that will generate a P&L.

```
Telerate                                          Mon Aug 09 11:10:37 1999
                              Analytics/Pages

US Economic Indicators -- BRIDGE
   Based on survey of 20 economists. na = not available, R = revised.
A = prior year. **Unemployment claims: For week ended Saturday

          Time                        Median
   Due     ET      Indicators         Forecast   Range    Previous   Actual
  08/06   0830  Jul Unemplymnt-Civil/Rate   4.2    4.1/4.4    4.3      4.3
  08/06   0830  Jul Payroll Jobs (000)      200    100/250    273R     310
  08/06   0830  Jul Avg Hrly Earnings (%)   0.3    0.2/0.4    0.4      0.5
  08/06   1500  Jun Consumer Credit(bln $)  6.4    3.5/8.0    11.7R    2.8
  08/12   0830  Jul Retail Sales            0.3    0.2/0.8    1.0
  08/12   0830  Jul Retail Sales/Ex-auto    0.4    0.2/0.6    0.4
  08/12   0830  **Unemployment Claims(000)  290    280/320    279
  08/13   0830  Jul Producer Price Index    0.3    0.1/0.7    -0.1
  08/13   0830  Jul PPI Core Rate           0.1    0.0/0.2    -0.2
  08/13   0830  Jun Business Inventories    0.2   -0.1/0.4    0.3
  08/17   0830  Jul Consumer Price Index    0.3    0.2/0.6    0.0
  08/17   0830  Jul CPI Core Rate           0.1    0.0/0.3    0.1
  08/17   0915  Jul Industrial Production   0.5    0.3/1.0    0.2
                     (CONTINUED ON PAGE 698)
```

Figure 17.4. The U.S. economic calendar on page 697. *(Source: Bridge Information Systems, Inc.)*

CHARACTERISTICS OF THE ECONOMIC DATA RELEASE

Economic data is generally released on a monthly basis. The exceptions are the Gross Domestic Product and the Employment Cost Index, which are released quarterly. (See Figure 17.5.)

Several indicators are released weekly, on a preliminary basis. (See Figure 17.6.) However, the indicators released weekly are not important to foreign exchange traders, as the data is not complete and, consequently, the indicators are not market shakers.

All economic indicators are released in pairs. The first number reflects the latest period. The second number is the revised figure for the month prior to the latest period.

For instance, in July, economic data is released for the month of June, the latest period. In addition, the release includes the revision of the same economic indicator figure for the month of May. The reason for the revision is that the department in charge of the economic statistics compilation is in a better position to gather more information in a month's time.

This feature is important for traders. If the figure for an economic indicator is better than expected by 0.4 percent for the past month, but the previous month's number is revised lower by 0.4 percent, then traders are likely to ignore the overall release of that specific economic data.

Economic indicators are released at different times. In the United States, economic data is generally released at 8:30 and 10 AM ET. It is important to remember that the most significant data for foreign exchange is released at 8:30 AM ET. In order to allow time for last-minute adjustments, the United States currency futures markets open at 8:20 AM ET.

SOURCES OF INFORMATION

Information on upcoming economic indicators is published in all leading newspapers, such as the *Wall Street Journal*, the *Financial Times*, and the *New York Times*; and business magazines, such as *BusinessWeek*. More often than not, traders use the monitor sources—Bridge Information Systems, Reuters, or Bloomberg—to gather information both from news publications and from the sources' own up-to-date information.

THE GROSS NATIONAL PRODUCT (GNP)

The *Gross National Product* is perhaps the most significant economic indicator. According to professor Paul Samuelson, GNP "measures the economic performance of the whole economy." This indicator consists, at macro scale, of the sum of consumption spending, investment spending, government spending, and net trade.

CATEGORY		-1999-			-1998-
		Q2	Q1	Q4	Q3
	Level	change	Level	Level	Level
Gross domestic product	7803.6	44.0	7759.6	7677.7	7566.5
Personal consumption expenditures	5384.7	52.8	5331.9	5246.0	5181.8
Durable goods	809.8	10.9	798.9	775.0	733.7
Motor vehicles and parts	280.3	1.4	278.9	279.3	252.6
Furniture and household equipment	391.0	9.4	381.6	362.1	352.0
Other	150.1	1.4	148.7	141.0	139.1
Nondurable goods	1612.7	11.8	1600.9	1565.1	1549.1
Food	738.5	4.2	734.3	730.1	718.9
Clothing and shoes	335.2	2.1	333.1	312.5	309.8
Gasoline and oil	121.9	0.5	121.4	121.5	121.1
Fuel oil and coal	11.4	0.7	10.7	9.5	9.9
Other	411.6	4.3	407.3	395.2	393.4
Services	2977.2	30.4	2946.8	2917.2	2904.8
Housing	750.9	4.1	746.8	741.5	737.1
Household operation	332.8	7.2	325.6	318.2	326.3
Electricity and gas	119.7	2.8	116.9	112.9	123.8
Other household operation	212.7	4.3	208.4	205.0	202.4
Transportation	225.0	1.4	223.6	221.8	220.5
Medical care	739.9	5.4	734.5	730.8	725.3
Other	931.2	12.8	918.4	906.3	898.2
Gross private domestic investment	1399.5	11.0	1388.5	1360.6	1331.6
Fixed investment	1373.6	29.6	1344.0	1311.0	1270.9
Nonresidential	1038.5	26.3	1012.2	991.9	958.7
Structures	207.2	-0.6	207.8	205.0	202.0
Nonresidential bldgs, inc farm	155.7	-2.1	157.8	153.8	150.1
Utilities	31.1	0.9	30.2	29.7	29.7
Mining exploration, shafts, & we	13.3	-0.4	13.7	15.3	16.4
Other structures	7.2	1.3	5.9	6.0	5.8
Producers' durable equipment	849.6	29.8	819.8	801.5	769.3
Info prcsng and related equip	482.4	34.2	448.2	422.5	399.6
Computers and peripheral equip	494.0	41.1	452.9	413.0	370.5
Other	161.0	10.0	151.0	145.6	142.8
Industrial equipment	131.9	0.7	131.2	133.5	133.1
Transportation and related equip	173.7	7.5	166.2	168.7	151.7
Other	127.4	-1.5	128.9	122.5	125.8
Residential	340.1	4.2	335.9	324.1	316.5
Stuctures	331.3	4.0	327.3	315.7	308.3
Single family structures	165.8	-1.2	167.0	159.7	155.6
Multifamily structures	23.3	-0.3	23.6	21.7	20.8
Other	143.0	5.7	137.3	135.0	132.6
Producers' durable equipment	8.8	0.2	8.6	8.3	8.2
Change in business inventories	19.4	-19.3	38.7	44.2	55.7
Farm	3.8	0.2	3.6	7.2	9.1
Nonfarm	15.8	-19.3	35.1	37.5	47.0
Manufacturing	-2.7	0.6	-3.3	6.2	19.2
Wholesale trade	9.1	-0.3	9.4	13.7	29.6
Retail trade	1.1	-15.0	16.1	10.9	-5.3
Other	8.2	-4.1	12.3	6.6	4.0
Net exports of goods and services	-323.0	-19.4	-303.6	-250.0	-259.0
Exports	1007.6	11.1	996.5	1009.6	965.3
Goods	760.0	8.8	751.2	768.4	727.3
Foods, feeds, and beverages	43.8	2.1	41.7	45.4	39.9
Industrial supplies and materials	129.2	2.6	126.6	131.1	127.9
Capital goods, except automotive	423.7	2.2	421.5	430.6	407.6
Auto vehicles, engines, and parts	69.0	2.2	66.8	70.0	62.1
Consumer goods, except automotive	76.6	0.0	76.6	76.1	76.6

Figure 17.5. The GDP components on Story 4740. (*Source: Bridge Information Systems, Inc.*)

```
         Other                                44.1    -0.8     44.9     42.3     38.7
         Services                            252.0     2.4    249.6    247.0    242.1
      Imports                               1330.6    30.5   1300.1   1259.6   1224.3
         Goods                              1158.4    30.8   1127.6   1091.7   1056.3
            Foods, feeds, and beverages       40.7     1.7     39.0     38.2     37.8
            Industrial supplies and materials 141.1    3.2    137.9    137.6    140.3
            Petroleum and products            75.6     3.6     72.0     70.8     73.4
            Capital goods, except automotive 483.2    27.4    455.8    442.3    426.2
            Auto vehicles, engines, and parts 158.9   -0.3    159.2    150.3    132.2
            Consumer goods, except automotive 227.2    2.2    225.0    216.8    216.1
            Other                             66.2     0.6     65.6     62.9     58.8
         Services                           177.0     0.5    176.5    171.6    170.8

   Gvt spending & gross invest             1320.0    -3.9   1323.9   1310.3   1299.6
      Federal                               454.7    -3.7    458.4    460.6    452.5
         National defense                   296.9    -2.5    299.4    304.6    303.5
            Consumption expenditures        256.9    -4.2    261.1    267.3    265.1
            Gross investment                 40.3     1.8     38.5     37.2     38.5
         Nondefense                         156.8    -1.2    158.0    155.2    148.4
            Consumption expenditures        136.3     1.2    135.1    134.6    128.4
            Gross investment                 20.3    -3.0     23.3     20.5     19.9
      State and local                       865.5    -0.3    865.8    850.0    847.3
         Consumption expenditures           704.2     3.4    700.8    695.6    691.6
         Gross investment                   161.2    -3.8    165.0    154.3    155.6

   Residual                                -259.2   -21.3   -237.9   -210.7   -175.7

   Addenda:
      Final sales of GDP (GDP less CBI)    7776.0    60.6   7715.4   7628.9   7507.6
      Gross domestic purchase              8087.0    59.2   8027.8   7901.3   7798.8
      Final sales to domestic purchasers   8059.7    76.1   7983.6   7852.5   7739.9
   Gross domestic product                  7803.6    44.0   7759.6   7677.7   7566.5
      Plus: Receipts of factor income        na       na    242.8    240.4    235.7
      Less: Payments of factor income        na       na    255.3    253.9    254.6
      Equals: Gross national product         na       na   7746.3   7663.3   7546.7
   End
```

Figure 17.5. (*Continued*)

```
-------------------------- Thursday, Aug 12 --------------------------

    --0830 ET: State unemployment claims for week ended Aug 7; (Week
ended Jul 31: +4,000 to 279,000)
```

Figure 17.6. Weekly jobs on Story 55. (*Source: Bridge Information Systems, Inc.*)

$$GNP = C + I + G + T$$

where

C = consumption spending

I = investment spending

G = government spending

T = net trade (exports and imports)

THE GROSS DOMESTIC PRODUCT (GDP)

Whereas the gross national product refers to the sum of all goods and services produced by United States residents, either in the United States or abroad, the *Gross Domestic Product* (GDP) refers to the sum of all goods and services produced in the United States, either by domestic or foreign companies. The differences between the two are nominal in the case of the economy of the United States. GDP figures are more popular outside the United States. (See Figure 17.7.) In order to make it easier to compare the performances of different economies, the United States also releases GDP figures.

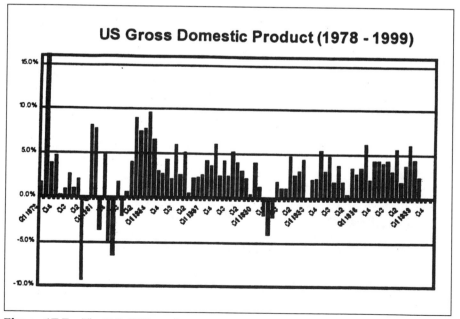

Figure 17.7. The U.S. GDP performance.

CONSUMPTION SPENDING

Consumption is made possible by personal income and discretionary income. The decision by consumers to spend or to save is psychological in nature. Consumer confidence is also measured as an important indicator of the propensity of consumers who have discretionary income to switch from saving to buying.

INVESTMENT SPENDING

Investment—or gross private domestic spending—consists of fixed investment and inventories.

GOVERNMENT SPENDING

Government spending is very influential in terms of both sheer size and its impact on other economic indicators, due to special expenditures. For instance, United States military expenditures had a significant role in total U.S. employment until 1990. The defense cuts that occurred at the time increased unemployment figures in the short run.

NET TRADE

Net trade is another major component of the GNP. Worldwide internationalization and the economic and political developments since 1980 have had a sharp impact on the United States' ability to compete overseas. The U.S. trade deficit of the past decades has slowed down the overall GNP. GNP can be approached in two ways: flow of product and flow of cost. (See Figure 17.8.)

CHARACTERISTICS

GDP is released on a quarterly basis, unlike the rest of the economic indicators. Its release is automatically paired with the release of the implicit GDP deflator, which is an important method used to adjust the GDP for inflation. The GDP deflator is calculated by dividing the current dollar GDP figures by the constant GDP figures.

Due to its quarterly release, the revision of the GDP performance from previous terms is often disregarded by foreign exchange traders, because they find it difficult to design future trading strategies based on fundamentals that occurred as long as six months ago.

Flow of Product Approach	*Flow of Cost Approach*
Personal consumption spending	Wages
Durable goods	
Nondurable goods	Proprietors' income
Services	
	Rental income of persons
Gross private domestic investment	
	Corporate profits
Government spending	
	Net interest
Net trade	
Exports	Business transfer payments
Imports	
	Capital consumption allowances

Figure 17.8. The two approaches summarized here are used by the U.S. Department of Commerce. This method is known as the National Income and Product Accounts (NIPA). The two sides must balance.

INDUSTRIAL SECTOR INDICATORS

The industrial sector indicators consist of industrial production, capacity utilization, National Association of Purchasing Managers (NAPM) Index, factory goods orders, and durable goods orders.

INDUSTRIAL PRODUCTION

Industrial production consists of the total output of a nation's plants, utilities, and mines. (See Figure 17.9.) From a fundamental point of view, it is an important economic indicator that reflects the strength of the economy, and by extrapolation, the strength of a specific currency. Therefore, foreign exchange traders use this economic indicator as a potential trading signal. The industrial production figures are released on a monthly basis.

CAPACITY UTILIZATION

Capacity utilization consists of total industrial output divided by total production capability. (See Figure 17.10.) The term refers to the maximum level of output a plant can generate under normal business conditions.

```
US Industrial Output-STATS-Summary --

   Changes in percent from prior month except where noted. Source:
Federal Reserve. R-denotes revision.

--Industrial Production--
                                                                    Jun 98-
                          Jun   May(R) Apr(R) Mar(R)  Feb    Jan   Jun 99
Total                     0.2    0.2    0.3    0.7    0.1    0.0    2.7
Total products           -0.1    0.1    0.4    0.5    0.1    0.1    1.6
   consumer goods         0.0    0.0    0.3    0.0    0.1    0.2    0.4
   business equipment     0.1    0.6    0.8    1.0    0.2   -0.4    5.1
   construction supplies -0.6   -0.1    0.4   -0.8    0.2    1.1    4.1
Materials                 0.5    0.3    0.2    1.0    0.2   -0.2    4.5
Manufacturing             0.1    0.3    0.4    0.4    0.3   -0.2    3.6
   excluding motor vehicles 0.0  0.2    0.4    0.4    0.3   -0.2    2.4
   motor vehicles         1.6    1.3    0.1    0.9    1.8   -0.9   27.0
   durable               0.4    0.6    0.6    0.9    0.2   -0.1    7.1
   nondurable           -0.2   -0.2    0.1   -0.2    0.5   -0.4   -0.7
Mining                    0.4    0.4   -0.6    0.1    0.4   -0.5   -5.4
Utilities                 0.4   -1.7   -0.4    4.9   -3.0    2.7   -3.4
```

Figure 17.9. Industrial production statistics on Story 4753. *(Source: Bridge Information Systems, Inc.)*

```
--Capacity Utilization--
                          Jun   May(R) Apr(R) Mar(R)  Feb    Jan
Total                    80.3   80.4   80.5   80.5   80.2   80.3
Manufacturing            79.4   79.6   79.6   79.5   79.5   79.5
   Durable goods         79.6   79.7   79.5   79.4   79.1   79.3
     Primary metals      84.1   84.0   83.8   83.8   81.5   83.2
     Industrial machinery 82.1  82.4   82.9   83.0   82.3   82.5
     Motor vehicles/parts 82.2  80.9   79.9   79.8   79.2   77.9
     Autos/light trucks  91.9   80.3   87.4   85.8   86.5   86.8
   Nondurable goods      79.7   79.9   80.1   80.2   80.4   80.1
Mining                   81.7   81.4   81.2   81.8   81.8   81.5
Utilities                90.2   89.9   91.5   91.9   87.7   90.5
```

Figure 17.10. Capacity utilization statistics on Story 4753. *(Source: Bridge Information Systems, Inc.)*

In general, capacity utilization is not a major economic indicator for the foreign exchange market. However, there are instances when its economic implications are useful for fundamental analysis. A "normal" figure for a steady economy is 81.5 percent. If the figure reads 85 percent or more, the data suggests that the industrial production is overheating, that the economy is close to full capacity. High capacity utilization rates precede inflation, and expectation in the foreign exchange market is that the central bank will raise interest rates in order to avoid or fight inflation.

THE NATIONAL ASSOCIATION OF PURCHASING MANAGERS INDEX

The *National Association of Purchasing Managers Index (NAPM)* is a survey of 250 industrial purchasing managers, conducted to gauge the changes in new orders, production, employment, inventories, and vendor delivery speed. A reading under 45 to 50 percent indicates a worsening economy. From a trader's point of view, the NAPM Index is a mixed bag. The survey is based more on psychology than on facts; it excludes California; and industrial production does not automatically generate consumer demand.

FACTORY ORDERS

Factory orders refer to the total of durable and nondurable goods orders. Nondurable goods consist of food, clothing, light industrial products, and products designed for the maintenance of durable goods. Durable goods orders are discussed separately. The factory orders indicator has limited significance for foreign exchange traders.

DURABLE GOODS ORDERS

Durable goods orders consist of products with a life span of more than three years. (See Figure 17.11.) Examples of durable goods are autos, appliances, furniture, jewelry, and toys. They are divided into four major categories: primary metals, machinery, electrical machinery, and transportation.

In order to eliminate the volatility pertinent to large military orders, the indicator includes a breakdown of the orders between defense and nondefense.

This data is fairly important to foreign exchange markets because it gives a good indication of consumer confidence. Because durable goods cost more than nondurables, a high number in this indicator shows consumers' propensity to spend. Therefore, a good figure is generally bullish for the domestic currency.

BUSINESS INVENTORIES

Business inventories consist of items produced and held for future sale. The compilation of this information is facile and holds little surprise for the market. Moreover, financial management and computerization help control business inventories in unprecedented ways. Therefore, the importance of this indicator for foreign exchange traders is limited.

```
US Durable Goods-STATS-Seasonally adjusted data --

   Levels are in millions of dollars. Pct changes are from
previous month. R denotes revision. Source: US Commerce Department.
```

--DURABLE GOODS--	-----Percent Change-----			------Level-------		
Total:	Jun	May	Apr	Jun	May	Apr
shipments	0.9	1.1	-0.5	201,048	199,353	197,246
new orders	0.3	0.8	-2.4	196,948	196,308	194,674
unfilled orders	-0.8	-0.6	-0.5	493,465	497,565	500,610
Excluding defense:						
shipments	1.0	1.1	-0.5	194,715	192,779	190,720
new orders	0.5	0.5	-1.0	191,374	190,512	189,614
unfilled orders	-0.8	-0.6	-0.3	399,377	402,718	404,985
With unfilled orders:						
shipments	-0.1	1.0	0.0	163,820	163,998	162,442
new orders	-0.8	0.7	-2.3	159,720	160,953	159,870
Primary metals:						
shipments	0.8	2.0	-1.9	14,626	14,506	14,225
new orders	0.0	0.5	1.6	14,848	14,846	14,767
unfilled orders	0.7	1.1	1.8	30,417	30,195	29,855
Machinery, except electrical:						
shipments	-1.5	0.1	1.0	36,958	37,504	37,464
new orders	-5.4	-4.5	3.2	35,737	37,757	39,556
unfilled orders	-1.5	0.3	2.7	77,880	79,101	78,848
Electrical machinery:						
shipments	0.8	0.7	1.9	34,162	33,875	33,655
new orders	2.1	-0.8	0.3	34,818	34,096	34,364
unfilled orders	1.0	0.3	1.1	65,829	65,173	64,952
Transportation equipment:						
shipments	2.7	2.2	-3.1	50,160	48,818	47,755
new orders	2.7	9.0	-12.5	46,617	45,378	41,616
unfilled orders	-1.5	-1.4	-2.5	231,453	234,996	238,436
--CAPITAL GOODS INDUSTRIES--						
Total:						
shipments	-2.2	1.5	0.6	60,807	62,163	61,257
new orders	-4.5	2.0	-5.7	56,067	58,718	57,585
unfilled orders	-1.4	-1.0	-1.0	346,066	350,806	354,251
Non-defense:						
shipments	-2.0	1.6	0.9	54,474	55,589	54,731
new orders	-4.6	0.8	-1.5	50,493	52,922	52,525
unfilled orders	-1.6	-1.0	-0.8	251,978	255,959	258,626
Excluding aircraft and parts:						
shipments	0.1	0.9	0.8	46,455	46,421	46,016
new orders	-4.0	-2.8	0.3	44,244	46,089	47,437
unfilled orders	-2.0	-0.3	1.3	109,602	111,813	112,145
Defense:						
shipments	-3.7	0.7	-2.2	6,333	6,574	6,526
new orders	-3.8	14.5	-34.9	5,574	5,796	5,060
unfilled orders	-0.8	-0.8	-1.5	94,088	94,847	95,625

Figure 17.11. Durable goods orders statistics on Story 4727. (*Source: Bridge Information Systems, Inc.*)

CONSTRUCTION DATA

Construction indicators constitute significant economic indicators that are included in the calculation of the GDP of the United States. Moreover, housing has traditionally been the engine that pulled the U.S. economy out of recessions after World War II. These indicators are classified into three major categories:

1. housing starts and permits (see Figure 17.12);
2. new and existing one-family home sales; and
3. construction spending.

Private housing is monitored closely at all the major stages: permits, starts, completion, and sales. (See Figure 17.13.) Private housing is classified based on the number of units (one, two, three, four, five, or more); region (Northeast, West, Midwest, and South); and inside or outside metropolitan statistical areas.

```
US Housing Starts-STATS --

    In thousands of units, seasonally adjusted except actuals.
p-preliminary, r-revised. Source: Commerce Department.


--Starts--      Jun 99p  Jun-May  May 99r  May-Apr  Apr 99r  Mar 99r
Actual starts     152.4    -1.9    155.4      6.1    146.5    149.3
Annual rate       1,571    -5.6    1,665      5.6    1,577    1,746
 One-family       1,274    -8.7    1,395     10.7    1,260    1,394
 2-4 units           30    11.1       27    -10.0       30       33
 5 units or more    267     9.9      243    -15.3      287      319
  Northeast         159     0.0      159     16.1      137      147
  Midwest           359     0.3      358      6.9      335      381
  South             701    -4.6      735      4.1      706      821
  West              352   -14.8      413      3.5      399      397
--Permits--
Actual            163.2    15.2    141.7     -5.0    149.1    152.1
Annual rate       1,621     1.9    1,591      1.2    1,572    1,654
 One-family       1,231    -1.0    1,243      2.4    1,214    1,242
 2-4 units           60     1.7       59    -11.9       67       69
 5 units or more    330    14.2      289     -0.7      291      343
  Northeast         168     8.4      155     -4.3      162      163
  Midwest           332    -1.8      338      0.0      338      356
  South             717     3.6      692      0.0      692      744
  West              404    -0.5      406      6.8      380      391

--Mobile Homes--  May 99            Apr 99                     May 98
Shipments           365               368                        372
```

Figure 17.12. Housing starts on Story 4749. (*Source: Bridge Information Systems, Inc.*)

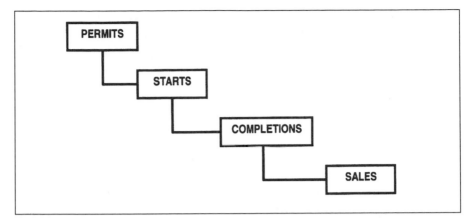

Figure 17.13. Diagram of construction of private housing.

Construction indicators are cyclical and very sensitive to the level of interest rates (and consequently mortgage rates) and the level of disposable income. Low interest rates alone may not be able to generate a high demand for housing, though. As the situation in the early 1990s demonstrated, despite historically low mortgage rates in the United States, housing increased only marginally, as a result of the lack of job security in a weak economy.

Housing starts between one and a half and two million units reflect a strong economy, whereas a figure of approximately one million units suggests that the economy is in recession.

Despite their economic significance, construction indicators are not favorites of the foreign exchange traders. Their unusual volatility is further exacerbated by weather patterns. As a trader, it is difficult to gauge whether sunny summer weather is better for housing shopping or going to the beach. The numbers tend to fluctuate significantly from one month to another. Therefore, few traders use the construction figures for their fundamental analysis.

INFLATION INDICATORS

Few other economic problems have the same infamous connotation as does inflation. The rate of inflation is the widespread rise in prices. Therefore, gauging inflation is a vital macroeconomic task.

Traders watch the development of inflation closely, because the method of choice for fighting inflation is raising the interest rates, and higher interest rates tend to support the local currency. Moreover, the inflation rate is used to "deflate" nominal interest rates and the GNP or GDP to their real values in order to achieve a more accurate measure of the data.

The values of the real interest rates or real GNP and GDP are of the utmost importance to the money managers and traders of international financial instruments, allowing them to accurately compare opportunities worldwide.

Generally, traders use seven economic tools:

- Producer Price Index (PPI)
- Consumer Price Index (CPI)
- GNP Deflator
- GDP Deflator
- Employment Cost Index (ECI)
- Commodity Research Bureau's Index (CRB Index)
- Journal of Commerce Industrial Price Index (JoC)

The first four are strictly economic indicators; they are released at specific intervals. The commodity indexes provide information on inflation quickly and continuously.

Other economic data that measure inflation are unemployment, consumer prices, and capacity utilization.

PRODUCER PRICE INDEX (PPI)

The *producer price index* has been compiled since the beginning of the twentieth century and was called the wholesale price index until 1978. (See Figure 17.14.) Currently, the PPI gauges the average changes in prices received by domestic producers for their output at all stages of processing. The PPI data is compiled from most sectors of the economy, such as manufacturing, mining, and agriculture. The sample used to calculate the index contains about 3400 commodities. The weights used for the calculation of the index for some of the most important groups are: food—24 percent; fuel—7 percent; autos—7 percent; and clothing—6 percent. Unlike the CPI, the PPI does not include imported goods, services, or taxes. This index is released on a monthly basis.

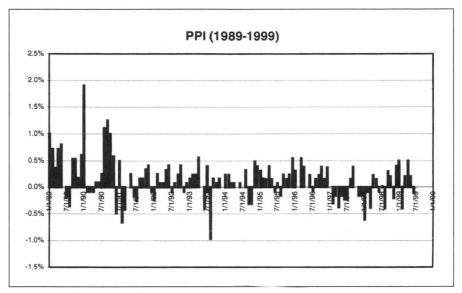

Figure 17.14. The U.S. PPI performance.

CONSUMER PRICE INDEX (CPI)

The *consumer price index* (CPI) gauges the average change in retail prices for a fixed market basket of goods and services. The CPI data is compiled from a sample of prices for food, shelter, clothing, fuel, transportation, and medical services that people purchase on daily basis. (See Figure 17.15.) The weights attached for the calculation of the index to the most important groups are: housing—38 percent; food—19 percent; fuel—8 percent; and autos—7 percent. The consumer price index is released monthly.

The two indexes, PPI and CPI, are instrumental in helping traders measure inflationary activity, although the Federal Reserve takes the position that the indexes overstate the strength of inflation.

GROSS NATIONAL PRODUCT IMPLICIT DEFLATOR

The nominal GNP figure is not in itself helpful to the trading community. A large number may or may not be good, depending on the level of inflation in the specific economy. Therefore, the nominal GNP figure must be "deflated" by some price index.

There are several GNP deflators, but the most commonly used is the *implicit deflator*. The implicit deflator is calculated by dividing the current dollar GNP figure by the constant dollar GNP figure.

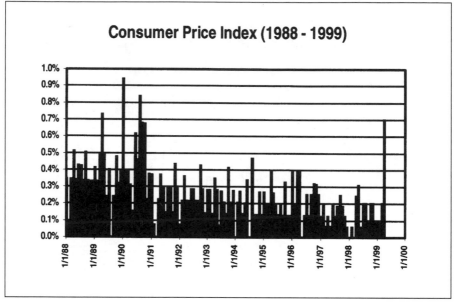

Figure 17.15. The U.S. CPI performance.

GROSS DOMESTIC PRODUCT IMPLICIT DEFLATOR

In the same manner, the *gross domestic product implicit deflator* is calculated by dividing the current dollar GDP figure by the constant dollar GDP figure.

Both the GNP and GDP implicit deflators are released quarterly, along with the respective GNP and GDP figures. The implicit deflators are generally regarded as the most significant measure of inflation.

COMMODITY RESEARCH BUREAU'S FUTURES INDEX (CRB INDEX)

The Commodity Research Bureau's Futures Index makes watching for inflationary trends easier. The CRB Index consists of the equally weighted futures prices of 21 commodities. The components of the CRB Index are:

- Precious metals: gold, silver, platinum
- Industrials: crude oil, heating oil, unleaded gas, lumber, copper, and cotton
- Grains: corn, wheat, soybeans, soy meal, soy oil

- Livestock and meat: cattle, hogs, and pork bellies
- Imports: coffee, cocoa, sugar
- Miscellaneous: orange juice

The preponderance of food commodities makes the CRB Index less reliable in terms of general inflation. Nevertheless, the index is a popular tool that has proved quite reliable since the late 1980s.

THE JOURNAL OF COMMERCE INDUSTRIAL PRICE INDEX (JoC)

The Journal of Commerce Index consists of the prices of 18 industrial materials and supplies processed in the initial stages of manufacturing, building, and energy production. It is more sensitive than other indexes, as it was designed to signal changes in inflation prior to the other price indexes.

A Trader's Point of View

Traders have the luxury of a multitude of tools to measure inflation. However, traders cannot expect the central banks to either raise the discount rate every time one of the indicators shows a higher figure, signaling inflation, or to cut it when the opposite occurs. As illustrated in the accompanying figures, the indexes spiked up several times, such as the CPI figure in 1991 due to the short-lived speculation of high oil prices following the Iraqi invasion of Kuwait. One month's economic figures grab attention, but they do not generally trigger the action of a central bank, because one number does not make a trend. Central banks need confirmation of long-term changes in the inflation trend before they will counteract with equally long-term measures.

Even a trend does not guarantee the central bank's action in the short term. For instance, the low inflation in the United States in the early 1990s allowed the Federal Reserve to maintain a low discount rate of 3 percent, which was instrumental in the steady process of economic recovery.

At times, the discount rate is not perceived by the markets as being sensitive to the low or lower readings of the price indexes. If the nominal discount rate is already very low, the markets expect the discount rate to be sensitive only on the upside, when inflation is perceived to have picked up. From the point of view of foreign exchange, the inflation indicators are significant at their most when they either increase after a period of stagnation, and when they decrease after a series of gains.

BALANCE OF PAYMENTS

The *balance of payments* consists of all the international commercial and financial transactions of the residents of one country. The familiar indicator is the merchandise trade balance. In the long term, the competitiveness of a country is a function of its natural resources, industrial base, skill of the labor force, and cost structure. In the short term, international trade is impacted by changes in spending patterns generated by the business cycles. Other factors affecting the balance of payments are domestic and foreign investments in both goods and services. The data has a limited following by traders. However, the data is important for foreign exchange on a longer-term statistical basis.

MERCHANDISE TRADE BALANCE

The *merchandise trade balance* is one of the most important economic indicators. Its value may trigger long-lasting changes in monetary and foreign policies. The trade balance consists of the net difference between the exports and imports of a certain economy. The data includes six categories:

1. food,
2. raw materials and industrial supplies,
3. consumer goods,
4. autos,
5. capital goods, and
6. other merchandise.

The typical example of the impact of the merchandise trade balance in the financial markets must refer to the coordinated change in foreign exchange, backed by changes in interest rates conceived at the historic Plaza Accord in New York on September 1985 by the G-5 countries. At the time, the U.S. dollar was at post–World War II record highs against the European and Japanese currencies. The United States felt that the American exporters were at a disadvantage, as their high-priced products were hardly competitive in the international markets. The devaluation of the U.S. dollar was therefore earmarked to rebalance this economic disequilibrium in the medium term. Trade deficits were not something new in the United States. As a matter of fact, the last time the United States had registered a positive trade balance was in 1975. The economic theory behind this strategy was the purchasing power parity theory. The extent of the success of the U.S. dollar devaluation strategy in order to reduce and eventually reverse the trade deficit has been minuscule. (See Figure 17.16.)

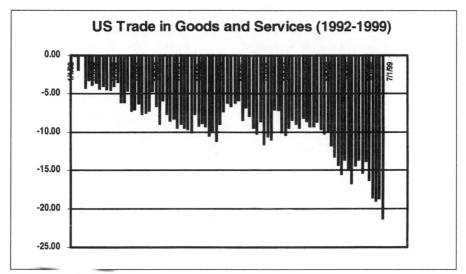

Figure 17.16. The U.S. trade deficit.

THE UNITED STATES–JAPAN MERCHANDISE TRADE BALANCE

With the trade balance hitting record deficits despite the devaluation of the dollar between 1985 and 1995, it is easy to understand why friction over the trade gap between the United States and Japan can be intense. (See Figure 17.17.) The dollar devaluation, which cut the dollar by 1995 to one-third from its 1985 value, failed to generate a sound turnaround of the U.S. trade balance in the early 1990s. (See Figure 17.18.) Technically, changes in the value of currencies take six to nine months to translate into changes in the trade balance. But in this case, nearly 10 years failed to make a significant dent, so politicians folded their tents and buried the issue.

A Trader's Point of View

Important as it may be in general, the trade deficit has been of variable importance for foreign exchange traders. In the 1980s, both before and after the Plaza Accord, the trade figure was one of the most sought-after pieces of fundamental data.

Before the Accord, the U.S. dollar was an easy but temporary sell, as the number was worse by the month. The release of the data created a perfect opportunity to take profit on the almighty dollar. After the Accord, the release of the figure generated perfect opportunities to enter new short U.S. dollar positions based on disappointment in the lack of quick translation of the dollar devaluation into trade deficit improvements.

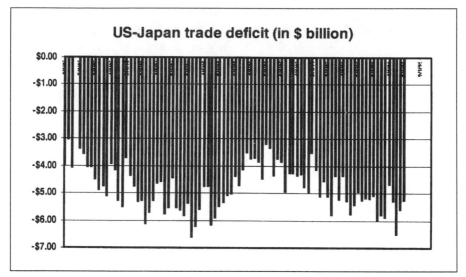

Figure 17.17.   The U.S.–Japan trade deficit.

Figure 17.18.   The dollar/yen chart between 1985 and 1995. *(Source: Bridge Information Systems, Inc.)*

However, the trade figure eventually lost its panache. After all, no happy ending was in sight. Traders took positions based on expectations or facts that did not materialize.

In 1992, the newly elected Clinton Administration suddenly brought the trade deficit's importance to the foreign exchange community into the limelight. A series of well-timed statements from President Clinton and then Treasury Secretary Lloyd Bentsen regarding the relative weakness of the yen vis-à-vis the dollar and its negative impact on the U.S.–Japan balance of trade sent the dollar/yen on a fast downward spiral, from 126.00 to 80.00, a post–World War II record.

Fundamentally, this situation created a tremendous USD/JPY long-term selling opportunity for foreign exchange traders around the world. But the U.S. merchandise trade deficit continued.

EMPLOYMENT INDICATORS

The employment rate is an economic indicator with significance in multiple areas. The rate of employment, naturally, measures the soundness of an economy. (See Figure 17.19.) In addition, the indicator is used as a major

Figure 17.19. The U.S. unemployment rate.

component in the calculation of other economic indicators, such as GNP and GDP.

Generally, the most commonly used employment figure is not the monthly unemployment rate, which is released as a percentage, but the nonfarm payroll rate. (See Figure 17.20.) The rate figure is calculated as the ratio of the difference between the total labor force and the employed labor force, divided by the total labor force. The data is more complex, though, and it generates more information. The report consists of two separate surveys: business firms and households.

- The Business Firms (Establishments) Survey consists of the payroll, workweek, hourly earnings, and total hours of employment in the nonfarm sector. The nonfarm sector refers to jobs in government, manufacturing, services, construction, mining, retail, and others.
- The Households Survey consists of the unemployment rate, the overall labor force, and the number of people employed.

In foreign exchange, the standard indicators monitored by traders are the unemployment rate, manufacturing payrolls, nonfarm payrolls, average earnings, and average workweek. Generally, the most significant employ-

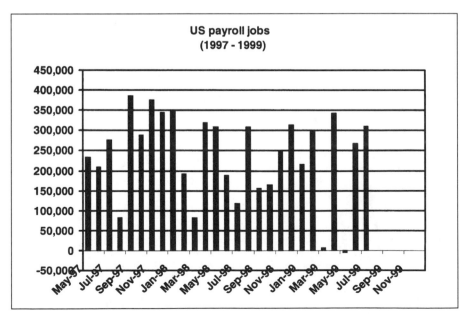

Figure 17.20. The U.S. payroll jobs rate.

ment data are manufacturing and nonfarm payrolls, followed by the unemployment rate.

This data is released on a monthly basis. Although initial unemployment claims are available on a weekly basis, they are not important to the market because they are not complete. The claims understate the real figures, because not all workers are covered by unemployment insurance.

The household data is generally less reliable. This survey tends to show overly optimistic figures due either to individual reluctance to admit being unemployed or to discouraged unemployed workers who stop seeking work or claiming unemployment.

The unemployment rate is a lagging economic indicator. It is an important feature to remember, especially in times of economic recession. Whereas people focus on the health and recovery of the job sector, employment is the last economic indicator to rebound. When economic contraction causes jobs to be cut, it takes time to generate psychological confidence in economic recovery at the managerial level before new positions are added. At individual levels, the improvement of the job outlook may be clouded when new positions are added in small companies and thus not fully reflected in the data.

The employment reports are significant to the financial markets in general and to foreign exchange in particular. In foreign exchange, the data is truly affective in periods of economic transition—recovery and contraction. The reason for the indicators' importance in extreme economic situations lies in the picture they paint of the health of the economy and in the degree of maturity of a business cycle. A decreasing unemployment figure signals a maturing cycle, whereas the opposite is true for an increasing unemployment indicator.

EMPLOYMENT COST INDEX (ECI)

The Employment Cost Index measures wages and inflation and provides the most comprehensive analysis of worker compensation, including wages, salaries, and fringe benefits. The ECI is one of the Fed's favorite quarterly economic statistics.

CONSUMER SPENDING INDICATORS

RETAIL SALES

Retail sales is a significant consumer spending indicator for foreign exchange traders, as it shows the strength of consumer demand as well as consumer confidence. (See Figure 17.21.)

U.S. Retail Sales—STATS—Summary

Percent change from prior month except where noted. Seasonally adjusted. (a)
denotes Ex-leased department stores.

	June	May	Apr	Mar	Feb	May 99	Apr 99
		May 98–April 98					
Total retail sales	0.1	1.2	0.5	0.0	1.7	8.0	8.3
Non-automotive sales	0.4	0.5	0.8	0.4	1.3	8.0	7.7
Durable goods	-0.4	2.3	-0.2	-0.8	2.6	8.5	9.7
Building materials	0.4	0.0	1.0	-1.7	3.6	13.4	11.6
Automotive dealers	-1.0	3.5	-0.4	-1.2	2.9	7.8	10.0
Furniture	0.2	0.7	0.0	0.5	1.5	8.0	8.8
Durable ex-autos	0.3	0.6	0.0	-0.3	2.2	9.7	9.3
Non durable goods	0.4	0.5	1.0	0.7	1.0	7.5	7.2
General merchandise	0.5	0.3	-0.5	0.8	0.6	8.0	7.5
Department stores (a)	0.6	0.3	-0.7	0.8	0.4	7.2	6.3
Food stores	0.1	1.2	0.0	-0.1	1.3	5.1	5.4
Gasoline stations	-0.4	-1.0	5.0	2.6	0.5	5.8	6.2
Apparel	0.2	0.7	1.9	0.1	0.5	8.8	8.2
Eating and drinking	0.2	0.3	1.3	-0.2	1.4	6.9	7.2
Drug Stores	1.5	0.3	0.9	1.0	1.9	13.0	11.4
End							

Figure 17.21. Retail sales statistics on Story 4865. *(Source: Bridge Information Systems, Inc.)*

As an economic indicator, retail sales is particularly important in the United States. Unlike other countries such as Japan, the focus in the U.S. economy is the consumer. If the consumer has enough discretionary income, or enough credit for that matter, then more merchandise will be produced or imported. Retail sales figures create an economic process of "trickling up" to the manufacturing sector.

The seasonal aspect is important for this economic indicator. The retail sales months that are most watched by foreign exchange traders are December, because of the holiday season, and September, the back-to-school month. Increasingly, November is becoming an important month, as a result of the shift in the former after-Christmas sales to pre-December sales days.

Another interesting phenomenon occurred in the United States. Despite the economic recession in the early 1990s, the volume of retail sales was unusually high. The profit margin, however, was much thinner. The reason is the consumer's shift toward discount stores.

Traders watch retail sales closely to gauge the overall strength of the economy and, consequently, the strength of the currency.

This indicator is released on a monthly basis.

CONSUMER SENTIMENT

Consumer sentiment is a survey of households that is designed to gauge the individual propensity for spending. The University of Michigan and National Family Opinion Conference Board conduct the two studies in this area. The confidence index measured by the Conference Board is sensitive to the job market, whereas the index generated by the University of Michigan is not.

In the early 1990s, consumer confidence increased sharply twice: after the successful allied intervention against Iraq and following the 1992 United States presidential election. Both times, however, the increases were short-lived, as they occurred against a bleak economic background.

AUTO SALES

Despite the importance of the auto industry in terms of both production and sales, the level of auto sales is not an economic indicator widely followed by foreign exchange traders. The American automakers experienced a long, steady market share loss, only to start rebounding in the early 1990s. But car manufacturing has become increasingly internationalized, with American cars being assembled outside the United States and Japanese and German cars assembled within the United States. Because of their confusing nature, auto sales figures cannot easily be used in foreign exchange analysis.

LEADING INDICATORS

The *leading indicators* consist of the following economic indicators:

Average workweek of production workers in manufacturing

Average weekly claims for state unemployment

New orders for consumer goods and materials (adjusted for inflation)

Vendor performance (companies receiving slower deliveries from suppliers)

Contracts and orders for plant and equipment (adjusted for inflation)

New building permits issued

Change in manufacturers' unfilled orders, durable goods

Change in sensitive materials prices

Index of stock prices

Money supply, adjusted for inflation

Index of consumer expectations

This index is designed to offer a 6- to 9-month future outlook of economic performance. (See Figure 17.22.) Unlike the unemployment rate, which is a lagging economic indicator, the leading indicators are, as the name implies, leading. In addition to its forecasting value, the data can be used in times of slow economic performance to gauge whether the economy is in recession. Three consecutive negative monthly readings are generally considered to indicate recession. The index, which was set up during the Depression, when the structure of the U.S. economy was vastly different than it is now, carries little FX significance.

```
US Leading Economic Indicators Report-STATS --


Change in percent. R denotes revision. Source: Conference Board.
                          Jun   chg  May   chg  Apr    chg    Mar    chg
  Leading indicators index 107.7  0.3  107.4  0.3  107.1 -0.1   107.2r -0.1r
  Coincident index         124.6  0.4  124.1  0.2  123.8r 0.0r  123.8   0.3
  Lagging index            108.0 -0.4  108.4  0.0  108.4  0.3   108.1   0.1


    Contributions of US leading index components.
                                                   Mar    Apr   May    Jun
Average workweek, production, manufacturing       -0.03   0.03  0.03   0.00
Average weekly state unemployment claims          -0.01  -0.07  0.01   0.02
New orders: manufactured consumer goods/materials  0.04  -0.02r 0.02r  0.08
Vendor performance, companies receiving slower     0.06  -0.10  0.08   0.04
  vendor deliveries
Manufacturers' new orders, nondefense capital goods 0.0  -0.01  0.01r -0.04
Building permits                                  -0.06  -0.06  0.01   0.03
Stock prices: 500 common stocks                    0.05   0.08  0.00  -0.01
Real money supply (M2)                             0.04   0.02r 0.07   0.07
Interest rate spread, 10-yr Treasury less fed funds 0.04  0.00  0.07   0.07
Consumer expectations                             -0.05  -0.02  0.00   0.02
```

Figure 17.22. Leading economic indicators statistics on Story 4761. (*Source: Bridge Information Systems, Inc.*)

PERSONAL INCOME

Personal income is simply the income received by individuals, nonprofit institutions, and private trust funds. Components of this indicator include wages and salaries, rental income, dividends, interest earnings, and transfer payments (Social Security, state unemployment insurance, and veterans' benefits). The wages and salaries reflect the underlying economic conditions.

This indicator is vital for the sales sector. Without an adequate personal income and a propensity to purchase, consumer purchases of durable and nondurable goods are limited.

For FX traders, personal income is not significant.

CONCLUSION

Economic fundamentals provide the most significant information to traders. The time of release is known in advance, a feature specific to the economic indicators. The impact of the economic data tends to be longer-term, with an impact measurable in months. This effect is generated not only by the need for a deeper understanding of the changes reflected by the data, but also by the flow of the market. The old saying, "Buy on the rumor, sell on the fact," may in the short run stir in the wrong direction. Traders go long in dollars on expectation of strong U.S. economic data. They take profit by selling their long positions once the good economic data is released. The data is not truly disregarded, because it will create a buying opportunity later on.

Not all economic data is significant for the foreign exchange market. We have discussed the most important economic indicators. However, these indicators do not have the same impact on the market every time. Traders react to expectations of change or to actual changes. If the economic data fails to show changes in the economy, then the traders will have a mute reaction. If one country's economy overperforms or underperforms relative to other economies, that specific currency will be bought or sold, respectively, generating long-term trends. If the correlation between economies is high, then currency will be less volatile as the overall change is limited.

The relativity of economic performance among countries is particularly important to foreign exchange. Whereas in other financial markets domestic data suffices, that is not the case in foreign exchange. Any FX transaction consists of simultaneous transactions in two currencies, so it is easy to grasp the importance of comparing individual economies in the international arena.

The significance of economic data tends to be cyclical. In the United States, where the trade balance has had an abysmal showing for years, that indicator has been in and out of the limelight, depending on the market's perception of what the government can do and what it actually does about it.

Also in the United States, the foreign exchange markets generally disregarded inflation numbers in the early 1990s. Because they were low for so long, these indicators allowed the Federal Reserve to maintain low interest rates. Little change, if any, was expected, so the inflation numbers, excellent otherwise for the economy, were non-events for traders. However, interest in those numbers rose steeply in the late 1990s on fear that the record bull market might show signs of waning.

Although there are quite a few economic indicators released in any given month, they do not provide all the information necessary to trade. The information is not always relevant, either because the change is insignificant or because the market has already discounted it. What these economic indicators do, however, is provide an overall background. The "feeling" of the market is the vital element in trading. If the market focuses on an aspect askew from the theoretical truth, it may be difficult for an individual trader to stop the tidal wave. That is why traders must stay close to the market, trying to gauge any change in other traders' opinions.

This is not an argument to follow the flock, but an attempt to emphasize the importance of understanding and "feeling" the market. In the contemporary environment, access to information and the processing of information are at unprecedented levels of sophistication and speed. The monitors crowding the traders' desks display a continuous flow of information. Currency traders have become information traders.

It is up to the trader to discern what data is important, how to interpret it, and what weights to apply—instantly.

18 Financial and Sociopolitical Factors

C urrency exchange rates are greatly influenced by financial factors, particularly by interest rates. In fact, some market observers consider interest rates to be the primary determinant of a currency's value. It is a misconception, however, to think that all increases in interest rates automatically trigger a rally in the domestic currency. This chapter analyzes the importance of interest rates vis-à-vis the exchange rates and explains how traders use interest rate changes in their trading.

THE ROLE OF FINANCIAL FACTORS

Financial factors are vital to fundamental analysis. Changes in a government's monetary or fiscal policies are bound to generate changes in the economy, and these will be reflected in the exchange rates. Financial factors should be triggered only by economic factors. Is that always the case? Regrettably, no. When governments focus on different aspects of the economy or have additional international responsibilities, financial factors may have priority over economic factors. This was painfully true in the case of the European Monetary System in the early 1990s. The realities of the marketplace revealed the underlying artificiality of this approach. Using the interest rates independently from the real economic environment translated into a very expensive strategy. The European economies came under undue pressure by 1992, and the EMS was in complete disarray by July 1993, delaying currency unification plans to 1999 from 1997.

Let's take a look at the financial factors affecting currency exchange rates.

MONEY SUPPLY

According to Paul Samuelson, the supply of money, M1, incorporates "the sum of coins and currency in circulation outside the banks, plus checkable demand deposits (after various routine adjustments have been made in this magnitude)." (Paul Samuelson, *Economics*, 11th ed., McGraw-Hill, 1980.) The broader M2 also includes time and savings accounts. In addition, the Fed publishes another, broader money supply figure, M3, which also includes large denomination time deposits and term repurchase agreements. For further details please refer to Chapter 6.

Money supply is a major factor of the *Quantity Equation of Exchange*:

$$MV = PQ$$

where

M = money supply

V = velocity

P = prices

Q = real transactions

Velocity of money is the rate at which money is turning over on an annual basis to facilitate income transactions. Samuelson states that MV "equals GNP."

The money supply data is released in the United States on a weekly basis. This data comes in handy in revealing the cyclical phase of economic recovery. For example, a larger money supply reflects a strengthening economy. Despite their implied importance, the money supply figures have lost some of their panache since the 1980s. This is due to distortions created by newer types of bank deposits, such as interest-bearing checking accounts and money market accounts. By 1993, the Federal Reserve Bank of the United States found the money supply no longer useful for gauging the state of the economy, because of the statistical distortions.

INTEREST RATES

Interest rates are of paramount importance for foreign exchange. Generally, the first advice on fundamental analysis given to the junior foreign exchange trader is to "watch the interest rates." This is easier said than done, though, as central banks are not particularly eager to change discount rates often. The realities of the international and domestic economic environment, however, dictate more maneuvering of the discount rates. (See Figure 18.1.)

The rule of thumb is that higher interest rates generate a stronger currency, and vice versa. However, the investor must focus on the real interest rate rather than on the nominal interest rate. Nominal interest rates, unlike the real ones, take inflation into account. Also, it is critical to gauge the impact of a change in the rates on that country's asset markets. A rate hike might hurt those markets, and the dollar would be sold. Moreover, in foreign exchange, it takes two to tango, especially when it comes to interest rates. Because foreign exchange, by definition, consists of simultaneous transactions in two currencies, then it follows that the market must focus on two respective interest rates as well. This is the *interest rate differential*, a basic factor in the markets. (See Figures 18.2 and 18.3.)

Traders react when the interest rate differential changes, not simply when the interest rates themselves change. For example, if all the G-5 countries decided to simultaneously lower their interest rates by 0.5 percent, the move would be neutral for foreign exchange, because the interest rate differentials would also be neutral. Of course, most of the time the discount rates are cut unilaterally, a move that generates changes in both the interest differential and the exchange rate.

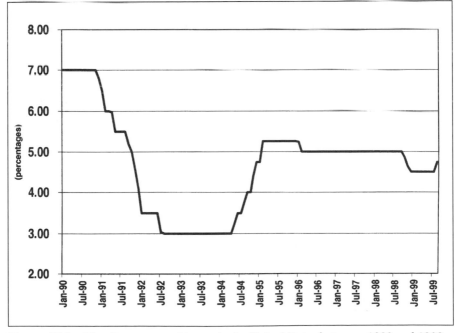

Figure 18.1. The discount rate history in the United States between 1990 and 1999.

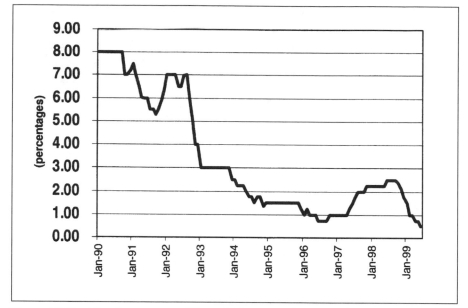

Figure 18.2. The discount rate differential between the U.S. and the U.K. between 1990 and 1999.

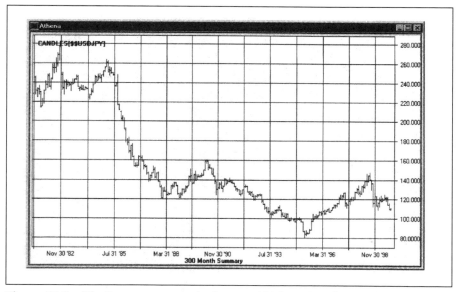

Figure 18.3. The Japanese yen reached a record high against the U.S. dollar in 1995, as a result of the United States' government call for a more equitable trade balance between the United States and Japan. *(Source: Bridge Information Systems, Inc.)*

Traders approach the interest rates like any other factor, trading on expectations and facts. For example, if rumor says that a discount rate will be cut, the respective currency will be sold before the fact. Once the cut occurs, it is quite possible that the currency will be bought back, or the other way around. An unexpected change in interest rates is likely to trigger a sharp currency move. "Buy on the rumor, sell on the fact..." Things are not that easy in a market as complex as the foreign exchange market. Other factors affecting the trading decision are the time lag between the rumor and the fact, the reasons behind the interest rate change, and the perceived importance of the change.

The market generally prices in a discount rate change that was delayed. Since it is a fait accompli, it is neutral to the market. If the discount rate was changed for political rather than economic reasons, a common practice in the European Monetary System, the markets are likely to go against the central banks, sticking to the real fundamentals rather than the political ones. This happened in both September 1992 and the summer of 1993, when the European central banks lost unprecedented amounts of money trying to prop up their currencies, despite having high interest rates. The market perceived those interest rates as artificially high and, therefore, aggressively sold the respective currencies.

Finally, traders deal on the perceived importance of a change in the interest rate differential. Is the differential divergent from the economic balance of two countries? If so, is it likely that the respective governments, or at least one of them, will do anything about it? Was the change in the discount rate significant enough to help the economy? These are just some of the important questions for which a trader must find answers. In order to be successful on the cutting edge of foreign exchange, a trader must rely on a keen analytical ability, sensitivity to the market "feeling," and fast execution.

POLITICAL EVENTS

Political events represent an open-ended category of fundamental factors affecting the global currency market. While certain political events, such as the United States presidential elections, can be anticipated well in advance, most are nearly impossible to forecast. By and large, traders have to "play it by ear," adjusting their reactions relative to each event. As a rule of thumb, the financial instruments, which are perceived worldwide as safe havens in times of international uncertainty, are the U.S. dollar and the Swiss franc among currencies, and gold among commodities. Of course, like any other rule of thumb, investors do not follow this course blindly.

Let's take a look at several real-life political events and examine what the reactions have been in the foreign exchange markets.

THE JAPANESE ELECTIONS OF 1993

In 1992, when the United States elected its first Democrat president in 12 years, the impact in the foreign exchange market was neutral. After all, the polls had predicted Bill Clinton's victory long before the elections. The FX markets also shrugged off the replacement of German Chancellor Helmut Kohl in 1998, on the eve of the introduction of the euro, despite his significant contribution to the success of the currency convergence.

On the other hand, an unexpected event occurred in Japanese politics in 1993. After 38 years of uninterrupted power, a coalition government replaced the Liberal Democratic Party. The Liberal Democratic Party had been plagued by an astounding number of political scandals since the mid-1980s. Yet, through thick and thin, they had managed to hold onto the political reins. How did the foreign exchange market react to this surprising turn of events?

Let's take a look back at the foreign exchange climate prior to the event. Clinton, the new American president, had unleashed a wave of Japanese yen buying, by stating that the U.S.–Japan trade balance was in deep disequilibrium. The Japanese yen was rising fast, from above 120 Japanese yen per U.S. dollar to around 105 Japanese yen per U.S. dollar. Coming in the middle of this yen revaluation, the foreign exchange impact of the Japanese elections was strong. The Japanese yen fell to around 111 per U.S. dollar. Within two months, however, the Japanese yen reached a temporary post–World War II record of 100.35 per U.S. dollar. (See Figure 18.3.) The dollar/yen bottomed out at around 80.00 in 1995.

Two questions come to mind: Why did the Japanese elections have such a strong impact on the currency? And, although the impact on the currency was so strong, why was it so short-lived?

The Japanese yen fell on the surprising results of the elections due to genuine shock overseas, and immediate international assumptions regarding potential Japanese changes over a variety of issues linked to trade. But the yen quickly rebounded when traders took a closer look at the realities of Japanese politics. On one hand, Morihiro Hosokawa was hardly a new face on the political scene; he had been a top member of the deposed Liberal Democratic Party. On the other hand, the Japanese government had been perceived over the years as very weak, relative to Japan's economic might. The markets obviously doubted that sweeping changes were around the corner and refocused on the stronger fundamentals, specifically, Mr. Clinton's call for a stronger yen to rebalance the American trade deficit with Japan. In addition, the revaluation of the Japanese yen was not just a call in the wild. The Japanese economy is formidable and the currency should reflect its might.

THE CLINTON–LEWINSKY AFFAIR

The markets were utterly confused when proof finally emerged in 1998 that U.S. President Bill Clinton had indulged in extramarital affairs even after entering the White House. Rumors and accusations had been haunting him for years, since his days as a young governor in Arkansas. Confusion was fueled by the very international structure of the currency markets: While many European and South American traders hold a liberal philosophy of life, morals are markedly more strict in the U.S. Thus, the market lacked a single voice in this matter, and traders kept their eyes on the U.S. asset markets for clues. But it was still difficult to distinguish between the smoke of the emerging markets' economies and the spots on the infamous dress that turned White House intern Monica Lewinsky into a trademark for Bill Clinton's presidency. While his affairs won him the dubious distinction of being only the second U.S. President to be impeached, Clinton managed to keep the rudder straight. All in all, his alleged and proven adultery triggered only two minor sell-offs, both on Fridays, which were corrected on the following Mondays.

POLITICAL CRISES

Political events generally take place over a period of time, but political crises strike suddenly. They are almost always, by definition, unexpected. Currency traders have a knack for responding to crises. Speed is essential; shooting from the hip is the only fighting option. The traders' reflexes take over. Without fast action, traders can be left out in the cold. There is no time for analysis, and only a split second, at best, to act. As volume drops dramatically, trading is hindered by a crisis. Prices dry out quickly, and sometimes the spreads between bid and offer jump from 5 pips to 100 pips. Getting back to the market is difficult, as few traders want to get caught on the wrong foot.

THE IRAQI INVASION OF KUWAIT

The Iraqi invasion of Kuwait remains a significant international event because of the way currencies reacted to the exceptional situation of so many major international forces united against a common aggressor. The event was different from NATO's intervention in Kosovo to stop the ethnic slaughter in Yugoslavia in 1999. The reaction in the foreign exchange markets to the August 1990 Iraqi invasion of Kuwait was quick: Buy the dollar against the Japanese yen. The Japanese economy was perceived as worst suited to a reduction of oil supply. The dollar/yen rate rallied to 160 from 150. By the beginning of 1991, with the allied troops at the height of the operations against Iraq, the dollar/yen reversed to a meek 125. How did the Japanese yen manage this mighty comeback?

Japan was not directly involved in the military confrontation in the Persian Gulf. In accordance with its Constitution, it maintained a neutral stand, and only reluctantly contributed financially to the allies' effort. As a major customer of gulf oil, Japan was allowed to continue its oil transports throughout the crisis. Moreover, Japan had already stockpiled large quantities of oil. Once they realized that the doomsday scenarios bore little relation to the reality of the situation, traders turned around and started buying Japanese yen. In the end, it wasn't the U.S. dollar that had gained but the pound and the Canadian, Australian, and New Zealand dollars, which benefited from their specific double-digit deposit rates.

CONCLUSION

Fundamental analysis must take into account numerous events that occur in a multitude of areas. Whether they are economic, financial, or political, different fundamental factors can have a vastly different impact on foreign exchange. Sometimes the reaction is quick. At other times, the effects only appear within a time frame of six to nine months, or they occur on the "wrong" side. Astute traders learn to interpret all of these continuously evolving factors, weigh them properly, and act on them appropriately. This concerted effort, along with the technical signals, can generate accurate forecasts in an increasingly competitive trading environment.

19 Technical Analysis

One of the most significant tools available for the forecasting of financial markets is technical analysis, which is the chart study of past behavior of commodity prices in order to forecast their future performance. Although the use of chart analysis has increased significantly since the mid-1980s, it is nothing new. Such analysis has been an increasingly utilized forecasting tool over the last two centuries. Seiki Shimizu, a famous Japanese commodity trader and the author of a comprehensive study on candlestick charting, speculated that technical analysis could have occurred in Europe in the sixteenth century and in Japan in the seventeenth century. He believes that the beginning of the rice market in 1750 parallels the establishment of charting in Japan.

THE EVOLUTION OF TECHNICAL ANALYSIS

Commodity traders started to analyze past price behavior because they felt that commodity prices reflect the action of all available factors. In other words, commodity prices reflect all the changes in the balance between supply and demand as caused by traders' reaction to economic, political, or psychological changes. Later, observations on the seasonality of crops evolved into the idea of historical repetition in the market. Finally, the empirical evidence showed that, once the market starts moving one way, the direction and momentum are likely to continue for a while, before new forces are able to change the balance between buyers and sellers and turn the tide.

351

These three factors—the price as the ultimate result of all the market forces; the repetition of the market price behavior; and the market tendency to move in trends—slowly crystallized in traders' minds to set up the basis of chart analysis. Since then, there has been a vigorous and continuous effort to refine the process of technical analysis in order to profitably forecast future market behavior.

To the untrained eye, technical analysis may seem confusing at times. On one hand, it seems that everybody is talking about it, using it, and profiting from it. On the other hand, certain academicians compare it with the structure of a house of cards.

Where is the truth?

PROS

The main strengths of technical analysis may be summarized as flexibility, flexibility, and flexibility. There is flexibility with regard to the underlying instrument. A trader who deals several currencies but specializes in one may easily apply the same technical expertise to trading another currency. Traders do this when trading activity in the currency in which they specialize slows down temporarily.

There is also flexibility regarding the markets. A trader who specializes in spot trading can make a smooth transition to dealing currency futures by using chart studies, because the same technical principles apply over and over again, regardless of the market.

Finally, there is flexibility regarding the time frame. Different players have different trading styles, objectives, and time frames. Yet the same technical principles apply, as they easily adapt to many different points of view.

Technical analysis also has a user-friendly feature: It is easy to compute and the technical services are becoming increasingly sophisticated and reasonably priced. Currently, the market enjoys a multitude of financial information services that offer printed and electronic charts. Technically inclined traders have only to focus on interpreting them, not on producing them.

. . . AND CONS

All good things seem to get their share of criticism, and so does technical analysis. Criticism is healthy, as it keeps the object of its attention "lean and mean." Criticism is good for technical analysis in general and for foreign exchange analysis in particular, because it helps newcomers better understand its characteristics and the ways it can help their performance.

The technical analysis naysayers usually focus on two general aspects: the random walk theory and the self-fulfilling prophecy.

The Random Walk Theory

Developed by Paul Cooner in 1964, this theory is based on the efficient market hypothesis, which states that prices move randomly versus their intrinsic value. The random walk theory has three versions: the strong version, the semistrong version, and the weak version.

1. The strong version holds that it is impossible to forecast anything based on past or current information. Therefore, past chart information is completely meaningless.

2. The semistrong version states that forecasting is impossible if it is based on publicly available information. By extrapolation, since most information in foreign exchange—including the charts reflecting that information is publicly available, forecasting is generally precluded. Exceptions are allowed in the case of proprietary information. A trading desk receiving an order to buy a very large amount of currency will therefore be able to "forecast" the behavior of the market.

3. The weak version maintains that an efficient market with instantaneous access to information will discount everything, so past data is useless for forecasting.

Among financial markets, academicians have labeled foreign exchange as the most efficient market. If the hypothesis of market efficiency holds, then all past information has already been reflected in the price and, therefore, there is no niche for an individual trader to speculate at the expense of the rest of the market. Any "turf advantage" or any other type of "inside information" will be instantly gathered and digested by the markets. Consequently, all market participants are precluded from consistently having any advantage over the rest of the market. The instantaneous access to information around the world should only add to the validity of this theory.

All markets do have a degree of randomness. This is perhaps even more true in the foreign exchange market, which has such large volume that no individual player can have a consistent or long-term impact on the direction of a currency. Until very recently, the academic community has generally been unable to prove the existence of any particular patterns governing price activity. However, new academic studies, such as tests conducted at the University of Wisconsin that take advantage of unprecedented computer capability, fully contradict the random walk theory. Let's take an example to see if charting philosophy clears the reality check.

In the 1985 Plaza Accord, the G-3 countries decided that, since the unchecked rise of the U.S. dollar was damaging American exporters' competitiveness abroad and the enormous exchange rate disequilibrium had already triggered a dangerously high trade deficit for the United States, the dollar must be devalued. A dollar devaluation was achieved over time by massive central bank intervention.

Prior to this historic open market intervention, technical analysis provided ample selling signals. The outcome was proven over the next two years. In addition, the USD/JPY daily chart shows an interesting pattern. (See Figure 19.1.) The dollar/yen spot rate moves in increments of 2000 pips in the long term. From its high at around 240, the currency dropped to 220, to 200, 180, 160, 140, back up to around 160, and then down to 140 and 120. After reaching the 120 level the third time, the dollar/yen spot rate reached and broke the 100 barrier to reach 79.75, or just about 80, in April 1995. Every 2000 pips, the U.S. dollar/Japanese yen spot rate found a trading plateau. This pattern was not an exception; in fact, it is still continuing.

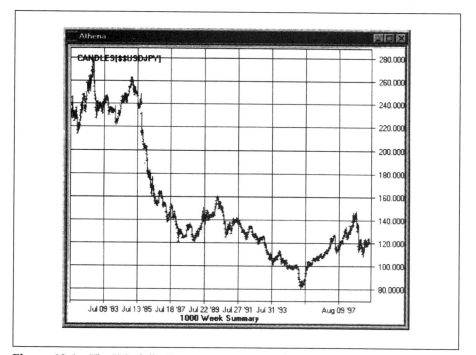

Figure 19.1. The U.S. dollar/Japanese yen spot exchange rate chart shows that the currency follows a price pattern of 2000 pips in the long term, 1982–1999. *(Source: Bridge Information Systems, Inc.)*

The Self-Fulfilling Prophecy

Criticism has been around for a long time and technical analysts wouldn't actually mind this theory—should it hold. Not only would it be the fastest way of getting rich overnight, but think of all the trader-size egos that would be touched.

The self-fulfilling prophecy, however, has too many holes to support anything but the most superficial criticism, because chart interpretation is very subjective and personal. It requires an individual, innate talent mixed with personally acquired and refined research and understanding. Also, since different traders have different objectives, time frames, and trading styles, it is rather difficult to predict which prophecy will be fulfilled. Moreover, if the time-honored law of supply and demand does not provide the backing, any technical-related price overshooting will be short-lived.

Chartists are not trying to create an artificial environment in which financial instruments may be maneuvered at will. They are merely trying to identify in the already existing environment any signals in price behavior that indicate future price activity.

How Past Information Impacts the Future

This brings us to the matter of whether past information can predict the future. Yes, it can. One does not have to venture all the way to the foreign exchange world to see this, because the strategy of using past information to build forecasting models is rather the standard in most industries. Currency trading is not a game of darts, so precedent is very important in helping a chartist forecast a currency's way into the future. It is the lack of historic information, not its availability, that is detrimental. It may be lack of understanding of the lessons of the past, rather than the past itself, that triggered the debate.

Technical analysis has been proved over and over again in the financial markets. The majority of currency traders use it extensively. Very rarely, if ever, was a consistently useful tool such as charting able to make such a powerful impact on the traders' decision process.

Despite all the technological breakthroughs, charting remains closer to art than to science. Yet the more refined a trader becomes, the better is his or her forecasting performance.

Arguments may continue to go back and forth. In the meantime, the technicians, in increasing numbers, focus their expertise on forecasting price activity in the future.

For those still interested in charting, let's move ahead, keeping several important ideas in mind:

1. Price is a comprehensive reflection of all the market forces.
2. Price movements are historically repetitive.
3. Price movements are trend followers.

TYPES OF CHARTS: A COMPARISON

There are four types of charts:

1. Line chart. (See Figure 19.2.)
2. Bar chart. (See Figure 19.3.)
3. Candlestick chart. (See Figure 19.4.)
4. Point-and-figure chart. (See Figure 19.5.)

LINE CHART

The *line chart* is the original type of chart. In order to plot it, a line connects single prices for a selected time period. The most popular line chart is the daily chart. Although any point in the day can be plotted, most traders focus on the closing price, which they perceive as the most important. (See Figure 19.6.) But an immediate problem with the daily line chart is the fact that it is impossible to see the price activity for the balance of the day.

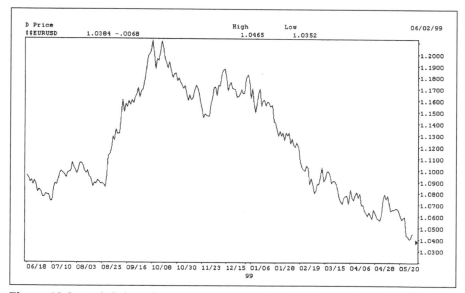

Figure 19.2. A daily line chart in euro/U.S. dollar. *(Source: Bridge Information Systems, Inc.)*

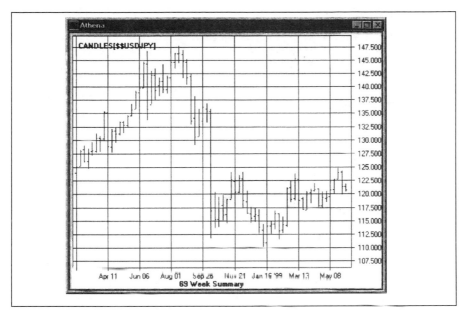

Figure 19.3. A bar chart in U.S. dollar/Japanese yen. *(Source: Bridge Information Systems, Inc.)*

Figure 19.4. A candlestick chart in U.S. dollar/Canadian dollar. *(Source: Bridge Information Systems, Inc.)*

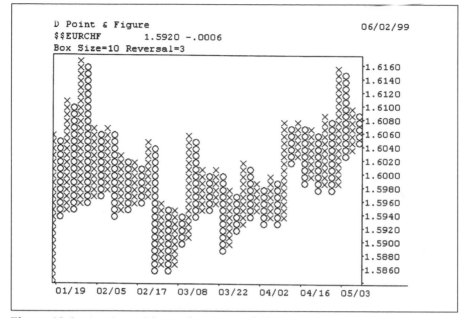

Figure 19.5. A point-and-figure chart in U.S. dollar/Japanese yen. *(Source: Bridge Information Systems, Inc.)*

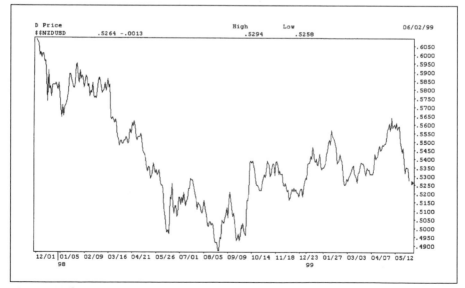

Figure 19.6. An example of a daily line chart in U.S. dollar/Japanese yen. *(Source: Bridge Information Systems, Inc.)*

With so much information missing, should line charts even be considered for technical analysis?

Yes, because due to the sophistication of current charting services, daily price activity does not need to be lost. Simply change the time span for which you need to see the price fluctuation to a very short period by selecting a tick chart, and virtually all prices will be plotted for you to analyze. (See Figure 19.7.)

Daily line charts are also useful when looking for the big picture or the major trend because, without line charts, intraday activity would become an unimportant detail. When plotted over a long stretch of time, such as several years, a line chart is easier to visualize. (See Figure 19.1.) Also, technical analysis goes well beyond chart formation; in order to execute certain models and techniques, line charts are better suited than any of the other charts.

However, like the point-and-figure chart, the line chart is a continuous chart, and this is a disadvantage because price gaps cannot be charted on a continuous chart.

BAR CHART

The *bar chart* is arguably the most popular type of chart currently in use. It consists of four significant points:

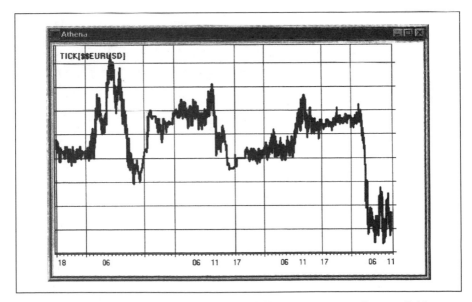

Figure 19.7. Example of a tick chart in U.S. dollar/Japanese yen. *(Source: Bridge Information Systems, Inc.)*

- the high and the low prices, which are united by a vertical bar;
- the opening price, which is marked with a little horizontal line to the left of the bar; and
- the closing price, which is marked with a little horizontal line to the right of the bar. (See Figure 19.8.)

The opening price is not always important for analysis.

Bar charts have the obvious advantage of displaying the currency range for the period selected. The most popular period is daily, followed by weekly. Other periods may be selected as well.

An advantage of this chart is that, unlike line and point-and-figure charts, the bar chart is able to plot price gaps that are formed in the currency futures market. Although the currency futures market trades around the clock, the currency futures market is physically open for only about a third of the trading day. (Chicago IMM is open for business 7:20 AM to 2 PM CDT.) Therefore, price gaps may occur between two days' price ranges. Incidentally, the bar chart is the chart of choice among currency futures traders.

This chart, however, is unable to plot the whole price fluctuation, even when plotted for short time periods. (See Figure 19.9.)

CANDLESTICK CHART

The *candlestick chart* was probably developed in Japan around 1750. Despite its venerable age, it was only in the 1980s that it became popular

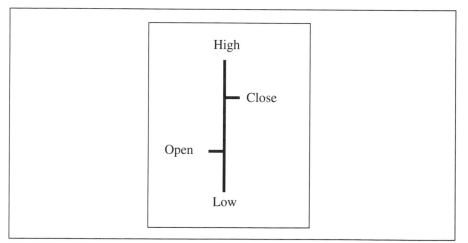

Figure 19.8. The structure of a price range bar.

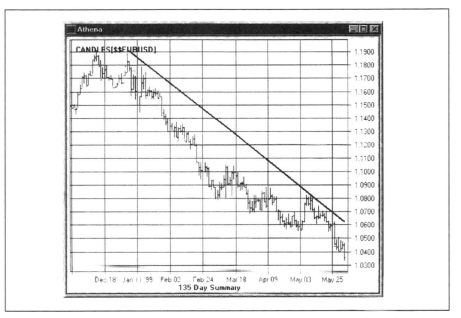

Figure 19.9. Bar charts cannot show every price fluctuation, even when plotted for very short-term time periods.

among non-Asian traders. This exposure was largely possible because of breakthroughs in electronic charting.

The candlestick chart is closely related to the bar chart. It also consists of four major prices: high, low, open, and close. (See Figure 19.10.) In addition to the common readings, the candlestick chart has a set of particular interpretations. It is also easier to view.

The opening and closing prices form the *body* (*jittai*) of the candlestick. To indicate that the opening was lower than the closing, the body of the bar is left blank. (See Figure 19.10-A.) In its original form, the body was colored red. Current standard electronic displays allow you to keep it blank or select a color of your choice. If the currency closes below its opening, the body is filled. (See Figure 19.10-B.) In its original form, the body was colored black, but the electronic displays allow you to keep it filled or to select a color of your choice.

It is very easy to see the intraday (or weekly) direction on a candlestick chart. When the high and the low differ from the opening and closing levels, the rest of the range is marked by two "shadows": the *upper shadow* (*uwakage*) and the *lower shadow* (*shitakage*).

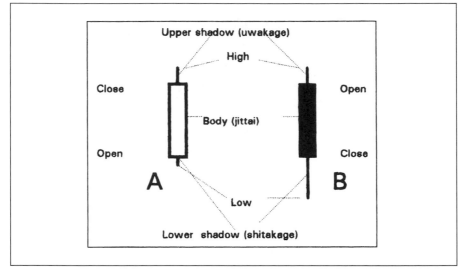

Figure 19.10.   The structure of a candlestick.

For illustration purposes, we may assume that in Figure 19.10, the following price activity took place:

> The GBP/USD opened at 1.7000 and closed at 1.7200. The high was 1.7230 and the low was 1.6980 (A.)
>
> The GBP/USD opened at 1.7200 and closed at 1.7000. The high was 1.7250 and the low was 1.6900 (B.)

Just as with a bar chart, the candlestick chart is unable to trace every price movement during a day's activity.

POINT-AND-FIGURE CHART

The *point-and-figure chart* takes a different approach. All other types of charts have one thing in common: The prices are always plotted against certain periods of time. The point-and-figure chart completely disregards time, concentrating fully on the price activity. When the currency moves up, the fluctuations are marked with X's. Moves on the downside are plotted with O's. This chart was also designed to minimize the amount of statistical noise. The direction on the chart will only change if the currency is reversed by a certain number of pips.

A popular point-and-figure chart is 1 X 3—1 box to continue the previous direction and 3 boxes to reverse the current direction. (See Figure 19.11.) With most traders selecting 10 pips per box, it means that the currency must advance 10 pips to mark an X, or reverse by 30 pips before 3 O's are plotted. In this way, minor activities are ignored, allowing the trader to concentrate solely on the price fluctuation.

This chart is very popular among intraday futures traders because the trading signals are easier to see on the chart, they are more precise, and no personal interpretation is necessary. It has become more popular since the late 1980s, due to the electronic charting exposure. Point-and-figure charting is discussed in more detail in Chapter 23.

Not all traders use all of the chart types, nor is it a prerequisite of a successful trader. It will be up to you to choose the best chart or set of charts for yourself.

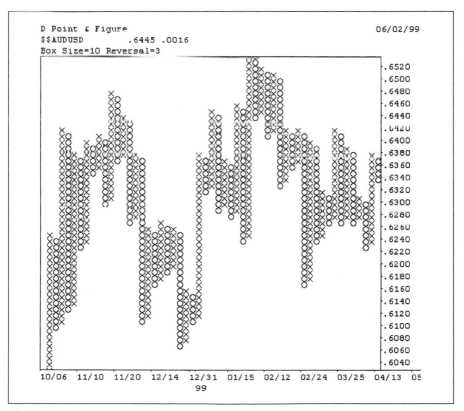

Figure 19.11. A market example of a point-and-figure chart in Australian dollar/U.S. dollar. *(Source: Bridge Information Systems, Inc.)*

VOLUME AND OPEN INTEREST

Volume consists of the total amount of currency traded within a period of time, usually one day. For example, by year 2000, the total foreign currency daily trading volume was $1.4 trillion. But traders are naturally more interested in the volume of specific instruments for specific trading periods, because large trading volume suggests that there is interest and liquidity in a certain market, and low volume warns the trader to veer away from that market.

The risks of a low-volume market are usually very difficult to quantify or hedge. In addition, certain chart formations require heavy trading volume for successful development. An example is the head-and-shoulder formation, which is discussed in Chapter 20.

Therefore, despite its obvious importance, volume is not easy to quantify in all foreign exchange markets. Volume figures can be calculated for futures and for options on futures markets, because both take place on centralized exchange floors and all the trades go through the clearinghouse. It is a different situation for the spot, forwards, and cash options markets, because trading is completely decentralized and therefore almost impossible to gauge.

In order to minimize this problem, traders have to learn how to estimate volume. One method is to extrapolate the figures from the futures market. Another is "feeling" the size of volume based on the number of calls on the dealing systems or phones, and the "noise" from the brokers' market. It isn't the easiest job in the world, but who ever thought it would be?

Open interest is the total exposure, or outstanding position, in a certain instrument. The same problems that affect volume are also present here. As I have already mentioned, figures for volume and open interest are available for currency futures. If you have access to printed or electronic charts on futures, you will be able to see these numbers plotted at the bottom of the futures charts. As demonstrated in Figure 19.12, volume is represented by a bar chart, and open interest is plotted as a line chart.

Volume and open interest figures are available from different sources, although one day late. These figures may be obtained from:

1. Newswires: Bridge Information Systems, Reuters, Bloomberg
2. Newspapers: the *Wall Street Journal*, the *Journal of Commerce*
3. Weekly printed charts: Commodity Perspective, Commodity Trend Service

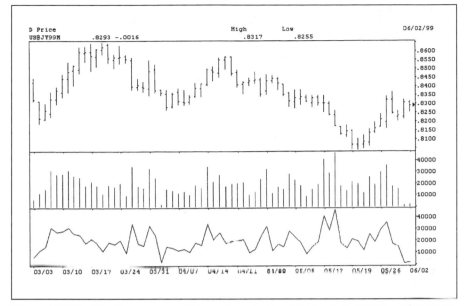

Figure 19.12. The Japanese yen futures bar chart and its trading volume and open interest. *(Source: Bridge Information Systems, Inc.)*

A Trader's Point of View

The open interest figures from the futures market are not foolproof. The foreign exchange markets are a zero-sum game, and this is more evident in the futures markets, where every outstanding contract must be offset by an opposite contract. So, on an individual basis, the figures may be misleading.

For instance, if an investment bank or a fund opens a position in the open futures market by buying a large amount of euro futures, it is not fully clear whether the real position of that player is long euro futures. It may also be a hedge for an option position or a cash position, or simply a strategy of throwing the dogs off the scent by showing one hand where everybody sees it, and doubling it up on the opposite side in the cash market.

TREND

The concept of trend is paramount to technical analysis. The familiar quote, "The trend is my friend," is deeply rooted in the experience of the markets. It should be respected and attentively observed. A trend simply shows the direction of the market. Therefore, a trend may be:

1. Upward, such as the trend in the yen against the U.S. dollar between January 1985 and May 1988. (See Figure 19.13.)

2. Downward, such as the euro trend against the U.S. dollar between January and June 1999. (See Figure 19.14.)

3. Sideways, also known as a "flat market" or "trendless." (See Figure 19.15.)

Because the markets do not move in a straight line in any direction, but rather in zigzags, it is the direction of these peaks and troughs that creates the market trend.

In addition to direction, trends are also classified by time frame: *major* or *long-term trends*, *secondary* or *medium-term trends*, and *near-term* or *short-term trends*. Any number of secondary and near-term trends may occur within a major trend.

The time frames for each class vary widely. The Dow Theory, developed at the end of the nineteenth century by Charles Dow, suggests a one-year length for a major trend. Currently, for a major trend, the market expects a time span of over one year. (See Figures 19.13 and 19.14.) Secondary trends should last for a matter of months, and short-term trends for a matter of weeks.

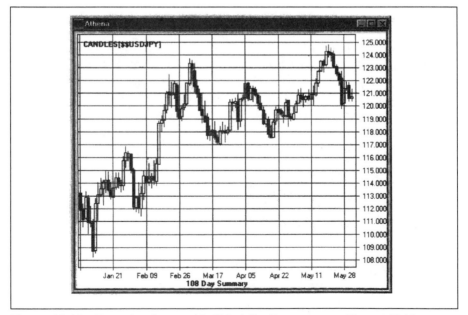

Figure 19.13. Example of uptrend in U.S. dollar/Japanese yen. *(Source: Bridge Information Systems, Inc.)*

Figure 19.14. Example of downtrend in euro/U.S. dollar. *(Source: Bridge Information Systems, Inc.)*

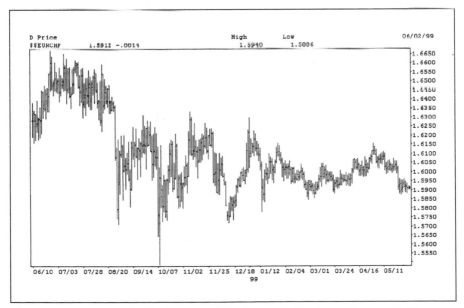

Figure 19.15. Example of sideways trading in euro/Swiss franc. *(Source: Bridge Information Systems, Inc.)*

SUPPORT AND RESISTANCE LEVELS

The peaks represent the price levels at which the selling pressure exceeds the buying pressure. They are known as *resistance levels*. The troughs, on the other hand, represent the levels at which the selling pressure succumbs to the buying pressure. They are called *support levels*. In an uptrend, the consecutive support and resistance levels must exceed each other respectively. The reverse is true in a downtrend. Although minor exceptions are acceptable, these failures should be considered as warning signals for trend changing.

The significance of trends is a function of time and volume. The longer the prices bounce off the support and resistance levels, the more significant the trend becomes. Trading volume is also very important, especially at the critical support and resistance levels. When the currency bounces off these levels under heavy volume, the significance of the trend increases.

The importance of support and resistance levels goes beyond their original functions. If these levels are convincingly penetrated, they tend to turn into just the opposite. A firm support level, once it is penetrated on heavy volume, will likely turn into a strong resistance level. (See Figure 19.16.) Conversely, a strong resistance turns into a firm support after being penetrated. (See Figure 19.17.)

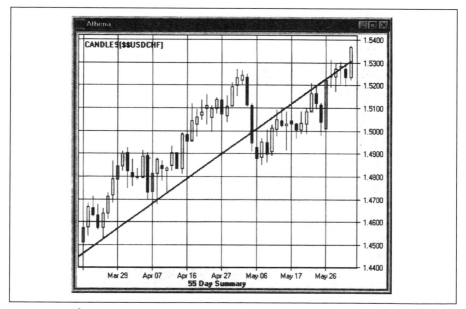

Figure 19.16. Example of support turned into resistance. *(Source: Bridge Information Systems, Inc.)*

Figure 19.17. Example of resistance turned into support. *(Source. Bridge Information Systems, Inc.)*

TRENDLINE

A *trendline* is the natural development in tracking a trend. It simply consists of a straight line connecting the significant highs (peaks) or the significant lows (troughs.) Following in the tracks of the trend directions, the trendlines may be classified as:

1. Rising trendlines. (See Figure 19.18.)
2. Declining trendlines. (See Figure 19.19.)
3. Sideways trendlines. (See Figure 19.20.)

Drawing the trendline is rather easy, as only two points are necessary. But this trendline is merely "tentative." Most traders expect a *third contact point confirmation*. When a trend seems to be securely set in its tracks, we must recall an important point made in the beginning of this chapter.

Financial markets are trend followers. Therefore, we can expect the currency to maintain its general direction and velocity. The most significant trendlines occur around an angle of 45°. (See Figure 19.21.) W. D. Gann, the renowned investor and technical analyst, established this important technique. He noted that a trendline at a sharper angle suggests that the rally is unsustainable. Conversely, a trendline at a low level indicates that the trend is close to reversing. He also noted that a longevity of one month or more would provide the trendline with increased weight.

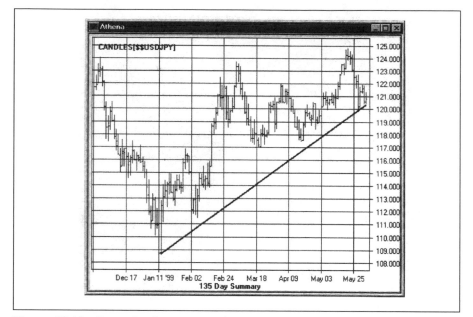

Figure 19.18. Example of a rising trendline in U.S. dollar/Japanese yen. *(Source: Bridge Information Systems, Inc.)*

Figure 19.19. Example of a declining trendline in euro/dollar. *(Source: Bridge Information Systems, Inc.)*

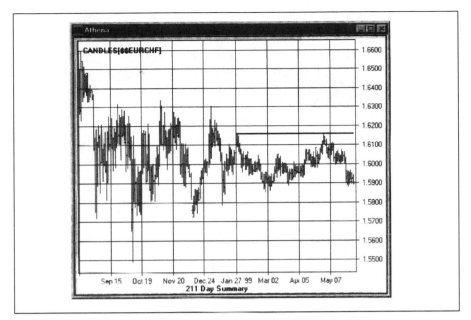

Figure 19.20. Example of a flat trendline in euro/dollar. *(Source: Bridge Information Systems, Inc.)*

Figure 19.21. Example of 45° line in U.S. dollar/Canadian dollar. *(Source: Bridge Information Systems, Inc.)*

Not only would we like to identify as many significant trendlines as possible, but we would also like the trendlines to provide "clean" support and resistance levels. However, since the market has a life of its own, this is not possible. Many times we see minor trendline penetrations. As a rule of thumb, this type of breakout should be disregarded.

A Trader's Point of View

1. *Anemic breakouts* (from a volume point of view) should be disregarded. Several players were perhaps forced to cut their losses, or attempted to spearhead a new trend but failed to stir sufficient market interest. (See Figure 19.22.)

2. A breakout from a rising trendline should be confirmed by a close above the high of the original trendline breakout range. Conversely, a breakout from a declining trendline should be confirmed by a close below the low of the range, one that penetrated the trendline. (See Figure 19.23.)

3. For more significance of the trend-changing signal, a breakout should be followed by two consecutive closes outside the trendline. (See Figure 19.24.)

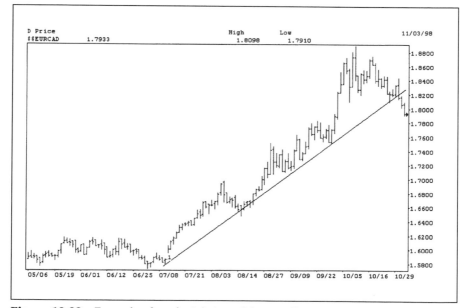

Figure 19.22. Example of weak violation of the trendline in euro/Canadian dollar *(Source: Bridge Information Systems, Inc.)*

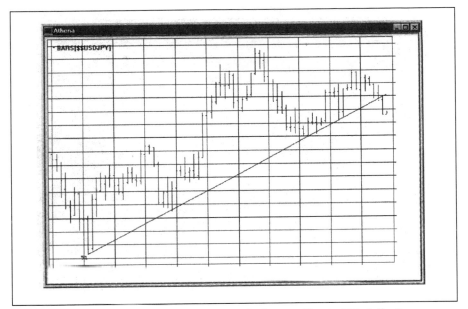

Figure 19.23. Example of one closing outside the trendline in U.S. dollar/Japanese yen. *(Source: Bridge Information Systems, Inc.)*

Figure 19.24. Trendline breakouts are confirmed by two or more closings outside the trendlines. On the euro/Canadian dollar chart, you can see an example of this rule of confirmation. *(Source: Bridge Information Systems, Inc.)*

4. Even after confirmation, the breakout is still likely to be followed by a period of consolidation. (See Figure 19.25.) It is relatively rare for a trendline to suddenly reverse its direction.

5. If a consolidation period does indeed occur, the longer it lasts, the steeper the following rally will be. (See Figure 19.26.)

6. Breakouts from up trendlines tend to test the strength of the former support line, now turned into a resistance line. (Figure 19.27.)

7. Use a price filter of 1 percent to test the validity of the breakout.

THE CHANNEL LINE

A *channel line* is a parallel line that can be traced against the trendline, connecting the significant peaks in an uptrend and the significant troughs in a downtrend. (See Figure 19.28.) Along with the trendline, the channel line creates a channel that borders the currency trend. In a downtrend, the channel line is at the bottom of the channel (the support line). In an uptrend, the channel line is at the top of the channel (the resistance line).

A Trader's Point of View

1. A channel is a very attractive chart pattern for traders, as the number of buying signals is approximately doubled by the number of selling signals, and vice versa. The price basically gyrates between the trendline and the channel line.

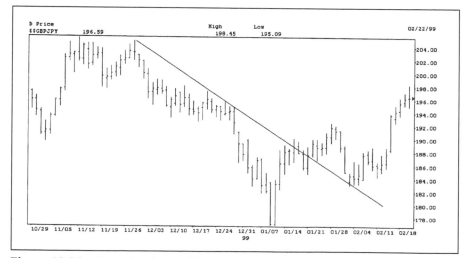

Figure 19.25. Example of a trendline breakout followed by a period of consolidation. *(Source: Bridge Information Systems, Inc.)*

Figure 19.26. Example of a sharp move following consolidation outside the trend-line. *(Source: Bridge Information Systems, Inc.)*

Figure 19.27. Example of a currency retesting its trendline after breakout. *(Source: Bridge Information Systems, Inc.)*

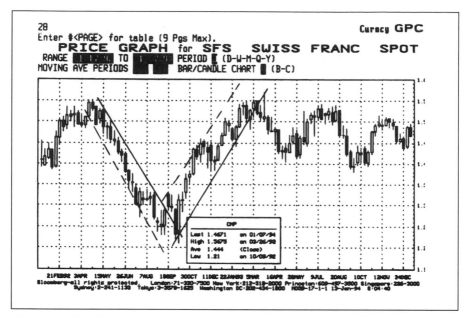

Figure 19.28. There are two channel lines traced against the trendlines. In our example, the U.S. dollar/Swiss franc channel lines are marked with dashed lines. *(Source: Bloomberg)*

2. The price failure to reach the trendline should be interpreted as a possible trend acceleration. (See Figure 19.29.)
3. The break of the channel line confirms trend acceleration. (See Figure 19.30.)
4. The price failure to reach the channel line should be construed as a case of a weakening trend. (See Figure 19.31.)
5. A channel breakout suggests a target for the currency price equal to the width of the channel.

SPEEDLINES

Speedlines provide an innovative method for trend analysis, perfected by Edson Gould and quickly embraced by the technicians. To calculate speedlines, the total range of a trend is divided into thirds on a vertical line. The two speedlines are plotted by connecting the origin of the range (bottom for an uptrend and top for a downtrend) and the 1/3 and 2/3 levels respectively.

A price fluctuation away from the trend, which finds support at the first (1/3) speedline, indicates that the trend continues smoothly ahead. The penetration of the first (1/3) speedline is a trend-weakening warning; the

Figure 19.29. The failure to reach the trendline is a signal that the downtrend is accelerating. *(Source: Bridge Information Systems, Inc.)*

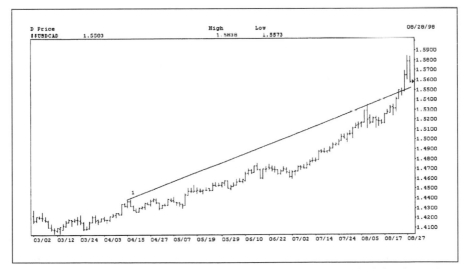

Figure 19.30. Example of trend acceleration signaled by the break of the channel line. *(Source: Bridge Information Systems, Inc.)*

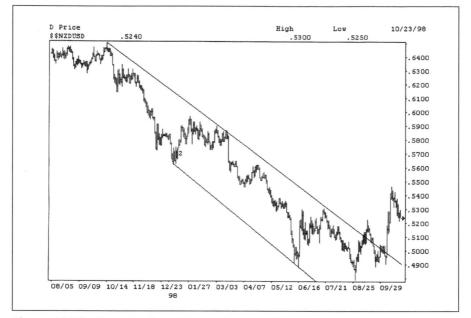

Figure 19.31. Example of trend reversal signaled by the failure to reach the channel line. *(Source: Bridge Information Systems, Inc.)*

next level to watch is the second speedline (2/3). If the currency price bounces back, we may be faced with an uncertain (or consolidation) period between the first (1/3) and second (2/3) speedlines. If the last speedline gives way as well, then the next target is the origin of the range. (See Figure 19.32.) The previous rule, that a penetrated support level will turn into a resistance level, and its converse, remain valid for speedlines.

Speedlines may be applied to all charts. Their significance in the medium and long term extrapolates well to short-term charts.

THE IMPORTANCE OF THE LONG-TERM CHARTS

As previously mentioned, the tools of technical analysis are flexible in terms of instruments, markets, and time frames. Although in terms of time frame the most popular charts are the daily charts, the longer period charts (weekly and monthly charts) are very important too. Electronic charting and weekly printed charts services offer maximum convenience to the traders.

Figure 19.32. An example of speedlines in the U.S. dollar/Japanese yen. *(Source: Bridge Information Systems, Inc.)*

Why are the weekly and monthly charts useful?

1. They make it possible to compress long-term information into a single chart. (See Figure 19.33.)

2. Long-term charts provide important information regarding long-term trends or cycles. The trader can get a correct perspective regarding the real direction of the market in the long run, the strength or direction of the current trend occurring within that trend, or the possibility of a breakout from the long-term trend. (See Figure 19.34.)

3. Long-term charts may also provide other technical signals that are lost in the daily charts. For instance, a long-term triple top in the British pound was approaching completion in September 1992. (See Figure 19.35.) The massive sell-off triggered by George Soros' Quantum Fund helped the British pound break the support line. This pattern was not evident on short-term charts.

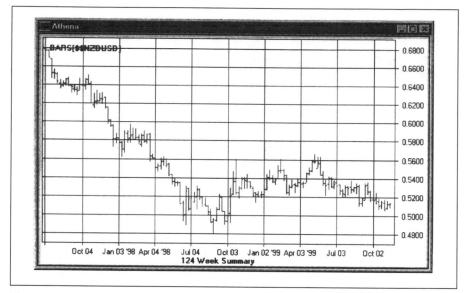

Figure 19.33. The bar weekly chart in New Zealand dollar/U.S. dollar. *(Source: Bridge Information Systems, Inc.)*

Figure 19.34. The weekly bar chart of U.S. dollar/Japanese yen between 1984 and 1993. The downtrend in this currency is obvious between the beginning of 1985 and the end of 1993. *(Source: Bridge Information Systems, Inc.)*

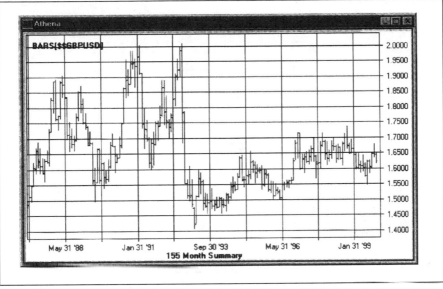

Figure 19.35. The monthly bar chart of the British pound/U.S. dollar between 1982 and 1998. *(Source: Bridge Information Systems, Inc.)*

PERCENTAGE RETRACEMENTS

As we are well aware by now, foreign currencies, like all the other financial instruments, do not move straight up or down, even in the healthiest of trends. Traders watch several percentage retracements, in search of price objectives.

There are three typical percentage retracements:

1. Charles Dow developed the traditional percentage retracements at the turn of the last century. They are 1/3, 1/2, and 2/3; or 33 percent, 50 percent, and 66 percent. A retracement past 66 percent is considered to be a trend failure. (See Figure 19.36.)

2. The Fibonacci ratios are very popular among Elliott Wave students. These ratios are .382, .50, and .618, or approximately 38 percent, 50 percent, and 62 percent. (See Figure 19.37.) Fibonacci ratios are discussed in more detail in Chapter 28.

3. The Gann percentages attach importance to the one-eighth breakdowns. (See Figure 19.38.)

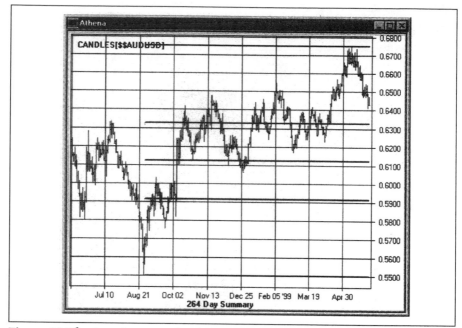

Figure 19.36. A market example of Charles Dow's retracement percentages in Australian dollar: 33% (A), 50% (B), and 60% (C). *(Source: Bridge Information Systems, Inc.)*

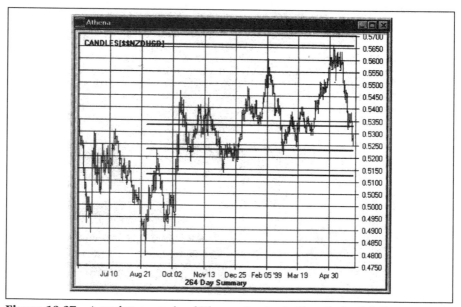

Figure 19.37. A market example of Fibonacci ratios in New Zealand dollar/U.S. dollar. *(Source: Bridge Information Systems, Inc.)*

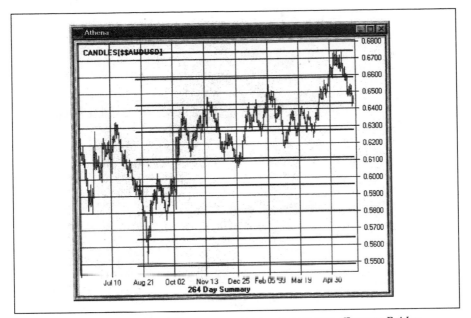

Figure 19.38. An example of Gann percentage retracements. *(Source: Bridge Information Systems, Inc.)*

20 Trend Reversal Patterns

C hart formations are generally sorted on the basis of their significance to the current trend of the underlying currency. Formations signaling the end of the trend are known as *reversal patterns*. Conversely, chart formations that confirm that the underlying currency trend is intact are called *continuation patterns*. This chapter presents trend reversal formations.

The most significant trend reversal patterns are:

1. Head-and-shoulders and inverse head-and-shoulders
2. Double tops and double bottoms
3. Triple tops and triple bottoms
4. V-formations

HEAD-AND-SHOULDERS

The head-and-shoulders pattern, one of the most reliable and well-known chart formations, hardly needs an introduction. As you can see in Figure 20.1, the underlying currency broke the trendline of the channel *xx'-yy'*. In a typical move, the currency rallied back to the previous support line, which turned into a resistance line. As the currency fell, the trend breakout was confirmed.

The head-and-shoulders pattern consists of three consecutive rallies. The first and third rallies—the *shoulders*—have about the same height, and the middle one—the *head*—is the highest. All three rallies are based on the same support line (or on the resistance line in the case of the reversed head-and-shoulders formation), known as the *neckline*.

Prior to point A, the neckline was a resistance line. (See Figure 20.1.) Once the resistance line was broken, it turned into a significant support line. The price bounced off it twice, at points B and C. The neckline was eventually broken in point D, under heavy volume, and the trend reversal was confirmed. As the significant support line was broken, a retracement could be expected to retest the neckline (E), now a resistance line again. If the resistance line held, the price was expected to eventually decline to around level F, which was the price target of the head-and-shoulders formation. The target was approximately equal in amplitude to the distance between the top of the head and the neckline. The price target was measured from point D, where the neckline was broken. (See the dotted lines.) A market example of a head-and-shoulders reversal formation is presented in Figure 20.2.

SIGNALS GENERATED BY THE HEAD-AND-SHOULDERS PATTERN

The head-and-shoulders formation provides excellent information:

1. The *support line*. This is based on points B and C.
2. The *resistance line*. After giving in at point D, the market may retest the neckline at point E.

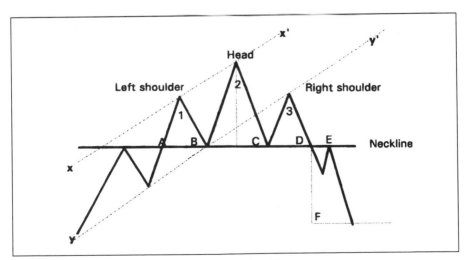

Figure 20.1. Diagram of a typical head-and-shoulders pattern.

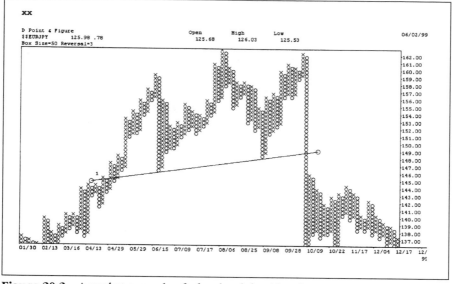

Figure 20.2. A market example of a head-and-shoulders formation. *(Source: Bridge Information Systems, Inc.)*

3. The *price direction*. If the neckline holds the buying pressure at point E, then the formation provides information regarding the price direction: diametrically opposed to the direction of the head-and-shoulders (bearish).

4. The *price target*. This is provided by the confirmation of the formation (by breaking through the neckline under heavy trading volume).

One of the main requirements of the successful development of this formation is that the breakout through the neckline occurs under heavy market volume. As you remember, though, gauging volume is only possible in the currency futures market. The trader will have to estimate the size of the cash market volume by extrapolating from the currency futures' volume and the trading "noise." A breakout on light volume is a strong warning that it is a false breakout and will trigger a sharp backlash in the currency price.

The time frame for this chart formation's evolution is anywhere from several weeks to several months. The intraday chart formations are not reliable. The longer the formation time is, the more significance should be attached to this pattern.

The target is unlikely to be reached in a very short time frame. Whereas there is no immediate suggestion regarding the length of target reaching time, common sense would link it to the duration of development of the chart pattern.

I want to emphasize the importance of measuring the target from the point where the neckline was broken. There is a tendency among new technicians to measure the target price not only from under the neckline but also from the middle of the formation. This may happen as they measure the height of the head.

Most head-and-shoulders formations, of course, look different from that in Figure 20.1. Prices fluctuate enough to forego any possibility of a clean-looking chart line. Also, the neckline is seldom a perfectly horizontal line.

POTENTIAL PROBLEMS

1. The height of the shoulders should be about equal. More important, though, the shoulders must not be taller than the head.

2. It is very important that the significant points A, B, C, and D are all tangential to the neckline. The failure of this requirement nullifies the characteristics of the formation.

3. The head-and-shoulders formation is confirmed only when the completion of the three rallies and their reversals is followed by a breach of the neckline. The failure of the price to break through the neckline on closing prices basis puts on hold or negates the validity of the formation.

A Trader's Point of View

1. Traders use many types of charts based on different time periods. It is important to remember that the breakout confirmation is a closing price outside the neckline. It is recommended that either a daily bar chart or a daily line chart be used.

2. Most traders wait for the formation to penetrate the neckline before attempting to jump on the bandwagon. Price quotes are likely to be very wide and any hesitation may make it difficult to get in the market, as it is possible that the market will retest the neckline.

3. A minority of the market, the high-risk traders, take positions prior to the breakout. If the market penetrates the neckline, they will have the highest profitability. In case the market fails, very tight stop-loss orders must be set, although the high speed and low

liquidity of the situation may make it almost impossible to execute them.

4. Due to the market expectation for imminent completion, it is likely that there are large positions outstanding in the direction of the future target. Therefore, the chart failure is likely to trigger steep position reversals.

5. The target should be considered as simply a suggested objective. The price will only accidentally stop exactly at the target price. Generally, it may fall somewhat short or overshoot. The trader must consider any additional information to fine-tune the profit-taking level.

6. Cash traders must remember both the importance of volume and the lack of volume information. The correct estimation of volume in the cash market is a matter of personal skill.

INVERSE HEAD-AND-SHOULDERS

The inverse head-and-shoulders formation is a mirror image of the previous pattern. (See Figure 20.3) Therefore, you can apply the same characteristics, potential problems, signals, and trader's point of view from the preceding presentation.

The underlying currency broke out of the downtrend ranged by the *xx'-yy'* channel. The currency retested the previous resistance line (the

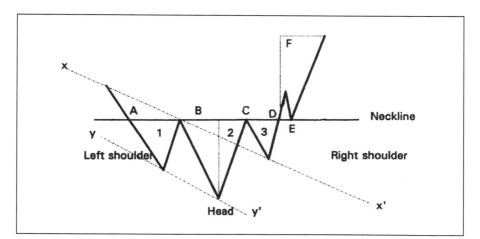

Figure 20.3. Diagram of a typical inverse head-and-shoulders pattern.

rally number 3), now turned into a support line. Among the three consecutive rallies, the shoulders (1 and 3) have approximately the same height, and the head is the lowest. Prior to point A, the neckline was a support line. Once this line was broken, it turned into a significant resistance line. The price bounced off the neckline twice, at points B and C. The neckline was eventually broken at point D, under heavy volume. As the significant resistance line was broken, a retracement could be expected to retest the neckline (E), now a support line again. If it held, the price was expected to eventually rise to around level F, which is the price target of the head-and-shoulders formation.

The price objective is approximately equal in amplitude to the distance between the top of the head and the neckline, and is measured from the breakout point, D.

Figure 20.4 presents an example of an inverse head-and-shoulders pattern at work in the foreign exchange markets.

DOUBLE TOP

Another very reliable and common trend reversal chart formation is the double top. As the name clearly and succinctly describes, this pattern consists of two tops (peaks) of approximately equal heights. (See Figure 20.5.)

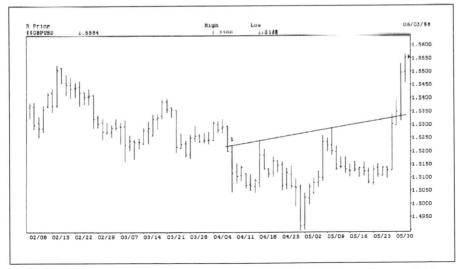

Figure 20.4. An example of an inverse head-and-shoulders pattern. *(Source: Bridge Information Systems, Inc.)*

A parallel line is drawn against a resistance line that connects the two tops. We should think of this line as identical to the head-and-shoulders' neckline.

As a resistance line, it is broken at point A. It turns into a strong support for price level at C, but eventually fails at point E. The support line turns into a strong resistance line, which holds the market backlash at point F. The price objective is at level G, which is the average height of the double top formation, measured from point E (See the dotted lines.)

SIGNALS PROVIDED BY THE DOUBLE TOP FORMATION

The double top formation provides information on:

1. The *support line*, set between points A and E.
2. The *resistance line*, set between points B and D.
3. The *price direction*. If the neckline holds the buying pressure at point F, then the formation provides information regarding the price direction: diametrically opposed to the direction of the peaks (bearish).
4. The *price target*, provided by the confirmation of the formation (by breaking through the neckline under heavy trading volume.)

Exactly as in the case of the head-and-shoulders pattern, a vital requirement for the successful completion of the double-top formation is that the breakout through the neckline occurs under heavy market volume. Again, please remember that gauging volume in traditional ways is only possible in the currency futures market. Therefore, the trader must estimate the size of the cash market volume by extrapolating from the currency fu-

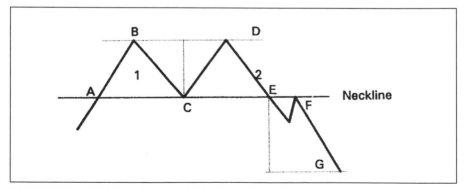

Figure 20.5. Diagram of a typical double-top formation.

tures' volume and the trading "noise." A breakout on light volume is a strong case for a false breakout, which would trigger a sharp backlash in the currency price.

The time frame for this chart formation's evolution is anywhere from several weeks to several months. The intraday chart formations are less reliable. There is a strong correlation between the length of time to develop the pattern and the significance of the formation.

The target is unlikely to be reached in a very short time frame. There is no direct suggestion regarding the length of target reaching time; but foreign exchange common sense links it to the duration of development.

It is important to measure the target from the point where the neckline was broken. Avoid the trap of measuring the target price from the middle of the formation under the neckline. This may happen as you measure the average height of the formation.

Most double-top formations look different from that in Figure 20.5. As shown in Figure 20.6, prices fluctuate enough to create a rather weathered-looking line, and the neckline is seldom a perfectly horizontal line.

POTENTIAL PROBLEMS

1. The height of the peaks should be about equal.
2. It is very important that the significant points A, C, and E are all tangential to the neckline. The failure of this requirement nullifies the characteristics of the formation.
3. The double-top formation is confirmed only when the full completion of the two rallies and their respective reversals is followed by a breach of the neckline (the closing price is outside the neckline.) The failure of the price to break through the neckline puts on hold or negates the validity of the formation.

A Trader's Point of View

1. It is important to remember that the breakout confirmation consists of a closing price outside the neckline. Therefore, it is recommended that a daily chart be used, rather than 5- or 15-minute charts.
2. The majority of the market will wait for the confirmation of the neckline's breaching before attempting to jump on the bandwagon. As the price quotes will likely be very wide and highly volatile, this makes it difficult to join in, especially since it is possible that the market will retest the neckline.

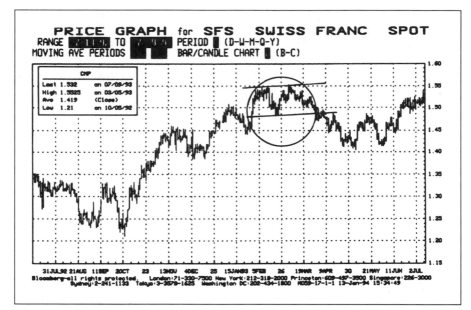

Figure 20.6. An example of a double-top formation in the U.S. dollar/Swiss franc daily chart. *(Source: Bloomberg)*

3. The high risk-takers will take positions prior to the breakout. If the market penetrates the neckline, they will have the highest profitability. Very tight stop-loss orders must be set, in case the market fails. Yet it may be nearly impossible to execute them, due to high speed and low liquidity.

4. Due to the market expectation for imminent completion, it is likely that there are large positions outstanding in the direction of the future target. Therefore, the chart failure is likely to trigger steep position reversals.

5. The target should be considered as simply a suggested objective. The price will only accidentally stop exactly at the target price. Generally it may either fall somewhat short or overshoot. The trader must consider any additional information in order to fine-tune the profit-taking level.

6. The cash traders must remember both the importance of volume and the lack of volume information. Correctly estimating volume in the cash market is a matter of personal skill.

DOUBLE BOTTOM

The double bottom formation is a mirror image of the previous pattern. (See Figure 20.7) Therefore, you may apply the same characteristics, potential problems, signals, and trader's point of view from the preceding presentation.

The bottoms have about the same amplitude. A parallel line (the neckline) is drawn against the line connecting the two bottoms (B and D.) As a support line, it is broken at point A. It turns into a strong resistance for price level at C, but eventually fails at point E. The resistance line turns into a strong support line, which holds the market backlash at point F. The price objective is at level G, which is the average height of the bottoms, measured from point E. (See the dotted lines.)

Figure 20.8 presents an example of a double-bottom pattern at work in the foreign exchange markets.

TRIPLE TOP AND TRIPLE BOTTOM

The triple top is a hybrid of the head-and-shoulders and double-top trend reversal formations. (See Figure 20.9.) Conversely, the triple bottom is a hybrid of the inverse head-and-shoulders and double-bottom formations. (See Figure 20.10.) Consequently, they have the same characteristics, potential problems, signals, and trader's point of view as the double top or double bottom, respectively.

As shown in Figure 20.9, in a typical triple-top formation, the tops have about the same height. A parallel line (the neckline) is drawn against

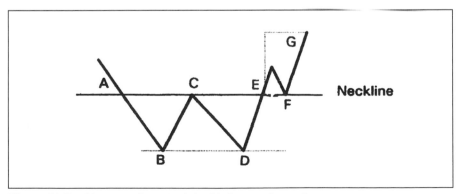

Figure 20.7. Diagram of a typical double-bottom formation.

the line connecting the three tops (B, D, and F.) As a resistance line, the neckline is broken at point A. It turns into a strong support for price levels at C and E, but eventually fails at point G. The support line turns into a strong resistance line, which holds the market backlash at point H. The price objective is at level I, which is the average height of the three tops formation, as measured from point D. (See the dotted lines.)

As a double top, the formation fails at point E. The price moves up steeply toward point F. The resistance line is holding once more and the price drops sharply again toward point G. At this level, the market pressure is able to penetrate the support line. After a possible retest of the neckline, the prices drop further, to eventually reach the price objective.

The opposite is true for the triple bottom.

As shown in Figure 20.10, in a triple-bottom formation, the bottoms have about the same amplitude. A parallel line (the neckline) is drawn against the line connecting the three bottoms (B, D, and F.) As a support line, the neckline is broken at point A. It turns into a strong resistance for price levels at C and E, but eventually fails at point G. The resistance line turns into a strong support line, which holds the market backlash at point H. The price objective is at level I, which is the average length of the triple-bottom formation, as measured from point D. (See the dotted lines.)

Figure 20.8. An example of a double-bottom formation. *(Source: CQG)*

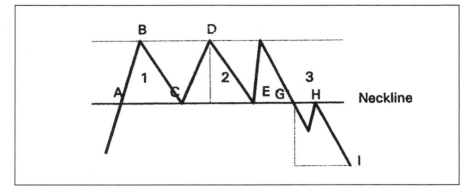

Figure 20.9. Diagram of a triple-top formation.

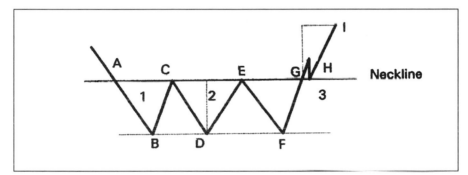

Figure 20.10.   Diagram of a typical triple-bottom formation.

Market examples of a triple top and triple bottom are presented in Figures 20.11 and 20.12.

V-FORMATIONS (SPIKES)

The V-formations—V-top and V-bottom seen in Figures 20.13 and 20.14—are different from the previous patterns because there is no consolidation prior to the trend reversal. In their case, the trend changes suddenly, and they are accompanied by heavy trading volume. Volume is significant because traders caught on the wrong foot are forced to reverse their positions.

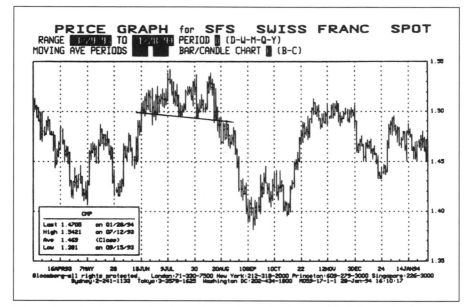

Figure 20.11. An example of a triple-top formation in the U.S. dollar/Swiss franc. *(Source: Bloomberg Financial Services)*

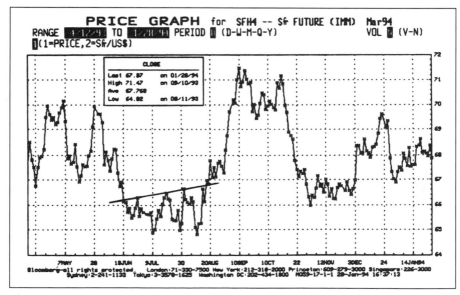

Figure 20.12. An example of a triple-bottom formation in the Swiss franc futures. *(Source: Bloomberg Financial Services)*

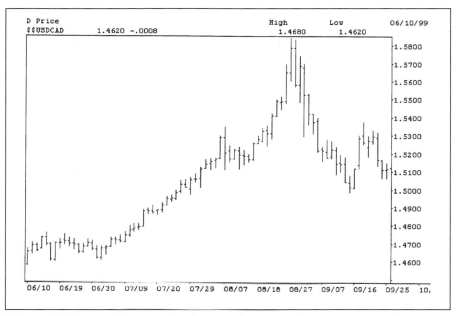

Figure 20.13. A market example of a V-top formation. *(Source: Bridge Information Systems, Inc.)*

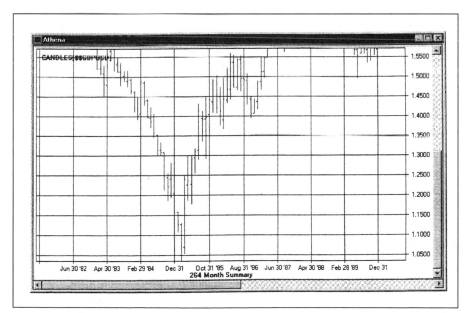

Figure 20.14. A market example of a V-bottom formation. *(Source: Bridge Information Systems, Inc.)*

OTHER PATTERNS

Other notable reversal patterns are the rounded and diamond formations.

ROUNDED TOP AND BOTTOM FORMATIONS

The rounded top and bottom, also known as saucers, are infrequent trend reversal chart patterns. (See Figures 20.15 and 20.16.) They consist of a very slow and gradual change in the direction of the market. These patterns reflect the indecision of the market at the end of a trend. The trading activity is slow. It is impossible to know when the formation is indeed completed, and not for a lack of trying. Like any other consolidation pattern, the longer it takes to complete, the higher the likelihood of a sharp price move in the new direction.

DIAMOND FORMATION

The diamond formation is a minor reversal pattern that tends to occur at the top of the trend. The price activity may be outlined by a shape resembling a diamond. (See Figure 20.17.) The increase and decrease in trading volume closely mimic the combination of divergent and convergent sup-

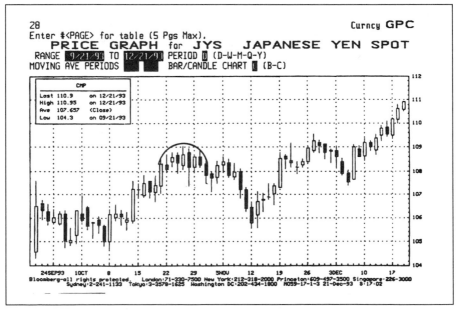

Figure 20.15. A market example of a rounded top formation in the U.S. dollar/Japanese yen daily chart. *(Courtesy of Bloomberg Financial Services)*

port and resistance lines. Upon breakout, volume picks up substantially. The price target is the height of the diamond, measured from the breakout point. An example of a diamond reversal formation is provided in Figure 20.18.

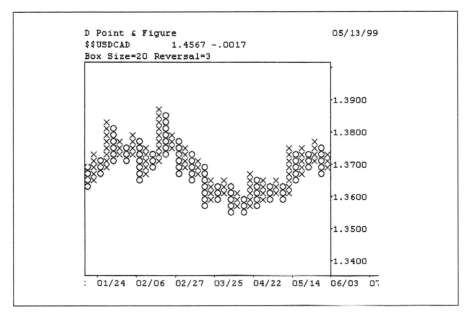

Figure 20.16. A market example of a rounded bottom formation. *(Source: Bridge Information Systems, Inc.)*

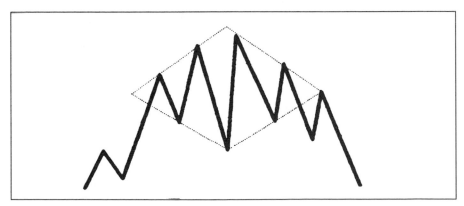

Figure 20.17. Diagram of a typical diamond formation.

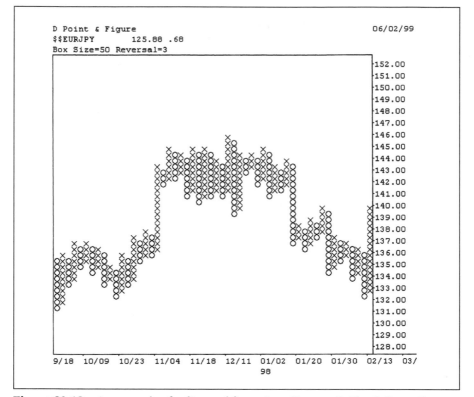

Figure 20.18. An example of a diamond formation. *(Source: Bridge Information Systems, Inc.)*

Among the reversal chart formations, the head-and-shoulders and the double top and bottom are by far the most common, followed by the V-formations and the triple top and bottom. Due to their significance in trend reversals, they are generally known as major reversal patterns.

21 Trend Continuation Patterns

W e have previously explored the major reversal patterns. Technical analysis also provides signals that reinforce the current trends. These chart formations are known as *continuation patterns*. Unlike the reversal patterns, they consist of fairly short consolidation periods. The breakouts occur in the same direction as the original trend. The most important continuation patterns are:

1. Flags
2. Pennants
3. Triangles
4. Wedges
5. Rectangles

FLAG FORMATION

The flag formation is a reliable chart pattern that provides two vital signals: direction and price objective. This formation consists of a brief consolidation period within a solid and steep upward trend or downward trend. The consolidation itself tends to be sloped in the opposite direction from the slope of the original trend, or simply flat. The consolidation is bordered by a support line and a resistance line, which are parallel to each other or very mildly converging, making it look like a flag (parallelogram.) The previous sharp trend is known as a flagpole.

Once the currency resumes its original trend by breaking out of the consolidation, the price objective is the total length of the flagpole, measured from the breakout price level. If the original trend is up, the formation is called a bullish flag. As Figure 21.1 shows, the original trend is sharply up. The flagpole is measured between points A and B. The consolidation period occurs between the support line D to E and the resistance line B to C. When the market penetrates the resistance line at point C, the trend resumes its rally, with the price objective F, measured from C. The price target is measured as the flagpole's length (A to B), calculated from the breakout point through the resistance line (B to C.)

In the numerical example, the height of the flagpole is measured as the difference between 1.7000 and 1.6000 equals 1000 pips. Once the resistance line is broken at 1.6800, the price target is 1.7800, as 1000 pips from 1.6800.

Conversely, if the original trend is going down, the formation is called a bearish flag. (See Figure 21.2.) As Figure 21.2 displays, the original trend is sharply down. The flagpole is measured between points A and B. The consolidation period occurs between the support line B to E and the resistance line C to D. When the market penetrates the support line at point E, the trend resumes its fall, with the price objective F, measured from E. The price target is of about equal amplitude with the flagpole's length (A to B), measured from the breakout point through the support line (B to E.)

In the numerical example, the height of the flagpole is measured as the difference between 140.00 and 120.00 equals 2000 pips. Once the support line is broken at 125.00, the price target is 105.00, as 2000 pips from 125.00.

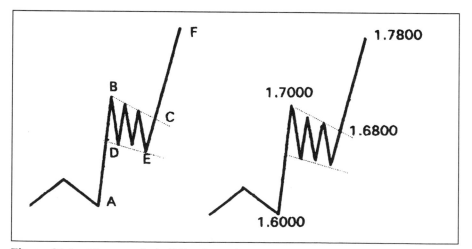

Figure 21.1. Diagram of a bull flag formation.

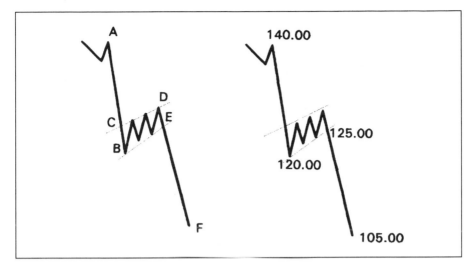

As you can see from Figures 21.3 and 21.4, the flag formations are very reliable. They tend to develop in a period of days to months. However, the support and resistance lines may have to be adjusted several times, due to false breakouts.

PENNANT FORMATION

The pennants are closely related to the flags. The same principles apply. The sole difference is that the consolidation area better resembles a pennant, as the support and resistance lines converge. If the original trend is bullish, then the chart pattern is a bullish pennant. In Figure 21.5, the pennant pole is A to B. The pennant-shaped consolidation is framed by C, B, and D. When the market breaks through the resistance line B to D, the price objective is E. The amplitude of the target price is D to E, and it is equal to the pennant pole A to B. The price target measurement starts from the breakout point.

In the numerical example, the height of the pennant pole is measured as the difference between 1.5500 and 1.4500, or 1000 pips. Once the resistance line is broken at 1.5200, the price target is 1.6200, as 1000 pips from 1.5200.

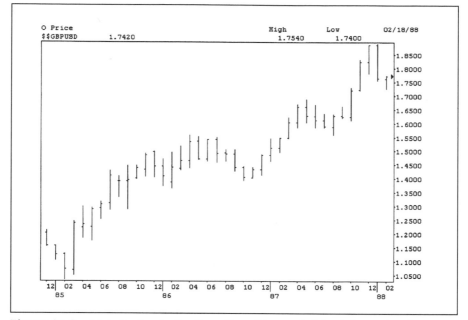

Figure 21.3. An example of a flag formation. *(Source: Bridge Information Systems, Inc.)*

Figure 21.4. An example of an inverse flag formation. *(Source: CQG)*

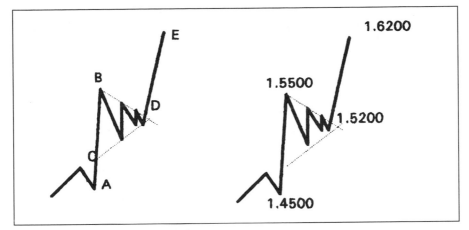

Figure 21.5. Diagram of a bullish pennant.

If the original trend is going down, then the formation is a bearish pennant. In Figure 21.6, the pennant pole is A to B. The pennant-shaped consolidation is framed by C, B and D. When the market breaks through the support line B to D, the objective price is E. The amplitude of the target price is D to E, and it is equal to the pennant pole A to B. The price target measurement starts from the breakout point.

In the numerical example, the height of the flagpole is measured as the difference between 139.00 and 119.00, or 2000 pips. Once the support line is broken at 120.00, the price target is 100.00, as 2000 pips from 120.00.

As you can see from Figure 21.7, the pennant formations are reliable. They may develop in different time frames, from days to months. However, the support and resistance lines may have to be adjusted, due to false breakouts.

TRIANGLE FORMATION

Triangles can be visualized as pennants with no poles. There are four types of triangles: symmetrical, ascending, descending, and expanding (broadening.)

A symmetrical triangle consists of two symmetrically converging support and resistance lines, defined by at least four significant points. (See Figure 21.8.) The two symmetrically converging lines suggest that there is a balance between supply and demand in the foreign exchange market. Consequently, a break may occur on either side. In the case of a bullish symmetrical triangle, the breakout will occur in the same direction, qualifying the formation as a continuation pattern.

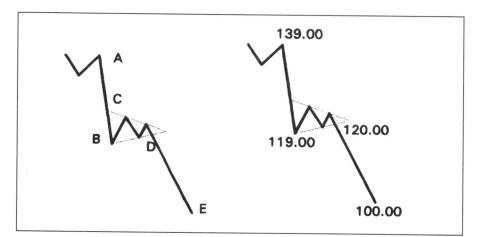

Figure 21.6.   Diagram of a bearish pennant.

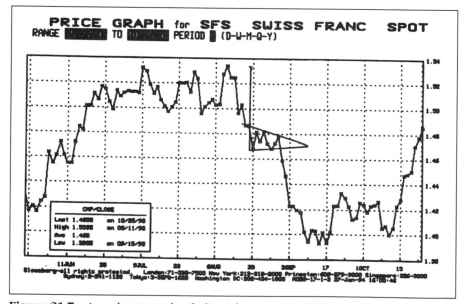

Figure 21.7.   A market example of a bearish pennant in the U.S. dollar/Swiss franc market. *(Source: Bloomberg Financial Services)*

As Figure 21.8 shows, the converging lines are symmetrical. The declining line is defined by points B, D, and F. The rising support line is defined by points A, C, E, and G. The price target is either (1) equal to the width of the base of the triangle BB', measured from the breakout point H (HH'); or (2) at the intersection of line BI (which is a parallel line to the rising line AG) with the price line.

Trading volume will visibly decrease toward the end of the triangle, suggesting the ambivalence of the market. The breakout is accompanied by a rise in volume.

In the numerical example, the price objective is either 1.5500, as the difference between 1.5000 and 1.4000, measured from 1.4500; or 1.5300, as the difference between 1.5000 and 1.4000, measured from 1.4300. A currency market example is presented in Figure 21.9.

The ascending triangle consists of flat resistance line and a rising support line. (See Figure 21.10.) The formation suggests that demand is stronger than supply. The breakout should occur on the upside, and it consists of the width of the base of the triangle as measured from the breakout point. As you can see in Figure 21.10, the resistance line defined by points A, C, and E is flat. The converging bottom line, defined by points B, D, and F, is sloped upward. The price objective is the width of the base of the triangle (AA') measured above the resistance line from the breakout point G (GG'.) In the numerical example, the price objective is 106.00, as the 200-pip difference between 105.00 and 103.00, measured from 104.00.

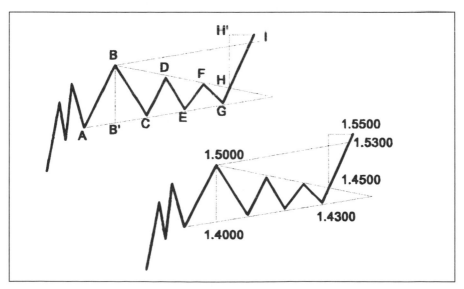

Figure 21.8. Diagram of a bullish symmetrical triangle.

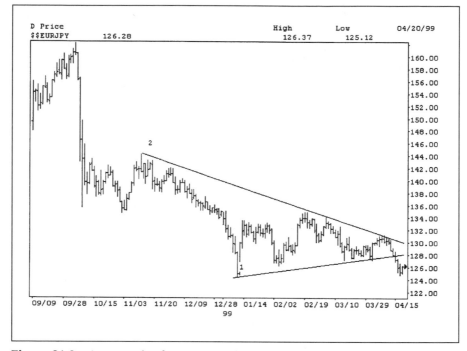

Figure 21.9.   An example of a symmetrical triangle. *(Source: Bridge Information Systems, Inc.)*

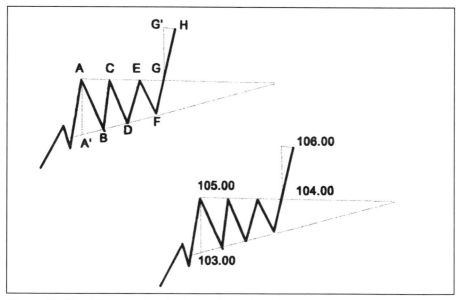

Figure 21.10.   Diagram of typical ascending triangle.

Trading volume is decreasing steadily toward the tip of the triangle, but increases rapidly on the breakout. Figure 21.11 presents a market example of an ascending triangle.

The descending triangle is simply a mirror image of the ascending triangle. It consists of a flat support line and a downward sloping resistance line. (See Figure 21.12.) This pattern suggests that supply is larger than demand. The currency is expected to break on the downside. The descending triangle also provides a price objective. This objective is calculated by measuring the width of the triangle base and then transposing it to the breakpoint. As shown in Figure 21.12, the support line, defined by points A, C, E, and G, is flat. The converging top line, defined by points B, D, F, and H, is sloped downward. The price objective is the width of the base of the triangle (AA'), measured above the support line from the breakout point I (II'.)

In the numerical example, the price objective is 1.3000, as the 1000-pip difference between 1.5000 and 1.4000, measured from 1.4000.

Trading volume is decreasing steadily toward the tip of the triangle, but increases rapidly on the breakout. Figure 21.13 displays an example of a descending triangle.

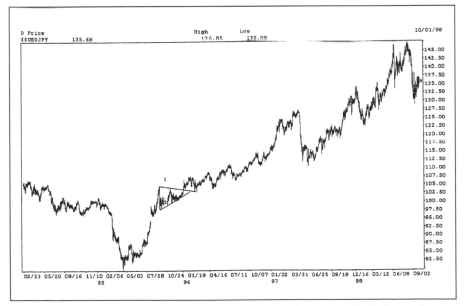

Figure 21.11. An example of an ascending triangle. *(Source: Bridge Information Systems, Inc.)*

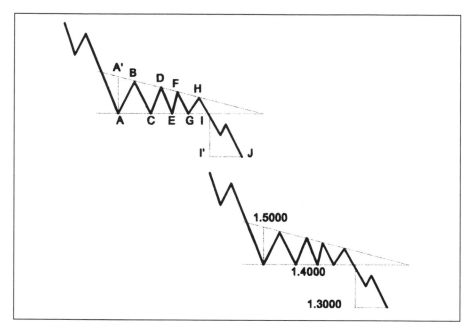

Figure 21.12. Diagram of a descending triangle.

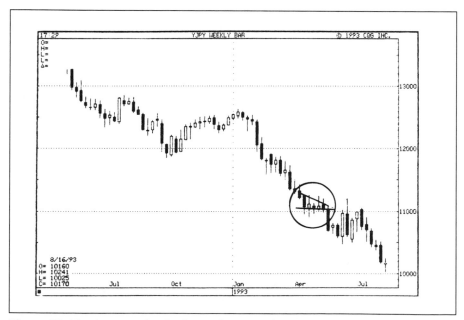

Figure 21.13. An example of a descending triangle. *(Source: CQG)*

The expanding (broadening) triangle is a fairly unusual pattern. It consists of a horizontal mirror image of a triangle, where the tip of the triangle is next to the original trend, rather than its base. (See Figure 21.14.) Volume also follows the horizontal mirror image switch and increases steadily as the chart formation develops. As shown in Figure 21.14, the bottom support line, defined by points B, D, and F, and the top line, defined by points A, C, and E, are divergent. The price objective should be the width, GG', of the base of the triangle, measured from the breakout point G.

In the numerical example, the price objective is 102.00, as the 100-pip difference between 101.00 and 100.00, measured from 101.00.

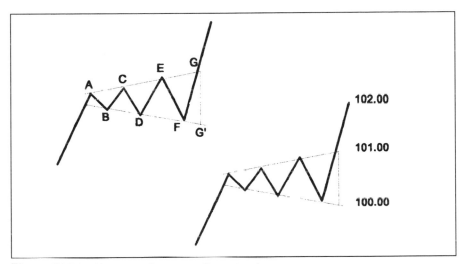

Figure 21.14. Diagram of an expanding triangle.

WEDGE FORMATION

The wedge formation is a close relative of the triangle and the pennant formations. It resembles both the shape and the development time of the triangles, but it really looks and behaves like a pennant without a pole. The wedge is markedly sloped, and the breakout occurs in the direction opposite to its slope (see Figures 21.15 and 21.17), but similar to the direction of the original trend. The signal we receive from the wedge formation is direction only. There is no reliable price objective. Depending on the trend direction, there are two types of wedges: falling (see Figures 21.15 and 21.16) and rising (see Figures 21.17 and 21.18).

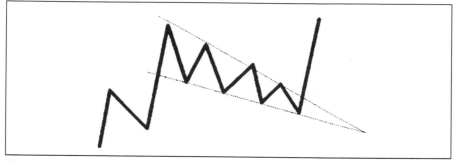

Figure 21.15. Diagram of a falling wedge.

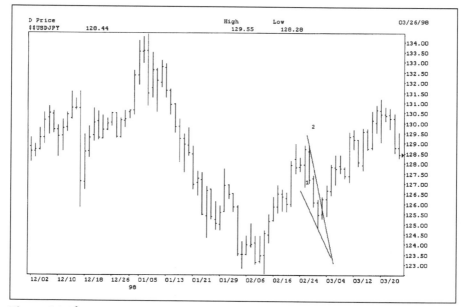

Figure 21.16. An example of a falling wedge. *(Source: Bridge Information Systems, Inc.)*

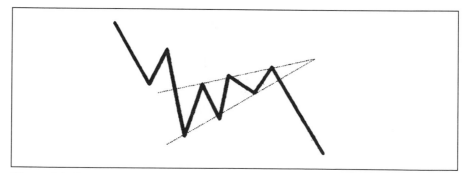

Figure 21.17. Diagram of typical rising wedge.

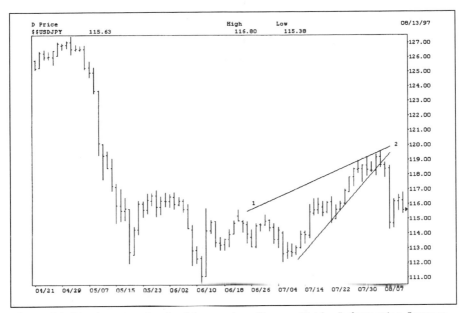

Figure 21.18. An example of a rising wedge. *(Source: Bridge Information Systems, Inc.)*

RECTANGLE FORMATION

Also known as a trading range (or congestion), the rectangle formation reflects a consolidation period. Upon breakout, it is likely to continue the original trend. Its failure will change it from a continuation to a reversal pattern. This pattern is easy to spot, as it can be considered a minor sideways trend.

If it occurs within an uptrend and the breakout occurs on the upside, it is called a bullish rectangle. (See Figure 21.19.) The price objective is the height of the rectangle. As Figure 21.19 shows, the currency moves between well-defined, flat support and resistance levels. A valid breakout may occur on either side from this consolidation period. Please note the failed double top (A, B, C, D, and E.) The price target (GH) is equal to the height of the rectangle (G'H), measured from the breakout point H. In the numerical example, the price objective is 1.6200, as the 100-pip difference between 1.6100 and 1.6000, measured from 1.6100.

If the consolidation occurs within a downtrend and the breakout continues the original trend, then it is called a bearish rectangle. (See Figure 21.20.) As shown in Figure 21.20, the currency moves between well-defined, flat support and resistance levels. A valid breakout may occur on either side of this consolidation period. Please note the failed double bottom (A, B, C, D, and E.) The price objective (HG') is equal in size to the height of the rectangle (GH), measured from the breakout point H. In the numerical example, the price objective is 100.00, as the 100-pip difference between 102.00 and 101.00, measured from 101.00. A market example of a rectangle is presented in Figure 21.21.

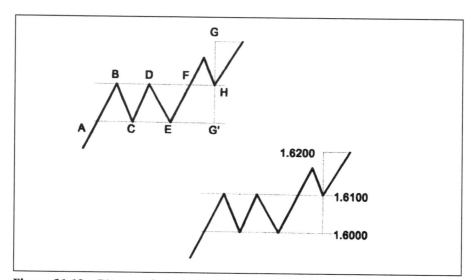

Figure 21.19. Diagram of a typical bullish rectangle.

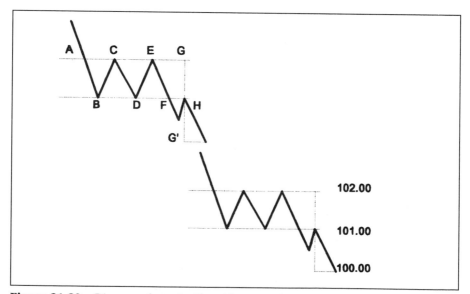

Figure 21.20. Diagram of a typical bearish rectangle.

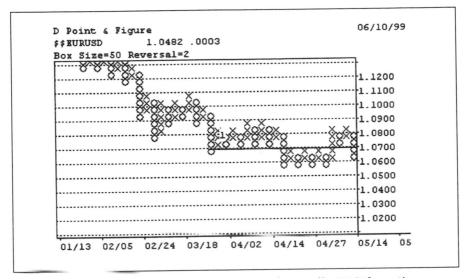

Figure 21.21. A market example of a rectangle. *(Source: Bridge Information Systems, Inc.)*

Volume should give further indication at or close to the points tangential to the support and resistance levels. As usual, heavier volume predicts or substantially increases the chance of a breakout.

A Trader's Point of View

1. Both the reversal and the continuation patterns are primarily used on line and bar charts. Somewhat similar readings may occur in the other types of charts. We will approach both the point-and-figure and the candlestick charts separately.

2. In the case of the continuation patterns, false breakouts tend to occur more often. Therefore, filters should be used.

3. As false breakouts are common, especially in the case of triangles, more adjustments may be necessary.

4. Traders should consider the term "continuation pattern" with restraint. A valid breakout on the "wrong" side will turn the formation into a reversal pattern.

5. Throughout the presentation, I mention the significance of volume. I have no choice but to remind you of the difficulty of gauging volume in foreign exchange markets other than the futures.

22 Formations Unique to Bar Charts for Futures

U nlike line and point-and-figure charts, which are continuous charts, bar and candlestick charts for futures are not. Currency futures trading sessions are shorter than cash trading sessions and price gaps may occur on a daily basis, if the overnight activity occurs outside of the previous day's range. Although the patterns presented here are applicable to both bar and candlestick charts, we analyze each type of chart separately.

The chart formations unique to bar charts are gaps, island reversals, and key reversals.

GAPS

Gaps refer to the price gaps between consecutive trading ranges. Price gaps occur when a range's low is higher than the previous range's high, or when the high of a range is lower than the preceding range's low.

In order to capture these price gaps, only certain bar charts may be used. Charts plotted for weekly, daily, or hourly periods generally fail to display the gaps, as they will show some inherent overlapping due to continuity. Exceptions might occur around the weekends and on short intraday periods, such as 1 minute, when the market moves very fast, or "gaps." Only currency futures markets provide the opportunity to chart these gaps on a regular basis. Since the currency futures are traded on centralized markets, which open and close at fixed times—trading roughly only a third of the day—they can naturally provide these price gaps between consecutive trading days.

The Chicago IMM trades between 7:20 AM and 2:00 PM CDT. If, for instance, the trading range for the previous day was 0.6000–0.6100, and today's opening price is 0.6150, because the market bought the marks overnight, then there is a 50-pip gap relative to yesterday's range.

There are four types of gaps: common, breakaway, runaway, and exhaustion.

THE COMMON GAP

Common gaps have the least technical significance. They do not give any indication of the market's direction or of price objective. (See Figure 22.1.) Common gaps tend to occur in relatively quiet periods or in illiquid markets. When they occur in illiquid markets, such as distant currency futures expiration dates, the common gaps must be completely ignored. When occurring within regular trading ranges, the word on the street has been that gaps must be filled.

Common gaps are short term. When currency futures open higher than yesterday's high, they will be quickly sold, targeting the level of the

Figure 22.1. Examples of common gaps. *(Source: Bridge Information Systems, Inc.)*

previous day's high. Should the sell-off fail, the market will turn on a dime, reversing the short-term position. For instance, if the previous day's range was 0.7030–0.7100 and today's opening price is 0.7130, traders tend to sell the futures contracts from 0.7130 to 0.7100 to fill the price gap. If they cannot reach 0.7100, then the market will quickly turn to buying the futures contracts. The reverse is true if the market opens lower than yesterday's low, as the traders will buy the futures contracts to fill the price gap between the current lower price and yesterday's low. For instance, if the previous day's range was 0.7030–0.7100 and today's opening price is 0.7000, traders tend to buy the futures contracts from 0.7000 to 0.7030 to fill the price gap. If they cannot reach 0.7030, then the market will quickly turn to selling the futures contracts.

Once again, the common gap lacks technical significance, a fact that is generally accepted among professional traders. However, at times, it is not clear whether a common gap is just a common gap or another type of gap. So the "gap-filling" temptation is likely to continue.

THE BREAKAWAY GAP

Breakaway gaps occur at the beginning of a new trend, many times at the end of a long consolidation period. They may also appear after the comple-

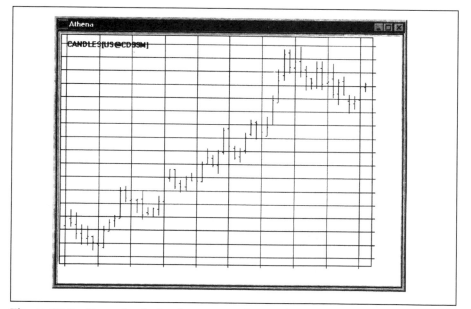

Figure 22.2.   Example of a breakaway gap. *(Source: Bridge Information Systems, Inc.)*

tion of some chart formations. They signify a brisk change in trading sentiment and they occur on very heavy trading. The price takes a secondary
place to participation. (See Figure 22.2.) For instance, if the Japanese yen
futures traded sideways in a 200-pip range—0.9520 to 0.9720—for two
months and a price gap occurred between 0.9720 and 0.9750, the market
would be likely to buy the yen futures further.

A Trader's Point of View

1. A breakaway gap provides the direction of the market.
2. Although there is no price objective per se, sustained demand for a
   currency will ensure a solid rally in the foreseeable future.

THE RUNAWAY OR MEASUREMENT GAP

Runaway or measurement gaps are special gaps that occur within solid
trends. They are known as measurement gaps because they tend to occur
about midway through the life of a trend. (See Figure 22.3.) For example,
if a 30-pip runaway gap occurs at the top of an uptrend measuring 200
pips—between 0.6250 and 0.6050—then the price objective for the trend
is 0.6480, as the previous 200-pip range is added to 0.6280.

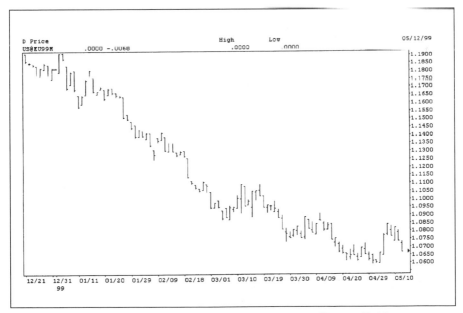

Figure 22.3. Example of a runaway or measurement gap. *(Source: Bridge
Information Systems, Inc.)*

A Trader's Point of View

1. The runaway or measurement gap provides the direction of the market. This gap confirms the health and velocity of the trend.

2. This is the only type of gap that also provides a price objective. The price objective is the previous length of the trend, measured from the runaway gap, in the same direction as the original trend.

THE EXHAUSTION GAP

Exhaustion gaps occur at the top or at the bottom of a V-reversal formation. Trends change direction in a rather uncharacteristically quick manner. There is no consolidation next to the broken trendline. The trend reversal is very sharp. (See Figure 22.4.)

A Trader's Point of View

1. The exhaustion gap provides the direction of the market.

2. In addition, this type of gap provides information on the high demand for a specific currency, which will ensure price velocity in the medium term.

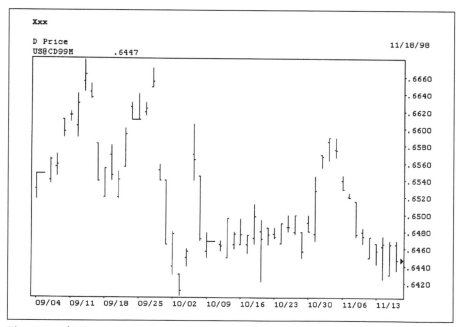

Figure 22.4. Example of an exhaustion gap. *(Source: Bridge Information Systems, Inc.)*

ISLAND REVERSALS

One or more day ranges will be separated from the ante and post ranges. These isolated ranges are known as island reversals and they are a direct result of exhaustion gaps. Occurring at the tip of a V-formation, an island reversal consists of one or more days' ranges, separated in an insular fashion from both the original trend and the new one. (See Figure 22.5.) The reversal signal is very strong. In the market example, in the Canadian dollar futures, the island reversal, which is separated by the exhaustion gap (D) from the rest of the range, consists of two days' ranges. The same principles from the exhaustion gap apply.

KEY REVERSAL DAYS

A reversal day consists of a trading range that reaches a new high in a bullish market but closes lower than the previous day. A key reversal day occurs when the daily price range on the bar chart of the reversal day fully engulfs the previous day's range, and the close is also outside the previous day's range.

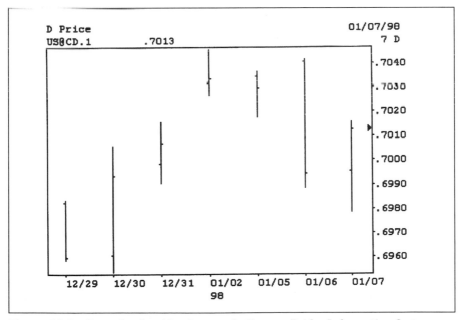

Figure 22.5. Example of an island reversal. *(Source: Bridge Information Systems, Inc.)*

Upgrading a reversal day to a key reversal day is not a fast process. Due to a fairly high rate of failure, a trader must wait several days for confirmation, which consists of a solid and sustained reversal of the previous trend.

A key reversal day example is illustrated in Figure 22.6.

Despite the difficulty in categorizing reversal days, the formation provides at least an excellent opportunity to spot a major trend reversal. In order to better and more quickly capitalize on this opportunity, a trader must use the signal only when it is supplemented with other information.

Figure 22.6. A market example of a key reversal day. *(Source: Bridge Information Systems, Inc.)*

23 Point-and-Figure Charting

The *point-and-figure chart* originated toward the end of the nineteenth century when it was known as the book method. Interest in this type of chart has been growing continuously, due to its accuracy in providing trading signals. But it was the electronic charting of the 1980s that brought this charting system into prominence.

The point-and-figure chart is the only type that plots only the price activity, whereas all the other charts plot the price in terms of time periods. Time is irrelevant for the purposes of this chart. If a chartist wants to make any personal notation regarding the time period, that is fine, of course. But time is a non-factor in the analysis. This means that, at times, there may be few or no entries for the standard periods of time used in other types of charts, if the market is flat. This is a different concept, as we are used to a flatter line or a short bar, but not to the prospect of no chart entry. That is why the point-and-figure chart represents a purer approach to charting. In addition, like the other continuous charts, including the line chart, it reveals price fluctuations missed by the bar chart.

The point-and-figure chart was designed to better plot price activity, and one of the important things this chart does is to *avoid plotting the lack of activity*. All irrelevant market activity, the so-called market noise, is filtered out. To understand how it works, let's remember how the chart is plotted. The rising prices are marked with X's and the falling prices are entered as O's. Therefore, a point-and-figure chart looks like a series of alternating columns of X's and O's columns. (See Figure 23.1.)

Let's take the very popular example of a 1 × 3 point-and-figure chart (also known as the *3-box reversal*), in which each box consists of 10 pips. Every 10-pip box that extends the original direction is entered on the chart.

When the market changes direction, no entry is posted before the price reverses by 30 pips. At that point, all three 10-pip sets are recorded, plus all the additional 10-pip sets that maintain the new direction. In this way, all the insignificant moves are tuned out, allowing the trader to focus on the real price behavior. (See Figure 23.2.)

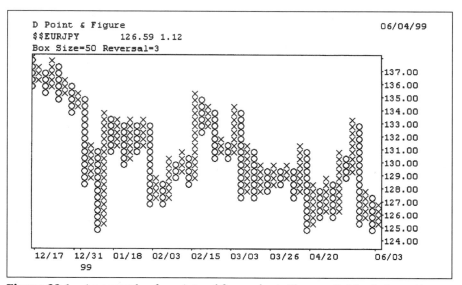

Figure 23.1. An example of a point-and-figure chart. *(Source: Bridge Information Systems, Inc.)*

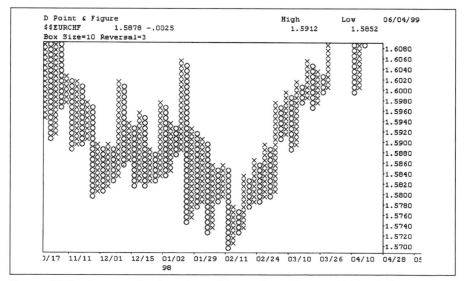

Figure 23.2. An example of a point-and-figure chart. *(Source: Bridge Information Systems, Inc.)*

Incidentally, it is quite possible to use a 1 × 1 reversal box, but it may not be the best possible choice. Because more activity will be charted, point-and-figure will fail to filter out inherent statistical noise.

Volume is not recorded or available in the FX cash market, yet it is an integral part of the chart. Because volume creates trading activity, the heavier the volume, the more activity will be charted. Therefore, volume is represented, albeit in this indirect manner.

Before we take a look at the popular point-and-figure chart formations to see how clear the trading signals are, let me point out the significance of the number 3 in technical analysis in general and for point-and-figure charting in particular. Previously, empirical evidence pointed to the importance of this number—the head-and-shoulders, triple-top, and triple-bottom formations, along with categorizing the trends in terms of importance and direction. The number 3 stands out as obvious in the point-and-figure chart formations. There is no known scientific reasoning behind it, but it is a reality that we have to observe.

It should also be noted that the 45° trendline is very important for point-and-figure analysis.

TRIPLE TOPS AND BOTTOMS

Notice the frequency of the 45° trendline in the charts presented here.

BREAKOUT OF A TRIPLE TOP

This formation is similar in aspect and behavior to a very short-term double-bottom formation, where the third upside attack results in the penetration of the resistance line. The breakout of the neckline is likely to be followed by a currency rally equal in size to the height of the bottoms. (See Figure 23.3.)

BREAKOUT OF A TRIPLE BOTTOM

This formation is similar in shape and performance to a very short-term double-top formation, where the third attack on the downside results in the penetration of the support line. A currency drop equal in size to the height of the tops should follow the breakout of the neckline. (See Figure 23.4.)

BREAKOUT OF A SPREAD TRIPLE TOP

The breakout of a spread triple top pattern is a spin-off of the breakout of a triple top. The difference consists of a failure of the third X's column to reach the resistance line. (See Figure 23.5.) However, the next attack (still the third), will break through the resistance level. The breakout of the neck-line is likely to be followed by a currency rally equal in size to the height of the bottoms.

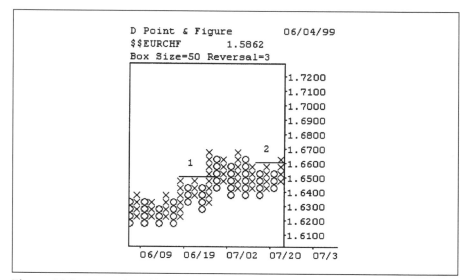

Figure 23.3. Examples of breakouts of triple tops. *(Source: Bridge Information Systems, Inc.)*

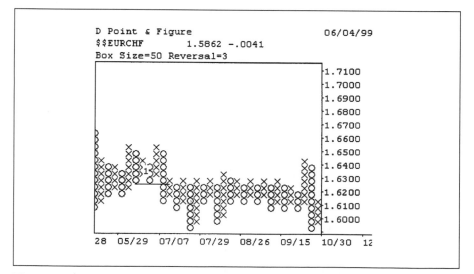

Figure 23.4. An example of a breakout of triple bottoms. *(Source: Bridge Information Systems, Inc.)*

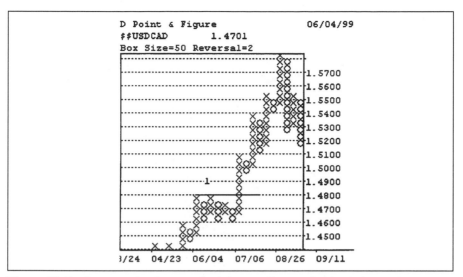

Figure 23.5. An example of a spread triple top. *(Source: Bridge Information Systems, Inc.)*

BREAKOUT OF A SPREAD TRIPLE BOTTOM

This formation is the mirror image of the breakout of a spread triple top. (See Figure 23.6.) A currency drop equal in size to the height of the tops will follow the breakout of the neckline.

THE ASCENDING TRIPLE-TOP FORMATION

The ascending triple-top formation is another spin-off of the breakout of a triple-top formation. Each new top is higher than the previous one. The third top is generally a buying signal. (See Figure 23.7.) The break of the resistance line confirms a buying signal.

UPWARD BREAKOUT OF A BULLISH RESISTANCE LINE

The upward breakout of a bullish resistance line pattern confirms the ascending triple-top formation by adding one or more X's to the chart. Although the same general rules apply, remember that the importance of this resistance line is enhanced by the larger number of significant tangential highs. (See Figure 23.7.)

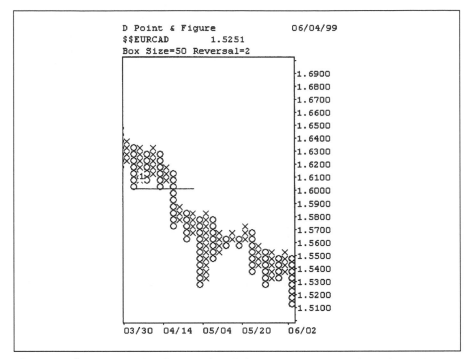

Figure 23.6. An example of a spread triple bottom. *(Source: Bridge Information Systems, Inc.)*

1		2		3			EUR/USD
				∠			1.0540
				∠			1.0530
				∠			1.0520
				∠			1.0510
							1.0500
				∠			1.0490
		∠		∠			1.0480
∠		∠	O	∠			1.0470
∠	O	∠	O	∠			1.0460
∠	O	∠	O	∠			1.0450
∠	O		O				1.0440
∠							1.0430
∠							1.0420

Figure 23.7. A diagram of the ascending triple-top formation.

THE DESCENDING TRIPLE-BOTTOM FORMATION

The descending triple bottom formation is a spin-off of the breakout of the triple-bottom formation. However, each consecutive bottom is lower than the preceding one. (See Figure 23.8.) The breakout of the support line generates a selling signal.

SUPPORT AND RESISTANCE LINES

DOWNWARD BREAKOUT OF A BEARISH SUPPORT LINE

The downward breakout of a bearish support line is a confirmation of the previous formation, the descending triple-bottom formation. Once the bearish support line is broken, one or several O's are entered.

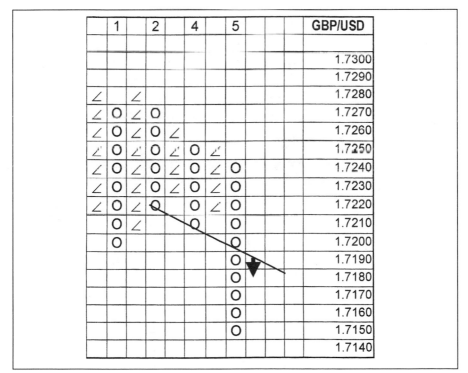

	1		2		4		5			GBP/USD
										1.7300
										1.7290
∠		∠								1.7280
∠	O	∠	O							1.7270
∠	O	∠	O	∠						1.7260
∠	O	∠	O	∠	O	∠				1.7250
∠	O	∠	O	∠	O	∠	O			1.7240
∠	O	∠	O	∠	O	∠	O			1.7230
∠	O	∠	O			O	∠	O		1.7220
	O	∠					O	O		1.7210
	O							O		1.7200
								O		1.7190
								O		1.7180
								O		1.7170
								O		1.7160
								O		1.7150
										1.7140

Figure 23.8. A diagram of the descending triple-bottom formation.

DOWNWARD BREAKOUT OF A BULLISH SUPPORT LINE

The downward breakout of a bullish support line pattern generates a selling signal. (See Figure 23.9.) In this pattern, the currency seems to be under a bullish bias as it moves within a bullish channel. However, if the currency has a valid breakout through the support line, the trader receives a bearish signal.

UPWARD BREAKOUT OF A BEARISH RESISTANCE LINE

The upward breakout of a bearish resistance line pattern occurs when the currency breaks out on the upside from the bearish channel. When the breakout is valid, this formation generates a buy signal. (See Figure 23.10.)

CONSOLIDATION FORMATIONS

UPWARD BREAKOUT FROM A CONSOLIDATION FORMATION

The upward breakout from a consolidation formation may be visualized as a bullish flag or pennant formation. (See Figure 23.11.) A valid upside breakout has a price objective equal in size to the total length of the flag-pole or pennant pole. If the pole is not obvious, the formation resembles a

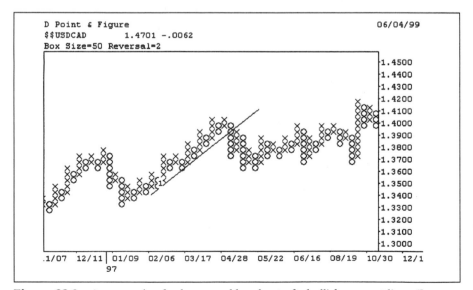

Figure 23.9. An example of a downward breakout of a bullish support line. *(Source: Bridge Information Systems, Inc.)*

symmetrical triangle or a rectangle. This is important to notice, because the currency may break out either way.

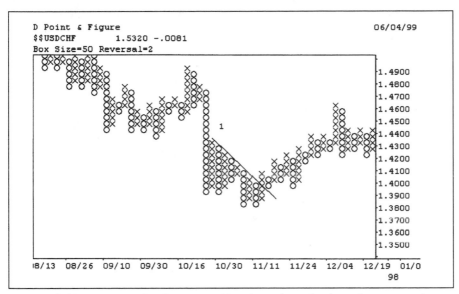

Figure 23.10. An example of an upward breakout through a bearish resistance line. *(Source: Bridge Information Systems, Inc.)*

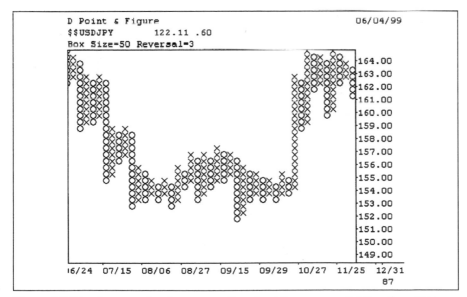

Figure 23.11. An example of an upward breakout from a consolidation formation. *(Source: Bridge Information Systems, Inc.)*

DOWNWARD BREAKOUT FROM A CONSOLIDATION FORMATION

The downward breakout from a consolidation formation resembles a bearish flag or a bearish pennant formation applied to point-and-figure charting. The breakout of the support line generates a selling signal. (See Figure 23.12.)

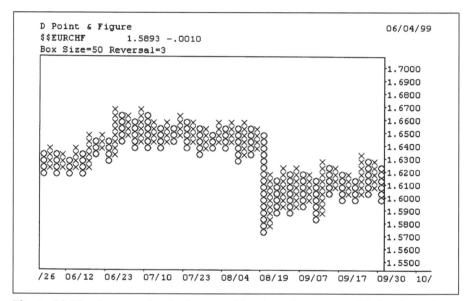

Figure 23.12. An example of a downward breakout from a consolidation formation. *(Source: Bridge Information Systems, Inc.)*

THE HORIZONTAL COUNT

The intraday one-box reversal charts offer yet another type of signal, specific only to point-and-figure: the horizontal count. The idea behind this approach is that a period of consolidation is generally followed by a sharp move. As you remember, the longer the consolidation period, the sharper the subsequent price activity. This method counts the number of columns that form the consolidation area (the horizontal count) and extrapolates this number vertically to the breakout price level. (See Figure 23.13.) The level thus obtained is the new price objective.

In addition to the above formations, all the classic reversal and continuation chart formations previously presented apply as well. Figure 23.14 displays a double-top formation.

													1.2490
												X	1.2480
												X	1.2470
												X	1.2460
												X	1.2450
		X										X	1.2440
X	O	X	O									X	1.2430
X	O	X	O									X	1.2420
X	O	X	O									X	1.2410
	O		O									X	1.2400
			O	X		X		X		X		X	1.2390
			O	X	O	X	O	X	O	X	O	X	1.2380
			O	X	O	X	O	X	O	X	O	X	1.2370
			O		O	X	O		O		O		1.2360

Figure 23.13. A diagram of the horizontal count.

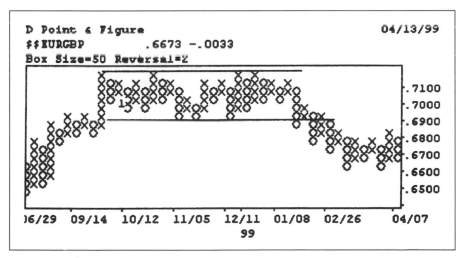

Figure 23.14. An example of a double-top formation. *(Source: Bridge Information Systems, Inc.)*

24 Candlestick Charting

One of the most fascinating types of chart is the candlestick chart. Used in Japan for over two hundred years, candlestick charting is becoming very popular around the world. In terms of structure, the charts are similar to the bar charts and consist of opening, high, low, and closing prices.

The body (*jittai*) consists of the range between the opening and closing price. A black body indicates that the currency closed lower than it opened. A white body indicates that the currency closed higher than it opened.

The Japanese consider the real body paramount in their technical interpretation. The candlestick's body provides the most significance regarding the direction of the market.

The high and low prices create the upper and lower shadows, respectively, when different from the open or close. The upper shadow (*uwakage*) occurs if the daily high is higher than either the closing price of a white body or the opening price of a black body. The lower shadow (*shitakage*) occurs if the daily low is lower than either the closing price of a black body or the opening price of a white body.

For example, let's assume that the dollar/yen opened at 100.00 and closed at 99.00, the high was 100.30, and the low was 98.50. The candlestick's body is black because the closing price (99.00) is lower than the opening price (100.00.) The candlestick has an upper shadow between 100.00 and 100.30 and a lower shadow between 99.00 and 98.50.

In their original form, the white bodies were colored red. Electronic services post them as white (they may be colored as well, depending on the system and printer used); we do likewise in this book.

Let's become familiar with the basic types of candlesticks, their characteristics, and their Japanese nicknames.

DAILY WHITE CANDLESTICKS

We focus first on the white candles, which show that the currency closed higher than it opened. (See Figure 24.1.)

Name	Nickname	Interpretation
A. Long white candle (no shadows)	White *marubozu*	Very bullish
B. Long white candle		Very bullish
C. White lower shadow		Bullish
D. Long white candle (lower shadow)	White closing *bozu*	Bullish
E. Long white candle (upper shadow)	White opening *bozu*	Moderately bullish
F. Short white candle		Stable to bullish

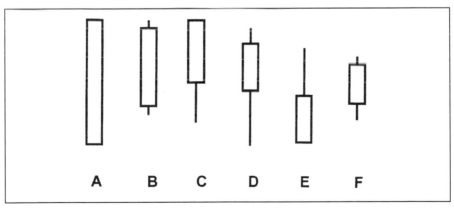

Figure 24.1.   Diagrams of white candlesticks.

Figure 24.2 displays several market examples of white candlesticks.

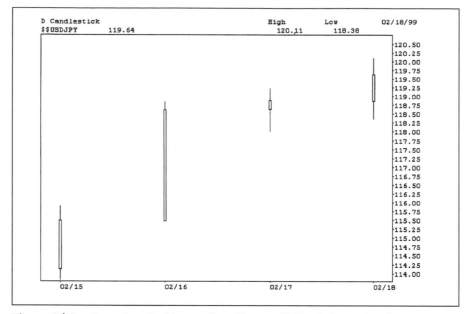

Figure 24.2. Examples of white candles. *(Source: Bridge Information Systems, Inc.)*

DAILY BLACK CANDLESTICKS

Let's take a look now at the black candles, which show that the closing price is lower than the opening. (See Figure 24.3.)

Name	Nickname	Interpretation
A. Long black candle (no shadows)	Black *marubozu*	Very bearish
B. Long black candle		Very bearish
C. Long black candle (upper shadow)	Black closing *bozu*	Bearish
D. Black upper shadow		Bearish
E. Black lower shadow		Stable to bearish
F. Short black candle		Stable to bearish

Several black candlestick market examples are shown in Figure 24.4.

A few words about the nicknames are in order. The Japanese are quite fond of nicknames, and this characteristic was also reflected in candlestick charting. Here are some of them: A *shaven head* (*marubozu*) is a candlestick with a full body, but no shadow. This means that in the case of a *white marubozu*, the opening price is similar to the low, and the closing price is the high. In the case of a *black marubozu*, the opening price is similar to the high (*yoritsuki takane*), and the closing price is the low (*yasunebike*).

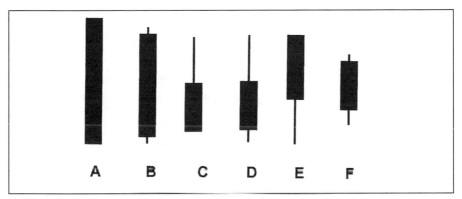

Figure 24.3. Diagrams of black candlesticks.

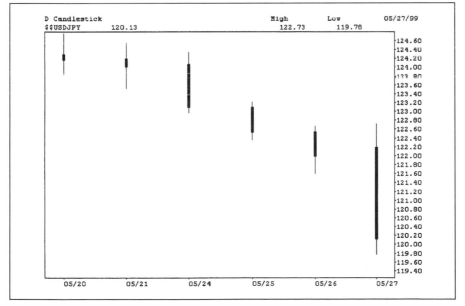

Figure 24.4. Market examples of black candlesticks. *(Source: Bridge Information Systems, Inc.)*

DAILY REVERSAL PATTERNS

Now we take a look at the daily reversal patterns, in Figure 24.5.

Name	Nickname	Interpretation
A. Opening and closing *doji* candlestick	Long-legged shadows' *doji*	Reversal
B. Opening and closing *doji* candlestick	*Tonbo* (dragonfly)	Reversal
C. Opening and closing *doji* candlestick	*Tonbo*	Reversal
D. Opening and closing *doji* candlestick	*Tohbo*	Reversal/stable
E. Black lower shadow	*Karakasa* (hangman at the top)	Sell at the top
F. White lower shadow	(hammer at the bottom)	Buy at the bottom
G. Short black candlestick	*Koma*	Either way
H. Short white candlestick	*Koma*	Either way

The nicknames, again, are very interesting. *Koma* is a spinning top, not quite sure which way to go. (See G and H.) *Tonbo* is a dragonfly; it signals a reversal, yet it may move either way. *Tohba* or *tohbu* is the gravestone doji. The *long legged shadows' doji* candlestick (Figure 24.5, A through D) is one of the most recognized candlestick reversal patterns outside Japan and also a very reliable reversal formation. A *doji* resembles a candlestick. The candlestick does not have a real body, as the opening and closing price are identical. (See Figure 24.6.) This shows that the market reached the end of the trend and temporarily balanced before reversing itself. The market tends to reverse immediately after the signal. At times, exceptional pressure on the opposite side was able to postpone the reversal by one day. A word of warning: To have reversal significance, the doji must occur at a relatively extreme high or low. When it appears midway through a trend, the reading is neutral, and the pattern is called a *rickshaw man*. (See Figure 24.7.)

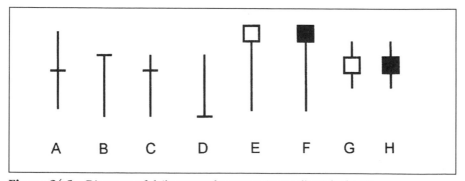

Figure 24.5. Diagrams of daily reversal patterns in candlestick charting.

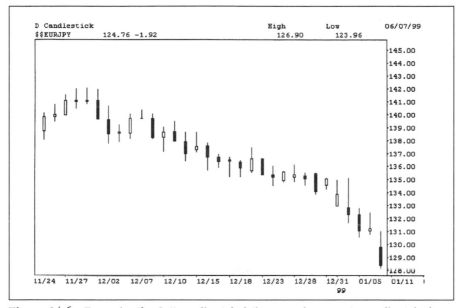

Figure 24.6. Example of a *doji* candlestick daily reversal pattern in candlestick charting. *(Source: Bridge Information Systems, Inc.)*

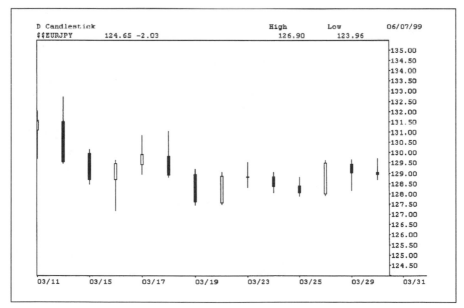

Figure 24.7. Example of a rickshaw man. *(Source: Bridge Information Systems, Inc.)*

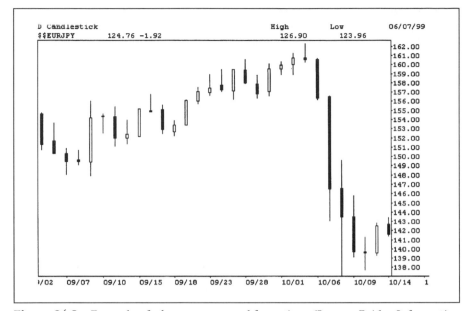

Figure 24.8. Example of a hangman reversal formation. *(Source: Bridge Information Systems, Inc.)*

Initially known as *karakasa*, the paper umbrella is better known now as the *hangman* when it occurs at the top of the trend, because the traders who may fall in the trap and buy that currency will be caught long at the top of the range. The opposite is true when this formation occurs at the bottom of the trend (Figure 24.5, E and F). The only difference is the name: the *hammer*. A market example of a hangman can be observed in Figure 24.8.

Although these candlesticks may seem to give either bullish signals at the top or bearish signals at the bottom, a closer look and a little caution should help. It is important to remember that the body is small—only one-half or one-third of the length of the shadow. Obviously, the signals are to sell at the top and buy at the bottom. (Don't we always want to do just that, anyway?)

The single candlesticks introduced so far are the fundamental tools, either by themselves or in combination. Now that we know their individual interpretations, let's move on and mix them up, in search of further signals.

TWO-DAY CANDLESTICK COMBINATIONS

When two consecutive candlesticks show the same direction, based on the momentum feature of the market, we tend to look for continuation. But can we get any signal when the consecutive candlesticks point out different directions? Let's find out.

THE BULLISH SIGNALS

The bullish candlestick signals are:

- piercing candlestick (*kirikomi*),
- bullish *tasuki*,
- upside gap *tasuki*, and
- bullish *tsutsumi* (the engulfing candlestick).

The piercing candlestick, or *kirikomi*, is a white candlestick that opens the second day lower than the previous low of a long black candlestick, and closes at or above the 50 percent level of the previous day's range of the candlestick. (See Figure 24.9.) The formation generates a powerful bullish signal.

The bullish *tasuki* candlestick is a much less reliable bullish pattern, whose logic is that a one-day decline on profit taking within a rising streak will not impede, but accentuate, the bullish momentum. It is less reliable because, while it makes sense from a medium-term point of view, the spot

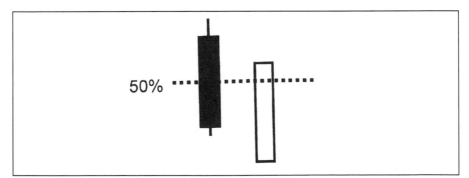

Figure 24.9.   Diagram of the piercing candlestick.

trader might get buried going long after seeing the pattern, while the currency extends its decline a little further in the short term. The formation consists of a long black candlestick that has a high above the 50 percent level of the previous day's long white body, and closes marginally below the previous day's low. (See Figure 24.10.)

The upside gap *tasuki* candlestick occurs in an uptrend. It is a second-day black candlestick that closes an overnight gap opened on the previous day by a white candlestick. (See Figure 24.11.) This is similar to a common gap in the currency futures candlestick chart that was indeed closed, but had little technical meaning otherwise, as it occurred against the direction

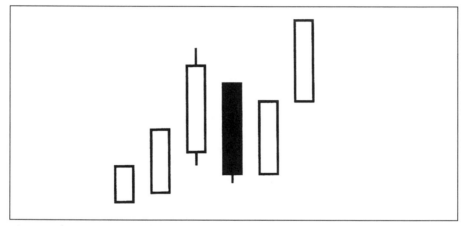

Figure 24.10.   Diagram of a bullish *tasuki* candlestick.

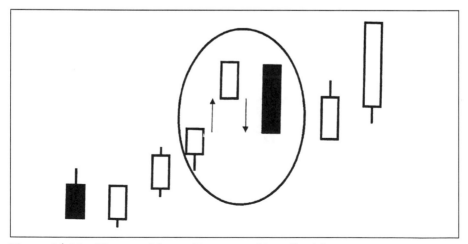

Figure 24.11.   Diagram of the upside gap *tasuki* candlestick.

of the trend. The signal of the upside gap tasuki candlestick is that the bull-ish momentum should continue.

The bullish engulfing pattern (bullish *tsutsumi*) consists of a second-day long white candlestick whose body surrounds the previous day's black body. (See Figure 24.12.) This is the equivalent of a bullish key reversal in the candlestick charts. A market example of the bullish engulfing pattern can be observed in Figure 24.13.

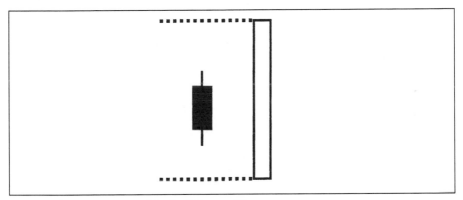

Figure 24.12.   Diagram of the bullish engulfing pattern.

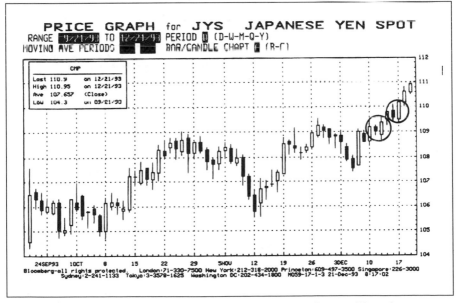

Figure 24.13.   Examples of the bullish engulfing pattern. *(Source: Bloomberg Financial Services)*

THE BEARISH SIGNALS

The bearish candlestick signals are:

- dark cloud cover (*kabuse*),
- *atekubi*,
- *irikubi*,
- *sashikomi*,
- bearish engulfing pattern (*tsutsumi*),
- bearish *tasuki*, and
- downside *tasuki* gap.

The dark cloud cover (a *kabuse* candlestick) is a second-day black candlestick that opens above the previous day's high and closes midway through the previous day's white long body. The dark cloud cover provides a deadly bearish reversal signal.

Based on the price behavior on the second day, there are three types of dark cloud cover (see Figure 24.14):

a. long black closing *bozu*, which settles under the 50 percent level of the original white candle;

b. black *marubozu*, and

c. long black opening *bozu*, which settles under the 50 percent level of the original white candlestick.

A market example of a *kabuse* candlestick can be observed in Figure 24.15.

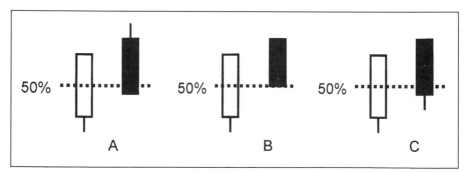

Figure 24.14. Diagrams of dark cloud cover.

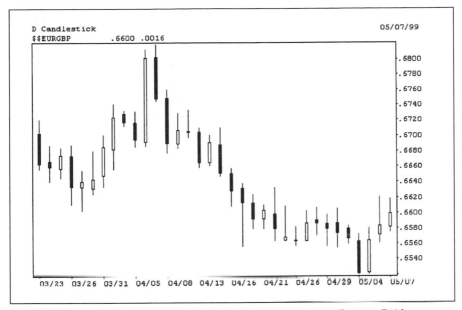

Figure 24.15. Market example of a dark cloud cover pattern. *(Source: Bridge Information Systems, Inc.)*

Atekubi, irikubi, and *sashikomi* are three varieties of the same pattern suggesting that weak rebound attempts via filling common gaps will not derail a solid decline.

The *atekubi* pattern, which is the most restrictive of the three, consists of a second-day white candlestick that closes at the daily high. (See Figure 24.16.) The current closing price equals the previous declining day's low. This is a typical case of the market closing an overnight gap in the currency futures market, with no impact on the previous trend. The *atekubi* candlestick suggests selling.

The *irikubi* candlestick is a modified *atekubi* candlestick. All the characteristics are the same, except that the second day's closing high is marginally higher than the original day's low. (See Figure 24.17.) The signal remains bearish.

The *sashikomi* candlestick is, in turn, a modified *irikubi* candlestick. (See Figure 24.18.) Therefore, all the characteristics are the same, and the signal remains bearish. The difference is that the opening of the second day's white candlestick is much lower than that of the *irikubi* candlesticks. Despite the wider gap thus formed, the white candlestick closes just above the previous day's low.

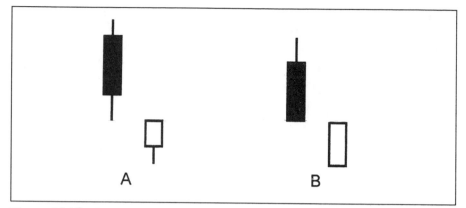

Figure 24.16.   Diagrams of *atekubi* candlesticks.

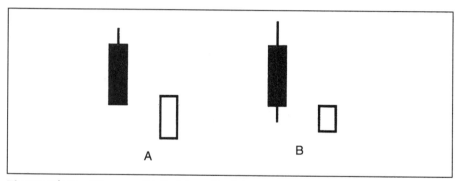

Figure 24.17.   Diagram of *irikubi* candlesticks.

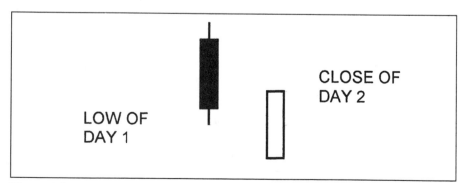

Figure 24.18.   Diagram of a *sashikomi* candlestick.

The bearish engulfing pattern (the bearish *tsutsumi*) is a second-day long black candlestick whose body "engulfs" the previous day's small white body, closing lower than the low of the first day. (See Figure 24.19.) This is the equivalent of a bearish key reversal in the candlestick charts. A market example of the bearish *tsutsumi* candlestick can be observed in Figure 24.20.

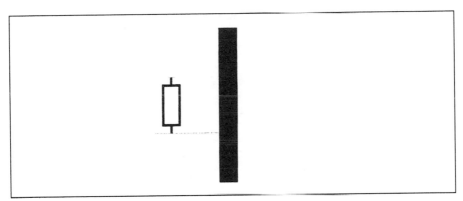

Figure 24.19. Diagram of the bearish engulfing pattern.

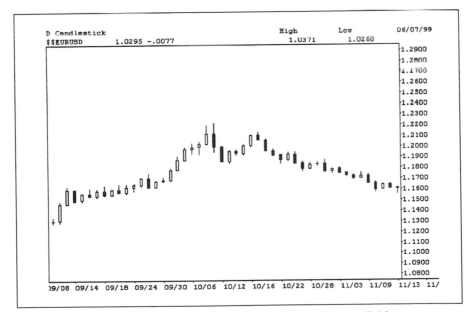

Figure 24.20. Example of the bearish engulfing pattern. *(Source: Bridge Information Systems, Inc.)*

The bearish *tasuki* candlestick is a long white candlestick that has a low above 50 percent of the previous day's long black body and closes marginally above the previous day's high. (See Figure 24.21.) The second day's rally is only temporary, as it is caused solely by profit taking. The sell-off is likely to continue the next day. The *tasuki* candlestick's signal is bearish.

The downside gap *tasuki* candlestick occurs in a downtrend. It is a second-day white candlestick that closes an overnight gap opened on the previous day by a black candlestick. (See Figure 24.22.) This is similar to a common gap in the currency futures candlestick chart that was indeed closed, but had little meaning otherwise because it occurred against the direction of the trend.

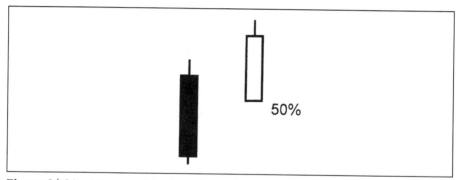

Figure 24.21. Diagram of the bearish *tasuki* candlestick.

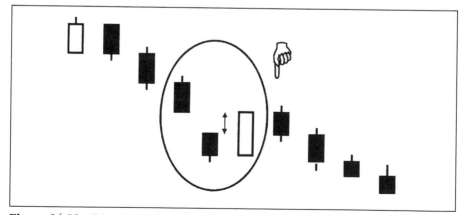

Figure 24.22. Diagram of the downside gap *tasuki* candlestick.

THE "WAIT AND SEE" SIGNALS

The "wait and see" candlestick signals are:

- *harami*,
- *star*, and
- *kenuki* (tweezers).

The *harami* pattern is just the opposite of the engulfing range. The second day's range occurs within the previous day's body; it's an inside range. The two consecutive ranges may have opposite directions, but it does not matter which one is first. (See Figure 24.23.) The market's focus remains on the activity of the first day, so the trading volume will slow down until further information becomes available. However, when the second day's range is a *doji* candlestick (C and D), then the *harami* candlestick becomes a reversal signal. A market example is presented in Figure 24.24.

The *hoshi* (star) candlestick is essentially identical in nature to the *harami* candlestick. It consists of a tiny body that appears the following day outside the original body. (See Figure 24.25.) It is not important whether the star reaches the previous day's shadows. The direction of the two consecutive ranges is also irrelevant. The reading is "wait and see." Market examples of stars are provided in Figures 24.26 and 24.27.

The *kenuki* (tweezers) refers to consecutive candlesticks that have matching highs or matching lows. (See Figure 24.28.) In a rising market, a tweezers top occurs when the highs match. The opposite is true for a tweezers bottom. The "wait and see" interpretation changes to reversal when the formation occurs after an extended move. A market example can be observed in Figure 24.29.

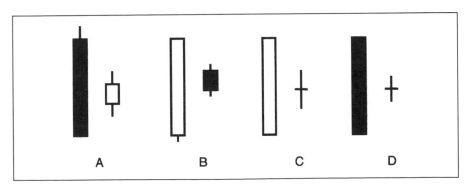

Figure 24.23. Diagrams of the *harami* candlesticks.

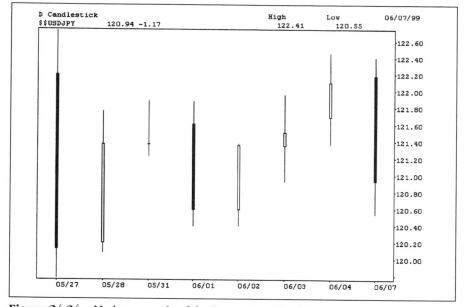

Figure 24.24. Market example of the *harami* candlestick. *(Source: Bridge Information Systems, Inc.)*

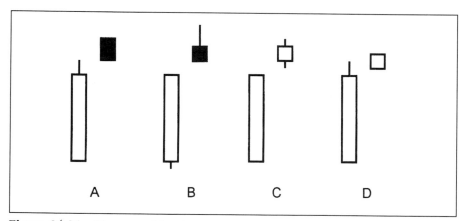

Figure 24.25. Diagrams of the star pattern.

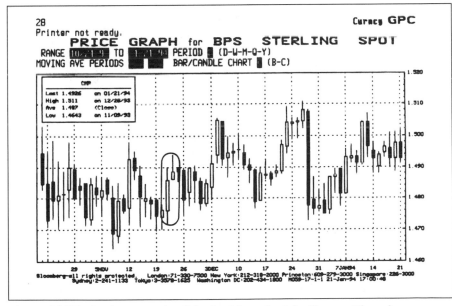

```
D Candlestick                                High      Low        06/07/99
$$EURJPY          124.88 -1.80               126.90    123.96
                                                                ┤140.00
                                                                ┤139.00
                                                                ┤138.00
                                                                ┤137.00
                                                                ┤136.00
                                                                ┤135.00
                                                                ┤134.00
                                                                ┤133.00
                                                                ┤132.00
                                                                ┤131.00
                                                                ┤130.00
                                                                ┤129.00
                                                                ┤128.00
                                                                ┤127.00
                                                                ┤126.00
                                                                ┤125.00
                                                                ┤124.00
                                                                ┤123.00

    06/18     06/19     06/23     06/24     06/25     06/26     06/27
```

Figure 24.26. Market example of the star. *(Source: Bridge Information Systems, Inc.)*

Figure 24.27. Market example of the *hoshi* candlestick. *(Source: Bloomberg Financial Services)*

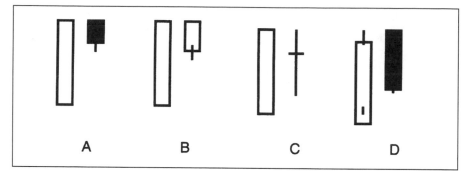

Figure 24.28. Diagrams of the tweezers.

Figure 24.29. Example of the tweezers pattern. *(Courtesy of CQG)*

SAKATA'S 5 METHODS

We have already come across several reliable reversal signals, such as the *doji* candlestick and the engulfing patterns. We observed that some of the uncertain signals may turn into reversal signals under certain conditions, for example, the tweezers candlesticks. Now we focus on other major patterns, mostly reversal formations, known as a whole as "Sakata's 5 methods." These strategies date back about 200 years. They are:

1. *sanzan* (three mountains),
2. *sansen* (three rivers),
3. *sangu* (three gaps),
4. *sanpei* (three parallel candlesticks), and
5. *sanpo* (three methods).

Please note the omnipresence of the number 3. It seems somehow that the number 3 holds a lot of attraction for technicians, regardless of geographical or time frames.

These reversal patterns generally have more daily entries than we have been accustomed to so far.

1. When considering three mountains (*sanzan*), think of the triple-top formation. (See Figure 24.30.) This strategy holds that prices move up in three waves and then descend in three waves. If the middle "mountain" is higher than the other two, the formation becomes a three Buddha top formation. This candlestick formation closely resembles the head-and-shoulders chart formation. (See Figure 24.31.)
2. The three-river method (*sansen*) is more commonly known as the three-river evening star or three-river morning star. It consists of three daily entries. In the three-river evening star, the first day is a long white candlestick (a bullish move). This pattern is followed by a rising, short-ranged, one-day island. It ends with a bearish long black candle. (See Figure 24.32.) It is easy to visualize if you remember the bearish exhaustion gap from the currency futures candlestick charts.

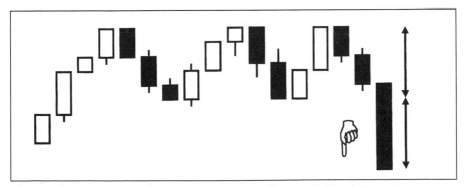

Figure 24.30.   Diagram of the three mountains. *(Source: Bridge Information Systems, Inc.)*

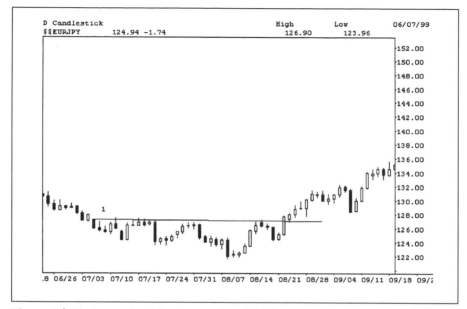

```
D Candlestick                                    High        Low        06/07/99
$$EURJPY          124.94  -1.74                 126.90      123.96
```

Figure 24.31. Example of the inverse three Buddha formation. *(Source: Bridge Information Systems, Inc.)*

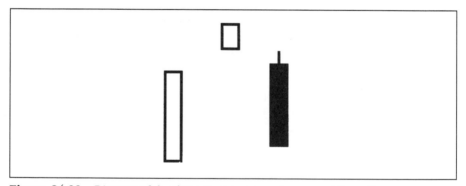

Figure 24.32. Diagram of the three-river evening star reversal formation.

A spin-off of the three-river evening star is a rather poetically named formation called the upside gap's two crows. (See Figure 24.33, A.) It differs in the second and third candlesticks, because they are both bearish yet unable to close the exhaustion gap in the very short term. It may be remembered from the exhaustion gaps, again, this time as the two- or three-day island.

There are several other versions of the three rivers, such as the evening Southern cross, in which the star is formed by a *doji*, and the two crows, but they have the same reversal function. (See Figure 24.33, B and C.)

The opposite of the three-rivers evening star is the three-rivers morning star. (See Figure 24.34.) The same rules apply, but it is at heart a bullish reversal pattern.

3. The three gaps (*sangu*) is a method applicable in a steeply trading commodity, not a currency market, when the daily limits will break the trading. The theory holds that after the third gap, the market will reverse to close at least the second gap. There is not much reason to focus on this method, as it is hardly applicable in the currency markets. Daily limits do not exist in the full sense in the currency futures markets. Therefore, it is highly unlikely that this formation would appear on the charts.

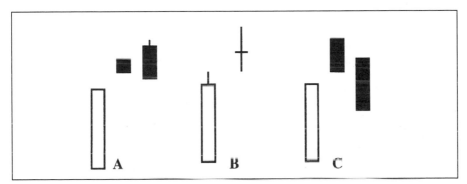

Figure 24.33. Diagram of the upside gap's two crows, evening Southern cross, and the two-crow reversal formation.

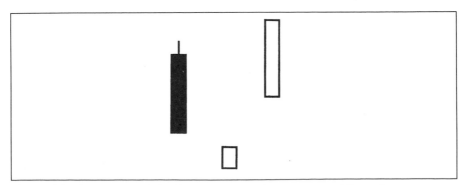

Figure 24.34. Diagram of the three-rivers morning star reversal formation.

4. Three parallel candlesticks (*sanpei*) refers to the similarity of direction and velocity of three consecutive candles, because otherwise all the entries are parallel. (See Figure 24.35.) They generate a reversal formation after an extended rally. When bullish, the formation is known as the three soldiers; when bearish, the name switches to three crows because calling it the inverted three soldiers may have caused confusion over the years. A market example of the three soldiers is presented in Figure 24.36.

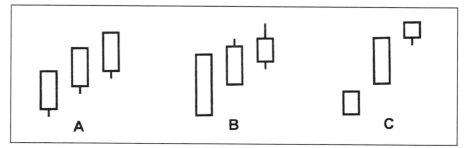

Figure 24.35. Diagram of the three soldiers and the three crows reversal formations.

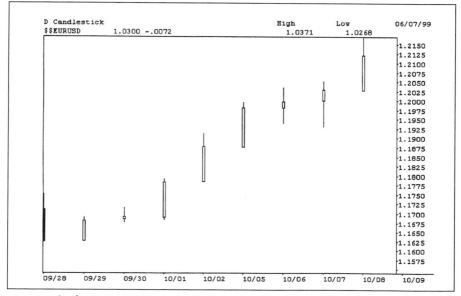

Figure 24.36. Market example of the three soldiers. *(Source: Bridge Information Systems, Inc.)*

5. Three methods (*sanpo*) advises a trader to pause occasionally when following a trend. In direct translation, no market will go straight up or down. Retracements are in order before the market will make new highs, and, respectively, new lows. (See Figure 24.37.) These formations are basically continuation patterns. The formations may be either bullish or bearish. A market example of the three rising method is provided in Figure 24.38.

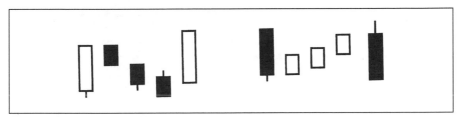

Figure 24.37. Diagram of the three rising method and the three falling method formations.

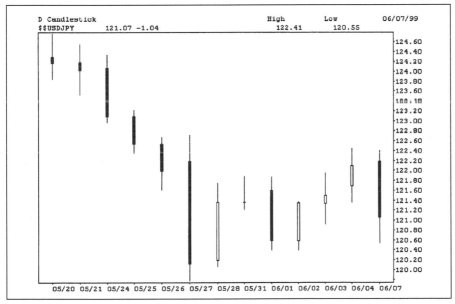

Figure 24.38. Example of the three rising method. *(Courtesy of Bloomberg)*

25 Quantitative Trading Methods

Now that we have been introduced to all the major chart types and chart formations, we move from chart interpretation to the quantitative, or mathematical, trading methods that provide a more objective view of price activity. In addition, the quantitative methods tend to provide signals prior to their occurrence on the currency charts.

The tools of the quantitative methods are moving averages, discussed in this chapter, and oscillators, discussed in Chapter 26.

MOVING AVERAGES

A *moving average* is an average of a predetermined number of prices over a number of days, divided by the number of entries. The higher the number of days in the average, the smoother the line is. A moving average makes it easier to visualize currency activity without daily statistical noise. It is a common tool in technical analysis and is used either by itself or as an oscillator.

As you can see from Figure 25.1, a moving average has a smoother line than the underlying currency. The daily closing price is commonly included in the moving averages. The average may also be based on the midrange level or on a daily average of the high, low, and closing prices.

It is important to observe that the moving average is a follower rather than a leader. Its signals occur after the new movement has started, not before.

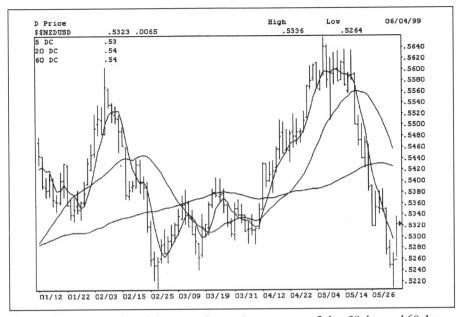

Figure 25.1. Examples of three simple moving averages—5-day, 20-day, and 60-day—traced along the New Zealand/U.S. dollar daily bar chart. *(Source: Bridge Information Systems, Inc.)*

There are three types of moving averages:

1. The simple moving average or arithmetic mean.
2. The linearly weighted moving average.
3. The exponentially smoothed moving average.

As described, the *simple moving average* or *arithmetic mean* is the average of a predetermined number of prices over a number of days, divided by the number of entries. If you want a three-day average, you simply add the closing prices of the last three days and divide their sum by three. In order to make the average "move," each day you add the new closing price to the previous sum and deduct the oldest price.

$$\text{Simple moving average} = \frac{P4 + P3 + P2 + P1 - P4}{3}$$

You now have a simple moving average.

Traders who dislike allocating equal weights to each of the daily prices considered always have the option of using a *linearly weighted mov-*

ing average. (See Figure 25.2.) This type of average assigns more weight to the more recent closings. This is achieved by multiplying the last day's price by one, and each closer day by an increasing consecutive number. In our previous example, the fourth day's price is multiplied by 1, the third by 2, the second by 3, and the last one by 4; then the fourth day's price is deducted. The new sum is divided by 9, which is the sum of its multipliers.

$$\text{Weighted moving average} = \frac{(P4 \times 1) + (P3 \times 2) + (P2 \times 3) + (P1 \times 4) - P4}{9}$$

The most sophisticated moving average available is the *exponentially smoothed moving average.* (See Figure 25.3.) In addition to assigning different weights to the previous prices, the exponentially smoothed moving average also takes into account the previous price information of the underlying currency.

Traders choose a number of averages to use with a currency. A suggested number is three, as more signals may be available. But be wary of using three very close moving averages, in order to avoid confusing signs. It may be helpful to use intervals that better encompass short-term, medium-term, and long-term periods, to arrive at a more complex set of signals.

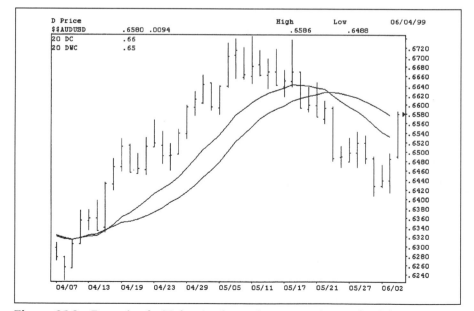

Figure 25.2. Example of a 20-day simple moving average (top at the right) as compared to a 20-day weighted moving average (bottom at the right.) *(Source: Bridge Information Systems, Inc.)*

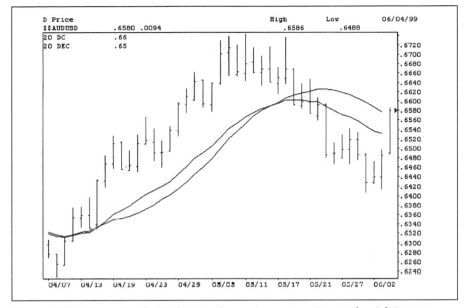

Figure 25.3. Example of a 20-day simple moving average (top at the right) as compared to a 20-day exponential moving average (bottom at the right). *(Source: Bridge Information Systems, Inc.)*

Some of the more popular periods are 4, 9, and 18 days; 5, 20, and 60 days; and 7, 21, and 90 days. Unless you focus on a specific combination of moving averages (for instance, 4, 9, and 18 days), the exact number of days for each of the averages is less important, as long as they are spaced far enough apart from each other to avoid insignificant signals.

TRADING SIGNALS

A *buying signal* on a two–moving average combination occurs when the shorter term of two consecutive averages intersects the longer one upward. A *selling signal* occurs when the reverse happens, and the longer of two consecutive averages intersects the shorter one downward. (See Figure 25.4.)

A signal involving three moving averages is generated by a moving averages combination of 4, 9, and 18 days. The *buying warning* occurs when the 4-day moving average crosses upward both the 9-day and 18-day averages, and the *buying signal* is confirmed when the 9-day moving average also crosses upward the 18-day average. (See Figure 25.5.)

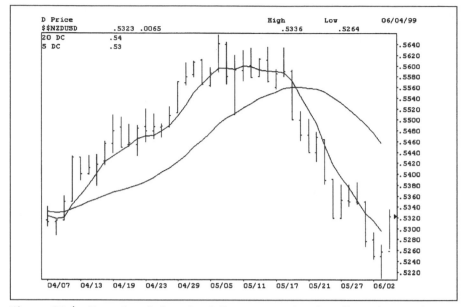

Figure 25.4. Examples of a buy signal (first crossover) and a sell signal (second crossover) provided by the 5-day and 20-day moving averages. *(Source: Bridge Information Systems, Inc.)*

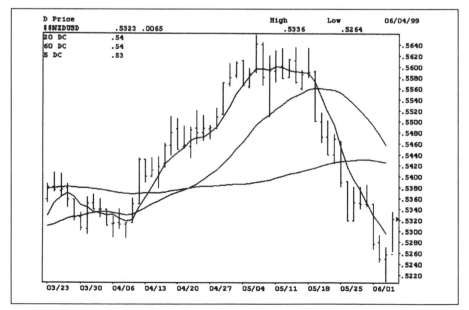

Figure 25.5. Examples of a buy signal (first crossover) and a sell signal (second crossover) provided by the 5-, 20-, and 60-day moving averages. *(Source: Bridge Information Systems, Inc.)*

The reverse is true for the selling signal. The *selling warning* appears when the 4-day average intersects downward the 9-day and 18-day moving averages. This warning becomes a *selling signal* when the 9-day moving average falls below the 18-day average as well. (See Figure 25.5.)

A type of signal based on a two–moving average combination, and more popular in Japan, is known as the *cross*. There are two kinds of crosses. When two consecutive moving averages intersect each other as they move in opposite directions, this is called a *dead cross*, and the intersection should be disregarded. However, if the two consecutive moving averages intersect as they move in the same general direction, this is called a *golden cross*, and it is a signal that the currency will move in the same direction. (See Figure 25.6.)

Single moving averages are frequently used as price and time filters, mirroring the filters first described under the trendline breakout confirmation rules.

- As a *price filter*, a short-term moving average has to be cleared by the currency closing price, the entire daily range, or a certain percentage (chosen at the discretion of the trader).

- As a *time filter*, a short number of days may be used to avoid any false signals.

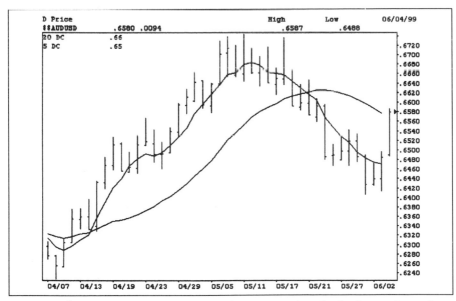

Figure 25.6. Example of a golden cross (first crossover) and a dead cross (second crossover) between the 5- and 20-day moving averages. *(Source: Bridge Information Systems, Inc.)*

Two very popular versions of the price filters are the envelope model and the high-low band.

The *envelope model* consists of a short-term (perhaps 5-day) closing price based moving average to which you add and subtract a small percentage (2 percent is suggested for foreign currencies.) The two winding parallel lines above and below the moving average will create a band bordering most price fluctuations. When the upper band is penetrated, a selling signal occurs. When the lower band is penetrated, a buying signal occurs. Because the signals generated by the envelope model are very short-term and they occur many times against the ongoing direction of the market, speed of execution is paramount.

The *high-low band* is set up the same way, except that the moving average is based on the high and low prices. The resulting two moving averages define the edges of the band. A close above the upper band sends a buying signal and one below the lower band gives a selling signal.

Due to the comprehensive number of foreign exchange topics covered in this book, it is impossible to present all the formulas. In order to balance this shortcoming, I provide the appropriate sources of information, should you require a more detailed analysis. Note that, whereas it is very important to understand the concept behind the mathematical formulas, the calculations are provided by the charting services: Bridge Information Systems, Bloomberg, and CQG.

26 Oscillators and Studies

To the chagrin of fundamentalists and politicians, markets gyrate, and prices tend to overshoot targets and overextend trends. Oscillators were designed to provide signals regarding overbought and oversold conditions. They come in particularly handy during trading ranges, when traders have no available trends on which to focus. Despite small differences in the formulas, studies were also designed to gauge the health of the trend. As we present these tools in more detail, three rules will become apparent:

1. The signals are mostly useful at the extremes of their scales.
2. Warnings or signals are triggered when a divergence occurs between the price of the underlying currency and the oscillator.
3. Crossing the zero line, when applicable, usually generates direction signals.

The major types of oscillators are: stochastics, moving averages convergence-divergence (MACD), momentum, and relative strength index (RSI).

STOCHASTICS

Unlike moving averages, which constitute a lagging indicator, stochastics generate trading signals before they appear in the price itself. Unfortunately, though, it is rather hard to know how long in advance the signal is appearing.

The stochastics concept is based on George Lane's observations that, as the market gets toppish, the closing prices tend to approach the daily highs; whereas in a bottoming market, the closing prices tend to draw near the daily lows.

The oscillator consists of two lines called %K and %D. Visualize %K as the plotted instrument, and %D as its moving average.

The formulas for calculating the stochastics are:

$$\%K = [(CCL - L9)/(H9 - L9)] * 100$$

where

CCL = current closing price

$L9$ = the lowest low of the past 9 days

$H9$ = the highest high of the past 9 days

and

$$\%D=(H3/L3) * 100$$

where

$H3$ = the three-day sum of $(CCL - L9)$

$L3$ = the three-day sum of $(H9 - L9)$

The resulting lines are plotted on a 1 to 100 scale, with overbought and oversold warning signals at 70 percent and 30 percent, respectively. The buying (bullish reversal) signals occur under 10 percent, and conversely the selling (bearish reversal) signals come into play above 90 percent after the currency turns. (See Figure 26.1.) In addition to these signals, the oscillator–currency price divergence generates significant signals.

The intersection of the %D and %K lines generates further trading signals. There are two types of intersections between the %D and %K lines:

1. The *left crossing*, when the %K line crosses prior to the peak of the %D line.
2. The *right crossing*, when the %K line occurs after the peak of the %D line.

Lane suggests using only the right intersection trading signals.

THE SLOW STOCHASTICS

The slower version of the stochastics is popular among many traders, as they believe that the signals are more accurate. The new slow %K line con-

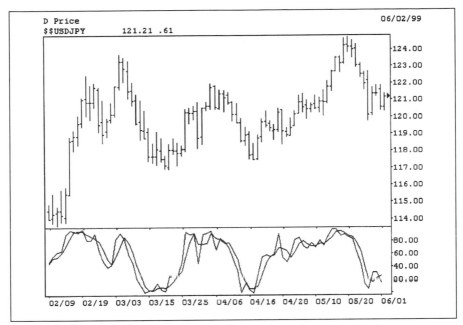

Figure 26.1. An example of the fast stochastic study. *(Source: Bridge Information Systems, Inc.)*

sists of the original %D line. The new slow %D line formula is calculated off the new %K line. (See Figure 26.2.)

A Trader's Point of View

It is important to remember that the scale of the stochastics ranges from 0 to 100. As the %K line reaches the extremes of the scale, it should not be interpreted to mean that the currency will necessarily reverse in the immediate period. The currency will indeed reverse, but it may do so at any time between the next day and the next several days (in the case of a daily chart). This is important to remember, since most traders have loss-limit constraints that may inadvertently be triggered in the very short run. The correct price reaction, even a day later, may offer little comfort and sympathy.

MOVING AVERAGE CONVERGENCE-DIVERGENCE

The *moving average convergence-divergence (MACD)* oscillator, developed by Gerald Appel, is built on exponentially smoothed moving aver-

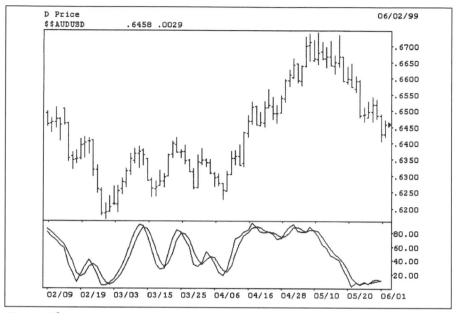

Figure 26.2. An example of slow stochastics. *(Source: Bridge Information Systems, Inc.)*

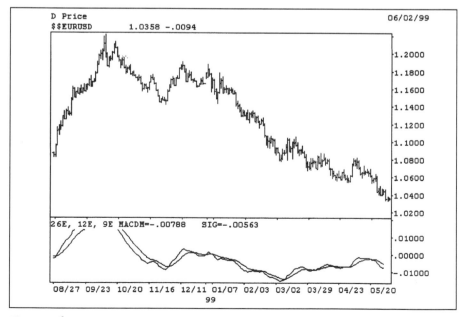

Figure 26.3. An example of MACD. *(Source: Bridge Information Systems, Inc.)*

ages. The MACD consists of two exponential moving averages that are plotted against the zero line. The zero line represents the times the values of the two moving averages are identical.

In addition to the signals generated by the averages' intersection with the zero line and by divergence, additional signals occur as the shorter average line intersects the longer average line. The buying signal is displayed by an upward crossover, and the selling signal by a downward crossover. (See Figure 26.3.)

MOMENTUM

Momentum is an oscillator designed to measure the rate of price change, not the actual price level. This oscillator consists of the net difference between the current closing price and the oldest closing price from a predetermined period.

The formula for calculating the momentum (M) is:

$$M = CCP - OCP$$

where

CCP = current closing price

OCP = old closing price for the predetermined period

The new values thus obtained will be either positive or negative numbers, and they will be plotted around the zero line. At extreme positive values, momentum suggests an overbought condition, whereas at extreme negative values, the indication is an oversold condition. (See Figure 26.4.) The momentum is measured on an open scale around the zero line.

This may create potential problems when a trader must figure out exactly what an extreme overbought or oversold condition means. On the simplest level, the relativity of the situation may be addressed by analyzing the previous historical data and determining the approximate levels that delineate the extremes.

In terms of time frame, needless to say, the shorter the number of days included in the calculations, the more responsive the momentum will be to short-term fluctuations, and vice versa.

The signals triggered by the crossing of the zero line remain in effect. However, they should be followed only when they are consistent with the ongoing trend.

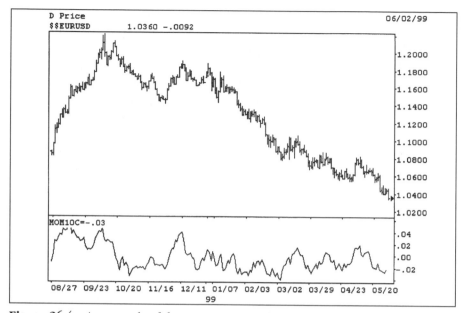

Figure 26.4. An example of the momentum oscillator. *(Source: Bridge Information Systems, Inc.)*

THE RELATIVE STRENGTH INDEX (RSI)

The *relative strength index* is a popular oscillator devised by Welles Wilder. The RSI measures the relative changes between the higher and lower closing prices. (See Figure 26.5)

The formula for calculating the RSI is:

$$RSI = 100 - [100/(1 + RS)]$$

where

RS = (average of X days up closes/average of X days down closes)

X = predetermined number of days

The original number of days, as used by its author, was 14 days. Currently, a 9-day period is more popular.

The RSI is plotted on a 0 to 100 scale. The 70 and 30 values are used as warning signals, whereas values above 85 indicate an overbought condition (selling signal) and values under 15 indicate an oversold condition (buying signal.) Wilder identified the RSI's forte as its divergence versus the underlying price.

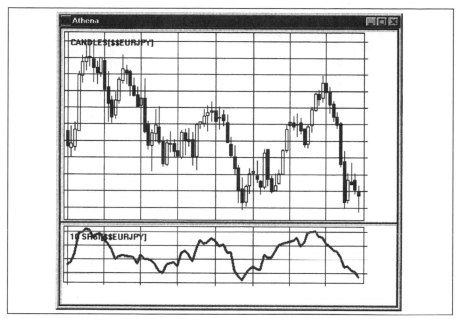

Figure 26.5. An example of the relative strength index (RSI). *(Source: Bridge Information Systems, Inc.)*

OTHER OSCILLATORS

Rate of Change (ROC)

The *rate of change* is another version of the momentum oscillator. The difference consists in the fact that, while the momentum's formula is based on subtracting the oldest closing price from the most recent, the ROC's formula is based on dividing the oldest closing price into the most recent one. (See Figure 26.6)

$$ROC = (CCP/OCP) * 100$$

where

CCP = current closing price

OCP = old closing price for the predetermined period

In the case of the ROC, the former zero line becomes the 100 line. The standard momentum rules of interpretation apply.

Larry Williams %R

The *Larry Williams %R* is a version of the stochastics oscillator. It consists of the difference between the high price of a predetermined number of days

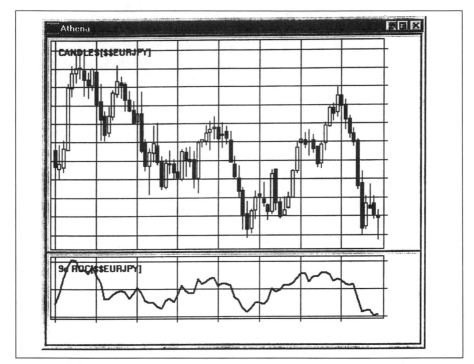

Figure 26.6. An example of the rate of change (ROC) oscillator. *(Source: Bridge Information Systems, Inc.)*

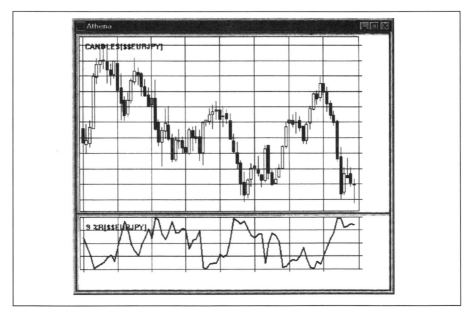

Figure 26.7. An example of the Larry Williams %R oscillator. *(Source: Bridge Information Systems, Inc.)*

and the current closing price, which difference in turn is divided by the total range. This oscillator is plotted on a reversed 0 to 100 scale. Therefore, the bullish reversal signals occur at under 80 percent, and the bearish signals appear at above 20 percent. The interpretations are similar to those discussed under stochastics. (See Figure 26.7.)

Commodity Channel Index (CCI)

The *commodity channel index* (*CCI*) was developed by Donald Lambert. It consists of the difference between the mean price of the currency and the average of the mean price over a predetermined period of time. A buying signal is generated when the price exceeds the upper (+100) line, and a selling signal occurs when the price dips under the lower (−100) line. (See Figure 26.8.)

Swing Index (SI)

The *swing index* (*SI*) is an oscillator developed by Welles Wilder. This momentum is plotted on a scale of 2100 to 1100. The spikes reaching the extremes suggest reversal.

Accumulation Swing Index (ASI)

The *accumulation swing index* (*ASI*) is based on the swing index (SI.) A buying signal is generated when the daily high exceeds the previous SI significant high, and a selling signal occurs when the daily low dips under the significant SI low.

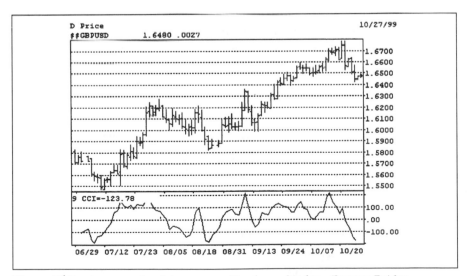

Figure 26.8. An example of the commodity channel index. *(Source: Bridge Information Systems, Inc.)*

Trix Index

The *Trix index* was devised by Jack Hutson. As analyzed by Martin Pring, it consists of a one-day ROC calculation of a triple exponentially smoothed moving average of the closing price. This momentum oscillator may be plotted in several ways. Because we do not have the space to analyze it here, I will only mention that it is useful either for indicating that a minor downward move following the completion of a chart formation means a reversal of the uptrend, or for indicating that its own top reversal is a warning that a head-and-shoulders formation will have an extended lower target.

OSCILLATORS WRAP-UP

Oscillators are favorite tools among traders. Some use them as the "main dish," and take the majority of their trading signals from oscillators. However, most traders use them as a "side dish," and try to avoid acting prematurely on a reversal signal. Regardless of the importance each individual trader attaches to them, oscillators are vital to the continuous search for more accurate technical forecasting.

STUDIES

BOLLINGER BANDS

The *Bollinger bands*, named after John Bollinger, combine a moving average with the instrument's volatility. The bands were designed to gauge whether prices are high or low on a relative basis via volatility. The two are plotted two standard deviations above and below a 20-day simple moving average.

The bands look a lot like an expanding and contracting envelope model. When the band contracts drastically, the signal is that volatility is low and thus likely to expand in the near future. An additional signal is a succession of two top formations, one outside the band followed by one inside. If it occurs above the band, it is a selling signal. When it occurs below the band, it is a buying signal. (See Figure 26.9.)

THE PARABOLIC SYSTEM (SAR)

This is another technical tool designed by Welles Wilder. The *parabolic system* is a stop-loss system based on price and time. The system was devised to supplement the inadvertent gaps of the other trend-following sys-

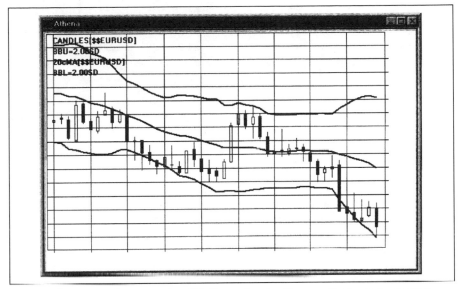

Figure 26.9. A market example of Bollinger bands. *(Source: Bridge Information Systems, Inc.)*

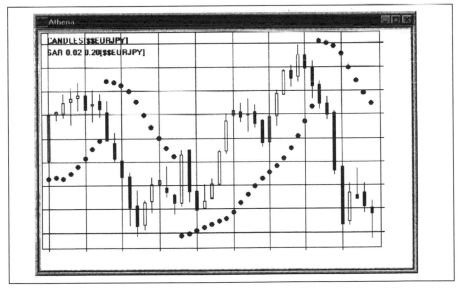

Figure 26.10. An example of the SAR parabolic study. *(Source: Bridge Information Systems, Inc.)*

tems. Although not technically an oscillator, the parabolic system can be used with oscillators.

SAR stands for *stop and reverse*. The stop moves daily in the direction of the new trend. The built-in acceleration factor pushes the SAR to catch up with the currency price. If the new trend fails, the SAR signal will be generated.

The name of the system is derived from its parabolic shape, which follows the price gyrations. It is represented by a dotted line. When the parabola is placed under the price, it suggests a long position. Conversely, when placed above the price, the parabola indicates a short position. (See Figure 26.10.)

SAR performs well in trending markets, but it is not quite reliable in trading ranges. John Murphy suggests as a possible solution another device from Welles Wilder: the directional movement index.

THE DIRECTIONAL MOVEMENT INDEX (DMI)

The *directional movement index* provides a signal of trend presence in the market. The line simply rates the price directional movement on a scale of

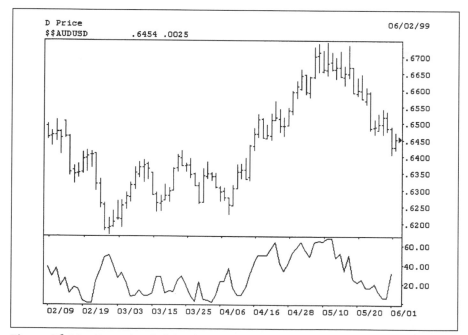

Figure 26.11. Example of of the directional movement index (DMI). *(Source: Bridge Information Systems, Inc.)*

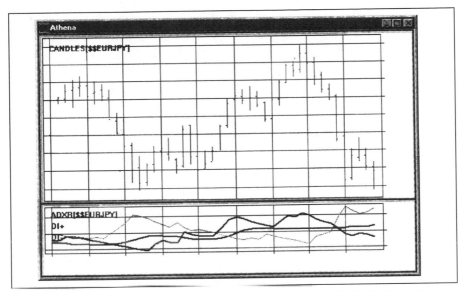

Figure 26.12. Example of ADXR with +DI and −DI. *(Source: Bridge Information Systems, Inc.)*

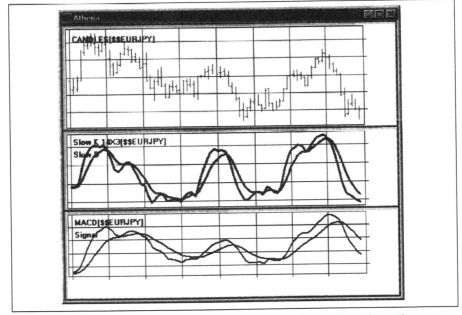

Figure 26.13. Example of oscillator combinations used for daily trading. *(Source: Bridge Information Systems, Inc.)*

0 to 100. The higher the number, the better the trend potential of a movement, and vice versa. (See Figures 26.11 and 26.12.) This system can be
used by itself or as a filter to the SAR system. DMI is beyond the scope of
our discussion here, but is described in full detail by Welles Wilder in *New
Concepts in Technical Analysis*, by John Murphy in *Technical Analysis of
the Futures Markets*, and by Martin Pring in *Market Momentum*.

Traders use different combinations of technical tools in their daily trading and analysis. Some of the more popular oscillators are the stochastics and
the MACD, as shown in Figure 26.13, and the relative strength index, the fast
and slow stochastics, and the MACD, as shown in Figure 26.14.

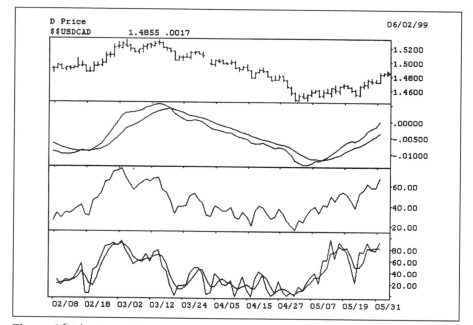

Figure 26.14. Example of oscillator combinations used for daily trading. *(Source:
Bridge Information Systems, Inc.)*

27 W. D. Gann Analysis

One of the most influential approaches to technical analysis was developed by William D. Gann (1878–1955), the eminent stock and commodity trader. The Gann analysis is a complex approach based on traditional chart formations. His mathematical approach to technical analysis generates unique trading signals.

The most important features of Gann analysis are:

1. the cardinal square,
2. the squaring of price and time, and
3. geometric angles.

THE CARDINAL SQUARE

The *cardinal square* is a technique for forecasting future significant chart points by counting from the all-time low price of the currency. It consists of a square divided by a cross into four quadrants. The all-time low price is housed in the center of the cross. All of the following higher prices are entered in clockwise order. The numbers positioned in the cardinal cross are the most significant chart points because they are 50-pip pivot points.

Let's take the example of the 124.00 50-pip pivot point in dollar/yen at a time when the spot rate is 123.35. A rally should be thwarted at 124.00, and the downside target is 123.50. However, if this level is penetrated on good volume, the currency is likely to rally to 124.50, its upside target. Figure 27.1 shows an application of the cardinal square to the U.S. dollar/Japanese yen.

150.05	150.10	150.15	150.20	150.25	150.30	150.35	150.40	150.45	150.50	150.55	150.60	150.65	150.70	150.75	150.80	150.85	150.90	150.95	151.00	151.05	151.10	151.15	151.20	151.25	151.30	151.35	151.40	151.45	151.50	151.55	151.60	151.65	151.70	151.75	151.80	151.85	151.90
150.00	142.75	142.80	142.85	142.90	142.95	143.00	143.05	143.10	143.15	143.20	143.25	143.30	143.35	143.40	143.45	143.50	143.55	143.60	143.65	143.70	143.75	143.80	143.85	143.90	143.95	144.00	144.05	144.10	144.15	144.20	144.25	144.30	144.35	144.40	144.45	144.50	144.55
149.95	142.70	135.85	135.90	135.95	136.00	136.05	136.10	136.15	136.20	136.25	136.30	136.35	136.40	136.45	136.50	136.55	136.60	136.65	136.70	136.75	136.80	136.85	136.90	136.95	137.00	137.05	137.10	137.15	137.20	137.25	137.30	137.35	137.40	137.45	137.50	137.55	144.60
149.90	142.65	135.80	129.35	129.40	129.45	129.50	129.55	129.60	129.65	129.70	129.75	129.80	129.85	129.90	129.95	130.00	130.05	130.10	130.15	130.20	130.25	130.30	130.35	130.40	130.45	130.50	130.55	130.60	130.65	130.70	130.75	130.80	130.85	130.90	130.95	137.60	144.65
149.85	142.60	135.75	129.30	123.25	123.30	123.35	123.40	123.45	123.50	123.55	123.60	123.65	123.70	123.75	123.80	123.85	123.90	123.95	124.00	124.05	124.10	124.15	124.20	124.25	124.30	124.35	124.40	124.45	124.50	124.55	124.60	124.65	124.70	124.75	131.00	137.65	144.70
149.80	142.55	135.70	129.25	123.20	117.55	117.60	117.65	117.70	117.75	117.80	117.85	117.90	117.95	118.00	118.05	118.10	118.15	118.20	118.25	118.30	118.35	118.40	118.45	118.50	118.55	118.60	118.65	118.70	118.75	118.80	118.85	118.90	118.95	124.80	131.05	137.70	144.75
149.75	142.50	135.65	129.20	123.15	117.50	112.25	112.30	112.35	112.40	112.45	112.50	112.55	112.60	112.65	112.70	112.75	112.80	112.85	112.90	112.95	113.00	113.05	113.10	113.15	113.20	113.25	113.30	113.35	113.40	113.45	113.50	113.55	119.00	124.85	131.10	137.75	144.80
149.70	142.45	135.60	129.15	123.10	117.45	112.20	107.35	107.40	107.45	107.50	107.55	107.60	107.65	107.70	107.75	107.80	107.85	107.90	107.95	108.00	108.05	108.10	108.15	108.20	108.25	108.30	108.35	108.40	108.45	108.50	108.55	113.60	119.05	124.90	131.15	137.80	144.85
149.65	142.40	135.55	129.10	123.05	117.40	112.15	107.30	102.85	102.90	102.95	103.00	103.05	103.10	103.15	103.20	103.25	103.30	103.35	103.40	103.45	103.50	103.55	103.60	103.65	103.70	103.75	103.80	103.85	103.90	103.95	108.60	113.65	119.10	124.95	131.20	137.85	144.90
149.60	142.35	135.50	129.05	123.00	117.35	112.10	107.25	102.80	98.75	98.80	98.85	98.90	98.95	99.00	99.05	99.10	99.15	99.20	99.25	99.30	99.35	99.40	99.45	99.50	99.55	99.60	99.65	99.70	99.75	104.00	108.65	113.70	119.15	125.00	131.25	137.90	144.95
149.55	142.30	135.45	129.00	122.95	117.30	112.05	107.20	102.75	98.70	95.05	95.10	95.15	95.20	95.25	95.30	95.35	95.40	95.45	95.50	95.55	95.60	95.65	95.70	95.75	95.80	95.85	95.90	95.95	99.80	104.05	108.70	113.75	119.20	125.05	131.30	137.95	145.00
149.50	142.25	135.40	128.95	122.90	117.25	112.00	107.15	102.70	98.65	95.00	91.75	91.80	91.85	91.90	91.95	92.00	92.05	92.10	92.15	92.20	92.25	92.30	92.35	92.40	92.45	92.50	92.55	96.00	99.85	104.10	108.75	113.80	119.25	125.10	131.35	138.00	145.05
149.45	142.20	135.35	128.90	122.85	117.20	111.95	107.10	102.65	98.60	94.95	91.70	88.85	88.90	88.95	89.00	89.05	89.10	89.15	89.20	89.25	89.30	89.35	89.40	89.45	89.50	89.55	92.60	96.05	99.90	104.15	108.80	113.85	119.30	125.15	131.40	138.05	145.10
149.40	142.15	135.30	128.85	122.80	117.15	111.90	107.05	102.60	98.55	94.90	91.65	88.80	86.35	86.40	86.45	86.50	86.55	86.60	86.65	86.70	86.75	86.80	86.85	86.90	86.95	89.60	92.65	96.10	99.95	104.20	108.85	113.90	119.35	125.20	131.45	138.10	145.15
149.35	142.10	135.25	128.80	122.75	117.10	111.85	107.00	102.55	98.50	94.85	91.60	88.75	86.30	84.25	84.30	84.35	84.40	84.45	84.50	84.55	84.60	84.65	84.70	84.75	87.00	89.65	92.70	96.15	100.00	104.25	108.90	113.95	119.40	125.25	131.50	138.15	145.20
149.30	142.05	135.20	128.75	122.70	117.05	111.80	106.95	102.50	98.45	94.80	91.55	88.70	86.25	84.20	82.55	82.60	82.65	82.70	82.75	82.80	82.85	82.90	82.95	84.80	87.05	89.70	92.75	96.20	100.05	104.30	108.95	114.00	119.45	125.30	131.55	138.20	145.25
149.25	142.00	135.15	128.70	122.65	117.00	111.75	106.90	102.45	98.40	94.75	91.50	88.65	86.20	84.15	82.50	81.25	81.30	81.35	81.40	81.45	81.50	81.55	83.00	84.85	87.10	89.75	92.80	96.25	100.10	104.35	109.00	114.05	119.50	125.35	131.60	138.25	145.30
149.20	141.95	135.10	128.65	122.60	116.95	111.70	106.85	102.40	98.35	94.70	91.45	88.60	86.15	84.10	82.45	81.20	80.35	80.40	80.45	80.50	80.55	81.60	83.05	84.90	87.15	89.80	92.85	96.30	100.15	104.40	109.05	114.10	119.55	125.40	131.65	138.30	145.35
149.15	141.90	135.05	128.60	122.55	116.90	111.65	106.80	102.35	98.30	94.65	91.40	88.55	86.10	84.05	82.40	81.15	80.30	79.85	79.90	79.95	80.60	81.65	83.10	84.95	87.20	89.85	92.90	96.35	100.20	104.45	109.10	114.15	119.60	125.45	131.70	138.35	145.40
149.10	141.85	135.00	128.55	122.50	116.85	111.60	106.75	102.30	98.25	94.60	91.35	88.50	86.05	84.00	82.35	81.10	80.25	79.80	79.75	80.00	80.65	81.70	83.15	85.00	87.25	89.90	92.95	96.40	100.25	104.50	109.15	114.20	119.65	125.50	131.75	138.40	145.45
149.05	141.80	134.95	128.50	122.45	116.80	111.55	106.70	102.25	98.20	94.55	91.30	88.45	86.00	83.95	82.30	81.05	80.20	80.15	80.10	80.05	80.70	81.75	83.20	85.05	87.30	89.95	93.00	96.45	100.30	104.55	109.20	114.25	119.70	125.55	131.80	138.45	145.50
149.00	141.75	134.90	128.45	122.40	116.75	111.50	106.65	102.20	98.15	94.50	91.25	88.40	85.95	83.90	82.25	81.00	80.95	80.90	80.85	80.80	80.75	81.80	83.25	85.10	87.35	90.00	93.05	96.50	100.35	104.60	109.25	114.30	119.75	125.60	131.85	138.50	145.55
148.95	141.70	134.85	128.40	122.35	116.70	111.45	106.60	102.15	98.10	94.45	91.20	88.35	85.90	83.85	82.20	82.15	82.10	82.05	82.00	81.95	81.90	81.85	83.30	85.15	87.40	90.05	93.10	96.55	100.40	104.65	109.30	114.35	119.80	125.65	131.90	138.55	145.60
148.90	141.65	134.80	128.35	122.30	116.65	111.40	106.55	102.10	98.05	94.40	91.15	88.30	85.85	83.80	83.75	83.70	83.65	83.60	83.55	83.50	83.45	83.40	83.35	85.20	87.45	90.10	93.15	96.60	100.45	104.70	109.35	114.40	119.85	125.70	131.95	138.60	145.65
148.85	141.60	134.75	128.30	122.25	116.60	111.35	106.50	102.05	98.00	94.35	91.10	88.25	85.80	85.75	85.70	85.65	85.60	85.55	85.50	85.45	85.40	85.35	85.30	85.25	87.50	90.15	93.20	96.65	100.50	104.75	109.40	114.45	119.90	125.75	132.00	138.65	145.70
148.80	141.55	134.70	128.25	122.20	116.55	111.30	106.45	102.00	97.95	94.30	91.05	88.20	88.15	88.10	88.05	88.00	87.95	87.90	87.85	87.80	87.75	87.70	87.65	87.60	87.55	90.20	93.25	96.70	100.55	104.80	109.45	114.50	119.95	125.80	132.05	138.70	145.75
148.75	141.50	134.65	128.20	122.15	116.50	111.25	106.40	101.95	97.90	94.25	91.00	90.95	90.90	90.85	90.80	90.75	90.70	90.65	90.60	90.55	90.50	90.45	90.40	90.35	90.30	90.25	93.30	96.75	100.60	104.85	109.50	114.55	120.00	125.85	132.10	138.75	145.80
148.70	141.45	134.60	128.15	122.10	116.45	111.20	106.35	101.90	97.85	94.20	94.15	94.10	94.05	94.00	93.95	93.90	93.85	93.80	93.75	93.70	93.65	93.60	93.55	93.50	93.45	93.40	93.35	96.80	100.65	104.90	109.55	114.60	120.05	125.90	132.15	138.80	145.85
148.65	141.40	134.55	128.10	122.05	116.40	111.15	106.30	101.85	97.80	97.75	97.70	97.65	97.60	97.55	97.50	97.45	97.40	97.35	97.30	97.25	97.20	97.15	97.10	97.05	97.00	96.95	96.90	96.85	100.70	104.95	109.60	114.65	120.10	125.95	132.20	138.85	145.90
148.60	141.35	134.50	128.05	122.00	116.35	111.10	106.25	101.80	101.75	101.70	101.65	101.60	101.55	101.50	101.45	101.40	101.35	101.30	101.25	101.20	101.15	101.10	101.05	101.00	100.95	100.90	100.85	100.80	100.75	105.00	109.65	114.70	120.15	126.00	132.25	138.90	145.95
148.55	141.30	134.45	128.00	121.95	116.30	111.05	106.20	106.15	106.10	106.05	106.00	105.95	105.90	105.85	105.80	105.75	105.70	105.65	105.60	105.55	105.50	105.45	105.40	105.35	105.30	105.25	105.20	105.15	105.10	105.05	109.70	114.75	120.20	126.05	132.30	138.95	146.00
148.50	141.25	134.40	127.95	121.90	116.25	111.00	110.95	110.90	110.85	110.80	110.75	110.70	110.65	110.60	110.55	110.50	110.45	110.40	110.35	110.30	110.25	110.20	110.15	110.10	110.05	110.00	109.95	109.90	109.85	109.80	109.75	114.80	120.25	126.10	132.35	139.00	146.05
148.45	141.20	134.35	127.90	121.85	116.20	116.15	116.10	116.05	116.00	115.95	115.90	115.85	115.80	115.75	115.70	115.65	115.60	115.55	115.50	115.45	115.40	115.35	115.30	115.25	115.20	115.15	115.10	115.05	115.00	114.95	114.90	114.85	120.30	126.15	132.40	139.05	146.10
148.40	141.15	134.30	127.85	121.80	121.75	121.70	121.65	121.60	121.55	121.50	121.45	121.40	121.35	121.30	121.25	121.20	121.15	121.10	121.05	121.00	120.95	120.90	120.85	120.80	120.75	120.70	120.65	120.60	120.55	120.50	120.45	120.40	120.35	126.20	132.45	139.10	146.15
148.35	141.10	134.25	127.80	127.75	127.70	127.65	127.60	127.55	127.50	127.45	127.40	127.35	127.30	127.25	127.20	127.15	127.10	127.05	127.00	126.95	126.90	126.85	126.80	126.75	126.70	126.65	126.60	126.55	126.50	126.45	126.40	126.35	126.30	126.25	132.50	139.15	146.20
148.30	141.05	134.20	134.15	134.10	134.05	134.00	133.95	133.90	133.85	133.80	133.75	133.70	133.65	133.60	133.55	133.50	133.45	133.40	133.35	133.30	133.25	133.20	133.15	133.10	133.05	133.00	132.95	132.90	132.85	132.80	132.75	132.70	132.65	132.60	132.55	139.20	146.25
148.25	141.00	140.95	140.90	140.85	140.80	140.75	140.70	140.65	140.60	140.55	140.50	140.45	140.40	140.35	140.30	140.25	140.20	140.15	140.10	140.05	140.00	139.95	139.90	139.85	139.80	139.75	139.70	139.65	139.60	139.55	139.50	139.45	139.40	139.35	139.30	139.25	146.30
148.20	148.15	148.10	148.05	148.00	147.95	147.90	147.85	147.80	147.75	147.70	147.65	147.60	147.55	147.50	147.45	147.40	147.35	147.30	147.25	147.20	147.15	147.10	147.05	147.00	146.95	146.90	146.85	146.80	146.75	146.70	146.65	146.60	146.55	146.50	146.45	146.40	146.35

Figure 27.1. Application of the Gann cardinal square to the U.S. dollar/Japanese yen. *(Source: © Copyright 1995 Cornelius Luca)*

THE SQUARING OF PRICE AND TIME

In his analysis, Gann used basic forms of geometry such as the square, the circle, and the triangle. The concept of 360 degrees is a staple in his time analysis. In order to reach his time targets, he counted forward from the significant chart points by 30, 90, 120, 180, and 360. These forward days are potential reversal days. In addition, Gann considered 7 a significant number.

The squaring of price and time refers to Gann's technique of converting a significant commodity dollar price into time units (from days to years) and adding these time periods to the day the significant price was reached. When the time targets were reached, time and price were squared, and the market was likely to reverse.

GEOMETRIC ANGLES

Gann divided price movements into both thirds and eighths, the same percentages he used to calculate price retracements. The resulting percentages are:

1/8	12.5%
2/8	25%
1/3	33.3%
3/8	37.5%
4/8	50%
5/8	62.5%
2/3	66.6%
6/8	75%
7/8	87.5%

The most important number is 50; the other numbers' importance decreases symmetrically on the upper and lower side. The 33.3 percent, 50 percent, and 66.3 percent levels coincide with the retracement percentages from the Dow Theory; and the 37.5 percent and 62.5 percent levels coincide with Fibonacci retracement ratios.

The geometric angles are trendlines drawn from significant highs and lows at specific angles. (See Figures 27.2 and 27.3.) As mentioned in Chapter 19, the most important one is the 45° angle. A currency divergence from the 45° line signals a change in the trend.

The 45° angle is the result of a combination of price and time ratio of 1 × 1. Steeper trendlines are determined by a ratio of 1 × 2, 1 × 3, 1 × 4, and 1 × 8. Due to their steepness, they have little applicability. Flatter fan lines are determined by price and time ratios of 2 × 1, 3 × 1, 4 × 1, and 8 × 1. These lines work in the same manner as the speedlines. The penetration of one line suggests that the price will move to the next line. They tend to work best on medium- and long-term charts.

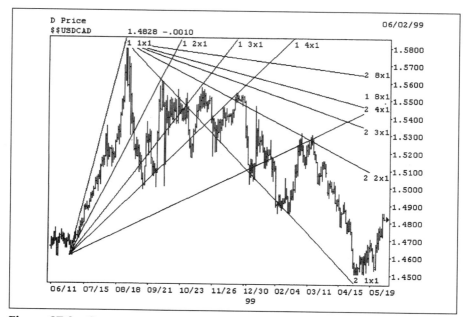

Figure 27.2. Gann geometric angles. *(Source: Bridge Information Systems, Inc.)*

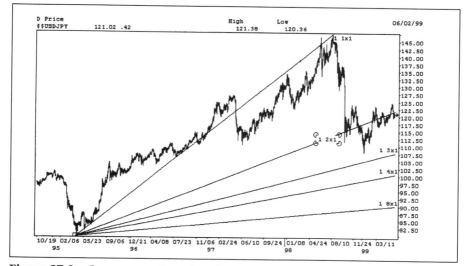

Figure 27.3. Gann geometric angles. *(Source: Bridge Information Systems, Inc.)*

28 The Elliott Wave

R alph Nelson Elliott (1871–1948) developed his approach to technical analysis in the latter part of a life he spent as an accountant.
Elliott discovered—through an exhaustive study of the DJIA—that
the ever-changing stock market reflects a basic harmony found in nature.
From this discovery, he developed a rational system of stock market analysis. He postulated that price movements in financial markets are repetitive
in form but not necessarily in time or amplitude, and he claimed predictive
value for what is now called the *Elliott Wave Principle*.

In essence, the Elliott Wave Principle is a system of empirically derived rules for interpreting action in the markets. It is a tool of unique
value, whose most striking characteristics are generality and accuracy. Its
generality gives market perspective most of the time, and its accuracy in
identifying changes in direction is at times remarkable. For the trader, it is
important to know that the rules of wave analysis have stood the test of
time and that market action can be understood usefully within the context
of Elliott's principles.

BASICS OF WAVE ANALYSIS

The basic objective of wave analysis is to follow and interpret correctly the
development of patterns in the markets. The Wave Principle's rules and
guidelines provide an objective basis both for making these interpretations
and for trading signals.

In a series of articles published in 1939 by *Financial World* magazine,
Elliott pointed out that the stock market unfolds according to a basic
rhythm or pattern of five waves in the direction of the trend at one larger
scale and three waves against that trend. In a rising market, this five-

wave/three-wave pattern forms one complete bull market/bear market cycle of eight waves. The five-wave upward movement as a whole is referred to as an *impulse wave*, while the three-wave countertrend movement is described as a *corrective wave*. This basic structure is illustrated in Figure 28.1.

Within the five-wave bull move, waves 1, 3, and 5 are themselves impulse waves, subdividing into five waves of smaller scale; while waves 2 and 4 are corrective waves, subdividing into three smaller waves each. As shown in Figure 28.1, subwaves of impulse sequences are labeled with numbers, while subwaves of corrections are labeled with letters.

Following the cycle shown in the illustration, a second five-wave upside movement begins, followed by another three-wave correction, followed by one more five-wave upmove. This sequence of movements constitutes a five-wave impulse pattern at one larger degree of trend, and a three-wave corrective movement at the same scale must follow. Figure 28.2 shows this larger-scale pattern in detail. As the illustration shows, waves of any degree in any series can be subdivided and resubdivided into waves of smaller degree or expanded into waves of larger degree. This structure is an example of "fractal" geometry, incorporating self-similarity and scaling symmetry, and is consistent with numerous scientific insights into the nature of growth and evolution.

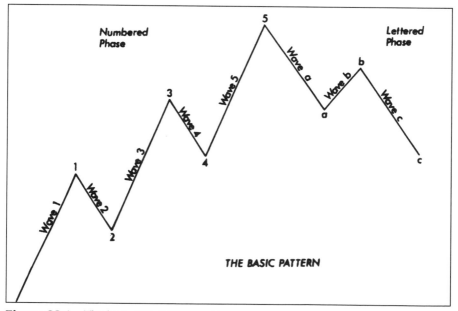

Figure 28.1. The basic Elliott Wave pattern.

Three essential rules govern the interpretation of these patterns:

1. A second wave may never retrace more than 100 percent of a first wave; for example, in a bull market, the low of the second wave may not go below the beginning of the first wave.
2. The third wave is never the shortest wave in an impulse sequence; often, it is the longest (see Extensions in the next section).
3. A fourth wave can never enter the price range of a first wave, except in one specific type of wave pattern (see the section on Diagonal Triangles).

Overall, the form of market movements is essentially the same, irrespective of the size or duration of the movements. Furthermore, smaller-scale movements link up to create larger-scale movements possessing the same basic form. Conversely, large-scale movements consist of smaller-scale subdivisions with which they share a geometric similarity. Because these movements link up in increments of five waves and three waves, they generate sequences of numbers that the analyst can use (along with the rules of wave formation) to help identify the current state of pattern development, as shown in Figure 28.3.

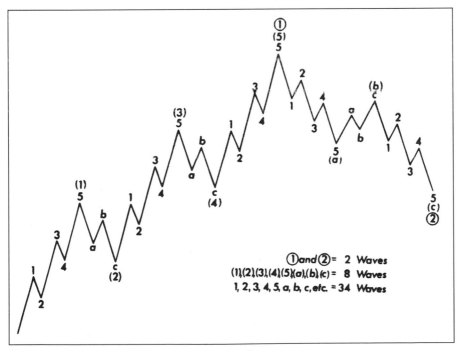

Figure 28.2. The larger scale pattern in detail.

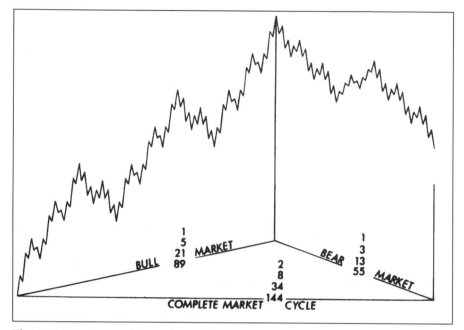

Figure 28.3. A complete market cycle.

IMPULSE WAVES—VARIATIONS

EXTENSIONS

In any given five-wave sequence, a tendency exists for one of the three impulse subwaves (i.e., wave 1, wave 3, or wave 5) to be an *extension*—an
elongated movement, usually with internal subdivisions. At times, these
subdivisions are of nearly the same amplitude and duration as the larger degree waves of the main impulse sequence, giving a total count of nine
waves of similar size rather than the normal count of five for the main sequence. In a nine-wave sequence, it is sometimes difficult to identify which
wave is extended. However, this is usually irrelevant, because a count of
nine and a count of five have the same technical significance. Figure 28.4
shows why this is so; examples of extensions in various wave positions
make it clear that the overall significance is the same in each case.

Extensions can provide a useful guide to the lengths of future waves.
Most impulse sequences contain extensions in only one of their three impulsive subwaves. Thus, if the first and third waves are of about the same
magnitude, the fifth wave probably will be extended, especially if volume
during the fifth wave is greater than during the third. On the other hand, if

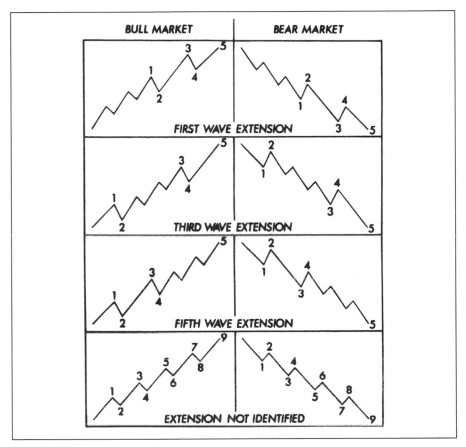

Figure 28.4. Wave extensions.

wave three has already extended, wave five should simply be constructed and should resemble wave one.

Extensions can also occur within extensions. Although extended fifth waves are not uncommon, extensions of extensions occur most often within third waves, as shown in Figure 28.5.

DIAGONAL TRIANGLES

Two types of diagonal triangle have been identified. Both types are found relatively rarely, and each has highly specific implications for future market movements. (These formations should not be confused with the more common corrective triangles found in fourth-wave positions within im-

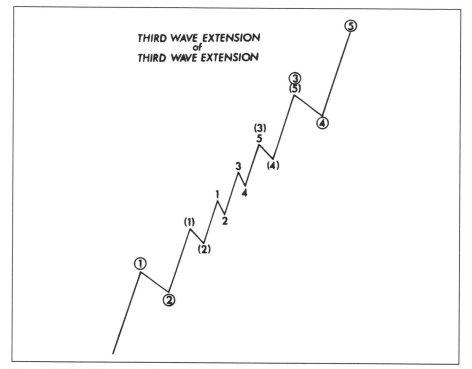

Figure 28.5. Wave extensions.

pulse waves and B-wave positions within corrections; see Corrective Waves in the next section.)

The diagonal triangle type 1 occurs only in fifth waves and in C waves, and it signals that the preceding move has "gone too far, too fast," as Elliott put it. Essentially a rising wedge formation defined by two converging trendlines, type 1 diagonal triangles indicate exhaustion of the larger movement. Unlike other impulse waves, all of the patterns' subwaves, including waves 1, 3, and 5, consist of three-wave movements, and their fourth waves often enter the price range of their first waves, as shown in Figures 28.6 and 28.7.

A rising diagonal triangle type 1 is bearish, because it is usually followed by a sharp decline, at least to the level where the formation began. In contrast, a falling diagonal type 1 is bullish, because an upward thrust usually follows.

The diagonal triangle type 2 occurs even more rarely than type 1. This pattern, found in first-wave or A-wave positions in very rare cases, re-

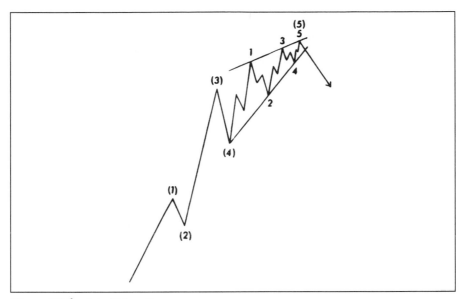

Figure 28.6. A bullish pattern.

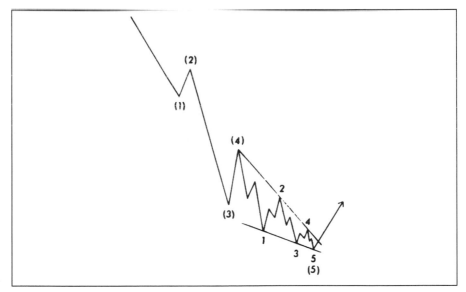

Figure 28.7. A bearish pattern.

sembles a diagonal type 1 in that it is defined by converging trendlines and its first wave and fourth wave overlap, as shown in Figure 28.8. However, it differs significantly from type 1 in that its impulsive subwaves (waves 1, 3, and 5) are normal, five-wave impulse waves, in contrast to the three-wave subwaves of type 1. This is consistent with the message of the type 2 diagonal triangle, which signals continuation of the underlying trend, in contrast to the type 1's message of termination of the larger trend.

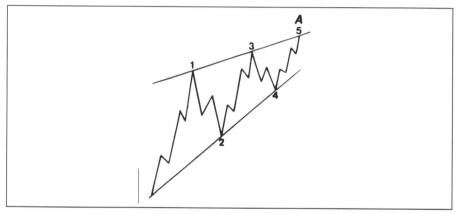

Figure 28.8.

FAILURES (TRUNCATED FIFTHS)

Elliott used the word *failure* to describe an impulse pattern in which the extreme of the fifth wave fails to exceed the extreme of the third wave. Figures 28.9 and 28.10 show examples of failures in bull and bear markets. As the illustrations show, the truncated fifth wave contains the necessary impulsive (i.e., five-wave) substructure to complete the larger movement. However, its failure to surpass the previous impulse wave's extreme signals weakness in the underlying trend, and a sharp reversal usually follows.

CORRECTIVE WAVES

Stock market swings of any degree tend to move more easily *with* the trend of one larger degree than *against* it. As a result, corrective waves can be highly complex and "choppy" and often are difficult to interpret precisely until they are finished. Thus, the terminations of corrective waves are less predictable than those of impulse waves, and the wave analyst must exercise greater caution when the market is in a meandering, corrective mood than when prices are in a clearly impulsive trend. Moreover, while only three main types of impulse wave exist, there are a total of ten basic corrective wave patterns, and all can link up to form extended corrections of great complexity.

The single most important thing to remember about corrections is that they can never be "fives." Only impulse waves can be fives. Thus, an initial five-wave movement against the larger trend is never a complete correction, but only part of it.

Corrective patterns fall into four main categories:

1. zigzags (5-3-5);
2. flats (3-3-5);
3. triangles (3-3-3-3-3); and
4. combined structures.

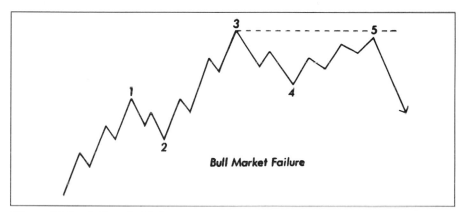

Figure 28.9. Bull market failure.

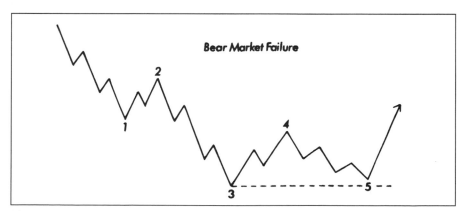

Figure 28.10. Bear market failure.

Zigzags

A *zigzag* is a simple three-wave pattern, subdivided into a 5-3-5 structure, in which the extreme of wave B remains a significant distance from the beginning of wave A. Figures 28.11 to 28.14 show examples in bull and bear markets. (A zigzag rally within a bear market is sometimes referred to as an *inverted zigzag*.)

Occasionally, in larger formations, two zigzags can occur in succession, separated by intervening three-wave structures of any type. This produces a *double zigzag*, illustrated in Figure 28.15. Although double zigzags are uncommon, they occur often enough that the analyst should be aware of their existence.

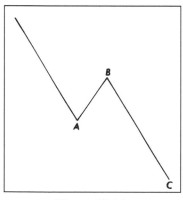

Figure 28.11.

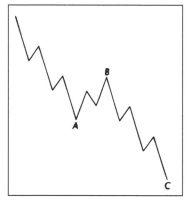

Figure 28.12.

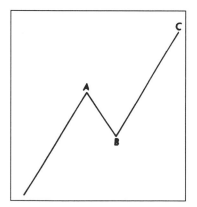

Figure 28.13.

Figure 28.14.

Flats

Flat corrections subdivide as 3-3-5 structures, as shown in Figures 28.16 to 28.19. The initial movement, wave A, seems to lack sufficient force to develop into a full five waves, as in a zigzag. Wave B appears to share this lack of countertrend pressure and often ends at or beyond the start of wave A; and wave C usually terminates near the extreme of wave A, rather than significantly beyond it, as in a zigzag.

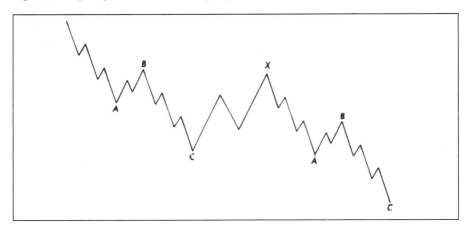

Figure 28.15. Double zigzag.

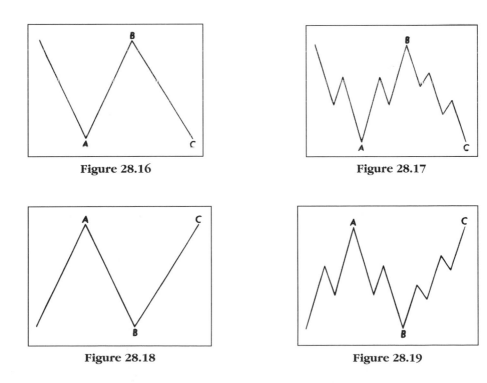

Figure 28.16   **Figure 28.17**

Figure 28.18   **Figure 28.19**

Flat corrections, overall, do less damage than zigzags to the larger trend. They appear to indicate strength underlying the larger trend and thus often precede or follow extensions. As a rule, the longer the flat, the more dynamic the next impulse wave.

Four types of flats have been identified:

1. *Regular*, in which wave B ends at or very slightly beyond the level of the start of wave A, and wave C ends at or slightly beyond the level of the extreme of wave A.

2. *Expanded*, in which wave B significantly exceeds the level of the start of wave A, and wave C significantly exceeds the level of the extreme of wave A. (See Figures 28.20 to 28.23.)

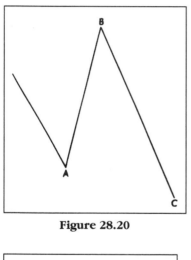

Figure 28.20

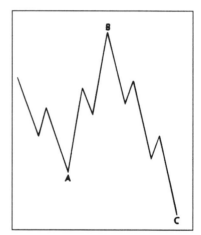

Figure 28.21

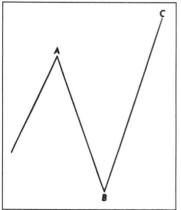

Figure 28.22

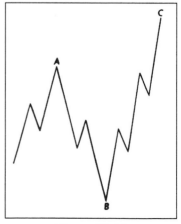

Figure 28.23

3. *Irregular*, in which wave B ends near the start of wave A, as in a regular flat, but wave C fails to move all the way to the extreme of wave A. (See Figures 28.24 to 28.27.)

4. *Running*, a rare formation in which wave B carries well beyond the level of the start of wave A and wave C fails to carry back past that level. In other words, the end of wave C in a downward correction ends above the beginning of wave A, and in an upward correction below the level of the beginning of wave A. (See figure 28.28.)

This formation signals strength in the larger trend and occurs when the market moves so quickly that corrective patterns have no time to develop normally. It is essential that the internal subdivisions of a running correction adhere to the Wave Principle's rules. For example, the B wave must contain only three subwaves and not five, which would probably make it, instead, the first wave of an impulse pattern of the next larger degree.

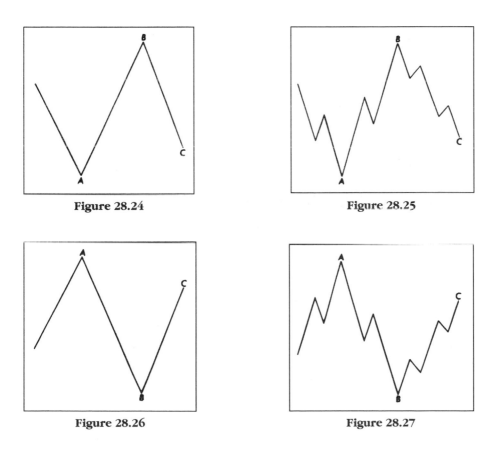

Figure 28.24   Figure 28.25

Figure 28.26   Figure 28.27

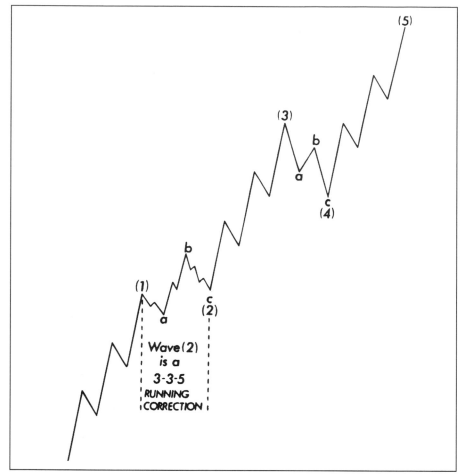

Figure 28.28

Triangles

Generally, triangles occur only in positions just prior to the final movement in the direction of the larger trend. They tend to be protracted and reflect a balance of forces that creates a sideways movement, usually associated with relatively low volume and low volatility. All triangles consist of five waves, labeled A-B-C-D-E, subdivided into three waves each. Four main types exist, as shown in Figure 28.29. (Corrective triangles must not be confused with the impulsive patterns called diagonal triangles. See Impulse Waves—Variations earlier in this chapter.

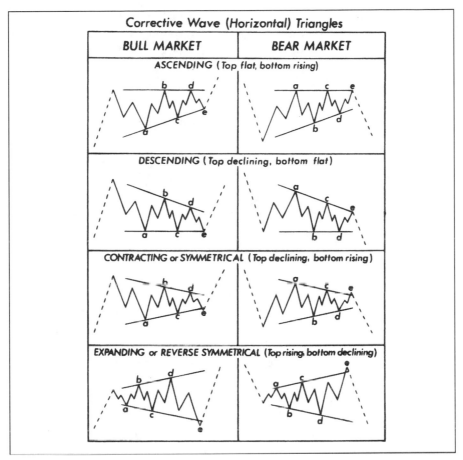

Figure 28.29

The trendlines that contain a triangle usually are highly accurate; that is, touchpoints rarely fall short of or exceed these boundaries. The one exception is wave E, which often overshoots the trendline, especially in expanding and contracting triangles.

After completion of a triangle, the final impulse wave of the larger trend is usually swift and travels a distance approximately equal to the widest part of the triangle. This movement is known as a *thrust*.

Combined Structures
In wave analysis, a zigzag or flat is often referred to as a *three*. Occasionally, these patterns, as well as triangles, may combine into more complex *double three* or *triple three* formations, consisting of two or more

"threes" separated by smaller three-wave movements labeled as X waves. Figures 28.30 and 28.31 illustrate the basic structure of these formations. A double three may consist of a flat, a smaller zigzag forming wave X, and a second flat; or of a zigzag, a smaller flat in wave X, and a second zigzag; or of any similar combination.

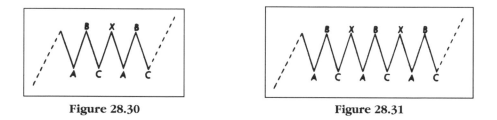

Figure 28.30   **Figure 28.31**

The combined structures appear to reflect hesitation in the market, as if stock prices are waiting for economic fundamentals to catch up with investor expectations. Usually, these formations move generally sideways, although Elliott indicated that the entire formation could slant against the larger trend. Action subsequent to a double or triple three often is quite strong.

As far as has been determined, the formations listed here are all that can be identified in the movements of financial markets. As a result of detailed study of a large number of charts at every conceivable time frame, from 15-minute bar charts covering a few days' action to monthly charts covering nearly three centuries of market history, we are convinced that no other formations exist.

FIBONACCI ANALYSIS

Perhaps Elliott's most important contribution to the study of patterns in the markets was his discovery that movements of the same degree tend to be related to one another by a specific mathematical ratio, known variously as the *Fibonacci ratio*, the *golden ratio*, or *phi*. With this discovery, Elliott was able to place social change, as reflected in the financial markets, into a continuum of evolution reaching from the molecular scale to the cosmological.

The Fibonacci ratio is named after Leonardo Fibonacci of Pisa, an Italian mathematician of the late twelfth and early thirteenth centuries, who introduced Hindu-Arabic numerals to Western Europe in a work titled

Liber Abaci. In the same book, in a problem concerning the dynamics of population growth in rabbits, he introduced an additive numerical series that has come to be called the *Fibonacci sequence* in his honor.

To obtain the Fibonacci sequence, begin with 1 and add 1 to it. Take the sum of this operation (2) and add it to the previous term in the sequence (1). Then take the sum of his second operation (3) and add it to the previous term in the sequence (the sum of the first operation, i.e., 2). Continue iterating in this manner, adding the most recent sum to the previous term, which is itself the sum of the two previous terms, etc. This yields the following series of numbers:

$$1, 1, 2, 3, 5, 8, 13, 21, 34, 55, 89, 144, 233, 377,$$
$$610, 987, 1597, 2584, 4181, (etc.)$$

These numbers exhibit several remarkable relationships, in particular the ratio of any term in the series to the next higher term. This ratio tends asymptotically to 0.618. . . . In addition, the ratio of any term to the next lower term in the sequence tends asymptotically to 1.618, which is the inverse of 0.618. Similarly constant ratios exist between numbers two terms apart, three terms apart, and so on. The ratio 0.618, referred to as the Fibonacci ratio, is an irrational number (i.e., it never resolves to a single solution no matter how many decimal places one carries it to), calculated as

$$\sqrt{5} - 1 / 2 = 0.6180339$$

Because 3 and 5 are Fibonacci numbers (i.e., numbers in the basic Fibonacci sequence), combinations of 3s and 5s will tend to add up to larger Fibonacci numbers. For example, Elliott's basic 5-3-5-3-5 impulse wave sequence adds up to 21, which is a Fibonacci number. Adding a 5-3-5 corrective wave sequence raises the total to 34, which is also a Fibonacci number. Thus, there are Fibonacci numbers and ratios embedded in the number of waves at various degrees.

The Fibonacci ratio underlies the geometry of the logarithmic spiral, a geometric form found widely in nature. The log spiral's expansion (or contraction) is determined by the cotangent of the angle of the radius vector to the tangent. In the case when that cotangent equals

$$- \pi / 2 \times \log (0.618)$$

the figure is sometimes referred to as the golden spiral. This figure also possesses the noteworthy property that the ratio of the length of the arc to its diameter is 1.618, the inverse of 0.618.

Golden spirals appear in a variety of natural objects, from seashells to hurricanes to galaxies. Many other natural forms exhibit additional Fibonacci proportions in various ways. In the human body, the bronchial tubes branch fractally in a pattern that exhibits the Fibonacci ratio. The double helix of the DNA molecule possesses precise Fibonacci geometry. Indeed, the Fibonacci ratio occurs at every scale from the molecular to the cosmological, and it is most associated with processes of growth.

The financial markets exhibit Fibonacci proportions in a number of ways. As noted earlier, most five-wave sequences contain an extension in one impulse wave. The two nonextended waves tend to be approximately equal in magnitude, and the extended wave tends to be a Fibonacci multiple (most often 1.618 times) of the nonextended waves. Corrective waves tend to retrace a Fibonacci percentage (most often 61.8 percent, 38.2 percent, or 23.6 percent) of the preceding impulse wave. Within corrective waves, Fibonacci relationships often exist among the subwaves.

These relationships, combined with Elliott's detailed rules and guidelines, constitute a powerful tool for calculating price targets and placing stops. For example, if a corrective wave is expected to retrace 61.8 percent of the preceding impulse wave, an investor might place a stop slightly below that level. This will ensure that if the correction is of a larger degree of trend than expected, the investor will not be exposed to excessive losses. On the other hand, if the correction ends near the target level, this outcome will increase the probability that the investor's preferred wave interpretation is accurate.

FURTHER STUDY

This discussion has touched on only the most basic concepts of wave analysis. Successful forecasting and trading using the Wave Principle require a thorough knowledge of the method's rules and guidelines. *Elliott Wave Principle: Key to Stock Market Profits*, by A.J. Frost and Robert R. Prechter, Jr. (Elliott Wave International, PO Box 1618, Gainesville, GA 30503, USA, 404-536-0309), is the standard textbook of wave analysis, presenting the highly sophisticated technical analysis method in comprehensive detail.

CONCLUSION

This concludes our exploration of the main tools currently used by traders. We have covered all types of charts, major chart formations, quantitative methods, theories, and studies. Some of these topics may look more familiar to you than others. Few traders are familiar with all the technical tools.

Perhaps the mere analysis of all the formations would take too much away from trading time. Luckily, most traders will be able to reach significant signals from a much lighter load of technicals. Even more, our analysis time has been greatly reduced and our analytical sharpness seriously enhanced by the splendid on-line electronic charting services and weekly printed charts.

What the best technical combination is for you is really only up to you. You have the opportunity to see for yourself what is available in the fascinating world of technical analysis. If you feel familiar and confident with certain techniques, and especially if they prove profitable to you, then you have probably got it.

Glossary

Accumulation swing index (ASI) An oscillator based on the swing index (SI.) A buying signal is generated when the daily high exceeds the previous SI significant high, and a selling signal occurs when the daily low dips under the significant SI low.

American style currency option An option that may be exercised at any valid business date throughout the life of the option.

Arbitrage A risk-free type of trading in which the same instrument is bought and sold simultaneously in two different markets in order to cash in on the divergence between the two markets.

Ascending triangle A triangle continuation formation with a flat upper trendline and a bottom sloping upward trendline. (*See* Triangle.)

Ascending triple top A bullish point-and-figure chart formation that suggests that the currency is likely to break a resistance line the third time it reaches it. Each new top is higher than the previous one.

Atekubi A bearish two-day candlestick combination. It consists of a blank bar that closes at the daily high; the current closing price equals the previous day's low. The original day's range is a long black bar.

At par forward spread Forward price is zero; therefore, the spot price is similar to the forward price. It reflects the fact that the foreign interest rate is similar to the U.S. interest rate for that particular period.

At-the-money (ATM) option An option whose present currency price is approximately equal to the strike price.

At the price stop-loss order A stop-loss order that must be executed at the precise requested level, regardless of market conditions.

Average options Options that refer to the average rate of the underlying currency that existed during the life of the option. This rate becomes the strike in the case of the average strike options; or it becomes the underlying, determining the intrinsic value when compared to a predetermined fixed strike in the case of average rate options. Average options can be based on the spot rate (spot style) or on the forward underlying the option (forward style.) The average can be calculated arithmetically or geometrically, and the rates can be tabulated with a variety of frequencies.

Balance-of-payments All the international commercial and financial transactions of the residents of one country.

Bank of Canada (BOC) The central bank of Canada.

Bank of England (BOE) The central bank of the United Kingdom. It is a less independent central bank. The government may overwrite its decision.

Bank of France (BOF) The central bank of France.

Bank of Italy (BOI) The central bank of Italy.

Bank of Japan (BOJ) The Japanese central bank. Although its Policy Board is still fully in charge of the monetary policy, changes are still subject to the approval of the Ministry of Finance (MOF). The BOJ targets the M2 aggregate.

Bar chart A type of chart that consists of four significant points: the high and the low prices, which form the vertical bar; the opening price, which is marked with a little horizontal line to the left of the bar; and the closing price, which is marked with a little horizontal line to the right of the bar.

Barrier options (trigger options, cutoff options, cutout options, stop options, down/up-and-outs/ins, knockups) Options very similar to European style vanilla options, except that a second strike price (the trigger) is specified that, when reached in the market, automatically causes the option to be expired (knockout options) or "inspired" (knockin options).

Bearish tasuki A bearish two-day candlestick combination. It consists of a long blank bar that has a low above 50 percent of the previous day's long black body, and closes marginally above the previous day's high. The second day's rally is temporary, as it is caused only by profit-taking. The sell-off is likely to continue the next day.

Bearish tsutsumi (the engulfing pattern) A bearish two-day candlestick combination. It consists of a second-day bearish candlestick whose body "engulfs" the previous day's small bullish body.

Bilateral grid An exchange rate system that links all the central rates of the EMS currencies in terms of the ECU.

Black closing bozu A bearish candlestick formation that consists of a long black bar (upper shadow).

Black marubozu (shaven head) A bearish candlestick formation that consists of a long black bar (no shadow).

Black opening bozu A bearish candlestick formation that consists of a long black bar (lower shadow).

Black-Scholes fair value model The original option pricing model, which holds that a stock and the call option on the stock are comparable investments and thus a riskless portfolio may be created by buying the stock and selling the option on the stock, as a hedge. The movement of the price of the stock is reflected by the movement of the price of the option, but not necessarily by the same amplitude. Therefore, it is necessary to hold only the amount of the stock necessary to duplicate the movement of the price of the option.

Blank closing bozu A bullish candlestick formation that consists of a long blank bar (lower shadow).

Blank marubozu (shaven head) A bullish candlestick formation that consists of a long blank bar (no shadows).

Blank opening bozu A bullish candlestick formation that consists of a long blank bar (upper shadow).

Bollinger bands A quantitative method that combines a moving average with the instrument's volatility. The bands were designed to gauge whether the prices are high or low on a relative basis. They are plotted two standard deviations above and below a simple moving average. The bands look like an expanding and contracting envelope model. When the band contracts drastically, the signal is that volatility will expand sharply in the near future. An additional signal is a succession of two top formations, one outside the band followed by one inside. If it occurs above the band, it is a selling signal. When it occurs below the band, it is a buying signal.

Book method Point-and-figure chart's original name.

Box spread A compound option strategy that consists of four options with a common expiration date: a long call and a short put at one strike price, and a long put and a short call at a different strike price.

Breakaway gap A price gap that occurs in the beginning of a new trend, many times at the end of a long consolidation period. It may also appear after the completion of major chart formations.

Breakout of a spread triple bottom A bearish point-and-figure chart formation that suggests that the currency is likely to break a support line the third time it reaches it. The currency failed to reach the support line once.

Breakout of a spread triple top A bullish point-and-figure chart formation that suggests that the currency is likely to break a resistance line the third time it reaches it. The currency failed to reach the resistance line once.

Breakout of a triple bottom A bearish point-and-figure chart formation that suggests that the currency is likely to break a support line the third time it reaches it.

Breakout of a triple top A bullish point-and-figure chart formation that suggests that the currency is likely to break a resistance line the third time it reaches it.

Bullish tasuki A bullish two-day candlestick combination. It consists of a long black bar that has a high above 50 percent of the previous day's long blank body, and closes marginally below the previous day's low.

Bullish tsutsumi (the engulfing bar) A bullish two-day candlestick combination. It consists of a second bullish candlestick whose body "engulfs" the previous day's small bearish body.

Bundesbank The German central bank. In addition to its domestic obligations, the Bundesbank has had international obligations since 1979 as the front player of the European Monetary System. The Bundesbank is a very independent central bank.

Business firms (establishment) survey Survey of the payroll, workweek, hourly earnings, and total hours of employment in the nonfarm sector.

Business Inventories An economic indicator that consists of the items produced and held for future sale.

Butterfly spread A compound option strategy that consists of a combination of a bull spread and a bear spread, using either calls or puts.

Calendar combination A compound option strategy that consists of the simultaneous call calendar spread and put calendar spread, in which the strike price of the calls is higher than the strike price of the puts.

Calendar spread A combination option of two similar types of options, either calls or puts, with the same strike price but different expiration dates. The dissimilarity between the expiration dates allows this type of spread to capitalize on both the impact of the time decay and the interest rate differentials.

Calendar straddle A compound option strategy that consists of simultaneous buying of a longer-term straddle and a near-term straddle with a common strike price.

Call ratio backspread A compound option strategy that consists of short calls with a lower strike price and more long calls with a higher strike price. The profit is twofold. The maximum upside profit potential is unlimited. The downside profit potential consists of the total premium received. The maximum loss potential occurs when the currency price reaches the higher strike price at expiration.

Candlestick chart A type of chart that consists of four major prices: high, low, open, and close. The body (*jittai*) of the candlestick bar is formed by the opening and closing prices. To indicate that the opening was lower than the closing, the body of the bar is left blank. If the currency closes below its opening, the body is filled. The rest of the range is marked by two "shadows": the upper shadow (*uwakage*) and the lower shadow (*shitakage*).

Capacity utilization An economic indicator that consists of total industrial output divided by total production capability. The term refers to the maximum level of output a plant can generate under normal business conditions.

Cardinal square A Gann technique for forecasting future significant chart points by counting from the all-time low price of the currency. It consists of a square divided by a cross into four quadrants. The all-time low price is housed in the center of the cross. All of the following higher prices are entered in clockwise order. The numbers positioned in the cardinal cross are the most significant chart points.

Channel line A parallel line that can be traced against the trendline, connecting the significant peaks in an uptrend, and the significant troughs in a downtrend.

Chaos theory A theory that holds that statistically noisy behavior may occur randomly, even in simple environments. This seemingly random behavior may be predicted with decreasing accuracy if the source is known.

CHIPS (Clearing House Interbank Payments System) A computerized system used for foreign exchange dollar settlements.

Christmas tree spread A compound option strategy that consists of several short options at two or more strike prices.

Classes of options The types of options: calls and puts.

Combination spread (synthetic future) A compound option strategy that consists of a long call and a short put, or a long put and a short call, with a common expiration date.

Commodity Channel Index (CCI) An oscillator that consists of the difference between the mean price of the currency and the average of the mean price over a predetermined period of time. A buying signal is generated when the price exceeds the upper (+100) line, and a selling signal occurs when the price dips under the lower (-100) line.

Commodity Futures Trading Commission (CFTC) An independent agency created by Congress in 1974 with a mandate to regulate commodity futures and options markets in the United States. The CFTC's responsibilities are to ensure the economic utility of futures markets, via competitiveness and efficiency; ensure the integrity of these markets; and protect the participants against manipulation, fraud, and abusive practices. The Commission, based in Washington, D.C., regulates the activities of 285 commodity brokerage firms; 48,211 salespeople; 8017 floor brokers; 1325 commodity pool operators (CPOs); 2733 commodity trading advisers (CTAs); and 1486 introducing brokers (IBs).

Commodity Research Bureau's (CRB) Futures Index Index formed from the equally weighted futures prices of 21 commodities. The preponderance of food commodities makes the CRB Index less reliable in terms of general inflation.

Common gap A price gap that occurs in relatively quiet periods or in illiquid markets. It has limited technical significance.

Condor spread A compound option strategy that consists of either four same-type options with a common expiration date—two long options with consecutive strike prices, one short option with an immediately lower strike price, and one short option with an immediately higher strike price; or four same-type options with a common expiration date—two short options with consecutive strike prices, one long option with an immediately lower strike price, and one long option with an immediately higher strike price.

Consumer Price Index (CPI) An economic indicator that gauges the average change in retail prices for a fixed market basket of goods and services.

Consumer sentiment A survey of households designed to gauge the individual propensity for spending. There are two studies conducted in this area, one survey by the University of Michigan, and the other by the National Family Opinion for the Conference Board. The confidence index measured by the Conference Board is sensitive to the job market, whereas the index generated by the University of Michigan is not.

Continuation patterns Technical signals that reinforce the current trends.

Cost of carry The interest rate parity, whereby the forward price is determined by the cost of borrowing money in order to hold the position.

Council of Ministers The legislative body of the European Economic Community in charge of making the major policy decisions. It is composed of ministers from all the 12 member nations. The presidency rotates every six months by all the 12 members, in alphabetical order. The meetings take place in Brussels or in the capital of the nation holding the presidency.

Country (sovereign) risk A trading risk emerging from a government's interference in the foreign exchange markets.

Covered interest rate arbitrage An arbitrage approach that consists of borrowing currency A, exchanging it for currency B, investing currency B for the duration of the loan, and, after taking off the forward cover on maturity, showing a profit on the entire set of deals.

Covered long A compound option strategy that consists of selling a call against a long currency position. A covered long is synonymous with a short put.

Covered short A compound option strategy that consists of shorting a put against a short currency position. A covered short is synonymous with a short call.

Cox, Ross, and Rubinstein pricing model An option pricing model that takes into consideration the early exercise provision of the American style options. As it assumes that early exercise will occur only if the advantage of holding the currency exceeds the time value of the option, their binomial method evaluated the call premium by estimating the probability of early exercise for each successive day. The theoretical premium is compared to the holding cost of the cash hedge position, until the option's time value is worth less than the forward points of the currency hedge and the option should be exercised.

Credit risk The possibility that an outstanding currency position may not be repaid as agreed, due to a voluntary or involuntary action by a counterparty.

Cross rates Currencies traded against currencies other than the U.S. dollar. A cross rate is a non-dollar currency.

Currency call A contract between the buyer and seller that holds that the buyer has the right, but not the obligation, to buy a specific quantity of a currency at a predetermined price and within a predetermined period of time, regardless of the market price of the currency. The writer assumes the obligation of delivering the specific quantity of a currency at a predetermined price and within a predetermined period of time, regardless of the market price of the currency, if the buyer wants to exercise the call option.

Currency fixings An open auction executed in Europe on a daily basis in which all players, regardless of size, are welcome to participate with any amount.

Currency futures A specific type of forward outright deal with standardized expiration date and size of the amount.

Currency option A contract between a buyer and a seller, also known as writer, that gives the buyer the right, but not the obligation, to trade a specific quantity of a currency at a predetermined price and within a predetermined period of time, regardless of the market price of the currency; and gives the seller the obligation to deliver or buy the currency under the predetermined terms, if and when the buyer wants to exercise the option.

Currency put A contract between the buyer and the seller that holds that the buyer has the right, but not the obligation, to sell a specific quantity of a currency at a predetermined price and within a predetermined period of time, regardless of the market price of the currency. The writer assumes the obligation to buy the specific quantity of a currency at a predetermined price and within a predetermined period of time, regardless of the market price of the currency, if the buyer wants to exercise the call option.

Current account balance The broadest current dollar measure of U.S. trade, which incorporates services and unilateral transfers into the merchandise trade data.

Daylight position limit The maximum amount of a certain currency a trader is allowed to carry at any single time, between the regular trading hours.

Dead cross An intersection of two consecutive moving averages that move in opposite directions and should technically be disregarded.

Dealing systems On-line computers that link the contributing banks around the world on a one-on-one basis.

Delta (Δ) (1) The change of the currency option price relative to a change in the currency price; (2) the hedge ratio between the option contracts and the currency futures contracts necessary to establish a neutral hedge; (3) the theoretical or equivalent share position. In the third case, delta is the number of currency futures contracts a call buyer is long or a put buyer is short. Delta ranges between 0 and 1.

Descending triangle A triangle continuation formation with a flat lower trendline and a downward-sloping upper trendline. (*See* Triangle.)

Descending triple bottom Bearish point-and-figure chart formation that suggests that the currency is likely to break a support line the third time it reaches it. Each new bottom is lower than the previous one.

Diagonal spread A compound option strategy that consists of several same-type options, in which the long side and the short side have different strike prices and different expirations.

Diamond A minor reversal pattern that resembles a diamond shape.

Direct dealing An aggressive approach in which banks contact each other outside the brokers' market.

Directional Movement Index A signal of trend presence in the market. The line simply rates the price directional movement on a scale of 0 to 100. The higher the number, the better the trend potential of a movement, and vice versa.

Discount forward spread A forward price that is deducted from a spot price to calculate a forward price. It reflects the fact that the foreign interest rate is lower than the U.S. interest rate for that particular period.

Discount rate The interest rate at which eligible depository institutions may borrow funds directly from the Federal Reserve Banks. The rate is controlled by the Federal Reserve and is not subject to trading.

Discretion for range to trader stop-loss order A stop-loss order that gives the trader a number of discretionary pips within which the order has to be filled.

Double bottoms A bullish reversal pattern that consists of two bottoms of approximately equal heights. A parallel (resistance) line is drawn against a line that connects the two bottoms. The break of the resistance line generates a move equal in size to the price difference between the average height of the bottoms and the resistance line.

Double tops A bearish reversal pattern that consists of two tops of approximately equal heights. A parallel (support) line is drawn against a resistance line that connects the two tops. The break of the support line generates a move equal in size to the price difference between the average height of the tops and the support line.

Downside tasuki gap A bearish two-day candlestick combination. It consists of a second-day blank bar that closes an overnight gap opened on the previous day by a black bar.

Downward breakout of a bearish support line A bearish point-and-figure chart formation that confirms the currency's breakout of a support line the third time it reaches it.

Downward breakout of a bullish support line A bearish point-and-figure chart formation that confirms the currency's breakout of a support line the third time it reaches it. The support line is sloped upward.

Downward breakout from a consolidation formation A bearish point-and-figure chart formation that resembles the inverse flag formation. A valid downside breakout from the consolidation formation has a price target equal in size to the length of the previous downtrend.

Durable Goods Orders An economic indicator that measures the changes in sales of products with a life span in excess of three years.

Economic exposure Reflects the impact of foreign exchange changes on the future competitive position of a company.

Elliott Wave Principle A system of empirically derived rules for interpreting action in the markets. It refers to a five-wave/three-wave pattern that forms one complete bull market/bear market cycle of eight waves.

Envelope model A band created by two winding parallel lines above and below a short-term moving average that borders most price fluctuations. When the upper band is penetrated, a selling signal occurs; when the lower band is penetrated, a buying signal is generated. Because the signals generated by the envelope model are very short-term and occur many times against the ongoing direction of the market, speed of execution is paramount.

Eurocurrency Currency deposit outside the country of origin.

Eurodollars U.S. dollar deposits placed in commercial banks outside the United States.

European Coal and Steel Community European entity established in 1951 by the Treaty of Paris, with the purpose of promoting inter-European trade in general, and eliminating restrictions on the trade of coal and raw steel in particular. West Germany, France, Italy, the Netherlands, Belgium, Luxembourg, and Great Britain formed this community.

European Commission The executive body of the European Economic Community in charge of making and observing the enforcement of policy. It consists of 23 departments, such as foreign affairs, competition policy and agriculture. Each country selects its own representatives for four-year terms, but the commissioners may only act for the benefit of the community. The commission is based in Brussels and consists of 17 members.

European Court of Justice The European Economic Community body in charge of settling disputes between the EC and member nations. It consists of 13 members and is based in Luxembourg.

European currency unit A basket of the member currencies. As a composite unit, the ECU consists of all the European Community currencies, which are individually weighted. It was created by the European Monetary System with the eventual goal of replacing the individual European member currencies.

European Economic Community A community established by the Treaty of Rome in 1957, with the goal of eliminating customs duties and any barriers against the transit of capital, services, and people among the member nations. The signatories were West Germany, France, Italy, the Netherlands, Belgium, and Luxembourg.

European Joint Float Agreement European monetary system established in April 1972 by the EC members: West Germany, France, Italy, the Netherlands, Belgium, and Luxembourg. Great Britain, Ireland, and Denmark were admitted by January 1973. The agreement allowed the member currencies to move within a 2.25 percent fluctuation band (nicknamed *the snake*). As a joint group, the agreement allowed these currencies to gyrate within a 4.5 percent band (nicknamed *the tunnel*). The entire agreement was known as *the snake in the tunnel*.

European Monetary Cooperation Fund EMS fund established to manage the EMS credit arrangements.

European Monetary Institute (EMI) The new European Central Bank created to govern the EMS. As of March 1994, it did not have any power over inter-EMS monetary policy.

European Monetary System European monetary system established in March 1979 by seven full members: West Germany, France, the Netherlands, Belgium, Luxembourg, Denmark, and Ireland. Great Britain did not participate in all of the arrangements and Italy joined under special conditions. New members: Greece in 1981, Spain and Portugal in 1986. Great Britain joined the Exchange Rate Mechanism in 1990. Also in 1990, West Germany became Germany as a result of its political unification with East Germany.

European Parliament The European Economic Community body in charge of reviewing and amending legislative proposals. It has the power to reject the budget proposals. It consists of 518 members who are elected. It is based in Luxembourg, but the sessions take place in Strasbourg or Brussels.

European Payment Union European entity instituted in 1950 to facilitate the inter-European settlements of international trade transactions.

European-style currency option An option that may only be exercised on the expiration date.

European Union Treaty Treaty signed by the 12 EMS members in February 1992 in the Dutch city of Maastricht, with the stated goal of forming a "closer union among the peoples of Europe."

Exchange for physical (EFP) Consists of deals executed in the cash market, outside the exchanges, for amounts equivalent to the currency futures amount, on forward outright prices valued for the futures' expiration. EFPs are generally quoted by commercial and investment banks, even during regular trading hours.

Exchange rate risk (1) Foreign exchange risk that is the effect of the continuous shift in the worldwide market supply and demand balance on an outstanding foreign exchange position. (2) Trading risk pertinent to market fluctuation.

Exercise (strike) price The price at which the underlying currency will be delivered upon exercise.

Exhaustion gap Price gap that occurs at the top or the bottom of a V-reversal formation. The trend changes direction in a rather uncharacteristically quick manner.

Expanding (broadening) triangle A triangle continuation formation that looks like a horizontal mirror image of a triangle; the tip of the triangle is next to the original trend, rather than its base. (*See* Triangle.)

Expiration date The delivery date.

Exponentially smoothed moving average A moving average that also takes into account the previous price information of the underlying currency.

Factory Orders An economic indicator that refers to total orders for durable and nondurable goods. The nondurable goods orders consist of food, clothing, light industrial products, and products designed for the maintenance of the durable goods.

FASB # 8 (Financial Accounting Standards Board's Statement Number 8) The original accounting rules regarding foreign exchange were standardized in 1975, which set the procedures for foreign currency translations into U.S. dollars in the consolidated balance sheets of U.S. multinational corporations.

FASB # 52 (Financial Accounting Standards Board's Statement Number 52) A complex set of rules designed in 1981, whose main objective is to move the foreign exchange P&L from current income into shareholders' equity.

Federal funds (Fed funds) Immediately available reserve balances at the federal reserves. The Fed funds are widely used by commercial banks or large corporations to lend to each other on an overnight basis. Although their level is established by the Fed, the prices fluctuate because they are traded in the market.

Federal Open Market Committee (FOMC) A committee established in 1935, through the Banking Act, to replace the Open Market Policy Conference (OMPC.) Currently active.

Federal Reserve The central bank of the United States. It was established in 1913 when Congress passed the Federal Reserve Act. The Act held that role of the Federal Reserve was "to furnish an elastic currency, to afford the means of rediscounting commercial paper, to establish a more effective supervision of banking in the United States, and for other purposes."

Federal Reserve Board The board consists of a Governor and four other regular members. The Secretary of the Treasury and the Comptroller of the Currency are closely consulted. The 12 regional Federal Reserve Banks around the country have sufficient autonomy to manage financial conditions in their districts. They are also managed by governors.

Fedwire An automated communications and settlement system linking the Federal Reserve banks with other banks and with depository institutions.

Fence A compound option strategy that consists of either a long currency position—a long out-of-money put and a short out-of-the-money call, where the options have the same expiration date (risk conversion); or a short currency position—a short out-of-the-money put and a long out-of-the-money call, where the options have the same expiration date (risk reversal).

Fibonacci percentage retracements Price retracements of .382 and .618, or approximately 38 percent and 62 percent.

Fibonacci ratio 0.618 and 0.312.

Fibonacci sequence Takes a sequence of numbers that begins with 1 and adds 1 to it, then takes the sum of this operation (2) and adds it to the previous term in the sequence (1). Next it takes the sum of the second operation (3) and adds it to the previous term in the sequence (the sum of the first operation, i.e., 2). The Fibonacci sequence continues iterating in this manner, adding the most recent sum to the previous term, which is itself the sum of the two previous terms, etc. This yields the following series of numbers: 1 1 2 3 5 8 13 21 34 55 89 144 233 377 610 987 1597 2584 4181 (etc.).

FINEX A currency market that is part of the New York Cotton Exchange (NYCE), the oldest futures exchange in New York. The exchange lists futures on the European Currency Unit and the USDX, a basket of ten currencies: deutsche mark, Japanese yen, French franc, British pound, Canadian dollar, Italian lira, Dutch guilder, Belgian franc, Swedish krona, and Swiss franc.

Fisher effect A theory holding that the nominal interest rate consists of the real interest rate plus the expected rate of inflation.

Flag A continuation formation that resembles the outline of a flag. It consists of a brief consolidation period within a solid and steep upward trend or downward trend. The consolidation itself tends to be sloped in the opposite direction from the slope of the original trend, or simply flat. The consolidation is bordered by a support line and a resistance line, which are parallel to each other or very mildly converging, making it look like a flag (parallelogram). The previous sharp trend is known as the *flagpole*. When the currency resumes its original trend by breaking out of the consolidation, the price objective is the total length of the flagpole, measured from the breakout price level.

Floor brokers Any individuals on the exchange floor engaged in executing orders for another person. They may also trade for their own accounts, with the primary responsibility of executing the customers' orders first. Brokers are licensed by the federal government.

Floor traders (locals) Exchange members who execute their own trades by being physically present in the pit, or place for futures trading.

Foreign exchange The mechanism that values foreign currencies in terms of another currency.

Foreign exchange brokers Intermediaries among banks who bring together buyers and sellers to the market, optimize the prices they show to their customers, and do not take positions for themselves.

Foreign exchange exposure The potential effect of currency fluctuations on shareholders' equity.

Foreign exchange rate The price of one currency in terms of another.

Forward outright Foreign exchange deal that matures at a day past the spot delivery date (generally two business days).

Forward spread (forward points or forward pips) Forward price used to adjust a spot price to calculate a forward price. It is based on the current spot exchange rate, the interest rate differential, and the number of days to delivery.

Fractal geometry Geometry theory that refers to the fact that certain irregular objects have a fractal number of dimensions. In other words, an object cannot fill an integer number of dimensions.

French-West German Treaty of Cooperation A treaty signed in 1963 by President Charles de Gaulle and Chancellor Konrad Adenauer, which established that West Germany would lead economically through the cold war and France, the former diplomatic powerhouse, would provide the political leadership.

Fuzzy logic Method that attempts to weigh the quality of the patterns recognized by neural networks. Because not all patterns have equal financial significance for foreign currency forecasting, this method qualifies the degree of certainty of the results.

Gamma The rate of change of an option's delta, or the sensitivity of the delta.

Gann percentage retracements The Gann theory focuses mostly on the eighths, along with retracements in thirds.

Gap The price gap between consecutive trading ranges (i.e., the low of the current range is higher than the high of the previous range).

Genetic algorithms Method used to optimize a neural network. Trial and error are applied to an evolutionlike system, which mimics natural selection for financial forecasting purposes.

GLOBEX An electronic trading system conceived in 1987 as an after-hours trading system and geared toward global futures trading; created through a joint venture of the Chicago Mercantile Exchange (CME), the Chicago Board of Trade (CBT), and Reuters PLC.

Golden cross An intersection of two consecutive moving averages that move in the same direction and suggest that the currency will move in the same direction.

Gross Domestic Product The sum of all goods and services produced in the United States.

Gross National Product The sum of government expenditure, private investment, and personal consumption.

Gross National Product Implicit Deflator Deflator tool designed to adjust the Gross National Product for inflation. It is calculated by dividing the current dollar GNP figure by the constant dollar GNP figure.

Harami bar A "wait-and-see" two-day candlestick combination. It consists of two consecutive ranges having opposite directions, but it does not matter which one is first. The second day's range results fall within the previous day's body.

Head-and-shoulders A bearish reversal pattern that consists of a series of three consecutive rallies, such that the first and third rallies (the shoulders) have about the same height and the middle one (the head) is the highest. The rallies are based on the same support line, known as the neckline. When the neckline is broken, the price target is approximately equal in amplitude to the distance between the top of the head and the neckline.

Hedging A method used to minimize or eliminate the risk of exchange rate fluctuations.

High-low band A band created by two winding parallel lines above and below a short-term moving average that borders most price fluctuations. The moving average is based on the high and low prices. The resulting two moving averages define the edges of the band. A close above the upper band suggests a buying signal and a close below the lower band gives a selling signal.

Hoshi (star) A "wait-and see" two-day candlestick combination. It consists of a tiny body that appears the following day outside the original body. It is not important whether the star reaches the previous day's shadows. The direction of the two consecutive ranges is also irrelevant.

Households survey Consists of the unemployment rate, the overall labor force, and the number of people employed.

Implied volatility Method of measuring volatility by considering the premiums currently trading in the market and calculating the figure based on the level of the option premium.

In-the-money (ITM) call A call whose present currency price is higher than the strike price.

In-the-money (ITM) put A put whose present currency price is lower than the strike price.

Industrial Production An economic indicator that consists of the total output of a nation's plants, utilities, and mines.

Initiation margin A margin paid by the trading party in order to trade currency futures. A trader's daily loss cannot exceed the size of this margin.

Interest rate risk Amount of mismatches and maturity gaps among transactions in the foreign exchange book.

International Fisher effect Theory holding that investors will hold assets denominated in depreciating currencies only to the extent that interest rates are sufficiently high to balance the expected currency losses.

International Monetary Market The major currency futures and options on currency futures market in the world. It is a division of the Chicago Mercantile Exchange in Chicago.

Intrinsic value The amount by which an option is in-the-money. In the case of a call, the intrinsic value equals the difference between the underlying currency price and the strike price. In the case of the put, the intrinsic value equals the difference between the strike price and the present currency price, when beneficial.

Inverse head-and-shoulders A bullish reversal pattern that consists of a series of three consecutive sell-offs. Among the three consecutive sell-offs, the shoulders have approximately the same amplitude, and the head is the lowest. The formation is based on a resistance line called the neckline. After the neckline is penetrated, the target is approximately equal in amplitude to the distance between the top of the head and the neckline.

Irikubi A bearish two-day candlestick combination. It consists of a modified *atekubi* bar. All the characteristics are the same, except that the second day's closing high is marginally higher than the original day's low.

Island reversal An isolated range or ranges that occur at the tip of a V-formation.

ISO codes Standardized currency codes developed by the International Organization for Standardization (ISO).

J-Curve theory Devaluation of a currency will trigger export gains in the long term, rather than the short term, because of previous contracts, existing inventories, and behavior modification.

Jittai Body of the candlestick. (*See* Candlestick charts.)

Journal of Commerce Index Index that consists of the prices of 18 industrial materials and supplies used in the initial stages of manufacturing, building, and energy production. It is more sensitive than other indexes, as it was designed to signal changes in inflation prior to the other price indexes.

Kabuse (dark cloud cover) A bearish two-day candlestick combination. It consists of a second-day long black bar that opens above the high of the previous day's blank bar and closes within the previous day's range (in an uptrend).

Karakasa (hangman at the top, hammer at the bottom) A bearish candlestick at the top of the trend, bullish at the bottom of the trend. The candlestick can be either blank or black. The body of the candlestick is very small and only half the length of the shadow.

Kenuki (tweezers) A "wait-and-see" two-day candlestick combination. It consists of consecutive bars that have matching highs or lows. In a rising market, a tweezers top occurs when the highs match. The opposite is true for a tweezers bottom.

Key reversal day The daily price range on the bar chart of the reversal day fully engulfs the previous day's range; also, the close is outside the preceding day's range.

Kirikomi A bullish two-day candlestick combination. It consists of a blank marubozu bar that opens the second day lower (than the previous low of a long black line) and closes above the 50 percent level of the previous day's range.

Knockin A plain vanilla option that does not exist until the trigger is reached.

Knockout A plain vanilla option that goes away if the trigger is reached.

Koma (spinning tops) A reversal candlestick formation that consists of a short bar, either blank or black. This candlestick may also suggest lack of direction.

Larry Williams %R A version of the stochastics oscillator. It consists of the difference between the high price of a predetermined number of days and the current closing price; that difference in turn is divided by the total range. This oscillator is plotted on a reversed 0 to 100 scale. Therefore, the bullish reversal signals occur at under 80 percent and the bearish signals appear at above 20 percent. The interpretations are similar to those discussed under stochastics.

Leading Indicators Index An economic indicator designed to offer a six- to nine-month future outlook of economic performance. It consists of the following economic indicators: average workweek of production workers in manufacturing; average weekly claims for state unemployment; new orders for consumer goods and materials (adjusted for inflation); vendor performance (companies receiving slower deliveries from suppliers); contracts and orders for plant and equipment (adjusted for inflation); new building permits issued; change in manufacturers' unfilled orders for durable goods; change in sensitive materials prices; index of stock prices; money supply, adjusted for inflation; and the index of consumer expectations.

Line chart The line connecting single prices for each of the time periods selected.

Linearly weighted moving average A moving average that assigns more weight to the more recent closings.

Long legged shadows' doji A reversal candlestick formation that consists of a bar in which the opening and closing prices are equal.

Long straddle A compound option that consists of a long call and a long put on the same currency, at the same strike price, and with the same expiration dates. The maximum loss for the buyer is the sum of the premiums. The upside break-even point is the sum of the strike price and the premium on the straddle. The downside break-even point is the difference between the strike price and the premium on the straddle. The profit is unlimited.

Long strangle A compound option that consists of a long call and a long put on the same currency, at different strike prices, but with the same expiration dates. The profit is unlimited.

M1 Money supply measure that is composed of currency in circulation (outside the Treasury, the Fed, and depository institutions), traveler's checks, demand deposits, and other checkable deposits [negotiable order of withdrawal (NOW) accounts, automatic transfer service (ATS) accounts, etc.].

M2 Money supply measure that consists of M1 plus repurchase agreements, overnight Eurodollars, money market deposit accounts, savings and time deposits (in amounts under $100,000), and balances in general accounts.

M3 Money supply measure that is composed of M2 plus time deposits over $100,000, term Eurodollar deposits, and all balances in institutional money market mutual funds.

Margin The amount of money or collateral deposited by a customer with a broker, by a broker with a clearing member, or by a clearing member with the clearinghouse in order to insure the broker or clearinghouse against loss on outstanding futures positions.

Mark-to-market Daily cash flow system used by the U.S. futures exchanges to maintain a minimum level of margin equity for a specific currency future or option by calculating the profit and loss at the end of each trading day in each contract position resulting from the price fluctuation.

Matched sale-purchase agreements Daily operations executed by the Federal Reserve, in which the Fed sells a security for immediate delivery to a dealer or a foreign central bank, with the agreement to buy back the same security at the same price at a predetermined time in the future (generally within seven days). This arrangement amounts to a temporary drain of reserves.

Matching systems Electronic systems duplicating the traditional brokers' market. A price shown by a bank is available to all traders.

Maturity date The date when a foreign exchange contract expires.

Merchandise Trade Balance An economic indicator that consists of the net difference between the exports and imports of a certain economy. The data includes food, raw materials and industrial supplies, consumer goods, autos, capital goods, and other merchandise.

Momentum An oscillator designed to measure the rate of price change, not the actual price level. This oscillator consists of the net difference between the current closing price and the oldest closing price from a predetermined period. The momentum is measured on an open scale around the zero line.

Moving average An average of a predetermined number of prices over a number of days, divided by the number of entries.

Moving average convergence-divergence (MACD) An oscillator that consists of two exponential moving averages (other inputs may be chosen by the trader as well) plotted against the zero line. The zero line represents the times the values of the two moving averages are identical. A buying signal is generated when this intersection is upward, whereas a selling signal occurs when the intersection takes place on the downside.

Moving averages oscillator. An oscillator in which the values of two consecutive moving averages are subtracted from each other (the larger number of days from the previous one) and the new values are plotted.

Naked intervention (unsterilized intervention) A central bank intervention in the foreign exchange market that consists solely of the foreign exchange activity. This type of intervention has a monetary effect on the money supply and a long-term effect on foreign exchange.

National Association of Purchasing Managers Index (NAPM) A survey of 250 industrial purchasing managers, conducted in order to gauge the changes in new orders, production, employment, inventories, and vendor delivery speed.

National Futures Association (NFA) A self-regulatory organization that consists of futures commission merchants (FCMs), commodity pool operators (CPOs), commodity trading advisers (CTAs), introducing brokers (IBs), leverage transaction merchants (LTMs), commodity exchanges, commercial firms, and banks. It is responsible for certain aspects of the regulation of FCMs, CPOs, CTAs, IBs, and LTMs, focusing primarily on qualifications and proficiency, financial conditions, retail sales practices, and business.

Netting A process that enables institutions to settle only their net positions with one another at the end of the day, in a single transaction, not trade by trade.

Neural networks Computer systems that recognize patterns. They may be used to generate trading signals or to be part of trading systems.

Neutral spread (delta-neutral spread) A compound option strategy that consists of a long option position and a short option position whose respective total delta positions are relatively equal.

Next best price stop-loss order A stop-loss order that must be executed after the requested level is reached.

Nonfarm sector Jobs in government, manufacturing, services, construction, mining, retail and others.

Nostro account (clearing account) The account for each foreign currency in the country of origin maintained by the financial institutions for purchase and receiving (P&R) purposes.

Open interest The total outstanding position in a currency.

Open Market Investment Committee (OMIC) Committee established in 1923 in order to coordinate the Reserve Bank operations. It was composed of the Governors of the Federal Reserve Banks in New York, Boston, Philadelphia, Chicago, and Cleveland. Not currently active.

Open Market Policy Conference (OMPC) Committee established in 1930 to replace the OMIC. It consisted of 12 Federal Reserve Banks governors and the members of the Board. Not currently active.

Optimal options Options that refer to the most favorable rate of the underlying currency that existed (from the holder's perspective) during the life of the option. This rate becomes the strike in the case of optimal strike options, or it becomes the underlying, determining the intrinsic value when compared to a predetermined fixed strike in the case of optimal rate options. Optimals can be based on the spot rate (spot style) or the forward rate (forward style).

Option currency spread A long currency option and an offsetting short currency option, generally in the same currency.

Option writers Option sellers.

Oscillators Quantitative methods designed to provide signals regarding over-bought and oversold conditions.

Out-of-the-money (OTM) call A call whose present currency price is lower than the strike price.

Out-of-the-money (OTM) put A put whose present currency price is higher than the strike price.

Overnight position limit A position kept overnight by traders.

Parabolic system A stop-loss technical system, based on price and time. The system was devised to supplement the inadvertent gaps of the other trend-following systems. Although not technically an oscillator, the parabolic system can be used with the oscillators. *SAR* stands for stop-and-reverse. The stop moves daily in the direction of the new trend. The built-in acceleration factor pushes the SAR to catch up with the currency price. If the new trend fails, the SAR signal will be generated. The name of the system is derived from its parabolic shape, which follows the price gyrations. It is represented by a dotted line. When the parabola is placed under the price, it suggests a long position. Conversely, a price above the parabola indicates a short position.

Pennants A continuation formation that resembles the outline of a pennant. It consists of a brief consolidation period within a solid and steep upward trend or downward trend. The consolidation itself tends to be sloped in the opposite direction from the slope of the original trend, or simply flat. The consolidation is bordered by a support line and a resistance line, which converge, creating a triangle. The previous sharp trend is known as the pennant pole. When the currency resumes its original trend by breaking out of the consolidation, the price objective is the total length of the pole, measured from the breakout price level.

Personal Income An economic indicator that consists of the income received by individuals, nonprofit institutions, and private trust funds. Some of the components of this indicator are wages and salaries, rental income, dividends, interest earnings, and transfer payments (Social Security, state unemployment insurance, and veteran's benefits).

Philadelphia Stock Exchange (PHLX) The oldest U.S. securities exchange, it offers currency futures and options on currency futures.

Point-and-figure chart A type of chart that plots price activity without regard to time. When the currency moves up, the fluctuations are marked with X's. The moves on the downside are plotted with O's. The direction on the chart only changes if the currency reverses by a certain number of pips.

Premium The price of the option paid by the buyer to the seller.

Premium forward spread Forward price that is added to a spot price to calculate a forward price. It reflects the fact that the foreign interest rate is higher than the U.S. interest rate for that particular period.

Prime rate The rate that commercial banks charge customers, which is based on the discount rate.

Producer Price Index An economic indicator that gauges the average changes in prices received by domestic producers for their output at all stages of processing.

Purchasing power parity (PPP) Model of exchange rate determination stating that the price of a good in one country should equal the price of the same good in another country, exchanged at the current rate (the law of one price).

Put-call-forward exchange parity (PCFP) theory A relationship between a call option and a put option established through the forward market. The theory holds that the option of buying the domestic currency with a foreign currency at a certain price X is equivalent to the option of selling the foreign currency with the domestic currency at the same price X. Therefore, the call option in the domestic currency becomes the put option in the other, and vice versa.

Put ratio backspread A compound option strategy that consists of short puts with a higher strike price and more long puts with a lower strike price. The profit is twofold. The maximum upside profit potential consists of the total premium received. The downside profit potential is unlimited. The maximum loss potential occurs when the currency price reaches the lower strike price at expiration.

Random walk theory An efficient market hypothesis, stating that prices move randomly versus their intrinsic value. Therefore, no one can forecast market activity based on the available information.

Rate of change A momentum oscillator in which the oldest closing price is divided into the most recent one.

Ratio call spread A compound option strategy that consists of a number of long calls with lower strike prices and a larger number of short calls with a higher strike price. The maximum profit is realized when the currency price is at the higher strike price. This combination has two break-even points. The downside break-even point consists of the sum of the lower strike price and the debit, divided by the number of long calls. The upside break-even point consists of the sum of the higher strike price and the maximum profit potential, divided by the number of naked calls. The maximum loss is twofold. The maximum downside risk is the net premium. The upside risk is unlimited.

Ratio put spread A compound option strategy that consists of a number of long puts with higher strike prices and a larger number of short puts with a lower strike price. The maximum profit is realized when the currency price is at the lower strike price. This combination has two break-even points. The downside break-even point consists of the difference between the lower strike price and the maximum profit potential, divided by the number of naked puts. The upside break-even point consists of the difference between the higher strike price and the debit, divided by the number of long calls. The maximum loss is twofold. The maximum downside risk is unlimited. The upside risk is the net premium.

Ratio spread A compound option strategy in which the number of long options is different from the number of short options.

Rectangle A continuation formation that resembles the outline of a parallelogram. The price objective is the height of the rectangle.

Regulation Q Regulation passed by the Federal Reserve that prohibited payment of interest on demand deposits and prescribed maximum rates banks could pay on time deposits. These ceilings had been imposed since 1933 by the U.S. government. The regulation is not currently in effect.

Relative Strength Index An oscillator that measures the relative changes between the higher and lower closing prices. The RSI is plotted on a 0 to 100 scale. The 70 and 30 values are used as warning signals, whereas values above 85 indicate an overbought condition (selling signal), and values under 15 suggest an oversold condition (buying signal).

Replacement risk A form of credit risk that holds that counterparties of failed banks will find their books unbalanced to the extent of their exposure to the insolvent party. In order to rebalance their books, these banks must enter new transactions.

Repurchase agreements (repos) Daily operations executed by the Federal Reserve. A repurchase agreement between the Federal Reserve and a government securities dealer consists of the Fed's purchasing a security for immediate delivery, with the agreement to sell the same security back at the same price at a predetermined date in the future (usually within 15 days). This arrangement amounts to a temporary injection of reserves in the banking system.

Resistance level The peaks representing the price level at which supply exceeds demand.

Reversal patterns Patterns that occur at the end of the trend, signaling the trend change.

Rollover (tomorrow/next or tom/next) swap A swap designed for spot trades' maintenance. It was designed to change the old spot date to the current spot date (on the front office's side) and to enable the bank to make the payments to the counterparty (on the back office's side).

Rounded bottom A bullish reversal pattern that consists of a very slow and gradual change in the direction of the market.

Rounded top (saucer) A bearish reversal pattern that consists of a very slow and gradual change in the direction of the market.

Runaway or measurement gap A price gap that occurs within solid trends. It is also called a measurement gap because it tends to occur about midway through the life of a trend.

Sangu (three gaps) A reversal candlestick signal applicable in either a steeply rising or falling market, when the daily limits will break the trading. The theory holds that after the third gap, the market will reverse at least to the second gap.

Sanpei (three parallel bars) A reversal candlestick combination. It refers to the similarity in direction and velocity of three consecutive bars, as otherwise all the entries are parallel. They generate a reversal formation after an extended rally. When bullish, the formation is known as the *three soldiers*. When bearish, the name is the *three crows*.

Sanpo (three methods) A candlestick combination that advises that retracements are in order before the market will reach new highs and new lows.

Sansen (three rivers) method A reversal candlestick combination. It consists of three daily entries. The first day is a long blank bar (a bullish move), followed by a bullish but short-range one day island. The third entry is a bearish long black line.

Sanzan (three mountains) A reversal candlestick combination. It consists of a triple-top formation.

Sashikomi A bearish two-day candlestick combination. It consists of a modified *irikubi* bar. The difference is that the opening of the second day's blank bar is much lower than that of the *irikubi* bars. Despite the wider gap thus formed, the blank candlestick closes only slightly above the previous day's low.

Settlement risk A form of credit risk that may occur due to the time zones separating the nations. Payment may be made to a party who will declare insolvency (or be declared insolvent) immediately after receipt, but prior to executing its own payments.

Shitakage Lower shadow of the candlestick. (*See* Candlestick chart.)

Short straddle A compound option that consists of a short call and a short put on the same currency, at the same strike price, and with the same expiration dates. The maximum profit consists of the combined premium of the two individual options. The loss occurs when the level of the premium is overpassed by the currency swing, and the loss is unlimited.

Short strangle A compound option that consists of a short call and a short put on the same currency, with the same expiration dates, but with different strike prices. The maximum profit consists of the combined premium of the two individual options. The loss is unlimited.

Simple moving average or arithmetic mean An average of a predetermined number of prices over a number of days, divided by the number of entries.

Slow stochastics A version of the original stochastic oscillator. The new, slow %K line consists of the original %D line. The new, slow %D line formula is calculated from the new %K line.

Snake The nickname of the European Joint Float Agreement's 2.25 percent fluctuation band for the European currencies against each other, derived from its curvaceous movement.

Speedlines Support or resistance lines that divide the range of the trend into thirds on a vertical line. The two resulting speedlines are plotted by using as coordinates the origin and the 1/3 and 2/3 prices respectively.

Spot deal A foreign exchange deal that consists of a bilateral contract between a party delivering a certain amount of a currency against receiving a certain amount of another currency from a second counterparty, based on an agreed exchange rate, within two business days of the deal date. The exception is the Canadian dollar, in which the spot delivery is executed within one business day.

Spot next (S/N) A foreign exchange deal that matures one business day past the spot date, or three business days.

Sterilized intervention A central bank intervention in the foreign exchange market that consists of a sale of government securities that offsets the reserve injection which occurs due to the foreign exchange intervention. The money market activity sterilizes the impact of the foreign exchange intervention on the money supply. Sterilized interventions have a short- to medium-term effect.

Stochastics Oscillators that consist of two lines called %K and %D. Visualize %K as the plotted instrument and %D as its moving average. The resulting lines are plotted on a 1 to 100 scale. Just as in the case of the RSI, the 70 percent and 30 percent values are used as warning signals. The buying (bullish reversal) signals occur at under 10 percent and the selling (bearish reversal) signals come into play at above 90 percent.

Strike price *See* Exercise price.

Support level The troughs representing the level at which demand exceeds supply.

Swap deal A foreign exchange deal that consists of a spot deal and a forward outright deal. A party simultaneously buys and sells (or sells and buys) the same amount of a currency with another counterparty; the two legs of the transaction mature on different dates (one of the dates being the spot date) and are traded at different exchange rates (one of the exchange rates being the spot rate). Exceptions may be made with regard to the value dates (forward-forward) and amount (different amounts).

SWIFT (Society of Worldwide Interbank Financial Telecommunications) An automated system set up to send standardized payment instructions for foreign currencies among international banks.

Swing Index (SI) A momentum oscillator that is plotted on a scale of -100 to +100. The spikes reaching the extremes suggest reversal.

Symmetrical triangle A triangle continuation formation in which the support and resistance lines are symmetrical. (*See* Triangle.)

Synthetic call option A combination of a long currency and a long currency put.

Synthetic put option A combination of a short currency and a long currency call.

Tan Book An economic report prepared by the Federal Reserve for FOMC meetings.

Tankan Economic Survey The Japanese equivalent of the American Tan Book, which is released by the Federal Reserve. The survey is released on a quarterly basis.

Technical analysis The chart study of past behavior of commodity prices for purposes of forecasting their future performance.

Theory of elasticities A model of exchange rate determination stating that the exchange rate is simply the price of foreign exchange that maintains the BOP in equilibrium. The degree to which the exchange rate responds to a change in the trade balance depends entirely on the elasticity of demand to a change in price.

Theta (T) or time decay Occurs as the very slow or nonexistent movement of the currency triggers losses in the option's theoretical value.

Three Buddha top formation A reversal candlestick combination. It consists of a head-and-shoulders formation, or three consecutive rallies in which the first and the third are of approximately the same height, and the second is the highest.

Threshold of divergence A safety feature for the EMS that creates an emergency exit for currencies that become the singular focus of various adverse forces. The threshold of divergence indicates when the specific country with the pressured currency should take additional steps other than simple central bank intervention in the foreign exchange markets.

Time decay *See* Theta.

Time value (time premium or extrinsic value) The difference between the option premium and its intrinsic value.

Tohbu (gravestone doji) A reversal candlestick formation.

Tomorrow/next (T/N) deal A foreign exchange deal that matures the next business day, or one day prior to the spot date.

Tonbo (dragonfly) A reversal candlestick formation.

Traditional (Charles Dow) percentage retracements Occur at 33 percent, 50 percent, and 66 percent.

Transaction exposure Potential profit and loss generated by current foreign exchange transactions.

Translation exposure The risk of change of the consolidated corporate earnings as a result of past volatility in the base currency.

Trend The general direction of the market, as shown by the significant peaks and troughs of the currency fluctuations.

Trendline A straight line connecting the significant highs (peaks) in a downtrend, and the significant lows (troughs) in an uptrend.

Triangle A continuation formation that resembles the outline of a pennant, but without the pole. It consists of a brief consolidation period within a solid and steep upward trend or downward trend. The consolidation itself tends to be sloped in the opposite direction from the slope of the original trend, or simply flat. The consolidation is bordered by converging support and resistance lines, making it look like a triangle. When the currency resumes its original trend by breaking out of the consolidation, the price objective is the height of the triangle, measured from the breakout price level.

Triple bottom A bullish reversal pattern that consists of three bottoms of approximately equal heights. A parallel—resistance—line is drawn against a support line, which connects these tops. The break of the resistance line generates a move equal in size to the price difference between the average height of the bottoms and the resistance line.

Triple top A bearish reversal pattern that consists of three tops of approximately equal heights. A parallel—support—line is drawn against a resistance line, which connects these tops. The break of the support line generates a move equal in size to the price difference between the average height of the tops and the support line.

TRIX Index An oscillator that consists of a one-day ROC calculation of a triple exponentially smoothed moving average of the closing price.

Tunnel The nickname of the European Joint Float Agreement's total fluctuation band of the European currencies.

Unemployment Rate An economic indicator released as a percentage that is calculated as the ratio of the difference between the total labor force and the employed labor force, divided by the total labor force.

Upside gap tasuki Bullish two-day candlestick combination. It consists of a second-day black bar that closes an overnight gap opened on the previous day by a blank bar.

Upward breakout of a bearish resistance line Bullish point-and-figure chart formation that confirms the currency's breakout of a resistance line the third time it reaches it. The resistance line is sloped downward.

Upward breakout of a bullish resistance line Bullish point-and-figure chart formation that confirms the currency's breakout of a resistance line the third time it reaches it.

Upward breakout from a consolidation formation Bullish point-and-figure chart formation that resembles the flag formation. A valid upside breakout from the consolidation formation has a price target equal in size to the length of the previous uptrend.

USDX Currency index that consists of the weighted average of the prices of ten foreign currencies against the U.S. dollar: deutsche mark, Japanese yen, French franc, British pound, Canadian dollar, Italian lira, Dutch guilder, Belgian franc, Swedish krona, and Swiss franc.

Uwakage Upper shadow of the candlestick. (*See* Candlestick chart.)

Value at risk The expected loss from an adverse market movement, with a specified probability over a particular period of time.

Variation (maintenance) margin Margin paid by the trading party in order to fully cover any unrealized loss. Any trader holding an overnight position with a negative P&L must post it in cash. It must be kept on deposit at all times.

Vega The sensitivity of the theoretical value of an option to a change in volatility.

Velocity of money The rate at which money is turning over on an annual basis to facilitate income transactions.

Vertical bear call spread A compound option strategy of buying two options with a common expiration date; one option is a short call with a lower strike price and the other is a long call with a higher strike price. The seller's maximum profit is limited to the premium paid for the two options. The break-even point is calculated as the sum of the lower strike price and the total premium. The maximum loss consists of the dollar difference between the two strike prices, minus the total premium received.

Vertical bear put spread A compound option strategy of buying two options with a common expiration date; one option is a long put with a higher strike price and the other is a short put with a lower strike price. The buyer's maximum profit consists of the dollar difference between the two strike prices, minus the total premium paid. The break-even point is calculated as the difference between the higher strike price and the total premium. The maximum loss is limited to the premium paid for the two options.

Vertical bear spread An option combination whose theoretical value will decline to a predetermined maximum profit if the price of the underlying currency declines and whose maximum loss is also predetermined.

Vertical bull call spread A compound option strategy of buying two options with a common expiration date; one option is a long call with a lower strike price and the other is a short call with a higher strike price. The buyer's maximum profit consists of the dollar difference between the two strike prices, minus the total premium paid. The break-even point is calculated as the sum of the lower strike price and the total premium. The maximum loss is limited to the premium paid for the two options.

Vertical bull put spread A compound option strategy of buying two options with a common expiration date; one option is a long put with a lower strike price and the other is a short put with a higher strike price. The buyer's maximum profit consists of the net premium paid for the two options (one paid, the other received). The break-even point is calculated as the difference between the higher strike price and the total premium received. The maximum loss is limited to the dollar difference between the two strike prices, minus the total premium received.

Vertical bull spread An option combination whose theoretical value will rise to a predetermined maximum profit if the price of underlying currency rises, and whose maximum loss is also predetermined.

Vertical spread A compound option that consists of two similar options (i.e., calls or puts), one being bought and the other sold, on the same currency and with the same expiration date, but with different strike prices.

V-formation (spike) Reversal formation that shows sudden trend changes and is accompanied by heavy trading volume. This pattern may include a key reversal day, or an island reversal and an exhaustion gap.

Volatility The degree to which the price of currency tends to fluctuate within a certain period of time.

Volume The total amount of currency traded within a period of time, usually one day.

Vostro account A nostro account from the point of view of the counterparty.

Wedge A continuation formation that resembles the outline of a pennant, but without the pole. It consists of a brief consolidation period within a solid and steep upward trend or downward trend. The consolidation is sharply angled in the opposite direction from the slope of the original trend. The consolidation is bordered by a support line and a resistance line that converge, making it look like a sharply angled triangle. When the currency resumes its original trend by breaking out of the consolidation, the price objective is the height of the wedge, measured from the breakout price level.

Appendix A
World Currencies and Their Swift Codes

Afghanistan	Afghani	AFA
Albania	Lek	ALL
Algeria	Algerian dinar	DZD
American Samoa	U.S. dollar	USD
Andorra	Andorran peseta	ADP
	Spanish peseta	ESP
Angola	New kwanza	AON
Anguilla	E. Caribbean dollar	XCD
Antigua, Barbuda	E. Caribbean dollar	XCD
Argentina	Argentina peso	ARS
Armenia	Dram	AMD
Aruba	Aruban guilder	AWG
Australia	Australian dollar	AUD
Austria	Austrian schilling	ATS
Azerbaijan	Manat	AZM
Bahamas	Bahamian dollar	BSD
Bahrain	Bahraini dollar	BHD
Bangladesh	Taka	BDT
Barbados	Barbados dollar	BBD
Belarus	Belarus ruble	BYB
Belgium	Belgian franc	BEF
Belize	Belize dollar	BZD
Benin	CFA franc	XOF

Bermuda	Bermudian dollar	BMD
Bhutan	Ngultrum	BTN
	Indian rupee	INR
Bolivia	Boliviano	BOB
Bosnia-Herzegovina	Yugoslavia dinar	YUN
Botswana	Pula	BWP
Brazil	Real	BRL
Brunei Darusalam	Brunei dollar	BND
Bulgaria	Lev	BGN
Burkina Faso	CFA franc	XOF
Burundi	Burundi franc	BIF
Cambodia	Riel	KHR
Cameroon	CFA franc	XAF
Canada	Canadian dollar	CAD
Cape Verde	Capeverde escudo	CVE
Cayman Islands	Cayman Island dollar	KYD
Central African Republic	CFA franc	XAF
Chad	CFA franc	XAF
Chile	Chilean peso	CLP
China	Yuan renminbi	CNY
Colombia	Colombian peso	COP
Comoros	Comoro franc	KMF
Congo	CFA franc	XAF
Cook Islands	New Zealand dollar	NZD
Costa Rica	Costa Rica colon	CRC
Cote díIvoire	CF franc	XOF
Croatia	Kuna	HRK
Cuba	Cuban peso	CUP
Cyprus	Cyprus pound	CYP
Czech Republic	Koruna	CSK
Denmark	Danish Krone	DKK
Djibouti	Djibouti franc	DJF
Dominica	Caribbean dollar	XCD
Dominican Republic	Dominican peso	DOP
East Timor	Rupiah	IDR
	Timor escudo	TPE
Ecuador	Sucre	ECS
Egypt	Egyptian pound	EGP
El Salvador	El Salvador colon	SVC

Equatorial Guinea	CFA franc	XAF
Estonia	Kroon	EEK
Ethiopia	Ethiopian birr	ETB
European Union	Euro	EUR
Faeore Islands	Danish Krone	DKK
Falkland Islands	Falkland Islands pound	FKP
Fiji	Fiji dollar	FJD
Finland	Markka	FIM
France	French franc	FRF
French Guyana	French franc	FRF
Gabon	CFA franc	XAF
Gambia	Dalasi	GMD
Georgia	Russian ruble	RUR
Germany	Deutsche mark	DEM
Ghana	Cedi	GHC
Gibraltar	Gibraltar pound	GIP
Greece	Drachma	GRD
Greenland	Danish Krone	DKK
Grenada	Caribbean dollar	XCD
Guadeloupe	French franc	FRF
Guam	U.S. dollar	USD
Guatemala	Quetzal	GTQ
Guinea	Guinea franc	GNF
Guinea-Bissau	Guinea-Bissau peso	GWP
Guyana	Guyana dollar	GYD
Haiti	Gourde	HTG
	U.S. dollar	USD
Honduras	Lempira	HNL
Hong Kong	Hong Kong dollar	HKD
Hungary	Forint	HUF
Iceland	Icelandic krona	ISK
India	Indian rupee	INR
Indonesia	Rupiah	IDR
Iran	Iranian rial	IRR
Iraq	Iraqi dinar	IQD
Ireland	Irish pound	IEP
Isle of Man	Pound sterling	GBP
Israel	Shekel	ILS
Italy	Italian lira	ITL

Jamaica	Jamaican dollar	JMD
Japan	Yen	JPY
Jordan	Jordanian dinar	JOD
Kazakhstan	Tenge	KZT
Kenya	Kenyan shilling	KES
North Korea	North Korean won	KPW
Republic of Korea	Won	KRW
Kuwait	Kuwaiti dinar	KWD
Kyrygystan	Som	KGS
Lao	Kip	LAK
Latvia	Latvian lats	LVL
Lebanon	Lebanese pound	LBP
Lesotho	Loti	LSL
	Financial rand	ZAL
	Rand	ZAR
Liberia	Liberian dollar	LRD
Libyan Arab Jamahiriya	Libyan dinar	LYD
Liechtenstein	Swiss franc	CHF
Lithuania	Litas	LTL
Luxembourg	Belgian franc	BEF
	Luxembourg franc	LUF
Macao	Pataca	MOP
Macedonia	Denar	MKD
Madagascar	Malagasy franc	MGF
Malawi	Kwacha	MWK
Malaysia	Malaysia ringgit	MYR
Maldives	Rufiyaa	MVR
Mali	CFA franc	XOF
Malta	Maltese lira	MTL
Marshall Islands	U.S. dollar	USD
Martinique	French franc	FRF
Mauritania	Ouguiya	MRO
Mauritius	Mauritius rupee	MUR
Mexico	Peso	MXN
Micronesia	U.S. dollar	USD
Moldavia	Leu	MDL
Monaco	French franc	FRF
Mongolia	Tugrik	MNT
Monserrat	Caribbean dollar	XCD

Marocco	Maroccan dirham	MAD
Mozambique	Metical	MZM
Myanmar	Kyat	MMK
Namibia	Rand	ZAR
Nauru	Australian dollar	AUD
Nepal	Nepalese rupee	NPR
Netherlands Antilles	Netherlands Antilles guilder	ANG
Netherlands	Netherlands guilder	NLG
New Caledonia	CFP franc	XPF
New Zealand	New Zealand dollar	NZD
Nicaragua	Oro	NIO
Niger	CFA franc	XOF
Nigeria	Naira	NGN
Niue	New Zealand dollar	NZD
Norfolk Island	Australian dollar	AUD
Norway	Norwegian krone	NOK
Oman	Rial omani	OMR
Pakistan	Pakistan rupee	PKR
Palau	U.S. dollar	USD
Panama	Balboa	PAB
	U.S. dollar	USD
Papua New Guinea	Kina	PGK
Paraguay	Guarani	PYG
Peru	Nuevo sol	PEN
Philippines	Philippine peso	PHP
Poland	Zloty	PLZ
Portugal	Portuguese escudo	PTE
Puerto Rico	US dollar	USD
Quatar	Quatari Rial	QAR
Romania	Leu	ROL
Russia	Ruble	RUB
Rwanda	Rwanda franc	RWF
Saints Kitts & Nevis	Caribbean dollar	XCD
Saint Lucia	Caribbean dollar	XCD
Saint Vincent and the Grenadines	Caribbean dollar	XCD
Samoa	Tala	WST
San Marino	Italian lira	ITL
Sao Tome and Principe	Dobra	STD
Saudi Arabia	Saudi riyal	SAR

Senegal	CFA franc	XOF
Seychelles	Seychelles rupee	SCR
Sierra Leone	Leone	SLL
Singapore	Singapore dollar	SGD
Slovenia	Tolar	SIT
Solomon Islands	Solomon Islands dollar	SBD
Somalia	Somali shilling	SOS
South Africa	Rand	ZAR
Spain	Spanish peseta	ESP
Sri Lanka	Sri Lanka rupee	LKR
Sudan	Sudanese dinar	SDD
Suriname	Suriname guilder	SRG
Swaziland	Lilangeni	SZL
Sweden	Swedish krona	SEK
Switzerland	Swiss franc	CHF
Syria	Syrian pound	SYP
Taiwan	New Taiwan dollar	TWD
Tajikistan	Russian ruble	RUR
Tanzania	Tanzania shilling	TZS
Thailand	Baht	THB
Togo	CFA franc	XOF
Tonga	Paíanga	TOP
Trinidad and Tobego	Trinidad and Tobego dollar	TTD
Tunisia	Tunisian dinar	TND
Turkmenistan	Manat	TMM
Turkey	Turkish lira	TLR
Turks and Caicos Islands	U.S. dollar	USD
United Arab Emirates	UAE dirham	AED
Uganda	Uganda shilling	UGX
Ukraine	Karbovnet	UAK
United Kingdom	Pound sterling	GBP
United States of America	U.S. dollar	USD
Uruguay	Uruguayan peso	UYP
Uzbekistan	Sum	UZS
Vanuatu	Vatu	VUV
Vatican	Italian lira	ITL
Venezuela	Bolivar	VEB
Vietnam	Dong	VND
Virgin Islands	U.S. dollar	USD

Western Sahara	Moroccan Dirham	MAD
Yemen	Yemeni rial	YER
Yugoslavia	Dinar	YUN
Zaire	Zaire	ZRZ
Zambia	Kwacha	ZMK
Zimbabwe	Zimbabwe dollar	ZWD
*International Monetary Fund	Special Drawing Rights	XDR

*Designates no country assignment
Source: (Bridge Information Systems, Inc.)

Appendix B
The Financial Markets Association-USA (former Forex USA)

ACT CODE OF CONDUCT
SECTION 1 OF 6

The ACT Code of Conduct has been compiled by the Committee for Professionalism and issued by:
ACI - The Financial Markets Association, 8 rue de Mail, F-75002 Paris

INTRODUCTION

It was in January 1975 that the ACI published the first Code of Behaviour prepared by the Committee for Professionalism of Forex. Since that time, the world's foreign exchange and money markets have grown considerably both in size and complexity, and whilst ethical behaviour itself does not change, this new Code of Conduct takes into account the many technological changes which have taken place during that time, as well as the introduction of many new financial instruments. The instruments covered by this Code of Conduct are referred to in an appendix to the Code.

This Code cannot be a technical paper setting out the practicalities of dealing in each and every financial instrument—such information is covered by Terms and Conditions relating to each instrument which have been published by various authorities, and which are listed as an appendix to this paper.

Nor does this Code attempt to deal with legal matters. It is the responsibility of management and staff to ensure that they are aware of legal requirements applicable to transactions they undertake and to operate within them.

Rather, its aim is to set out the manner and the spirit in which business should be conducted in order that the market and its participants may continue to enjoy their current reputation for high standards of professionalism, integrity and ethical conduct. This can only be achieved by the determination of all personnel involved in the market (either directly or indirectly) to act in a manner consistent with these aims. This Code is therefore addressed, not only to dealers in both banks and brokers, but to the management of such institutions together with relevant operational support staff. This Code should therefore be distributed to all such personnel.

It must be every dealer's ambition to be known, not only for his/her professional expertise, but also for his/her sense of fair play and high standard of ethical behaviour. It is hoped this Code of Conduct will help toward achieving that aim. Inevitably, due to the complexity of the many instruments which comprise today's markets, misunderstandings will occur and disputes will arise. It is essential that the management of the parties involved take prompt action to settle any dispute quickly and fairly. The Chairman and members of the Committee for Professionalism are always ready to assist in resolving such disputes by giving impartial confidential advice to the parties concerned, if asked to do so. The names and addresses of the Chairman and members of the CFP are given in an appendix to this Code.

The vast majority of disputes referred to the Committee for Professionalism arise from (a) failure of dealers to use clear, unambiguous terminology resulting in the parties concerned having different ideas of the amount or the currency dealt in, the value date or period, or even who bought and who sold or (b) failure of back office staff promptly and accurately to check the counterparty's confirmation.

The Committee for Professionalism strongly advises management, dealers and back office staff to pay particular attention, in their own interests, to the above matters.

Where there are local restrictions in force or where differences exist between this Code of Conduct and a Code of Conduct or similar document issued by the Regulatory Authority governing the conduct of those transacting business in the financial markets in the centre for which it is responsible, the terms of the local Code of Conduct shall apply for transactions between institutions in that centre.

The Council of the ACT fully endorses this revised Code of Conduct and requests all national Forex Clubs to distribute copies to all relevant banks and brokers in their area for the attention of their management, dealing and support staff.

Finally, the Charter of ACT is set out as an appendix to this Code, together with "Some Warnings."

INTERNAL REGULATIONS OF THE CFP

1. COMPOSITION

The ACT Committee for Professionalism consists of a Chairman and up to a maximum of 10 international members who must represent the different markets and geographical areas: not less than five different countries and 3 continents.

2. ELECTIONS

2.1. The Chairman of the Committee for Professionalism, who must be an international member of a Club, will be nominated by the Central Committee and appointed by the Board of Councillors by simple weighted majority for a period of three years. Re-election for one term only of 3 years maximum is permissible. He cannot combine his office with that of Councillor of his own Club.

2.2. Members are nominated by the Central Committee and appointed by the Board of Councillors for a period of three years. Re-election for one term only of three years maximum is permissible.

2.3. The Committee for Professionalism will proceed to make its own distribution of tasks, and will appoint a Vice Chairman and a Secretary.

3. RESIGNATION

3.1. Six months notice is requested of a member's intention to resign or retire from the Committee.

4. MANDATE

The Committee for Professionalism is an advisory body of the ACT which shall act as follows:

4.1. To formulate and propose (through the Central Committee) guidelines—both technical and ethical—concerning the operations of the markets and the professional activities of ACT members (as defined in rule B 2 of chapter 1 Admission).

4.2. At the request of the parties concerned, both being represented by an international ACT member, to give advice on professional disagreements or problems having an international character, provided all parties to the disagreement are agreeable to giving the necessary mandate to the CFP and agree to waive any legal responsibility arising from the CFP's recommendations.

4.3. To formulate and propose policies and guidelines establishing the educational and professional standards for members of ACT.

5. MEETINGS

5.1. The Committee for professionalism shall hold a meeting either at the request of the chairman, or at the written request of at least three members of the Committee.

5.2. The Committee shall meet at least once a year and according to need.

5.3. The meetings shall be chaired by the Chairman or, in his absence, by the Vice Chairman.

5.4. The Committee shall meet in Paris at the headquarters of the ACT or elsewhere if designated by the Committee.

5.5. Following the Chairman's instructions, the Secretary shall notify members of the Committee, in writing, at least one month in advance of the subjects of the agenda and shall ask them if they wish to add any other subjects. The final agenda shall be sent out at least two weeks ahead of the meeting.

5.6. Resolutions may be adopted outside the agenda. Any member of the CFP may bring up any subject for resolution under the agenda item Any Other Business.

6. QUORUM

The Committee can meet validly only if more than half of its members are present.

7. VOTING PROCEDURE

7.1. The Committee shall take its decisions by a simple majority of members. In case of a tie, the Chairman shall have the casting vote. (Written votes received by the Chairman prior to the meeting are valid.)

7.2. The vote is generally by show of hands, unless a minimum of a third of the members present explicitly request a secret ballot.

8. MINUTES

The discussions of CFP are recorded in the minutes by the CFP-Secretary.

Minutes of each meeting must be kept and circulated by the CFP-Secretary to all the CFP-members. In the absence of comments from CFP-members within a month of the date of sending out the minutes, these are considered as having been approved, and will be sent to the Secretary General of the ACT and circulated to Central Committee Members.

Bibliography

Bank for International Settlements. "Central Bank Survey of Foreign Exchange Market Activity in April 1992." Basle, March 1993.

Bergstrand, Jeffrey H. "Selected Views of Exchange Determination after a Decade of 'Floating.'" *New England Economic Review*, Federal Reserve Bank of Boston, May/June 1983.

Frost, A.J. and Prechter Jr., Robert R. *Elliott Wave Principle*, 5th ed. New Classics Library, 1985.

Global Derivatives Study Group. "Derivatives: Practices and Principles." The Group of Thirty, Washington, D.C., 1993.

Levich, Richard. *Empirical Studies of Exchange Rates: Price Behavior, Rate Determination and Market Efficiency—Handbook of International Economics*. Elsevier Science Publishers B.V., 1985.

Meulendyke, Ann-Marie. "U.S. Monetary Policy and Financial Markets." Federal Reserve Bank of New York, 1989.

Murphy, John J. *Technical Analysis of the Futures Markets*. New York Institute of Finance, New York, 1986.

Plocek, Joseph E. *Economic Indicators*. New York Institute of Finance, New York, 1991.

Pring, Martin J. *Martin Pring on Market Momentum*. International Institute for Economic Research, Inc., 1993.

Samuelson, Paul A. *Economics*, 11th ed. McGraw-Hill, New York, 1980.

Shimizu, Seiki. *The Japanese Chart of Charts*. Tokyo Futures Trading Publishing Co., Tokyo, 1986.

Stigum, Marcia. *After the Trade: Dealer and Clearing Bank Operations in Money Market and Government Securities*. Dow Jones-Irwin, Chicago, 1988.

Sutton, W.H. *Trading in Currency Options*. New York Institute of Finance, New York, 1987.

CHART SERVICES

Inventure, 30 Broad Street, New York, NY 10004

Bloomberg Financial, 499 Park Avenue, New York, NY 10022

Bridge Information Systems, Inc., 3 World Financial Center, New York, NY 10284

Commodity Perspective, 30 S. Wacker Dr., Chicago, IL 60606

Commodity Trend Service, 1224 U.S. Highway 1, N. Palm Beach, FL 33408

CQG, Inc., PO Box 758, Glenwood Springs, CO 81602-0758

FutureSource, 955 Parkview Boulevard, Lombard, IL 60148

Index

543